After Leveson?

The Future for British Journalism

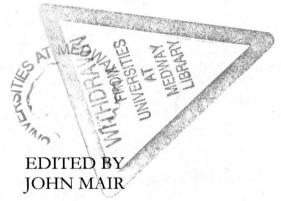

EDITED BY
JOHN MAIR

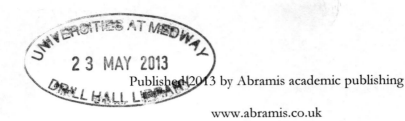
Published 2013 by Abramis academic publishing

www.abramis.co.uk

ISBN 978 1 84549 576 3

Printed and bound in the United Kingdom

Typeset in Garamond 11pt

Abramis is an imprint of arima publishing.

arima publishing
ASK House, Northgate Avenue
Bury St Edmunds, Suffolk IP32 6BB
t: (+44) 01284 700321

www.arimapublishing.com

Contents

Acknowledgements

These 'hackademic' texts are always a challenge and a joint effort. I am just the conductor standing in front of a very very talented orchestra of authors playing wonderful tunes. I suggest and guide, chivvy and harass but at the end of the day it is their golden words and their work.

I cannot thank the thirty – ten of them Professors of Journalism – who contributed to this volume enough.

My publishers Richard and Peter Franklin of Abramis provided their usual gold medal service. Nothing beats their fast turnaround which shows that the glacial pace of too much academic publishing is both un-necessary and a conspiracy against the informed reader. Academics need to look beyond the Research Excellence Framework panels to find real audiences and have some impact on public policy. I get a continual warm glow from hearing that Lord Justice Leveson read and took into account the first edition of Richard Keeble and my PHONE HACKING SCANDAL: JOURNALISM ON TRIAL published in the midst of his hearings in February 2012. Now, that's what I call impact!

Roy Greenslade and Richard Keeble deserve thanks for their work on this and other 'hackademic' volumes. Thanks are also due to my academic colleagues – now in journalism at Northampton and Napier, previously at the Coventry School of Cultural Studies. Their patience is appreciated.

Finally, some personal thanks.

My wife Susan has been (mainly) patient in sorting out the mess I presented to her as a typescript. She turned the sow's ear into this silk purse. It simply would not have been possible without her brilliant organisational skills. My heroine!

And to my late parents, John and Clara Eloise Mair. Both had the prescience to pass away at Christmas and ruin it forever for their children. It means I am always content to find a displacement exercise at Yuletide. Pulling this book together took up Christmas/New Year 2012. It beats watching endless repeats on TV.

I commend this book to you and leave you to judge the quality and depth.

John Mair, Oxford, January 2013

The Phone Hacking Scandal: Journalism on Trial
(Arima, February 2012; second edition October 2012)

Mirage in the Desert: Reporting the Arab Spring
(Arima, October 2011; second edition November 2011)

Investigative Journalism: Dead or Alive? (Arima, September2011)

Face the Future: Tools for the Modern Media Age (Arima, April 2011)

Afghanistan, War and Media: Deadlines and Frontlines (Arima, September 2010)

Playing Footsie with the FTSE: The Great Crash of 2008 and the Crisis in Journalism
(Arima, September 2009)

Beyond Trust (Arima, September 2008)

What Do we Mean by Local? Mair, John, Fowler, Neil and Reeves, Ian (eds)
(Arima, March 2012, second edition December 2012)

The Editor

John Mair is Head of Journalism/Subject Leader at the University of Northampton which he has just joined from the Coventry University School of Cultural Studies. He is a former BBC, ITV and Channel Four factual producer, a Royal Television Society winner (and judge) and the maker of over two hundred broadcast television programmes. He also judges other awards such as the Society of Editors local and the Muslim Young Writers.

John is the editor (or joint editor) of nine 'hackademic' texts in the last four and a half years. All achieve the holy grail of mixing academics and journalists informing each other between the same covers.

The subjects range from trust in television to the health of investigative journalism to reporting the 'Arab Spring' and more recently Leveson Studies. His and Richard Keeble's collection THE PHONE HACKING SCANDAL; JOURNALISM ON TRIAL was serialised In the *Media Guardian* by Roy Greenslade, went into a second and updated edition within six months and was chosen as a Guardian Kindle/E book, probably the first academic text to achieve this, It also has had very positive reviews from the likes of Sir Harry Evans 'every editor's dream-covers all angles' and Mark Thompson, formerly of the BBC, now CEO of the New York Times 'a brilliant piece of entrepreneurial journalism' he called it. John is always willing to consider ideas for new 'hackademic' collections.

John is married and lives in Oxford.

Preface

Sunlight really is the best disinfectant! Even I was shocked!

Dominic Ponsford is the Editor of the Parish magazine of the Fleet Street the Press Gazette. Day after day he chronicles triumph and disaster in the land of the hacks. But even one with a seasoned press watcher like Dominic was 'taken aback' at what came out in Lord Justice Leveson's court-room

Does former News International chief executive Rebekah Wade deserve to be burned at the stake?

Will the so-called feral beasts of Fleet Street be driven to extinction by the impact of Sir Brian Leveson's vast report on their behaviour.

Or will his Inquiry and report mark the moment at which the tabloid 'beasts' were finally tamed?

To find out the answers to these questions and many more - editor John Mair has drawn on the UK's leading media experts including 20 Professors of Journalism and 20 leading journalists. Those reporting back from the journalistic frontline include the Head of News and Current affairs at *Channel 4* Dorothy Byrne, former *Guardian* editor and doyen of UK media writers Peter Preston, seasoned media observer Raymond Snoddy and veteran crime and investigative reporter Duncan Campbell.

Contributors from the world of 'hackademia' include the former director of BBC News Professor Richard Sambrook and former tabloid editor turned Professor of journalism at City University and *Guardian* blogger Roy Greenslade and Professors Ivor Gaber,John Tulloch, Mick Temple, Chris Frost, Hugo De Burgh and Julian Petley .

Assembled with impressive speed in the wake of the publication on 29 November 2012 of the Leveson report on the culture, practice and ethics of the press, this volume takes stock at a historic moment for British journalism.

Will the papers accept a 'Leveson' type system?

At time of writing (January, 2013) the owners of Britain's major newspapers and magazines were thrashing out a deal to create a "Leveson-compliant" system of self-regulation in a bid to stave off, yet again, the threat of a solution being imposed on them by the politicians.

Time will tell whether the press owners responsible for an industry culture which bred inter alia: phone-hacking, the 'monstering' of the McCanns, the (alleged) bribing of public officials, inappropriate collusion with police and politicians, and other abuses; are capable of taking the philosophical leap towards doing the right thing this time. Or whether, as with the setting up of the Press Complaints Commission in 1991, and the Press Council before it in 1953, they will end up doing the politically and economically expedient minimum.

But any back-room deals between press owners and politicians to create a new settlement for press regulation in the UK will only form part of Lord Justice Leveson's legacy. His 97-days of public hearings and near 2,000-page report will only have really have succeeded if, to some extent, they change the hearts and minds of those involved in British journalism at all levels.

The power-brokers behind Britain's great newspaper titles give the impression at least that they have been deeply affected by the Leveson Inquiry and report. Chief 'fixer' and co-ordinator for press owners, *Telegraph* Media Group public affairs chief Lord Black, summed it up well when addressing Fleet Street's finest at the British Journalism Awards on 5 December 2012. Black described Leveson's report as "a remarkable piece of work, that will not only change the face of our industry for ever, but also - through the years - provide historians with a unique, encyclopaedic insight into our business at the moment when it is on the cusp of its final change from print to multi-platform. And that in itself has been a very important public service."

Sunlight was really the best disinfectant for the British press

As the editor of *Press Gazette*, the journalism trade magazine and website which has been 'guarding the guardians' since 1965, I know better than most that national newspapers are uniquely, and hypocritically, among the most secretive of our national institutions. So for every national press owner and editor to be interrogated forensically, on the record, and asked to account for their actions by Sir Brian and his counsel Robert Jay QC was a uniquely refreshing and healthy exercise. As journalists are so fond of saying, sunlight really is the best disinfectant!

It was, I am sure, a salutary experience for all concerned, and this book will help ensure that those lessons are not lost as the news and political agenda moves on. The Inquiry provided such an embarrasse de riches for students of journalism and the media that it is easy to forget quite how astonishing some of those evidence sessions were.

In December 2011 we had former *News of the World* editor Colin Myler explaining how his newspaper wrote to a sex-worker threatening her with public exposure unless she gave went on the record about Max Mosley's somewhat exotic sexual proclivities,

Lord Leveson: "You said it was unnecessary to have written in those terms, quite frankly it was outrageous wasn't it?"

Colin Myler: "It was totally inappropriate..."

Leveson: "What concerns me... [is] what it tells me about the thinking among extremely senior journalists working on the largest selling newspaper in the country."

Myler – now editor of the *New York Daily News* – clearly didn't grasp quite how distasteful his paper's conduct appeared in the cold light of day. Would any tabloid editor sanction such practices in the future? I think, and hope, not.

In February 2012 we had the rather more sympathetic figure of *Times* editor James Harding explaining why his paper published a story which we now know (but he did not, apparently, at the time) was based on information gained by illegally hacking the email account of the anonymous police blogger 'Nightjack' in 2008.

Going through a chain of events which revealed how senior staff at one of the most famous and admired newspapers in the world failed to grasp that computer-hacking was not only ethically highly dubious, but illegal under UK law, an excruciatingly embarrassed Harding told Leveson: "When you look back at all of this, sir – I really hope you understand – it's terrible. I really hope you appreciate that. I know that as keenly as you do."

Blogger Richard Horton was paid £42,500 in damages by the Times last October and at least one former *Times* reporter could yet face a criminal trial over their involvement in the affair.

Whatever new press regulator emerges - it will have powers to investigate and interrogate. The industry conceded that much in the first draft of Lord Black's plan for a new press regulator to succeed the PCC.

Follow the advice of Sir Harry ...

So all British journalists must henceforth learn to follow the advice of one of Harding's more famous predecessor in *The Times* editor's chair – Sir Harold Evans. Writing for *The Times* in 2011 he said: "In editing contentious stories, I always asked myself a simple question: are we ready, on publication, to describe the steps we took to make our revelations? If we cannot, we should not take them."

British journalists must learn the lessons of Leveson, not to stave off the threat of statutory control - but because if they are to survive in a digital world where they must compete for reader's attention with everyone who has a *Twitter* or *Facebook* account, they must hold themselves to a much higher ethical standard than the mob.

That's why this is such an important book for anyone who cares deeply about British journalism – and particularly those lucky enough to have gainful employment in the press or the academe. .It is also, as we say in the trade, a cracking read.

Fleet Street will, in my opinion, make the changes necessary to survive and thrive in the post-Leveson era because journalists are incredibly resourceful and determined characters. And far from being the 'feral beasts' of former Prime Minister Tony Blair's imagination – the vast majority are driven by honourable motives to report the truth and hold those in power to account, albeit in a competitive atmosphere that may appear feral to those in more genteel professions.

Note on the contributor
Dominic Ponsford started his career in regional newspapers and has been editor of Press Gazette since December 2006. Nowadays that involves running a rolling news website, a daily email newsletter, a weekly page-turning digital magazine and suite of events which include The British Journalism Awards for journalism in the public interest. He has been visiting fellow at City University London since 2010 and before that was journalist in residence at Kingston University.

Section A. After Leveson? What Now?

John Mair

Was Lord Justice Leveson really the harbinger of the new and the end of the newspaper world as we know it and as he was portrayed to be. The War for Leveson's Ear had been fought (and probably lost) by Britain's newspaper industry in the High Court in the Strand over eight months of open hearings. The cacophony surrounding his Report pre and post publication on November 29th 2012 was a sight and sound to behold. Megaphones to the fore. Two weeks before, the *Daily Mail* published a 12 page 'expose' of Leveson assessor (the wise men and women from journalism helping Lord Justice Leveson) Sir David Bell based on at most four facts – he was who he said he was, he was a senior British businessman a former Chairman of the *Financial Times* – he belonged to the Media Standards Trust and a body called Common Purpose and he had a lot of friends in high and low places. Ergo, he was a dangerous and uncontrolled Leftie weaving a spider's web around Sir Brian Leveson. It didn't quite compute and certainly did not sound convincing on paper. That was the nadir.

Sir Harold Evans is the Editors' Editor; the doyen of the trade. In his Cudlipp Lecture in January 2013 he very effectively took apart the arguments of the Leveson deniers.

There were those who made a living out of Leveson Studies, appearing in TV and Radio studios analysing every twist and turn of the Inquiry for public consumption. Paul Connew was in the van of those. He is the former editor of the *Sunday Mirror* and Deputy Editor of the *News of the World* and the *Daily Mirror*. He has been around the tabloid block many times. He himself was a hacking victim as a result of his post Fleet Street PR business. He is though firmly a Leveson sceptic

Nothing succeeds in the world on newspapers like a big alternative story. There are many 'days to bury bad news' in this world .The scandal over (now disgraced) Disc Jockey and TV presenter (Sir) Jimmy Savile was manna from heaven for both the black and red tops. Great story, a national idol with very nasty habits and feet of very soft clay and it also blew up right in the face of the 'bloated BBC' (*Daily Mail* and others copyright). It had all the ingredients for suburban shock and outrage apart from affecting (negatively) house prices in Leeds, Stoke Mandeville, Broadmoor, Staines and other stages for the paedophile practices of 'Sir Jimmy'. Savile was a very convenient and timely stick to beat the BBC who had come out of the Leveson Inquiry (and the London Olympics) smelling totally of roses.

Patrick Barrow looks at these intertwined narratives of the two 2012 big media events – the Leveson Inquiry and the scandals at the BBC over their coverage or non-coverage of the Jimmy Savile affair. Was one related to the other? Did the newspapers get the boot into the BBC as revenge? The jury on that is still out although no longer on Sir Jimmy.

As it is on the occupants of 'the last chance saloon' in the (one) memorable phrase from disgraced former Culture Minister David Mellor in 1991 .Many many last rounds have been bought consumed there by Fleet Street's finest since the Second World War. History is littered with Official Inquiries into the Press. Leveson was the latest in a long list of probes about the press and its role in society. All have failed to tame Tony Blair's 'feral beast'. John Jewell of the Cardiff School of Journalism examines the most important of these, their failure to lay a glove on the press and looks at just how we arrived at Leveson.

The whole Leveson process has been nothing if not cracking theatre-bad, sad and mad. The dramatis personae the great and good (and some not) of the Establishment of British public life – Media, Politics and even policemen. At times, it was like watching 'Who's Who' in the Leveson witness box. Some brought baggage with them, others took it away. Rebekah Brooks is a Cheshire working girl made good. She became Rupert Murdoch's surrogate daughter, the favourite editor of his two big papers in the UK the *Sun* and the *News of the World* and ultimately CEO of his News International company. The sheer pressure of unfolding events after the Dowler Affair and the setting up of Leveson got to her and she had to resign on July 15th 2011 but not before taking a pay-off of close to £11million pounds from her corporate sugar daddy. Rebekah (and friends including her husband) will now spend the next few years fighting off serious criminal charges against her.

Meanwhile, partly thanks to her 'Shaker' dress in the Leveson box, she is painted and constructed as a latter day witch. Is she a Saint or Sinned against? Witch or not? Professor John Tulloch of Lincoln University in a provocative piece (a version which also appears in the latest issue of '*Ethical Space*') argues the case for the defence of Ms Brooks against those who want to vilify her in the electronic Salem.

Amongst the more prominent defenders of the Press/Murdoch status quo ante was Tim Luckhurst, the Professor of Journalism at the University of Kent. Fellow Professor Julian Petley of Brunel University London is a firm sceptic of the Luckhurst Line, indeed he is a hostile critic of it. Petley finds Luckhurst's booklet *'Responsibility without Power'* simply unconvincing.

Finally, in what will I hope will prove to be the hallmark of this volume, active and open discussion of the issues from all (and some surprising) sides. A liberal journalist turns defender of 'Press Freedom'. Professor Peter Cole of Sheffield University, a former Editor of the *Sunday Correspondent* (a putative left wing Sunday paper that failed) and Deputy Editor of *The Guardian.* writes on the 'bonfire of the vanities of the chattering classes' what he sees as their rush to judgement in favour of regulation. He is hacked off by Hacked Off.

Ultimately you (and your political representatives) decide the future of the press.

'I regard the proposals on statutory underpinning – as an opportunity, not as a threat'

Sir Harold Evans, the former editor of *The Sunday Times* and *The Times*, is viewed by many professionals as one of the greatest newspaper editors of the modern age. He works now in the United States, but gave evidence to Leveson and as he showed in his Hugh Cudlipp lecture in London on January 28th 2013, he cares deeply about the British press and, as ever, is unafraid of controversy. The remarks, he said, were personal judgments and he did not speak for Reuters where he is editor at large.

"What is to prevent a newspaper from being the greatest organ of social life, the prime element of civilisation?"

That's a quote. This may seem an odd moment to attempt an answer to the question it poses. The focus, following all the scandals and the horrors so well documented by Lord Justice Leveson, is very much on a contrary question: What is to prevent a newspaper doing bad? What is to prevent a newspaper being the greatest agent of social disruption, the prime element of uncivilized conduct?

From doing bad again and again through decade after decade of rebukes and promises? The mood is not celebratory. It is punitive. Write it in 72 pt Franklin Gothic Bold condensed: Stop them before they kill again. Those of you familiar with the Cudlipp lexicon may wonder where the quotation came from. You probably have better luck with this passage from 1988:

"It was the dawn of the Dark Ages of tabloid journalism, when the proprietors and editors – not all but most- decided that playing a continuing role in public enlightenment was no longer the business of the popular press. Information about foreign affairs was relegated to a three inch yapping editorial insulting foreigners.

"It was the age when investigative journalism in the public interest shed its integrity and became intrusive journalism for the prurient, when nothing, however personal, was any longer secret or sacred and the basic human right to privacy was banished in the interest of publishing profit..." Hugh made that observation in 1988 at a time of sorrow, at the funeral of his lifelong friend and colleague Sydney Jacobson. He was also in mourning about what had become of the newspaper they created when they extinguished the *Daily Herald*, the paper IPC ran in conjunction with the Trade Union Congress, what you might expect when a racehorse cohabited with a carthorse. To Hugh, the *Herald* had become a "bloated, listless boa constrictor" and hopes were high for the successor they created. Alas, the parrot he'd trained to say "Buy the *Daily Mirror*!" just could not ever learn to say "Buy the *Sun*!"

The editor who asked the opening question in 1835 wasn't Hugh Cudlipp. It was a cross-eyed Scottish immigrant to America named John Gordon Bennett who got off the boat in New York in 1817 with only five pounds in his pocket. Eighteen years later he founded the model of the mass circulation daily, the New York Herald. By 1860, his newspaper had the world's largest circulation. His two eyes became ever more deviant as he tried to reconcile his loftier ambitions with the diet of sexy murders and Wall Street panics but the question he raised is one worth putting to ourselves when we have seen what misery an uncivilized newspaper can create.

Bennett's vision of the good a newspaper might do if it tried is one Hugh Cudlipp lived his life answering in his own vivid way. He cared about that. On its 50th birthday in 1953, when the *Daily Mirror* could claim the biggest sale on earth, he wrote a rollicking history, *Publish and Be Damned*, in which he celebrated the rows it had provoked – but they weren't rows about the way it had behaved. They were rows about its beliefs, blisteringly, openly stated, untainted by malice. They were honest rows about politics and public purposes, the espousal of unpopular causes, confrontations with authority and he was unabashedly proud: "It has always done a great deal of good," he wrote, "exerted much influence and bedevilled its rivals". Publisher Revel Barker captions a graph of the circulation heading for five million in 1952 with a tantalising question Cudlipp asked himself for the *Mirror* and its successive leaders:

"An immense power for good lies within its grasp. Can it increase its popularity and at the same time raise its prestige?"

An immense power for good! It sounds sententious, but as Geoffrey Goodman has reminded the millions who never felt the gust of Cudlipp's personality "journalism always meant fun much as anything else for Hugh Cudlipp." If you were at the receiving end of his wit and polemics it was hardly fun but these were big people – Winston Churchill for instance - who could take it, they were powerful and they gave as good as they got. In the service of both aims, profitable popularity and public esteem, Cudlipp deployed exhilarating talents. He was frequently mischievous but never mean spirited.

He had a depth of feeling for the way folk think and a consummate ability to translate an idea into the idiom of the tabloid, using the splash to address a princess or a dictator in the same breezy manner – "Come On Margaret, Make

Up your Mind"; and to Khrushchev, in sledgehammer type: "Mr K! if you will pardon the English phrase, "Don't be so bloody rude" with a tiny italic PS: Who do you think you are? Stalin?"

One can see Cudlipp exuberantly chomping on his Havana as he sent the page to press. There has never been a more challenging tabloid editor even to the point of partisan overkill – Whose Finger on the Trigger? infuriated Churchill in the 1951 election, and with justice. But Cudlipp was also a phenomenal public educator, risking pages in *Mirrorscope* without bias to explain inflation, NATO, the Common Market and no doubt, if he'd been around, the labyrinths of financial derivatives that were to wreak such havoc on our lives.

His techniques have been imitated, but alas, not so much the integrity. On the centenary of his birth, we should celebrate his brave – and vulnerable – aspiration to do well and do good.

The Dark Age of tabloid journalism! He ascribed Rupert Murdoch's success on acquiring the faltering *Sun* and then, mortifyingly, overtaking the *Mirror*, to "the daily nipple count and sleazy stories about bonking bimbos". There was much more to the *Sun*'s circulation success than that – several scoops honored from no less than the Cudlipp awards judges – but its contempt for the basic human right to privacy was a fair indictment even before the hacking scandal exposed the suppurating wound; I am told the *Sun* is now ahead of the late and lamented *News of the World* in the league table of arrests for bribery and hacking, but neither paper has had a monopoly of the disdain for personal privacy and other decencies set out in the Editor's code and so often disregarded. Long before the hacking scandal and the lies of the cover-up, it was obvious that press respect for private lives had all but vanished in the British press. So routine had become the trade in defamation, some bright spark on the tabs came up with a verb for the practice – to monster him or her. How bizarre it has been that private lives are exposed to irrelevant truths (and half truths) with no redeeming value and without real redress against the malefactors, while substantive journalism essential to a functioning democracy is restricted by law and its practitioners punished. The British press has been unduly restricted on matters of real public import. The Society of Editors recently reviewed what had happened since I suggested 38 years ago, in the Granada Guildhall lecture, that the British press was half-free by comparison with the free, but imperfect, press of the United States, which is protected by the First Amendment in the US Constitution. The Society found more regression than progress. Is there something about the ownership, tradition, structure and personnel of the British press that breeds a unique recidivism in which we seem doomed to experience what the economists call a negative multiplier effect? Every reform provoked by some abuse is followed by still grosser offences and, if we are to believe the defenders of the status quo, by still more extreme reformist assaults on the sacred freedom of the press bequeathed to us from time immemorial etc. Milton! Locke! Wilkes! Mill!

Have ever those who recruit you to their cause more reminded us of Queen Gertrude: they doth protest too much, methinks. Twenty years ago when from my American experience I was arguing here for a Freedom of Information Act, I was asked, reasonably enough, freedom for what? Freedom for exposing the records of a mental health therapist? Freedom for the clandestine taping of calls, the toxic seed of hacking yet to be fertilized by technology? Freedom to trespass in hospital wards? Freedom to ridicule a Minister because she has put on weight? Freedom to corrupt the police? Freedom to snoop on children at school? Freedom to blackmail and bribe?

Freedom of the press – importantly to inquire as well as to utter in the public interest – is too great a cause, too universal a value to a civilized society, to be cheapened as it is in the current debates. The *Wall Street Journal*'s Daniel Pearl paid a horrific price for exercising the freedom to search for truth, kidnapped and beheaded in Pakistan. So did Anna Politkovskaya sensationally murdered after investigating abuses by Russian troops in Chechnya, and we can never forget the courage of Marie Colvin who died trying to report the civil war in Syria. Otherwise the world barely notices. How many of us knew that the country which has the most journalists in prison just now is not Cuba or China or Iran, but Turkey?

Every year upwards of a hundred journalists, broadcasters and photographers die in the name of freedom of the press and thousands more live in daily peril. We tend to envisage those who die as chance victims of the roulette of covering war, and that is grievous enough, but the majority of deaths are not due to bad luck. According to the International News Safety Institute, they are the result of planned assassinations. Seven out of every ten have died in their own countries. Daily many risk assassination, beatings and imprisonment to report on drug cartels, expose police corruption, criticize predatory corporations, and resist arbitrary rule. The US-based Committee to Protect Journalists (CPJ) reports that 51 have been killed in Pakistan since 1992, and more than 50 journalists in Mexico, most of them murdered. Press freedom, as Rosemary Righter observed, is an indivisible whole so what we do in the name of the freedom of press here matters a great deal. When we abuse it, we give a licence to the oppressors and their protectors. Universally, 90% of the triggermen and their paymasters go unmolested, their crimes never investigated, let alone prosecuted, convicted and punished.

More than 2,000 names of journalists have been etched on the glass panels on a memorial tower at the Freedom Forum at the fabulous Newseum in Washington, DC. The common thread through the years is that these journalists died for the very simple reason that they did their jobs seeking truths relevant to the well being of their societies. The "most humble day of one's life" is to read the stories of our brethren around the world. They look to the freer societies of the West for example and inspiration. No doubt there are press transgressions in these countries, but they do not commonly confuse the public interest with prurience and public purpose with private profit, as the hackers and their bosses did so egregiously. Not that the sleaze merchants cared to make fine distinctions. The whole culture that fed them was rotten, corrupt, bullying, mean and cynical, inured to the misery caused by their intrusions, contemptuous of 'do-gooder' press codes. They betrayed the ideals and principles that have animated generations of journalists; they felt they were above the law. But they were merely detritus of what is now referred to as "too cosy" a relationship between politicians and the press. Cosy? How about corrupt?

As depressing as exposure of the dark arts has been, it is deepened by the cynicism and arrogance of much of the reaction to Leveson, coming from figures in the press who did nothing to penetrate – indeed whose inertia assisted – the cover-up conducted into oblivion by News International, a cover up which would have continued, but for the skill of Nick Davies and the courage of his editor. But let me be clear, as President Obama likes to say. I deplore pungent political reporting and commentary only when argument is augmented by lies unrelieved by the wit of *Private Eye*. The right to be free is not the duty to be perfect. I altogether rejoice in the vibrancy of the British press, its literacy, its vigour, its irreverence, its investigations of serious intent, its innovative design (though I do wonder whether the fatness and effluvia of multiple sections is not anachronistic, dinosauric in a digital age. The excess volume of weekly paper may dilute the compact story telling and news values so that impact is diffused). And while I find Lord Leveson convincing in his indictment of the crimes and misdemeanors, he fails to identify a number of elements that stand in the way of the press being 'a prime element of civilisation'. Indeed, in a number of proposals he makes that objective harder to achieve.

First, he glosses over the demonstrable effects of media concentration. I acknowledge that securing the plurality essential for discourse may be complicated in the digital age. The Internet is eroding the business model of the printed press and much of the Internet is devoted to opinion without the underpinning of reported fact. Still, Leveson's swift summary of what happened in 1981 in the fateful sale of Times Newspaper is inaccurate, inadequate and misleading. I don't propose to spell that out again – it is all in *Good Times, Bad Times*, a new edition published by Open Road Integrated Media – except to say that a representative democracy is undermined when the law is evaded to serve the political interests of a Prime Minister and the commercial interest of a media owner. The consequence for Times Newspapers and plurality of the secret and long denied meeting between Mrs Thatcher and Mr Murdoch on January 24, 1981, is well documented: infringement of the five key principles of editorial independence originally designed to protect the political independence of *The Times* and *Sunday Times* as separate titles. The recent surprise departure of Mr James Harding as editor of *The Times*, and now an argument over a merger of the two papers Mr Murdoch seeks against the wishes of the independent directors, gives me a sense, in the words of baseball great Yogi Berra, "it's déjà vu all over again."

Mr Murdoch has made great efforts to make *The Times* viable and the government may be impressed by the fact that such a redoubtable businessman cannot sustain the paper without merging it with the stronger *Sunday*. This will leave the awkward fact that Mr Murdoch pledged in 1981 that he would do no such thing, and the government of the day wrote that pledge into law as one of the ways to evade the reference to the Monopolies Commission enjoined by the Fair Trading Act. Nobody is entitled to inflict costs on Mr Murdoch he does not want to bear. At the same time, loss of the separate identity of *The Times* must be considered a setback to the vaunted democratic virtues of plurality. Perhaps the most straightforward way to resolve everyone's dilemmas is for Mr Murdoch to offer a grace period of six months in which a credible purchaser might relieve him of his burden.

A second unconvincing feature of the Leveson Report is that it is far too soft on the Metropolitan Police; that they were busy with terrorism is a lame excuse. Right at the start of my time as national editor in 1967, when William Rees Mogg at *The Times* risked outfitting a criminal with a wire to expose bribery and fitting-up, corruption at the Met has recurred with alarming frequency – outstripping Fleet Street, as it was, in the venality stakes.

Thirdly, while Leveon applauds instances of investigative journalism of value, he has insufficient appreciation how it works at the coal face. The changes in data protection, for instance, are dangerous. Insisting that an editor must tell a target where the newspaper has got an investigation, before it has formed any view of its validity, is a gift for the litigious and the cunning. In our early inquiries into the financial affairs of Mr Robert Maxwell, he stormed in to see Lord Thomson who, happily, told him he would not intervene. It was difficult enough following the money tree in Pergamon Press without affording Mr Maxwell another chance to fudge things.

So what use is the Leveson Report for the aspirations and the predicaments of our press? It's staggering to read his dissection of all the crimes and the futilities of "self-regulation" and then read the misrepresentation of his main remedial proposal. A certain rowdiness is a given, but to portray his careful construct for statutory underpinning as state control, licensing of the press, etc is a gross distortion. In that fine but poorly reported debate in the House of Lords, Norman Fowler expressed his discomfort at his transition from a defender of the press as a journalist and Conservative Minister to a critic. I know the feeling. He says he is confirmed in his conviction that there must be change, as I am, by "the dishonest campaign mounted against change by some of the most powerful figures in the industry."

"Rather than admit", he says, "that there has been abuse of power, they seem to feel they have been unfairly put upon. Before the Leveson report there were advertisements carrying pictures of Mugabe, Assad, Castro and Putin with the caption. 'These people believe state control of the press. Do you?'"

The anti-Leveson campaign invites the response, well, what do you believe in? We are brought right back to the exuberant opening question. What stops your newspaper from being the 'greatest organ of social life, the prime element of civilisation'?

The swift answer would be, what's it got to do with you mate? Newspapers are private enterprises so back off with your pretensions. Of course, the assumption in John Gordon Bennett's musing is that the press has a vital role in public life, that it claims its privileges, its freedoms, for the common good. Isn't it enough just to report the news objectively? There is great value in the apparently straightforward business of reporting what happens, who said what to whom and what happened where, but that is not as simple a task as implied by the term 'newspaper of record'. Deciding what to put on record from the cornucopia, and at what length and prominence, requires a value judgement. Otherwise, how do you choose? For instance, merely to record opposing statements in the name of "objectivity" may leave the reader bewildered. Recently in the United States, with the slaughter of the innocents at Sandy Hook, some newspapers have made an effort in the gun law debate not to be hostage to the false notion of objectivity epitomized in a fragment of verse by Chicago Tribune columnist Bert Leston Taylor:

Behold the mighty dinosaur
Famous in prehistoric lore,
You will observe by these remains
The creature had two sets of brains –
One in his head (the usual place),
The other in his spinal base.
If something slipped his forward mind
'Twas rescued by the one behind.
Thus he could think without congestion
Upon both sides of every question.
Oh, gaze upon this model beast;
Defunct ten million years at least.

Both Bennett and Cudlipp wanted a newspaper to have a strong point of view. They implied that an ethical purpose must motivate a good newspaper, a purpose not fulfilled simply by the making of money. The relevance of ethics is a truth in many areas of business, one brilliantly argued in Dr David Potter's analysis of the banking collapse. Profit is by no means an unworthy objective but it is no guide to conduct in public affairs, justifies no greater claim to attention and access than the manufacture of haberdashery. When making money is the primary goal, it tends to subsume all others. Arguably, that's what happened at the *News of the World*. It did much good journalism, but the bad killed the good. Now, everyone recognizes that commercial viability is an essential condition of independence unless there are other means of support with an affinity for the same principles. A newspaper that is broke or going broke is otherwise not well placed to be the 'prime element of civilization'. It may well be sustained by ownership, as *The Times* was in the family control of Astor and Thomson and has been under Mr Murdoch, until now at least, and the *Guardian* and *Observer*, too, under the Scott Trust. Having edited a profitable regional daily and a profitable national Sunday in Britain, directed a profitable news magazine in the United States, founded and edited a successful monthly glossy, and managed a profitable publishing house, I am acutely aware of the buoyancy provided by a good balance sheet – but in none of those enterprises was making money the primary objective. The conviction on all of them, shared by editor, publisher, staff and ownership, was that if they consistently and efficiently delivered the qualities they promised, commercial success would follow. And so it did. It was an example of what the great management guru, Roger Martin, called the Virtue Matrix – an enterprise building the trust of an audience and ultimately its power by adhering to the public values, no short cuts. On a newspaper, a Virtue Matrix is built by care for every assignment, every headline, by a commitment shared by the whole staff, and by the ownership.

And here is the overriding virtue of the Leveson Report. It charts a way to encourage high standards through incentives and penalties while enlarging, not diminishing, the essential freedom of the press.

Lord Leveson did not propose that a law should be passed laying down how the press should behave with civil servants as censors. No, he entirely accepted that it should regulate itself through an Independent Press Council or Trust, though with independent opinion dominant and certified by a Recognition Commission wholly independent of government. He more or less accepted the architecture proposed by the press but wanted a surveyor to check that its foundations were stable. Let me emphasise: he sees regulation of the press organized by the press, but with a statutory verification process as "essential" to ensure that the required levels of independence and effectiveness are met which they were not by the Press Council, though it did some good work mediating complaints.

Two well-meaning alternatives to a statutory Recognition Commission are being canvassed. One, a contractual agreement among publishers similar to the Advertising Authority, the second a Royal Charter. Neither offers the same assurances to the public or incentives and guarantees to a free press. The radiance of the monarch and the historic echo of Magna Carta are prayed for in aid of a Royal Charter. The BBC has one, why not the press? On the once upon a time radio program called the *BBC Brains Trust*, there was a certain Dr Joad who, asked what he thought on virtually any subject, meditated for minutes, it seemed, puffed his pipe and solemnly answered "Well, it all depends."

Parliamentary counsel can whistle up something that might look as good as the statutory underpinning of press freedom and high standards in three of the draft bills helpfully circulated by the Hacked Off campaign, but Lord Dow of Dalston expressed a reaction worthy of a Cudlipp headline. "It's a busted flush."

The BBC has a Royal Charter and a fine Trust. Yes, despite the blunders concerning Jimmy Savile and a defamed peer, it has a record of public service unmatched and envied around the world. It enjoys greater esteem than the national press. It is indispensable – but it is also incomplete. The doughty defender of its editorial achievements, then Director General Mark Thompson, now CEO of the *New York Times,* has said that the BBC could not have bought the compact disc that enabled the *Telegraph* to break the story of MP's expenses, and numerous other scandals in gray areas of press ethics would never have broken by the BBC including, I might add, the thalidomide investigation. Nor is the BBC invulnerable to government pressure. At its back it must always fear the paymaster hurrying near, especially in time of political strain – the long ordeal of Northern Ireland, the torments of the Iraq war come to mind. It would be surprising, would it not, if it were to tread lightly around landmines of political controversy in a way the press does not?

The BBC Royal Charter may be thought of as a rock but it is reviewed every decade or so and you don't have to be a geologist to find a fissure or two indicative of government attitudes in the 2006 review. It is hardly comforting to know that the behind the aura of all 900 Royal Charters, mostly ceremonial, there is the Privy Council, ancient in its history, and its composition of 600 members where a quorum of a handful of worthy Privy Councillors, many politicians and former politicians, can decide. The Prime Minister was bold and brave in setting up the Leveson Inquiry in the first place and endures with becoming grace the slings and arrows, but this wheeze won't work.

Some of my best friends are strongly opposed to statutory underpinning – let's say s.u. I respect the fears of those who have been honestly arguing that any flirtation with the state is an invitation to rape, but I don't see how what is being proposed in the draft bills helpfully circulated by the Hacked Off Campaign can be a mechanism for Westminster control over the press. "If MPs decide they do not like the press they are getting, they can easily amend the Act," writes the eloquent Timothy Luckhurst. Just how that is made any easier by an Act of Parliament arising from any of the draft bills? Even the government draft requires "Minister of the Crown to have regard to the importance of the right of the press to freedom of expression…" Lord Lester's clear little Bill calls for a Press Council "to act independently and in the public interest to promote and protect freedom of expression, including freedom of the press, communicating information and opinion to the public". Clause 1 of The Hacked Off campaign Bill is headed "Guarantee of media Freedom" and insists "Ministers of the Crown with responsibility for matters relating to media must uphold the freedom of the press and its independence from parliament and the executive."

Perhaps Mr Luckhurst and like-minded opponents of judicial underpinning are belt-and-braces men whose anxieties could be met by requiring a two-thirds majority for any amendment. Leveson fed the anxieties, of course, by assigning a key role to Ofcom. That was a mistake for a cause he otherwise argues well. The mention of Ofcom, dependent on government, has enriched the metaphors –

take your pick from 'slippery slope, thin end of the wedge, trapdoor, thin ice...' The metaphor I offer for target practice is our very own First Amendment, that Parliament should make no law abridging the freedom of the press. Of course, I recognize that there are large differences between the United States and Britain with its sovereign Parliament and its unwritten constitution but the attraction of the Leveson underpinning, for me, is that for the first time there would be a legal duty of the government to protect the freedom of the press. Many a time as a defendant editor on the hard benches of the law courts, when we have been attempting to publish a report in the public interest, I have wished we could refer to a binding precedent. Too many cases had turned on property rather than personal rights, hence our difficulties in achieving publication of the Crossman Diaries and of essential documents on the series of thalidomide challenges. Government and company alike resorted to the law of confidence to claim a proprietary right to the information we sought to publish, in the first case how political decisions were reached and in the other how a toxic medication was inflicted on mothers and babies. The courts agreed with government that the documents were not sufficiently "iniquitous" to justify breach of the law of confidence.

Coming back to that first question, I dare to risk a celestial rebuke in suggesting that the Cudlipp of his 1988 polemic would regard the Leveson proposals on statutory underpinning as an opportunity, not as a threat. What further might the vigorous British press do if it were free of internal and external restraints inimical to excellence – if the intellectual analysis and foreign reporting of the "heavies" and the tremendous flair in tabloid journalism, were alike bent to positive outcomes – such as Hugh Cudlipp dreamt in his youth and achieved so well in his prime.

Note
Cudlipp quotes reference: *Newspaperman* by Ruth Dudley Edwards (Pimlico, London, 2004)

Note on the contributor
Sir Harold Evans was editor of *The Northern Echo* (1961-1966), then *The Sunday Times* (1967-1981) and *The Times* (1981-1982) before emigrating to the USA where, inter alia, he founded the *Conde Nast Traveler* magazine which has just celebrated its 25th anniversary, presided over Random House and wrote two histories of America as well as his autobiography, *My Paper Chase*. He contributed to a previous volume in the 'hackademic' series *The Phone Hacking Scandal; Journalism on Trial* published last year and edited by John Mair and Richark Lance Keeble.

Confessions of a recovering tabloid hack (who has been phone hacked...)

Paul Connew is the former editor of the *Sunday Mirror* and Deputy Editor of the *News of the World* and the *Daily Mirror*. He has been around the tabloid block many times. Connew spent 2012 as an expert commentator on the Leveson Inquiry for broadcasters worldwide. He is firmly a Leveson sceptic

As anni horribuli go, 2012 certainly qualified at the top-end of the scale for both British journalism and the newspaper industry. It was the year when the press uncomfortably became the story rather than reporting it. In a year dominated by the all-embracing shadow of Lord Justice Leveson and a recession that has seen local papers and journalists' jobs vanish at the rate of casualty statistics from the Somme, it could hardly have been anything else.

So, is 2013 destined to produce anything other than more of the same depressing, debilitating picture? Let alone the slightest glimmer of an annus mirabilis? Well, unless George Osborne discovers miraculous powers on a Lazarus scale with the economy or my old boss David Montgomery's brave new Local World initiative can provide the elusive elixir of life, it's hard to see beyond more doom and gloom for Britain's local and regional press.

Look on the bright side

On the post-Leveson front, there are reasons to be more (cautiously) optimistic. Britain's national and local newspaper editors and owners seem reasonably united (a miracle in itself) in agreeing a plan for a tougher, more independent form of self-regulation that follows the more sensible road signs erected by Lord Justice Leveson while bypassing the unacceptably dangerous S-bend (that's S for statutory, of course) laid out in his Lordship's version of the Highway Code.

Ultimately, however, optimism may depend on the Prime Minister keeping his nerve at the wheel. Having apparently discovered a principle in his antipathy to statutory press regulation, David Cameron has to stick tight in the face of pressure from a considerable number of his own backbenchers, as well as his

Coalition partners and the Parliamentary Opposition, too many of whom would still relish seeing Leveson implemented lock, stock and press-freedom threatening barrel.

With the aid of his Number Ten 'fixer' Oliver Letwin, the Prime Minister initially came up with a system based on a Royal Charter that struck me as a possible building block better than the Leveson/Hacked Off plan, but still probably requiring a different degree of statutory underpinning with the potential to jeopardise future press freedom. Much better still was the 'charitable trust' proposal put forward by editors which, on the face of it, could avoid even the need for even a feather duster dab of statute. Having worked with charitable trusts, as part of my charity sector director role, I know how well it can work. God knows, it might (just) be possible, even in these depressed times, to extend the idea further and find a wealthy established charitable trust with sufficient interest in freedom of speech that might pick up all, or part, of the cost of the new regulatory system and underpin still further public confidence in its independence. Could the most zealous Hacked Off advocate undermine that one?

It wouldn't be unreasonable to suggest that the Prime Minister owes the principle of a free press a debt of honour by sticking to his guns on the post-Leveson battleground. But the newspaper industry also has to recognise the awkward reality that the political maths do not look good if the Prime Minister allows the pro-statutory argument to be put to a free vote in Parliament.

In truth, the very setting up of the Leveson Inquiry wasn't just a blatant example of political expediency, it was a disastrous PR strategy seized on in a blue funk moment of political panic.

How the Leveson Inquiry was conceived

Yes, there was a tsunami of public revulsion over the hacking of murdered schoolgirl Milly Dowler's phone by the *News of the World* as revealed in July 2011 by Nick Davies and the *Guardian* as the cherry on the cake of their three year investigation. But was there a genuine and irresistible public clamour for a judicial inquiry into the 'culture, practices and ethics of the British press' Leveson's terms and conditions)?

Probably not.

David Cameron's underlying Achilles heel was his flawed decision to appoint former *News of the World* editor Andy Coulson to the heart of government as his communications chief after the 2010 General Election. A decision that will haunt him up to, and beyond, the next general election if Coulson (who plans to plead not guilty) is convicted of any of the criminal charges that he now faces. Much the same scenario applies, of course, should his 'Chipping Norton set' friend and Rupert Murdoch protégé, Rebekah Brooks, a former *Sun* Editor, find herself convicted of the serious charges she faces.

For a former professional PR man, the PM's PR skills seemed to desert him in the face of an impressively opportunistic parliamentary onslaught by Ed

Miliband (who suddenly found his own feet as Labour leader in the face of Rupert Murdoch's embarrassment) in demanding a full public inquiry and linking it to the Coulson misjudgement and David Cameron's closeness to the Murdoch empire.

Instead of pointing out that phone-hacking was illegal and the outrageous hacking of Milly Dowler's phone was a matter for a criminal investigation and not an instant, kneejerk judicial inquiry, David Cameron buckled to the demands of Ed Miliband, Hacked Off and the febrile frenzy that had been whipped up.

Depending on who you talk to in Downing Street, it was either the Prime Minister's personal initiative to set up Leveson, or a decision he took reluctantly under pressure from his Coalition deputy, Nick Clegg, a man with no compunction about causing problems for a newspaper group to which he conveniently owed no favours and, unlike others in the political firmament, hadn't sought any either

Cameron and Murdoch wrong footed

Wearing my own PR adviser hat, I have a soupçon of sympathy for David Cameron's moment of weakness. It was pretty clear that, having been on a trip to Iraq as the Dowler hacking scandal escalated on the emotional Richter Scale, the Prime Minister was badly-briefed and out of touch as he arrived back in the UK. Just as Rupert Murdoch, jetting into London to take charge of the 'Hackgate' fallout, appeared so ill-briefed too that he initially indicated his first priority was survival of his two-legged red top favourite Rebekah Brooks rather than the Dowler family.

Sitting in a Sky TV studio as a media commentator and watching my onetime and sure footed boss door-stepped live to such devastating effect, my jaw dropped and I said, 'That's a PR own goal that Rupert will never live down.' Nothing that has happened since changes that view one iota.

In Rupert Murdoch's case swift realisation of a calamitously poor judgement call came with a personal apology, a meeting and a £2m pay out to the Dowler family and their favoured charities.

In David Cameron's case the reaction was to give the green light to a judicial inquiry that was so widely framed that it was always a hostage to (mis)fortune and a legalistic outcome that, in my view, imperilled a free press, free speech and misunderstood the practicalities of modern-day newsgathering.

Invited as a former tabloid editor and media commentator to submit written testimony at an early stage to Lord Justice Leveson's inquiry, I made those points. Together with expressing an opinion that, with a revived and comprehensive police investigation under way as a result of the *Guardian*'s diligent investigative journalism, the phone-hacking scandal that had precipitated the Inquiry could not be properly explored until the new police investigations were completed and any subsequent criminal trials decided. This view compounded by the Attorney General's warnings of potential prejudice emerging from testimony given to Leveson. (Unlike in the US, where I worked for a decade, and where Congressional hearings aren't inhibited by arguments over whether a future jury might be influenced by what emerges).

The net result being that the Leveson Inquiry had to pussyfoot around the whole area of phone-hacking (and alleged bribing of public officials) to such an extent with key witnesses that Joe and Jane Public learned next to nothing new about phone hacking but more about politicians and the police and their unhealthy interlinks and leaving them perplexed over why so many millions of pounds of taxpayers' money was being spent simultaneously on at least FOUR police investigations *and* a judicial inquiry. Despite the caution, it's still a strong likelihood that defence lawyers down the line will argue that even the limited evidence that emerged at Leveson will be prejudicial to their clients receiving a fair trial. Should any of those arguments succeed, it would prove a disservice to the public interest and an acute embarrassment to all those who pressed for public inquiry to plough ahead with uncharacteristically indecent haste.

Why only posh papers among Leveson advisers?
In my own submission to Leveson, I also pointed out what I believed was another serious flaw: the composition of his panel of assessors. The absence of a single panel member with a nanosecond of experience on a tabloid newspaper appeared unbalanced, to put it mildly. Retired political editors George Jones and Elinor Goodman are fine journalists, but neither had first-hand experience of the culture and demands of the tabloid sector, while, fairly or otherwise, former Financial Times chairman Sir David Bell's founding father role with the Media Standards Trust hardly inspired confidence at the popular end of the market.

For an Inquiry inspired by the misconduct of a section of the tabloid press, the lack of a tabloid-savvy assessor appeared perverse from the start and it was an impression that grew ever stronger as the Inquiry dragged on. The absence of an assessor with a regional or local press background seemed equally curious, as indeed did the lack of one from the online media as the impact of cyberspace recurrently became the elephant in Courtroom 73 at the Royal Courts of Justice.

Leveson as (im)pure theatre?
If, as a piece of judicial/media theatre, the Leveson Inquiry began as the hottest ticket in town, it sometimes lurched from high drama into variations on Whitehall Farce, The Theatre of the Absurd and you started to wonder if it might run longer than 'The Mousetrap'. The public, you sensed clearly, eventually grew bored long before the self-absorbed Westminster and media villages realised that on dull days of evidence they were flogging a dead horse -- and I don't mean the retired police nag the Met loaned to Mrs Brooks and which the Prime Minister belatedly owned up to riding.

Frequently covering Leveson (as a media commentator for the BBC, Sky, CNN and Al Jazeera among others) proved a curious, conflicting experience during a tumultuous 2012.

You would have needed a heart of stone not to feel moved and shamed by the powerful, poignant evidence of the Dowlers, the McCanns, Chris Jefferies and other 'civilian' victims of outrageous press misconduct. You only needed to be a father of daughters to wince at Sienna Miller's description of being chased down a dark street by a dozen large men whose only justification was that they were carrying cameras and she was a 'sleb'.

That said, you also wondered why the Leveson Inquiry, and much of the broadcast media coverage, didn't also fully reflect that the Dowlers were expensively compensated by Rupert Murdoch (eventually..), the McCanns received over £500,000 in libel damages *and* a front page apology from the Express group and Christopher Jefferies collected hefty libel settlements from several newspapers, with the *Sun* and the *Daily Mirror* also (rightly) being prosecuted and fined for Contempt of Court in that case.

In the Jefferies case, it's worth pointing out that those titles who breached the contempt laws were guilty of a kindergarten level of journalistic incompetence comparable to that displayed by the (regulated) BBC *Newsnight* team's failure to even show their main witness a photograph or give Lord McAlpine the opportunity to respond to the false child sex abuse allegations being levelled at him-though not by them directly but by the Twittersphere. Or on ITV's (regulated) *'This Morning'* show, presenter Philip Schofield ineptly ambushing Prime Minister Cameron with a list containing Lord McAlpine's name visible on screen. Both have since paid substantial damages to Lord McAlpine

Page 3 in Court 73?
And those moments of Leveson farce and Theatre of the Absurd? Well, witnessing *Sun* editor Dominic Mohan recalled for a second time to be quizzed about his paper's Page 3 girl counts as one. Was the issue of whether Page 3 is an affront to womankind and worthy of the *Sun* being banished to the top shelf of WH Smith really the stuff of Leveson?

As it happens, I gave Dominic Mohan his first national newspaper job on the *Sunday Mirror* and also think he's made a good fist of editing Britain's biggest-selling newspaper through a time of unprecedented trauma, but I disagree with him over Page 3. Simply because I consider her an anachronism I'd have dumped at least 20 years ago if I'd edited the *Sun*. She's as anachronistic and past her sell-by date as those old double entendre 'dirty' seaside postcards we once upon a time loved, rather than the still-beloved 'national institution' Mohan described to Lord Justice Leveson.

But the real absurdity was that Dominic Mohan was even sitting in the Royal Courts of Justice having this debate and that anti-Page 3 girl campaigners had been invited there to argue their case and that the best part of a half a day of the Leveson calendar was devoted to it.

That's not to challenge the right of 'ban Page 3' campaigners to protest outside Wapping or lobby advertisers to boycott the *Sun* until they drop her. But, ultimately, the continuing 'right' of 'Cindy from Coventry' to go topless in our top-selling paper in the hope of emulating Katie Price on the road to fame and fortune is a matter for Dominic Mohan and (doubtless) Rupert Murdoch to decide on commercial grounds rather than one for Lord Justice Leveson to even muse on.

Leveson as comedy?
Without particularly wishing to sound like a cheerleader for an ongoing *Daily Mail* campaign, I'm far more worried about what my schoolboy sons might be able to access porn wise on their smartphones and laptops behind the bike shed than I am about them perusing Page 3 of the *Sun*.

But the time I devoted to monitoring Leveson wasn't entirely a depressing experience. Who could forget Rebekah Brooks teasingly describing how she had to give David Cameron an embarrassing lesson in modern text speak, pointing out that 'LOL' means laugh out loud and not lots of love? (An episode that reduced the CNN studio where I was commentating live at the time to mild hysteria.)

Who could forget how lead counsel Robert Jay's predilection for the more arcane areas of the English language added to the gaiety of the nation? Thanks to Jay, QC, even my media-interested 12-year-old now knows what pellucidly (easy to understand) and propinquity (relationship) means, even if – like me – he is somewhat perplexed over how, having established the propinquity of senior politicians and policemen to sections of the press, Lord Justice Leveson's final report delivered such a softly, softly critique of politicians and policemen compared to his excoriating verdict on the press. Pellucid it was not.

A crisis in all institutions?
Significantly, perhaps, it's a contradiction that doesn't seem to have been lost on a wider public. Taking part as a media commentator on various radio phone-in programmes both during and post the Leveson Inquiry, I've been struck by a subtle but significant shift in public opinion. While there remains plenty of public hostility over what happened to the Dowlers and the McCanns, another mood is beginning to emerge. There is a much wider crisis of confidence in the traditional cornerstones of society, a crisis in which expenses-swindling politicians, bonus-greedy, rate-rigging bankers, lying and corrupt policemen, price-fixing energy cartels may well now stand nearer the front of the dock than journalists in the court of public opinion.

That's partly the result of the Hillsborough Independent Panel report and the child sex abuse scandal surrounding Jimmy Savile and others, including the serious question marks hanging over the BBC's role in 'Savilegate'. Suddenly the star struck celebrity culture that was too readily indulged during the Leveson Inquiry has lost its lustre.

Increasingly, ordinary phone-in programme callers reflect the view that, if the *News of the World* phone-hacking scandal was sufficient to trigger a full-scale judicial inquiry, then surely the multi-institutional failures and cover-ups surrounding Savile and its mushrooming fallout warrant it even more. The same strand of opinion is being echoed over the banks, the police and politicians who still don't appear to have 'got it' over the moral/legal issue of their expenses.

Increasingly, too, those ordinary phone-in callers are warming to the notion that, without a press free of a regulatory system open to political influence, the phone-hacking scandal and the MPs' expenses scandal would have remained hidden from public scrutiny.

There are encouraging signs that, despite the best efforts of Hacked Off, the British public might yet rally behind a beefed-up form of independent self-regulation.

It's a mood swing that might help explain the discrepancy – one firmly in favour one firmly against – between two YouGov polls (one commissioned by Hacked Off, the other by the *Sun*/'Currant Bun') over statutory regulation of the press. Or, perhaps, that might simply be down to a twist on the catchphrase of the late, lamented Irish comic Frank Carson – 'it's the way you ask 'em'.

I am a hacking victim too…

A funny thing happened to me after I'd submitted my own evidence to Leveson. It came with a call from Scotland Yard's Operation Weeting squad informing me I was another statistic on Glenn Mulcaire's voluminous list of hacking targets. This was nothing to do with my own journalistic history but was apparently linked to my role as a PR adviser to various celebrities, corporate clients and charities with prominent royal patrons.

I decided against sending LJL an addendum to my earlier evidence, and I also decided against referring to it during my broadcasting appearances commenting on the inquiry.

But it did force me to face the question whether it changed my mind about opposing statutory regulation of the press, not least because as a lifelong Labour supporter, it felt strange to be in bed with Michael Gove, Eric Pickles, David Cameron and George Osborne rather than my more natural bedfellows like Ed Miliband and Harriet Harman. (Thank God I eventually found myself sharing a metaphorical bed, after His Lordship delivered his report, with the more acceptable Shami Chakrabati, of Liberty and a Leveson assessor!)

For what it's worth, my verdict was that my belief in the principle of a free press outweighed personal grievances or my usual political loyalties.

It was a development I finally decided to go public about while appearing on a Hertford College Oxford University debate panel in November 2012 featuring Hugh Grant, Will Hutton and Baroness Helena Kennedy, QC, on the eve of publication of Lord Justice Leveson's much-anticipated report.

Afterwards Hugh Grant seemed to struggle with the very notion that a Labour-supporting victim of phone-hacking was arguing against the Hacked Off view rather than *for* it.

Similarly the otherwise genial actor suffered a minor sense of humour failure when I suggested being frontman for Hacked Off was his best role since the halycon days of *Four Weddings*, *Notting Hill*, *Bridget Jones's Diary* and *About a Boy*. (I've also several times felt compelled to question why Hacked Off, piously dismissive of the tabloids' fascination with celebrity stories, should be so eager to be publicly represented by an Anglo-Hollywood star on the campaign trail.)

Savile; my own failures

During the debate, Hugh Grant also appeared to consider it a low blow (whether under Queensbury or Leveson Rules, I'm not sure) when I ventured the opinion that, if he'd been alive, Jimmy Savile might well have joined the celebrity trek to the Royal Courts of Justice to complain about those pesky tabloids.

As the *Sunday Mirror* editor who only narrowly failed to expose Savile back in 1994 when two frightened former victims lost their nerve at the prospect of going to court, citing their doubt whether they'd be believed against the word of a powerful friend of Mrs Thatcher and members of the Royal family, I think I'm a better judge of the Savile factor than Hugh Grant.

Lest anyone get the wrong impression, I don't doubt the sincerity of Hugh Grant's involvement with the Hacked Off cause. But I do suggest that, in light of the compromises now being offered by the newspaper industry, Hacked Off's statutory demands smack of zealotry. And, despite his denials of any personal political career ambitions, I still fancy a modest wager with Betfair on Hugh Grant eventually standing for Parliament or some other form of public office!

So, is Leveson right or wrong?

On the day Lord Justice Leveson finally delivered his verdict, I spent several hours in various TV and radio studios, but the personal memory that lingers most doesn't feature the BBC, ITN, Sky or CNN. Instead it focuses on being buttonholed by small crews from Latin America and Eastern Europe, incredulous at the idea that Britain – a place they enviously associated with a free and robust press, holding power to account – would contemplate accepting even a 'dab of statute' around its newspapers.

In the days following publication, I was particularly struck by former *Guardian* editor and *Observer* columnist Peter Preston's perceptive December 2nd article, headlined 'An elephantine, sloppy exercise in cut-and-paste'

Preston wrote: 'The idea that politicians (and newspaper proprietors) will suddenly discover a perfect way of regulating the press is bunk. To see that, turn to the most single most depressing part of Brian Leveson's magnum opus and the paragraphs of chop-logic where he pretends that Twitter, Facebook and the rest don't exist.

'Who cares if Prince Harry's Vegas revels and Princess Kate's sunbathing are all over the net? Ethical, regulated newspapers are required to pretend that US privacy laws, French snappers and international celebrity websites that 90% of the British population can click to somehow don't exist. It's a ludicrous proposition'.

Peter Preston, it should be carefully noted, isn't a man who even Robert Jay, QC, could sniffily consider any sort of red-top ruffian.

But Preston had latched onto the massive flaw in the whole Leveson exercise. Given that the wild west of cyberspace was always the elephant in the room at the Royal Courts of Justice, the pitifully few pages devoted to it in the good judge's 1,987-page tome truly beggared belief. It was as if the whole Inquiry team had been hijacked by Dr Who and whisked off in the Tardis to a time before the internet had been invented and news depended solely on dead trees and a regulated broadcast media. (For Peter Preston's view see p 159 of this volume)

More than once during his 18-month long, near £5m inquiry, Lord Justice Leveson opined that he didn't want to see his report wind up 'gathering dust on the second shelf of an academic's bookcase'.

Not much fear of that, m'lud. But every chance it will be effectively be blown away in the near-future and rendered an irrelevance by the rapid, ever-evolving reality of cyberspace.

In the meantime, one of the big media stories of 2013 might well centre on whether the House of Commons' cross-party Culture, Media and Sport Select Committee (rumoured to be highly-sceptical about statutory regulation) press ahead with their idea of asking Lord Justice Leveson to appear before it and face questioning over his report and its conclusions.

So far it seems that Brian Leveson does not consider that a senior judge has any obligation to be cross-examined by MPs and that, having conducted a judicial inquiry and delivered his recommendations, it is up to the government who commissioned it, or Parliament as a whole, to decide how to handle his slippery balloon.

Onwards and upwards...
Almost inevitably, the Leveson marathon failed to nail the elusive butterfly of what constitutes the public interest. The tabloids, and the readers who exercise their right to buy them, will remain fascinated by the celebrity factor. The journalist in me remains convinced that exposing hypocrisy among the rich and famous is perfectly valid, provided the methodology is strictly legitimate. The PR in me will continue to advise celebrity clients along the following lines: If you do drugs, don't be tempted to front up a government anti-drugs campaign: if you are a serial adulterer don't trade on a idyllic marriage image: and if you choose to invest in perfectly legal, but morally questionable, tax avoidance schemes, don't promote yourself as a champion of the underprivileged. And, if you choose not to follow said advice, don't cry when the damage limitation exercise proves less than totally successful and the commercial sponsorship deals start to dry up.

Lord Justice Leveson was right to point out that, while there was little wrong with the PCC code, the now moribund watchdog was never truly a regulator. There are those of us committed to non-statutory regulation who have long argued the case for beefed-up independent self-regulation by a body with the power to levy fines, pro-actively investigate, rule on the prominence of apologies and corrections and with a minority of its members drawn from the press and without the involvement of serving editors in any complaint-judging capacity. The inclusion of some experienced newspaper hands would still be essential, but there is hardly a shortage of ex-editors and executives no longer reliant on the industry for their salaries or career ambitions to draw from.

Most of the above is already on the table in the delicate post-Leveson negotiations. Toss in an imposing independent chair like Sir Alistair Graham, the no-nonsense former head of the Committee on Standards in Public Life whose history of ruffling feathers in high places suggests he would be no patsy of either press barons or politicians while stoutly defending the public's reasonable right to know and we might just have a formula that only the most obdurate members of the pro-statute lobby could reject.

Truly, this bit of real life theatre could run and run…

Note on the contributor

Paul Connew is a media commentator who appears regularly on the BBC, Sky, CNN and Al-Jazeera, plus broadcasters in Australia, New Zealand, Canada and Russia. Connew is a former editor of the *Sunday Mirror*, deputy editor of the *Daily Mirror* and a former deputy editor of the *News of the World*. He is also a PR adviser to celebrity and corporate clients and charities with royal patrons. It was in his PR capacity that he was informed by Scotland Yard (during the Leveson Inquiry) that his phone had been targeted by the *News of the World*'s private investigator Glenn Mulcaire.

The Savile affair: The tabloids revenge for Leveson? Motives and mechanics of scandal at the BBC

Patrick Barrow looks at the intertwined narratives of two 2012 big media events-the Leveson Inquiry and the scandals at the BBC over their coverage or non-coverage of the Jimmy Savile affair. Was one related to the other? Did the newspapers get the boot into the BBC as revenge for the Corporation smelling of roses at the Leveson Inquiry?

When Lord Justice Leveson finally reported, few emerged with their reputations enhanced. Politicians and the police did rather better than perhaps they had expected, effectively cleared of considered wrong doing but certainly guilty of embarrassingly poor decision making.

For the media, however, the judgement was without mitigation: 'reckless prioritisation', 'ruthless pursuit of sensationalism', 'outrageous' behaviour, the results of which were 'devastation'.

All journalism was to hang its head in shame. All? No. One news organisation had, apparently, held out against the temptations of covert surveillance without public interest, shady and illegal practice and the systematic destruction of personal privacy. That organisation? The BBC.

The BBC emerges unscathed?
Not that the BBC was entirely alone in emerging un-spattered from the Leveson media gutter. The main TV news broadcasters – Sky, ITV News and so on – had all been largely protected as news operations either by moderated editorial inclinations or the tighter and more prescriptive nature of broadcast regulation.

But they weren't the BBC. In fact, in one instance they were owned and run by the man who had presided over some of the worst excesses of the press, Rupert Murdoch.

The BBC – a special case?
To many within the tabloid press however, the BBC was a special case; the Satan in a Pandemonium of left liberal media bias, uncompetitive subsidy, profligate

expenditure, Islington smugness, management speak, vested interest, ageism and social interference.

On no subject could it be trusted: politics, religion, Europe, climate change, the Middle East and, above all, press malpractice.

The suspicion abroad was that the BBC had revelled in the inquiry, not just in its blanket coverage or in its tone – though both became contentious when Cameron press aide Craig Oliver told Norman Smith, the BBC's chief political correspondent, he was "genuinely shocked" by the bias in his coverage, adding "I have rarely seen such partial reporting of the debate"[1] – but in the very evidence BBC management gave to the enquiry.

Sowing the wind; trust and complacency

Then Director General Mark Thompson poked the lion, telling Lord Justice Leveson: "The BBC is not a business and it might well be that someone running a media business might take a different view from the view that I took as Director General of the BBC."

He then added: "The BBC is a public service broadcaster. It is committed to be the most trusted, trustworthy source of news in the world and we want to maintain the highest possible standards in all matters, including matters relating to privacy."[2]

To anyone who has worked within BBC News (as I have) that kind of statement is Bible true, an article of faith and philosophy beyond question within the organisation and one on which the BBC has built and maintains its worldwide reputation.

To a BBC man (and woman) it is a commonplace, supported by survey after survey, trust index after trust index. It is a belief that is the very strength of the BBC and also its greatest weakness.

Veterans will testify to that earnest pride in the BBC's reputation, matched by a remorseless desire to live up to its ideals but matched equally by a wilful blindness to the facts of its own collective world and political view.

And anyone who has worked there will also tell you that the BBC's view of the way the world gazes back is one shaped by an odd naiveté and the certain knowledge that when it is important, 'the world turns to the BBC'.

It is, in the BBC mind, a public trust without nuance where criticism is largely confined to what BBC Media Correspondent Nick Higham described as the "'prejudiced' reader of *The Daily Mail* or the self-interested carping of News International."

Thompson, in that belief, then handed over this hostage to fortune: "It being undetermined how widespread some of these issues have been in the media, I think it was prudent to look at whether the BBC could, in its journalism and journalistic practice, hold its head up and say actually, we don't do these things."

In fact, the BBC's journalistic practices would soon be placed under the harshest scrutiny. Its respect for privacy would in one case prove over emphasised and in another horribly lax. Overlooking, some would suggest wilfully, the abuses of one man while falsely insinuating against another. In other words, the conceit on which BBC News based itself was about to be rocked to its very foundations.

Lord Patten goads the tabloids. Lord Patten goads everybody.

Meanwhile, and in parallel fashion, Lord Patten, Chairman of the BBC Trust, was winding the cord further round the Corporation's neck.

Perhaps believing himself, through his experience and positions, uniquely qualified to comment on both media and politics, Patten told Leveson that he was "in favour of talking to editors and journalists, but I am not in favour of grovelling". "I think the major political parties, and particularly their leaders, over the last 20 or 25 years have often demeaned themselves by the extent to which they have paid court to proprietors and editors," he said. "I think that politicians have allowed themselves to be kidded by editors and proprietors that editors and proprietors determine the fate of politicians. "I think that there is plenty of evidence that in some cases, particularly News International newspapers, will back the party that is going to win an election – so they give you what you don't need in return for more than a great deal of faith."[3]

What Lord Patten had to say may well have been true but speaking truth unto power was ever risky and newspaper editors, kidders or not, still possessed considerable power. Patten and Thompson, however unwittingly, were sowing the whirlwind.

Leaning to the Left?

The signs of the whirlwind they would reap were very clearly there. BBC Presenter Andrew Marr had conceded as far back as 2003 that the BBC has 'liberal preoccupations', veteran presenter Peter Sissons had written "At the core of the BBC, in its very DNA, is a way of thinking that is firmly of the Left"[4]. He added that "I lost count of the number of times I asked a producer for a brief on a story, only to be handed a copy of *The Guardian* and told 'it's all in there'". Thompson himself was later to admit to a 'massive left-wing bias' at the Corporation when he had first joined it.[5]

Those admissions were leading many to suggest that, far from standing smugly aloof from the Leveson process, the BBC should find itself subject to scrutiny for failing in its duty of impartiality.

That the BBC's contribution to Leveson was, in the minds of many, casting stones while believing itself sinless was hubris. An increasing number in the tabloid press were itching to be nemesis.

As Lord Justice Leveson himself said, there is "a cultural tendency within parts of the press vigorously to resist or dismiss complainants almost as a matter of course". They would, he said, exact revenge through "high-volume, extremely personal attacks on those who challenge them."[6]

It was a lesson the BBC and its management was about to learn in the most painful fashion.

Reaping the whirlwind; Savile and the Fates conspire

True to the highest forms of tragedy then, the makings of the BBC's downfall were inherent in its own character. And fate was working feverishly to have circumstances conspire to a point where the BBC's fault lines would be dreadfully exposed to its gathering enemies.

In October 2011 Jimmy Savile – DJ, fundraiser, *Top of the Pops* regular and host of the eponymous *Jim'll Fix It* – died. As the front man for various charities and by virtue of his sheer longevity as a national figure in entertainment his death was marked by warm news coverage and a memorial service from Leeds, marked by genuine popular affection. At the time, few in the media dissented from the public mood.

However, long-term rumours within journalism and on the showbiz circuit were effectively unleashed for repetition and investigation. That suspicions had existed about Savile for many years was fact. But he was a powerful figure and potentially litigious. With him dead, the dangers of libel disappeared and the testimony of his many victims became viable. First to publicly break cover was ITV in an *Exposure* documentary in October 2012 alleging that Savile was a regular abuser of children and the vulnerable and had misused his privileged position at high profile hospitals to perpetrate his crimes.

'Newsnight' takes centre stage

As the pre-publicity for the ITV exposé gathered momentum, it began to emerge that the flagship BBC current affairs programme *Newsnight* had shelved a similar investigation into Savile ten months previously.

The suggestion being that then *Newsnight* editor Peter Rippon had been placed under pressure to drop the film as it clashed with various retrospective hagiographies about the presenter and was an embarrassment to the BBC, much of the abuse had allegedly occurred on BBC premises and gone unchallenged by those who suspected it.

Rippon denied it, blogging that the programme had been shelved for editorial reasons and only on discovery that the Crown Prosecution Service (CPS) had dropped a similar investigation for lack of evidence.

However, in the aftermath of the ITV programme going to air and with more and more victims coming forward, tremendous pressure was exerted on the BBC to reveal not only what had happened with *Newsnight*'s investigation but what had happened to allow Savile to continue his allegedly paedophilic activities in the face of what now seemed to be widespread suspicion.

The roof simply fell in on the BBC

'BBC shelved Savile investigation to protect its own reputation'[7] accused the *Mail* and, amid a million more screaming and lurid headlines from across the tabloid piste in which the reader was never allowed to forget that Savile had been a 'BBC DJ', summed up precisely where the point of attack lay: the good name and trustworthiness of the BBC.

That many newspapers and police forces had embarked on investigations of Savile which never came to sufficiently robust conclusions to warrant either publication or arrest was beside the point. The BBC had failed and had covered it up was the top and bottom of tabloid interpretation.

The pressure became so intense that within a fortnight of the ITV broadcast the BBC had announced investigations into the dropping of the *Newsnight* story and the internal culture which had apparently indulged Savile's peccadilloes and discouraged belief in widespread concerns about him.

The BBC at (civil) war

On 23 October *Panorama* then performed the classically BBC trick of exposing the BBC, including sister programme *Newsnight* and its own (then) Director General George Entwistle. There are many ways to interpret this; variations round remarkably principled journalism based on genuine love of the organisation or simply crass disloyalty.

The BBC's coverage of itself can be remorseless as a later grilling of Entwistle by *Today* doyen John Humphrys[8] would demonstrate and is probably to its long-term reputational enhancement.

But while *Panorama* and Humphrys can claim proper journalistic imperatives, elsewhere the tabloids, the newspapers, have never been short of former BBC correspondents, or indeed press officers, eager to provide critical opinion of the Corporation.

By the end of the crisis, BBC notables such as world affairs editor John Simpson, former foreign correspondent Martin Bell and veteran presenter and *Question Time* Presenter David Dimbleby had all had a say and little in defence of their employer.

Either way, much as the English have always been able to rely on Celtic in-fighting to gather intelligence, the press have always had a steady stream of high profile BBC figures who, under whatever motivation, have provided grist to their mill.

Man down

On the eve of the *Panorama* broadcast, *Newsnight* editor Peter Rippon was forced to 'step aside' (in itself a strange BBC term...). In the event, it was a position he and his deputy would never recover. The first BBC victim was claimed.

Entwistle himself went on to give a deeply unconvincing display in front a Parliamentary Select Committee on October 23 and events shifted still further towards Westminster when, on the same day, Culture Secretary Maria Miller wrote to Entwistle raising 'concerns about trust and confidence in the BBC'.

Labour MP Tom Watson later stood up in the House of Commons on Oct 24 and suggested the existence of a high-level paedophile gang at the heart of the Tory Eighties government. In so doing, he set the scene for *Newsnight* to play another fateful part in facilitating tabloid revenge on the Corporation.

Once is unfortunate, twice starts to look like carelessness

Perhaps eager to make up for the shelving of the first Savile programme, *Newsnight* broadcast a Film on Nov 2 alleging abuse at a Welsh children's home in the 1970s in which it and an abuse victim, Steve Messham, implicated one-time Conservative treasurer Lord McAlpine not directly but by inference.

In so doing, they were aided and abetted by a former BBC Reporter Angus Stickler from the oddly monickered Bureau of Investigative Journalism. That it sounds like a self-aggrandising school gang comprising precocious sixth formers playing newspapers should have alerted *Newsnight* to say nothing of the track record of their main witness-Messham.

Even on the day of broadcast former *Newsnight* Political Editor Michael Crick had tweeted: "[A] 'senior political figure' due to be accused tonight by BBC of being paedophile denies allegations and tells me he'll issue a libel writ against the BBC." Crick had done his basic journalism, *Newsnight* had not. *The Guardian* later published a piece dismissing the long-whispered allegation as simply a case of mistaken identity; Messham had never seen a photo of the 'right' Lord McAlpine.

However eager to make up for missing the last war by starting this one, *Newsnight* pressed ahead without the apparent knowledge of its' Director General, who was later to claim that he had been too busy speech writing to read his cuttings, and without approaching Lord McAlpine to offer him a right of reply.

The result was catastrophic, setting off a Twitter storm that saw McAlpine outed and he out himself. He served a writ on the BBC and the tweeters and Steve Messham withdraw his allegations.

DG RIP

The whirlwind was about to reach its howling peak on November 9th with Director General George Entwistle savaged by a clearly angered John Humphrys on Radio 4's *Today*, conceding that *Newsnight* was 'fundamentally wrong' and claiming, fatally, that he had only known about the programme after broadcast. Entwistle resigned a little over 12 hours after the bloodbath on *Today*, a mere 54 days into the shortest tenure ever at the top of the BBC.

In the tabloids, the was joy unconfined: "Skewered by his own side: How just 24 minutes of the most humiliating interviews ever broadcast sealed the fate of the BBC's Director General" exulted the *Mail*.[9]

It may have been the BBC Brutus that had dealt the fatal blow but the tabloid senate had been screaming for it for days.

"BBC crisis: John Humphrys sealed George Entwistle's fate" agreed the *Telegraph*[10] but, broadsheet though it may be, it had a take on the farrago which went to the heart of the BBC's reputation and, in the eyes of many in the press, its real crime.

Boris says what many think?

Confronted with a bleeding Beeb, The Mayor of London and Wannabe Conservative Prime Minister Boris Johnson applied the boot to its prone figure without mercy: "They hadn't even put the allegations to McAlpine! Unbelievable! And why not? It was, as they say, a story that was too good to check. It wasn't just that it showed *Newsnight* taking up the cudgels against paedophiles, after the embarrassment of the axed Savile exposé. It went one better. It pushed all the buttons. It was like a dream come true for any vaguely resentful and Left-of-centre BBC producer. It was a chance to pour unlimited ordure on a man who – in their book – jolly well had it coming. He is rich, he is a toff, he is a Lord, he is a **Tory**, and – joy of joys – he is an EX-AIDE TO MRS THATCHER."[11]

The trouble for the BBC was, cock-up or conspiracy, it was just too damned hard to deny.

The BBC battered

Meanwhile on, on went the beating. Why wouldn't it? With less than a month to go before the 29 November publication date for Lord Leveson's report into press misconduct, the swot of the media class had been found cheating at exams, smoking and having an affair with teacher. It was simply too good to be true.

The BBC walked into punch after punch.

What was this odd Corporation phraseology 'stepped aside' when, on 12 Nov, Head of News Helen Boaden and her deputy Stephen Mitchell followed in Peter Rippon's footsteps and did just that?

On the same day, the MacQuarrie (the Director of BBC Scotland) Report into the second *Newsnight* gaffe concluded that "basic journalistic checks had not been completed".

Lord Patten conceded to MPs that Entwistle's £450,000 pay-off was twice as much as the figure to which he was entitled.

The BBC paid out £185,000 in agreed damages to Lord MacAlpine

The enquiry into the first *Newsnight* Savile farce, headed by former *Sky News* head Nick Pollard, eventually cost £2m. And each development was greeted by shrill press condemnation of the BBC's profligacy with licence payer's money, its evasive management-speak, its shoddy journalistic safeguards and so on *ad infinitum*.

All of which was a useful diversion from Lord Justice Leveson's condemnatory report on the press and his recommendation of statutory underpinning to newspaper regulation, something which all British newspapers detested and which they were determined to resist at any cost.

When the Pollard enquiry finally reported on December 19, its essential finding, that Peter Rippon had not been placed under undue pressure to drop the *Newsnight* Savile investigation, was drowned out in the clamour to report the serious management failings and the fact that while senior figures had resigned or been moved, nobody had actually been fired at BBC News.

Self-inflicted wound
So, the mechanics of a scandal. But tabloid revenge? Only up to a point, Lord Copper. That newspapers in all forms had screamed, yelled and criticised at every opportunity is undoubtedly true. That the tabloids had watched misfortune pile upon misfortune with undisguised glee, equally so. That the old criticisms had been rehearsed and interwoven into every new development, yes. That the whole shambles had proven a useful diversion and telling point to Leveson and those who supported his recommendations and findings, without doubt.

The cock-up that made conspiracy redundant
But none of that makes what happened tabloid revenge in the sense that there had been no active conspiracy or plot among the tabloids to make what happened happen. They hadn't needed to. The BBC had done it for them. All they had to do was sit back and cheer on the blood sport that followed.

The blood spilt had been considerable, whatever the tabloids or the press at large said.

Casualty report
Rippon, gone. Not from the BBC but from the editorship of the BBC's flagship current affairs output. His career blighted and, in effect, over.

Stephen Mitchell resigned and gone from the Corporation after a six month handover. The Head of BBC Radio 5Live, Adrian Van Klaveren, ostensibly holding oversight over Savile coverage, moved to a Corporation job away from News.

George Entwistle, DG, resigned in disgrace.

Newsnight's reputation sullied and damaged to the extent that rumours abounded that presenter Jeremy Paxman was planning a disgusted departure from the programme.

A decline in the BBC's trust rating. Its most treasured possession

Demands for the resignation of a 'petulant' Lord Patten.

Bafflement over the apparently unscathed return of BBC News boss Helen Boaden.

The list went on.

But it is an ill wind that blows nobody any good and, returning to the BBC fold as DG, the former head of news and current affairs, Tony Hall, in from a lauded tenure heading the revived Royal Opera House.

With a three month target of mapping out the BBC's reform and return to glory, Hall's appointment was widely seen as a good thing. A man who understands news and the BBC, the popular Hall had pushed through many of the Birt reforms which had seen the Corporation survive a previous bout of unwelcome scrutiny.

With many in the press watching and waiting for his first misstep, Hall will be keenly aware that, not for the first time, the future of the BBC is his to secure. The tabloids are watching.

Notes

All accessed on 24 December 2012

[1] http://www.guardian.co.uk/media/2012/may/28/cameron-media-chief-rebukes-bbc-reporter

[2] http://www.guardian.co.uk/media/interactive/2012/jan/23/mark-thompson-witness-statement-leveson-inquiry

[3] http://www.bbc.co.uk/news/uk-16677720

[4] http://www.dailymail.co.uk/news/article-1349506/Left-wing-bias-Its-written-BBCs-DNA-says-Peter-Sissons.html

[5] http://www.standard.co.uk/news/bbc-chief-mark-thompson-admits-leftwing-bias-6509105.html

[6] Leveson report http://www.official-documents.gov.uk/document/hc1213/hc07/0779/0779.pdf

[7] http://www.dailymail.co.uk/news/article-2099141/BBC-shelved-Savile-sex-abuse-investigation-protect-reputation.html

[8] John Humphrys interviews George Entwistle on Today http://www.youtube.com/watch?v=Q16kkOLvb4o

[9] http://www.dailymail.co.uk/news/article-2231286/George-Entwistle-The-disastrous-24-minutes-BBC-interviews-led-downfall-Director-General.html

[10] http://www.telegraph.co.uk/culture/tvandradio/bbc/9672270/BBC-crisis-John-Humphrys-sealed-George-Entwistles-fate.html

[11] http://www.telegraph.co.uk/comment/columnists/borisjohnson/9671346/BBC-investigation-Smearing-an-innocent-mans-name-is-the-real-tragedy-here.html

Note on the contributor

Patrick Barrow has more than 20 years experience at the sharp end of PR and corporate communications including time under Tony Hall as a senior press officer at BBC News in the Nineties. A former head of corporate affairs at the *Telegraph* he was also director general of the Public Relations Consultants Association. Now running his own agency, Reputation Communications, he is a regular commentator on topical reputational issues and media matters.

How many drinks in that 'Last Chance Saloon'? The history of official Inquiries into the British Press

The Leveson Inquiry was the latest in a long list of inquiries into the British press and its role in society since the Second World War. John Jewell of the Cardiff School of Journalism, examines the most important of these and looks at how we arrived at Leveson

When Lord Justice Leveson published his report on the 29th November, 2012[1] it was the culmination of the most sustained, intricate and comprehensive investigations into the culture, ethics and practices of the British press. It was an enquiry which, as Roy Greenslade states, 'had taken testimonies, either in person or in writing, from 650 witnesses, thus generating more than 6,000 pages of evidence. That is some achievement, given that the hearings did not begin until November 14, 2011.'[2]

The great, the good and the guilty appeared before Leveson – Prime Ministers past and present, proprietors, journalists and policeman all under public scrutiny as never before.

So let's not forget how we got here. In early July 2011 it was disclosed by the Guardian that journalists on the *News of the World* had hacked into the phone messages of murdered schoolgirl, Milly Dowler[3]. Not only this, messages were removed to make room for more. This was followed by the news that Scotland Yard detectives had contacted the families of Soham victims, Holly Wells and Jessica Chapman as part of their investigation into Private Investigator Glenn Mulcaire, who was previously employed by the paper[4]. Then came news that families of the victims of the 7/7 terrorist atrocities may also have had their messages monitored by Mulcaire[5]. The father of one of the victims, Graham Foulkes, said the prospect of these allegations being true 'fills me with horror'[6]. There was understandable public and political outrage at these allegations and Sunday 11th July 2012 saw the last ever edition of the *News of the World* after 168 years.

Events were moving very quickly indeed and on 13th July 2012, David Cameron announced that an Inquiry led by Lord Justice Leveson would investigate not only phone hacking but also he stated that the Inquiry would 'inquire into the culture, practices and ethics of the press; its relationship with the police; the failure of the current system of regulation; the contacts made, and discussions had, between national newspapers and politicians; why previous warnings about press misconduct were not heeded; and the issue of cross-media ownership. He will make recommendations for a new, more effective way of regulating the press – one that supports its freedom, plurality and independence from Government, but which also demands the highest ethical and professional standards. He will also make recommendations about the future conduct of relations between politicians and the press.'[7]

And so it was that Lord Justice Leveson opened the hearings on 14 November 2012, saying: "the press provides an essential check on all aspects of public life. That is why any failure within the media affects all of us. At the heart of this inquiry, therefore, may be one simple question: who guards the guardians?"[8]

But as the Hacked off [9] campaign pointed out in the days before the report was published, there have been, since the end of World War II, a succession of 'last chances' granted to the press and a number of inquiries into its probity and practices. In the chapter to follow I will examine some of the most significant.

The First Royal Commission on the Press

The First Royal Commission on the Press was established in 1947 'with the object of furthering the free expression of opinion through the press and the greatest practicable accuracy in the presentation of the news', and reported in 1949[10]. It proposed that the industry should set up a General Council of the Press to govern the behaviour of the press, from conditions of employment and training to issues of ownership, and to promote the interests of the consumers and conduct research into the long-term social and economic impact of the print industry.[11]

Let's not forget that in the years after the Second World War, the press was subject to the 'personal control of interventionist proprietors'[12] such as Beaverbrook and Rothermere, Indeed, the cultural and political similarities between then and now are remarkable. As Ian Jack[13] has pointed out, for two years the Commission took statements and examined witnesses. Michael Foot, Lord Beaverbrook and Tom Driberg were among those who turned up to testify. On the subject of journalists themselves, the report of 1949 concluded: 'some of the spokesmen of the press who gave evidence appeared to us unduly complacent and deficient in the practice of self-criticism.'[14]

The Commission also judged that the presentation of news was often misleading and that there was an inherent partisanship and political bias within much reporting. As Henry Irving[15] has noted, it was particularly critical of proprietors for offering an overly simplistic account of events rather than trying to educate their readers.

But the main recommendation of the report was the creation of a 'General Press Council'. In Parliament, Deputy Prime Minister, Herbert Morrison stated, 'This proposal for a General Council is a proposal that there should be a body which would watch the press, which would comment upon standards in the press, which would encourage good standards of journalism and of reporting and of presentation; a body to which complaints could be sent; and a body which also could represent the rights of the press to the Government and international organisations, and so on. In our judgment the recommendation of the Royal Commission is right.[16] Of great interest were these words, 'It is proposed that as to four-fifths of the membership, roughly, it should be composed of newspaper men of one sort and another, but as to about 20 per cent., including the chairman, it should be composed of outside people – fair minded, good citizens. It is proposed that they should be appointed by the Lord Chief Justice and the Lord President of the Court of Session.[17]

However, it was not until 1953, after the threat of political action to establish statutory regulation, that a General Council was actually set up. And then it included no lay membership. It was in the words of Tunstall, 'while claiming to be in the public interest, the Council was fairly transparently a defender of press interest.[18]

The Second Royal Commission on the Press

It was clear by 1961 that the General Council had failed to engage with the range of reforms and practices outlined in the recommendations of the Royal Commission. It never really acted in the public interest – its members were newspaper people and its funding came entirely from the industry. Crucially, it had no power at all to enforce any decisions it made. As Kevin Williams writes, 'it soon became apparent that the newspapers paid no attention to the Council'.[19]

So the 2nd Royal Commission on the Press (1961-1962), chaired by Lord Shawcross, was driven by the above issues, monopoly of ownership and by the closure of both national and provincial newspaper titles. Once again, observe the parallels with the present day.

More than this, when the Commission reported, it repeated the necessity – stated clearly in 1949 – 'of a voluntary basis for regulation, but stressed the need above all for an effective and credible body, with statutory backing if necessary'[20]: "If... the press is not willing to invest the Council with the necessary authority and to contribute the necessary finance the case for a statutory body with definite powers and the right to levy the industry is a clear one"[21].

This time the press was quick to action fearful of imposed radical changes. The General Council became the Press Council, dealing with complaints became a fundamental objective, in theory at least and the composition of the Council comprised 20% lay members, including its chairman, the judge Lord Devlin.[22]

But certain things had not changed. Though the Devlin years (1964-1969) were considered to be successful by some, the willingness of the press to pay for stories relating to high profile cases such as the Profumo affair and the Moors murders, meant that the perception of a wilfully powerless organisation continued. For one thing, it was still financially reliant on proprietors for funding and needed the approval and cooperation of the editors to function at all. It was difficult to dispel the notion that the 'long term purpose of the Press Council was to act as a public buffer, protecting the press from formal legislation and allowing it to carry on in much the same undisciplined way.'[23]

The Third Royal Commission on the Press

The third post war inquiry into the press (1974-1977) must be seen against the wider social and economic uncertainty of the times. The newspaper industry had its own economic problems[24] but still the concerns over the 'responsibilities, constitution and functioning 'of the Press Council persisted.[25]

Indeed, the 1977 Commission concluded that the Press Council 'has so far failed to persuade the knowledgeable public that it deals satisfactorily with complaints against newspapers, notwithstanding that this has come to be seen as its main purpose'.[26]

The report was highly disparaging of the Council overall and made twelve recommendations including the creation of a code of conduct on which it based its adjudications.

But the Royal Commission shied away from recommending statutory powers for enforcement of sanctions. That was in 1977. It was a full four years, in 1981, before the Council responded to the report and rejected the notion of a code. By this time the NUJ had withdrawn from membership of the Press Council on the grounds that it was 'incapable of reform'.[27]

The Calcutt Committee – 1

In 1989, Sir David Calcutt QC was tasked with heading a Privacy Committee looking into press intrusion. This measure had cross party support and came at a time when there was concerted public and political dissatisfaction with the perceived transgressions of the press. The 1980s had seen the *Sun* and the *Daily Mail* face adjudication from the Press Council on many occasions.[28] It was the era of tabloid expose, celebrity revelation and the Press Council was seemingly, once again, unable or unwilling to curb the many excesses of the newspapers.

The 1990 Calcutt report went over the same ground as its Royal predecessors – the Press Council was inefficient as an adjudicating body, it was still far too close to the proprietors, it continued to reject out of hand far too many complaints.

This time though, Calcutt recommended the setting up of a new Press Complaints Commission to replace the Press Council. The new Commission would be given 18 months to prove non-statutory self-regulation could work effectively and if it failed to do so, then a statutory system would be introduced.

Home Secretary, David Waddington, told the House, 'this is positively the last chance for the industry to establish an effective non-statutory system of regulation, and I strongly hope that it will seize the opportunity that the committee has given it. If a non-statutory commission is established, the Government will review its performance after 18 months of operation to determine whether a statutory underpinning is required. If no steps are taken to set up such a commission, the Government, albeit with some regret, will proceed to establish a statutory framework, taking account of the committee's recommendations.'[29]

On January 1st 1991, the Press Complaints Commission came into being.

The Calcutt Committee – 2

The first 18 months of the PCC was reviewed in the second Calcutt Report (*'Review of Press Self-Regulation'*) published in January 1993. The results could scarcely have been more damning. It was deemed to have been a total failure, with the pressing need for an independent body to be created which could restore public faith in critically damaged newspaper industry[30]. Calcutt wrote, 'The Press Complaints Commission is not, in my view, an effective regulator of the press. It has not been set up in a way, and is not operating a code of practice, which enables it to command not only press but also public confidence.

It does not, in my view, hold the balance fairly between the press and the individual. It is not the truly independent body which it should be. As constituted, it is, in essence, a body set up by the industry, financed by the industry, dominated by the industry, and operating a code of practice devised by the industry and which is over-favourable to the industry'[31]

For Calcutt, the press had had its final chance and the report recommended that the process toward creating a statutory Press Complaints Tribunal begin. There were a series of measures forwarded intended to improve standards, too – such as the idea that editors and journalists be obliged by contract to comply with industry codes of practice. Also forwarded was the notion that, 'individuals would have the right to appeal from the [new] Commission to a press ombudsman with statutory powers'[32] to supervise corrections, apologies and retractions.

In the event, The Government delayed making a decision about the proposals until 1995 when the Secretary of State for National Heritage, Virginia Bottomley MP, announced that statutory controls would not be introduced[33]; instead, in the manner of so many before her, she issued a series of recommendations for reform of the PCC.

That saloon, those chances...

In March 2012 the Chairman of the PCC, Lord Hunt, declared that it was closing down after 21 years of practice. To this day, though, it remains active while politicians debate the options for replacement.[34]

When Leveson delivered his report it was clear, like his predecessors, that he believed statute was necessary to underpin a completely new watchdog system, which would overseen by a judge. Also in the manner of his predecessors, David Cameron, disagreed.

On December 7th, 2012, days after the publication of the Leveson report, the *Daily Telegraph*[35] reported that the Prime Minister was considering establishing a new independent press watchdog by Royal Charter – the mechanism utilised when the BBC was set up in the 1920's. This means that politicians would be excluded from the operation of the watchdog and there would be no statutory regulation.

For their part, the newspapers editors could not have been any clearer. A prepared statement was issued in response to the report which finds us, yet again, on familiar ground. It read: 'the editors of all national newspapers met yesterday and unanimously agreed to start putting in place the broad proposals – save the statutory underpinning – for the independent self-regulatory system laid out by Lord Justice Leveson.'[36]

That self regulation has been allowed to continue for so long is remarkable given the recommendations of the Royal Commissions and the Calcutt reports. Time after time, the press has been offered the opportunities to reform or accept statutory regulation. Time after time reform has been negligible and government reaction merely to instigate further inquiries or reports. As the Media Standards Trust Submission to the Leveson Inquiry pointed out in reference to David Mellor's 1991 quip,[37] 'the phrase 'last chance saloon', when used with regard to the British press, has attained the status of parody.'[38]

Notes

[1] The report is available in full here: Leveson enquiry: Culture, practice and ethics of the press .http://www.officialdocuments.gov.uk/document/hc1213/hc07/0780/0780.asp accessed 29th December, 2012

[2] Greenslade, Roy (2012) Report in danger of gathering dust. British Journalism Review. Vol. 23, No. 3, 2012, pages 20-26. Available online at http://www.bjr.org.uk/data/2012/no3_greenslade accessed January, 2nd 2013.

[3] Missing Millie Dowler's voicemail was hacked by News of the World. The Guardian, 5th July, 2011. Available online at http://www.guardian.co.uk/uk/2011/jul/04/milly-dowler-voicemail-hacked-news-of-world?INTCMP=SRCH accessed on January 2nd 2013.

[4] News of the World phone hacking: Police review all child abduction cases. The Guardian, 5th July, 2011. Available online at http://www.guardian.co.uk/media/2011/jul/05/phone-hacking-police-review-child-murders?INTCMP=SRCH accessed on January 2nd 2013.

[5] Families of 7/7 victims 'were targets of phone hacking'. *The Guardian*, 6th July, 2011. Available online at http://www.guardian.co.uk/media/2011/jul/06/families-7-7-targets-phone-hacking?INTCMP=SRCH accessed on 2nd January 2013.

[6] 7/7 victim 'filled with horror' at phone hacking. BBC Radio 4 *Today programme*, 6th July, 2011. Available at

http://news.bbc.co.uk/today/hi/today/newsid_9531000/9531534.stm accessed 2nd January 2013.

[7] *Hansard*, 13th July, 2011. Available online at http://www.publications.parliament.uk/pa/cm201011/cmhansrd/cm110713/debtext/1 10713-0001.htm accessed 2nd January 2013. See also Phone hacking: David Cameron announces terms of phone-hacking inquiry. *The Daily Telegraph*, 13th July, 2011. Available online at http://www.telegraph.co.uk/news/uknews/phone-hacking/8634757/Phone-hacking-David-Cameron-announces-terms-of-phone-hacking-inquiry.html accessed 3rd January 2013

[8] The Leveson inquiry website. Available online at http://www.levesoninquiry.org.uk/ accessed 3rd January.

[9] From the Royal Commission to Leveson: the 65 year struggle over press regulation. *The Press Gazette*, 26th November, 2012. Available online at http://www.pressgazette.co.uk/content/royal-commission-leveson-65-year-struggle-over-press-regulation accessed 29th December 2012.

[10] The Royal Commission on the Press (1947 – 49): Evidence and Papers. Available online at http://discovery.nationalarchives.gov.uk/SearchUI/details?Uri=C9115 accessed January 2nd 2013.

[11] Media Wise – Press Complaints Commission: History and Procedural Reform. Available online at http://www.mediawise.org.uk/wp-content/uploads/2011/05/PCC-History-and-Procedural-Reform.pdf accessed January 3rd 2013.

[12] Curran, J and Jean Seaton (1981) *Power Without Responsibility*. London: Routledge, p 68.

[13] Leveson isn't unprecedented. The same issues came up 60 years ago. *The Guardian*, 22nd June, 2012. Available online at http://www.guardian.co.uk/commentisfree/2012/jun/22/do-failings-of-newspapers-matter accessed 2nd January 2013.

[14] *Hansard*, 28th July, 1949. Reference was made to this quote by Herbert Morrison, Deputy Prime Minister, in a debate about the findings of the report. Available online at http://hansard.millbanksystems.com/commons/1949/jul/28/royal-commission-on-the-press-report accessed 2nd January 2013.

[15] Irving, H (2012) Past Politics: The 1947-49 Royal Commission on the Press. 29th April, 2012. Available online at http://pastpolitics.wordpress.com/2012/04/29/1947-9-royal-commission-on-the-press/ accessed on January 3rd 2013.

[16] *Hansard*, 28th July, 1949.. Available online at http://hansard.millbanksystems.com/commons/1949/jul/28/royal-commission-on-the-press-report accessed 2nd January 2013.

[17] *Hansard*, 28th July, i1949 ibid.

[18] Tunstall, J (1996) *Newspaper Power*. Oxford: Clarendon p395.

[19] Williams, K (2010) *Read all about it!* London Routledge p180.

[20] Media Standards Trust, A Free and Accountable Media. June, 2012. Available online at http://mediastandardstrust.org/wp-content/uploads/downloads/2012/06/MST-A-Free-and-Accountable-Media-21-06-12.pdf accessed January 4th 2013.

[21] Royal Commission on the Press 1961-1962: (1962) Report, London: HMSO, p101

[22] O'Malley, T and Clive Soley (2000) *Regulating the Press*. London: Pluto.

[23] Tunstall, J (1996) *Newspaper Power.* Oxford: Clarendon p397.

[24] The decision in 1974 by Beaverbrook newspapers to close in Glasgow prompted calls by MP's to examine the long term future of the press. See O'Malley and Soley (2000), p72.

[25] Media Standards Trust, A Free and Accountable Media. p15.

[26] As quoted in the Law Society Gazette, 23rd October, 1991. Available online at http://www.lawgazette.co.uk/news/the-press-complaints-commission accessed Jan 4th 2013.

[27] Media Wise – Press Complaints Commission: History and Procedural Reform. Available online at http://www.mediawise.org.uk/wp-content/uploads/2011/05/PCC-History-and-Procedural-Reform.pdf accessed January 3rd 2013.

[28] Tunstall, J (1996) *Newspaper Power.* Oxford: Clarendon p404

[29] *Hansard,* 21st June, 1990. Available online at http://hansard.millbanksystems.com/commons/1990/jun/21/calcutt-report accessed Jan 4th 2013.

[30] O'Malley and Soley (2000) write that, 'by 1991 public confidence in the British press was low…those expressing confidence in the British press had dropped to only 14%.' p90.

[31] Department of National Heritage Review of Press Self Regulation. London: HMSO Available online at http://www.levesoninquiry.org.uk/wp-content/uploads/2012/06/Exhibit-SJM-6.pdf accessed January 5th 2013.

[32] O'Malley and Soley (2000) p93.

[33] Media Wise – Press Complaints Commission: History and Procedural Reform.

[34] The Press Complaints Commission website states that, 'In March 2012, the PCC announced that it will now move to a transitional phase, transferring its assets, liabilities and staff to a new regulatory body designed along the lines proposed by the PCC's Reform Committee and discussed by the newspaper and magazine industry in December 2011. Complaints can still be made in the normal way throughout the transition period., 'the terms of the Editors' Code of Practice remain the same, and members of PCC staff are available at any time to offer advice, including on an emergency out-of-hours basis for concerns relating to harassment or attention from journalists and photographers.' Available online at http://www.pcc.org.uk/faqs.html#faq_top1_1 accessed January 6th 2013.

[35] Leveson Report: PM Proposes Third Way to Regulate the Press. Daily Telegraph, 7th December, 2012. Available online at http://www.telegraph.co.uk/news/uknews/leveson-inquiry/9728849/Leveson-Report-PM-proposes-third-way-to-regulate-the-press.html accessed 7th January, 2013

[36] National Newspaper Editors 'Unanimous' Over New Press Watchdog Plans. The Press Gazette. 7th December 2012. Available online at http://www.pressgazette.co.uk/national-newspaper-editors-unanimous-over-new-press-watchdog-plans accessed January 7th 2013.

[37] In 1991, before the first Calcutt inquiry, the then Heritage Secretary, David Mellor, told the press that it was 'drinking in the last chance saloon'. The term has been used ad nauseadam ever since. See also Conditional Reprieve for the 'Last Chance Saloon' The

Independent. 1th July, 1995. Available online at
http://www.independent.co.uk/news/conditional-reprieve-for-the-lastchance-saloon-
cleaned-up-its-act-1591946.html accessed January 6th 2013.

[38] Media Standards Trust, A Free and Accountable Media. This document was incredibly
valuable in the writing of this chapter and provides a more rounded detailed exploration
of some of the themes explored here

Note on the contributor

Dr John Jewell is Director of Undergraduate Studies at Cardiff University School of
Journalism, Media and Cultural Studies. His research and teaching interests include war,
politics and propaganda and national identities. He is author of (2011) 'How the West
Waged the Propaganda War Against Gaddafi' in Richard Keeble and John Mair (eds)
Mirage in the Desert: Reporting The Arab Spring.

A distant prospect? The faults in the Luckhurst line

Professor Julian Petley of Brunel University London examines the arguments of Tim Luckhurst of the University of Kent against statute. Petley finds Luckhurst's pamphlet '*Responsibility without Power*' simply unconvincing

The British press loves nothing more than erecting straw men purely for the purpose of demolishing them with a few rhetorical flourishes. Thus before, during and after the time that Lord Justice Leveson delivered his report, every single suggestion for regulatory reform of the press which had the temerity to contain the word "statutory" was instantly castigated for threatening newspapers with "state control". Typical of the sentiments expressed in this febrile and overwrought atmosphere were these:

> Authoritarian rulers everywhere would exploit the slightest hint of state involvement in the regulation of the British press. Westminster's statutory backing for a press ombudsman would become President Putin's State Censorship Committee, Robert Mugabe's Ministry of Truth or Mahmoud Ahmadinejad's Board of Righteousness. Look, they would gloat, the mother of democracy understands the need for the state to ensure that journalists behave' (Luckhurst 2012: 28).

As it happens, this is not from a newspaper but from Professor Tim Luckhurst's pamphlet *Responsibility without Power: Lord Justice Leveson's Constitutional Dilemma*, which is a contribution to the Free Speech Network, formed by publishers and editors in the latter days of the Leveson Inquiry in the interests of "protecting freedom of expression against any threats to introduce a statutory backstop to press regulation"[1].

Nor is Luckhurst himself averse to scything at straw men. Thus any form of regulation containing a statutory element is characterised as "state supervision of newspapers" (ibid: 26), "statutory regulation" (28), "state-supervised regulation of British newspapers" (29), "an officially regulated press" (29), and so on. However, everything quoted thus far comes from the Conclusion of the pamphlet, in which its origin as a campaigning document is at its most obvious. What precedes it is a series of arguments, illustrated by examples taken from British press history, which are an attempt to define "the appropriate relationship between free speech and accountable government" (8). These are far more nuanced and considered, but they are nonetheless the product of a vision which sees the market as the best guarantor of free speech and the state as its main enemy. Both assumptions are, in fact, highly questionable, as I will attempt to show.

Knowing Their Place

Luckhurst gives a brief but lucid account of the development of the radical press in the first half of the nineteenth century, and also of government attempts to suppress it, by means of both laws and taxes. He notes that:

> newspapers would not be as popular again until parliament abandoned repression in the belief that a free market in newspapers might help high-quality titles to reach a wider audience and educate working class opinion away from revolutionary politics and towards reform. (15)

But he is silent about just why the radical press died, perhaps because this was in fact at the hands of the self-same "free market" which he espouses. Furthermore, it can be convincingly argued that the owners of the mass-market papers such as the *Daily Mail* which supplanted the radical press were less concerned with educating their readers about the benefits of "reform" than in encouraging them to know and accept their allotted place in English society, as well as in the capitalist system, more generally.

This is not leftist conspiracy theory but exactly what many of the proponents of repealing the press laws and taxes had intended. Thus, for example, in 1832 the MP Edward Bulwer-Lytton wondered whether "cheap knowledge may not be a better political agent than costly punishment" (quoted in Curran 1978: 55), whilst another MP, George Grote, argued that "a great deal of the bad feeling that was at present abroad among the labouring classes" was due to the "want of proper instruction, and correct information as to their real interests' (quoted in ibid.: 55), both of which resulted from the restraints upon the press. Similarly, in 1850, Thomas Milner-Gibson, the president of the Association for the Repeal of the Taxes on Knowledge, argued that repeal would "give to men of capital and respectability the power of gaining access by newspapers, by faithful record of the facts, to the minds of the working classes" (quoted in ibid.: 60).

The Market as a System of Control

With repeal, newspaper publishing became an attractive field for capital accumulation, and powerful commercial forces began to enter the press arena. Considerable technological development followed, and the craft system of newspaper production came to be replaced by an industrial one. This significantly increased both running costs and fixed capital costs, which made it difficult for those with limited funds to remain in, let alone break into, the press marketplace. The major operators benefited from economies of scale, offering attractive products while keeping cover prices low. In this they were greatly aided by the huge sums of advertising revenue which the commercial newspapers attracted, but which were unavailable to radical papers, either because advertisers disliked their politics or thought their readers too poor to matter to them, or both.

In this situation, radical newspapers had only two options: to move upmarket and try to draw in the kind of readers attractive to advertisers, or to attempt to offset their losses with donations from readers. But what they could not do, without incurring crippling losses, was to move unchanged into the mass market and sell themselves, without advertising, as cheaply as competitors now handsomely subsidised by the advertisers. Thus developed what was effectively a form of market censorship. The press may have been liberated from direct political controls, but the market to which it was delivered would reveal itself to be what James Curran calls a "system of control rather than an engine of freedom" (2002: 34) in which power was exercised by wealthy and frequently conservative-minded individuals and corporations, while the market itself operated in such a way as to generate an over-supply of papers characterised by soft news and populist politics and an under-supply of those specialising in hard news and espousing liberal values.

Politicians and the press

Luckhurst, however, ignores the depredations of the market, simply noting of the new arrivals in the press field that:

> These pioneers of popular journalism invented the art of selling news, opinion and entertainment to huge readerships. They helped make Britain a country in which, for a penny or less, millions of hard-working people could become better informed than they had ever been. They prepared the emerging electorate for transition between the partial suffrage of the Victorian era and the universal suffrage of the twentieth century. Above all, they made newspapers independent. They broke the sordid tradition of state subsidy and bribery that had tainted the industry since the young William Pitt first attempted to manipulate newspapers in his favour. (2012: 16)

However, this Whiggish view of early modern press history also fails to take account of the degree to which politicians and the press remained thoroughly inter-dependent. George Boyce (1978) has shown how, at the most basic level of inter-dependence, in 1901 Lloyd George engineered the purchase of the *Daily News* by the Cadbury family in the Liberal interest (not least to help in whipping up popular support for the Boer War); between 1911 and 1915 substantial funds from Unionist Central Office were channelled to the *Standard*, *Globe*, *Observer* and

Pall Mall Gazette; in 1918 Lloyd George arranged the purchase of the *Daily Chronicle* with monies accumulated from the sale of Honours; and in 1924 the *Morning Post* was bought by a Conservative syndicate headed by the Duke of Northumberland. Furthermore, Alan J. Lee (1976: 209) calculated that by 1885 no less than 22 MPs were also press proprietors.

At Home with the Governing Classes

But quite as important as these direct links between politicians, parties and newspapers were the indirect and systemic ones. Indeed, they are arguably more so, as it is these which characterise this crucial relationship today. So, for example, as Boyce (1978) has shown, Lord Palmerston established a close relationship with the *Morning Post* from 1838 to 1864, and various political grandees followed suit with successive editors of *The Times*. By the 1870s governments had come to realise that carrots were more effective than sticks for getting and keeping the press onside. As Lee put it: "The most successful way of doing this was by the provision of information and by making certain journalists feel at home with the 'governing classes', and even within the political system" (1976: 205). And if journalists could be seduced by the provision of information, the Honours system could have the same effect on proprietors. Boyce concludes that, by the early twentieth century, "the press was an extension of the political system, not a check or balance to Parliament and Executive, but inextricably mixed up with these institutions" (1978: 29).

Thus straightforward control of the press by the main political parties was gradually replaced not by the state of independence suggested by Luckhurst but by the modern machinery of media management and what we would now call 'spin', and politicians and media owners increasingly struck mutually beneficial deals in which the public interest counted for considerably less than the interests of the contracting parties. At its most egregious this has produced what Peter Oborne, who writes for the pro-Conservative *Daily Telegraph*, calls "client journalism" which, he argues, has become the dominant mode of political reporting:

> To put the matter at its simplest, journalists became instruments of government. Reporters and government joined a conspiracy against the public to create a semi-fictitious political world whose most striking features were media events and fabricated stories. (Oborne 2008: 242)

Oborne sees this process as "effectively a move to a kind of secondary reporting" in which journalists no longer concentrate on reporting events in their raw form but, rather, as mediated and interpreted by ministerial aides and 'spin doctors'. In this process, news stories emerge as "some kind of private deal between government and reporter" (ibid: 244), the political and media classes enter into a "conspiracy against the ordinary reader" (ibid.: 246), and, consequently, "much reporting of politics now amounts to an elaborate fraud perpetuated on the British public" (ibid.: 259).

News Pollution?

Oborne's jeremiad is aimed at British journalism as a whole, although it reserves particular venom for those journalists who, in his view, became overly close to "New Labour". But it is particularly applicable to press journalism in Britain, which, unlike broadcast journalism, is free from any obligation to remain impartial, and is thus a key player in the political arena. Newspapers may indeed be no longer directly funded and controlled by political parties, but the majority are highly partisan in a party political sense, and this most certainly affects the way in which they cover politics in the UK. As Harold Evans put it two decades ago: "The daily news print in Britain is more brilliantly polluted by partisan judgments than the press in most other democracies" (1983: 4), and since he wrote these words the pollution of news by views has become ever more pronounced, particularly, but no means entirely, in the popular press. Nor has it been beneficial to the political process and to public understanding of political issues that, historically, most of the pollution has blown in from one side, namely the Right.

Against this, it might be argued that, ever since the fall of Mrs Thatcher, much of the Tory press has frequently been less than friendly to the Party which it has traditionally supported. That, however, is simply because it could never forgive the Tories for ditching her in the first place, and it is now for the most part a *factional* Tory (and, in some cases, very probably proto-UKIP) press, thus narrowing ever further the range of political views espoused by newspapers.

Critics of the right-wing bias thesis might also point out that the Blair governments (1997-2007) enjoyed the support of the Murdoch press, but there are a number of rejoinders to this argument. Firstly, those governments were not exactly left-wing. Second, Murdoch, for largely commercial reasons, always wants to be seen as being on the winning side, and the Tories were for a long time simply unelectable. Third, Murdoch's papers' support was highly conditional on certain lines not being crossed – on the EU above all – and on certain policies, mostly notably on relaxing cross-media ownership rules, being adopted and put into practice.

Thus the changing political allegiances of the Murdoch press do not signify its liberation from proprietorial control but have ushered in an era in which, for reasons of pure self-interest, a significant section of the press backs whichever party it thinks most likely to win the next election and then supports it in power This is not exactly what the high-minded proponents of the Fourth Estate ideal had in mind, and casts considerable doubt on the extent to which the press can be considered as politically independent, except in the purely formal sense of not being owned and controlled by specific political parties.

Taking the Government's Side

It is precisely because of these and other problems with the press that commentators such as Steven Barnett (2011) have argued that broadcast journalism is rather more politically independent and trustworthy than is much newspaper journalism. This, they claim, is not despite the regulations governing broadcasting but largely due to them, and in particular to those requiring it to be balanced and impartial. However, Luckhurst claims that, from the 1926 General Strike onwards, the BBC's independence from the state has been, at least at times of national crisis, rather more apparent than real, and that during the strike, Reith defined impartiality "in a manner calculated to avoid offending the state" (2012: 19). Ever since this defining moment in the BBC's relationship with the state, Luckhurst notes, the BBC's relationships with governments of all parties "remain delicate. It is perpetually anxious to secure renewal of its charter and to obtain a generous licence fee settlement" (ibid: 20-1)

Luckhurst is quite correct, although the answer to this problem lies in the BBC interpreting its impartiality obligations differently rather than abandoning them. But what he does not mention is that every single time that the BBC has come into conflict with government – for example on the occasions of the Falklands War, *Real Lives: Edge of the Union* (1985), the 1986 bombing of Libya, *Secret Society* (1987), the run-up to the Iraq War in 2003 and the Hutton Report in 2004 – significant sections of the press, and especially the Murdoch press, have loudly and unhesitatingly taken the government's side. Whether it stems from ideological enmity or commercial rivalry, or both, the spectacle of press journalists backing government bullying of their colleagues in broadcasting is a bizarre and distasteful one, and it is one which must cast serious doubt on the sincerity of most newspapers' recent crusades on behalf of freedom of expression. Had those newspapers not vociferously supported successive governments' desire to decimate the BBC, its journalistic workforce might not have been so savagely slashed, and this might in turn have avoided the *Newsnight*/Savile saga (which, of course, gave the BBC's newspaper enemies yet more ammunition with which to attack it).(See Patrick Barrow, p 28 of this volume)

Second-hand Propaganda
Luckhurst does, however, discuss a different aspect of the relationship between newspaper and broadcast journalism, focusing on the impact on broadcast news of the way in which "popular newspapers invariably set the agenda with regard to human-interest stories about celebrities and people who are in the public eye". In his view, broadcasters "use these tales as pegs upon which to hang debates and discussions about economic and social trends" (2012: 23). This is surely a highly idealised view of what all too often actually happens in daily broadcasting practice, but, leaving that aside, the real problem here is that stories are not infrequently bounced onto the broadcasting agenda which have absolutely nothing to do with the news values proper to public service broadcasting and everything to do with the ideological agendas of the papers in which they first appeared. Such stories, which typically involve tabloid hate objects such as immigrants, asylum seekers, travellers, claimants, Muslims, human rights and "Europe"[2], all too often contain a great deal more in the way

of half-truth and indeed downright fiction than fact, and their only place in broadcasting should be in a news item examining their veracity. Where they most emphatically do not belong is in programmes whose presenters merely read out snippets from the morning's papers. Given the political complexion of the British press, this is almost inevitably a daily exercise in political imbalance and second-hand propaganda, and it is one made particularly acute by the lip-smacking relish with which John Humphrys on the BBC Radio Four *Today* programme habitually proclaims the latest outrages in "political correctness" which the *Mail* (to which he contributes) claims to have uncovered.

However, Luckhurst also believes that there are other reasons why broadcast journalism should take note of journalism in the popular press. Writing of his own time on *Today* he notes that:

> It was made plain to me that the *Daily Mail* was the most popular title among our listeners. I knew that for excellent coverage of topics including crime, popular culture and sport I had to read successful, popular newspapers. Mass-market journalism also helped me to understand the political priorities that motivate a majority of my fellow citizens. (23)

However, this is highly questionable, to put it mildly. First of all, much crime coverage in popular newspapers is so heavily inflected by editorialising that it is entirely unreliable as a record of anything other than of those papers' profoundly illiberal complexion. Meanwhile much of their coverage of popular culture is fatally compromised, as journalism, by its origins in the wholly commercial imperatives which caused it to be manufactured as "news" in the first place.

Second, it's highly questionable that what appears in the popular press does actually represent the "political priorities" of the majority of UK citizens. Politicians may choose to believe this, but that's an entirely different matter. In terms of sales figures, the two most popular papers in Britain are the *Sun* (2,582,301) and the *Mail* (1,945,496), both of which espouse profoundly right-wing views, particularly on social matters. The population of the UK at the last census in 2011 was 63,181,775. Even if we follow the newspapers' own dubious practice of assuming that each copy is read by three people (an archaic notion which harks back to a time when everyone was assumed both to live in families and to share papers at the workplace), their combined readership would account for only 13,583,391, namely 21% of the population – a long way off a majority, as it still would be even if one included the readership of other right wing newspapers. But the whole exercise would anyway be pointless as it cannot simply be assumed that readers share the views of their newspapers.

Liberal and Illiberal Values
Public opinion on any topic is notoriously difficult to measure, and newspapers are particularly prone to running the findings of largely spurious polls which merely "prove" the point for which they were designed in the first place. However, the annual *British Social Attitudes* survey is one of the most reliable

barometers of opinion, and this repeatedly shows that, in spite of the impression given by most of the press, public opinion remains predominantly and, perhaps surprisingly, liberal on most subjects. For example, the survey published in 2002 showed that the proportion of respondents who described themselves as "very" or "a little" prejudiced towards ethnic minorities had fallen from to two-fifths in 1987 to a quarter by 2001. And in terms of attitudes towards homosexuality, in the mid-1980s little more than one in ten respondents thought that homosexual behaviour was not wrong at all, but only fifteen years later the figure was around one third (Evans 2002). In this respect, it's also worth noting that the presence of liberal values in society at large is completely out of kilter with their presence in the press. If we define socially liberal papers as the *Mirror* (1,102,810), *Financial Times* (316,493), *Guardian* (215,988), and the *Independent* (105,160), we discover that their combined sales figures amount to a readership of 5,221,353, a mere 8.26% of the population. And whilst we're on the subject of just how unrepresentative is the British press of the political and ideological complexion of the UK, it's worth pointing out that at the 2010 election, the only paper to support the Liberal Democrats was the *Guardian,* which at that point had a sales figures of 302,285, giving a readership of 906,855, 1.44% of the population. By contrast, the party itself polled 6,836,248 votes, 23% of the total.

"Giving the Public What it Wants"

But if public attitudes to ethnic minorities and homosexuality are at variance with those of much of the national press, the same is true of public attitudes to privacy. This is particularly important in the present context, since newspapers repeatedly argue that in running privacy-busting stories they're simply "giving the public what it wants". For example, in a survey carried out by David Morrison and Michael Svennevig in 2002, although 61% of respondents agreed that celebrities have to accept some degree of intrusion into their personal lives, and 63% felt the same about people in important positions, 27% agreed strongly and 39% agreed that "the media should always respect people's privacy, even if this means not being able to cover an issue fully" (2002: 348). And according to an Ipsos MORI poll commissioned by the Media Standards Trust and conducted in 2009 before the phone hacking revelations came fully to light, 70% of the public believe that there are "far too many instances of people's privacy being invaded by newspaper journalists" (2009: 11) Much more specific, though, were responses to a poll conducted for the *British Journalism Review* by YouGov in 2012. This showed very low levels of support for publishing stories which invaded people's privacy for no discernible public interest reason. Thus 58% of respondents felt that a story about a well-known English footballer, who is married with young children, was a private matter and should not be published, 69% felt the same about a story concerning a leading politician's daughter being found drunk in public, 66% about a story featuring a member of a leading pop group having cosmetic facial surgery, and 80% about a story involving a finalist on *Britain's Got Talent* who once attempted suicide (Barnett 2012).

Press Regulation and the Separation of Powers

To be fair, Luckhurst himself does not actually suggest that the public supports newspapers for invading people's privacy for no good reason (other than a commercial one). However, he does argue that, "by taking the long view", his pamphlet "shows that state involvement in the regulation of journalism does not engender public trust" (2012: 26). But, in the present at least, the statistics again suggest otherwise. Thus a poll conducted by YouGov in October 2012 for the Hacked Off Campaign and the Media Standards Trust showed that 78% of those questioned favoured an independent body, established by law, to regulate the press[3]. In another YouGov survey carried out for the *Sun*, in November 2012, 63% of respondents said that they would not trust newspapers to establish a fair system of press regulation (although, entirely unsurprisingly, this was not reported by the paper itself)[4]. In the same month, when a Comres survey for BBC *Radio 5 Live* asked: "Who would you most like to see regulate newspapers in Britain?" 47% of respondents replied "a regulatory body with rules agreed and enforced by the courts", and 12% "a regulatory body with rules agreed and enforced by newspaper owners"[5].

One of the reasons why Luckhurst is so opposed to any form of statutory involvement in the regulation of the press is that in the UK, the executive and legislature are not legally separate, which

> gives a British government a level of executive power that is absent from other democratic traditions. To balance that power this country has evolved a system in which the electoral checks and balances are exercised in the public interest by the courts and the press. Statutory regulation [sic] of British newspapers would create a constitutional absurdity: parliamentary scrutiny of a body the electorate depends upon to scrutinise parliament. (27)

He is, of course, entirely correct about the power of the executive. But which institution is most in favour of retaining our archaic and over-centralised system of government? Which is the most vociferous defender of 'parliamentary sovereignty' (for which read the sovereignty of the executive) against the British courts, particularly in cases involving human rights? In other words, which is the most bitter enemy of the separation of powers which is the hallmark of any mature, modern democracy? Step forward the vast majority of the British press. And why is it such a stalwart defender of what has rightly been called an 'elective dictatorship?' Because it dreads a diminution of its ability to cajole and bully politicians if power should ever leak away from the incestuous Westminster bubble in which it lives – which is, of course, one of the main reasons for its visceral loathing of the idea of "Europe".

Why Luckhurst is Wrong

Luckhurst's pamphlet is, for the most part, an elegant and well-informed attempt to defend a certain conception of press freedom, one which sees state regulation as its main enemy. *Contra* Luckhurst I have argued that market forces regulate the press in a way which militates against diversity and privileges particular audiences and particular kinds of journalism over others; in doing so, it limits the public's freedom to be able access the wide range of accurate and dispassionate written news sources which are the hallmark of any self-respecting democracy. I have also argued that the press is far more deeply enmeshed in the political system than Luckhurst allows, and is indeed a major political player in our society. Such arguments lead to two main conclusions. Firstly, that if market forces limit press freedom then the state, in the interests of democracy, should regulate those forces in such a way as to produce a more diverse, accountable and independent press. It is thus a great pity that the Leveson Inquiry did not take more account of the whole question of press ownership and its impact on journalism. And second, politicians should forget outdated nineteenth century notions of newspapers as members of some kind of Olympian "Fourth Estate" and recognise them as the powerful, down-and-dirty and far-from-disinterested political force that they actually are. Above all, this entails standing firm in the face of howls of "state control" every time a measure is suggested which might help to engender a form of press freedom which is more than the freedom of press owners and their editors and managers to do with their papers whatever they damn well please.

However, the government's absolutely lamentable response to the Leveson report suggests that this is a very distant, if not thoroughly illusory, prospect.

Notes

[1] http://freespeechnetwork.wordpress.com/home/about/. Accessed 29 December 2012.

[2] The literature on press distortion is now quite considerable, but particularly recommended are Golding and Middleton (1982), Anderson and Weymouth (1999), Curran, Gaber and Petley (2005), and Petley and Richardson (2011).

[3] http://hackinginquiry.org/news/poll-shows-public-support-for-independent-regulator/. Accessed 29 December 2012.

[4] http://hackinginquiry.org/news/what-the-sun-didnt-report-today/. Accessed 29 December 2012.

[5] http://www.pressgazette.co.uk/new-comres-poll-finds-most-favour-statutory-regulator-full-polling-round. Accessed 29 December 2012.

Bibliography

Anderson, Peter J. and Weymouth, Tony (1999) *Insulting the public? The British press and the European Union*, London: Longman

Barnett, Steven (2012) Public interest: the public decides, *British Journalism Review*, Vol.23, No.2 pp.15-23.

Barnett, Steven (2011) *The rise and fall of television journalism: just wires and lights in a box?*, London: Bloomsbury.

Boyce, George (1978) The Fourth Estate: the reappraisal of a concept, Boyce, George, Curran, James and Wingate, Pauline (eds), *Newspaper history from the seventeenth century to the present day*, London: Constable pp.19-40.

Curran, James (1978) The press as an agency of social control: an historical perspective, Boyce, George, Curran, James and Wingate, Pauline (eds), *Newspaper history from the seventeenth century to the present day*, London: Constable pp.51-75.

Curran, James (2002) Press reformism 1918-98: a study of failure, Tumber, Howard (ed.), *Media power, professionals and policy*, London: Routledge pp.35-55.

Curran, James, Gaber, Ivor and Petley, Julian (2005) *Culture wars: the media and the British Left*.

Evans, Harold (1983) *Good times, bad times*, London: Weidenfeld & Nicolson.

Evans, Geoffrey (2002), In search of tolerance, Park, Alison, Curtice, John, Thomson, Katarina, Jarvis, Lindsey, Bromley, Catherine (eds), *British social attitudes: the 19th report*, London: Sage/National Centre for Social Research pp.213-30

Golding, Peter and Middleton, Sue (1982) *Images of welfare: press and public attitudes to poverty*, Oxford: Martin Robertson.

Lee, Alan J (1976) *The origins of the popular press 1855-1914*, London: Croom Helm.

Luckhurst, Tim (2012) *Responsibility without power: Lord Justice Leveson's constitutional dilemma*, Bury St Edmunds: Abramis.

Media Standards Trust (2009) *A more accountable press*, London: Media Standards Trust.

Morrison, David E., Kieran, Matthew, Svennevig, Michael and Ventress, Sarah (2002) *Media and values: intimate transgressions in a changing moral and cultural landscape*, Bristol: Intellect.

Oborne, Peter (2008), *The triumph of the political class*, London: Pocket Books.

Petley, Julian and Richardson, Robin (eds) (2011) *Pointing the finger: Islam and Muslims in the British media*, Oxford: Oneworld.

Note on the contributor

Professor Julian Petley is Professor of Screen Media at Brunel University London and a Co-chair of the Campaign for Press and Broadcasting Freedom.

'A little bit Salem': Rebekah Brooks, of News International, and the construction of a modern witch

Rebekah Brooks-Saint or Sinned against? Witch or not? Professor John Tulloch in a provocative piece (a version which also appears in the latest issue of 'Ethical Space') argues the case for the defence of Ms Brooks

Nothing in this chapter should be understood as having any bearing on current or future legal proceedings. My subject is emphatically *not* hacking of 'phones or computers, the alleged bribery of officials by journalists nor other wrong-doing. Rather, it is about one small aspect of how we make sense of the world – or rather, how we use the press to make sense of the world for us. And how that press reflects one of the most persisting sources of inequality that we negotiate day by day: the differential construction of images of men and women.

Last year, Rebekah Brooks positively willed herself to be my subject. She is, as many have seen fit to tell us, hard to resist. Not the Cotswold-living lady who rides retired police horses, or the tabloid editor and compulsive chum of celebrities, or the CEO of News International, the erstwhile 'most powerful woman in British media'. But the woman in the middle of the bizarre process that seems to happen regularly, when, for a short period, they become a subject of press interest, are objectified and, not be too dainty about it, 'monstered'.

Schadenfreude – taking pleasure in others' disasters – is too weak a word to describe the savouring of the extraordinary and delicious irony of Rebekah Brooks's fall by large sections of the media class and academia. That a person who had been responsible for editing the *News of the World* (2000-2003) and the *Sun* (2003-2009), those great engines for reproducing sexist stereotypes of women and promulgating the idea of human evil, should be herself turned into a witch or a Medusa, was a dream so wet, an irony of such purest poetry, that description was not just beggared, but hung, drawn and quartered. But rejoicing in the tokens of her fall, though delicious, diminishes all women – and Brooks has the same rights to imaginative fair-dealing as the most virtuous feminist. And apart from the too tempting opportunities for portentous moralising, her case is fascinating for what it can tell us about contemporary media culture, the persistence of class-based attitudes and a sexism so engrained into our public life as to appear 'natural', old boy.

The making of a witch

The process of 'witchifying' Brooks was given an elegant start signal on BBC2's *Newsnight* by Charlotte Harris, a prominent lawyer representing alleged victims of phone hacking. The occasion was the appearance by Rebekah Brooks in front of the Leveson Inquiry on 12 May 2012. Ms Harris, of course, might be construed to have ample grounds for anger:

> **Rebekah Brooks compared to witch by hacking lawyer: Critic says former News International chief looked 'a little bit Salem' Mail Online, 13 May 2012**
>
> Rebekah Brooks' outfit at the Leveson Inquiry has been compared to the clothes worn by 17th-century witches by a top phone-hacking lawyer. In an interview on BBC2's *Newsnight*, Charlotte Harris seized on the plain black dress with a white Peter Pan collar worn by the former News International chief executive as she gave evidence last week.
>
> Ms Harris, who has represented a series of phone-hacking victims, said: 'Her appearance was interesting because she appeared to be dressed quite innocently. But with the contrasting collar, it did look a little bit Salem.'
>
> The show's presenter, Gavin Esler, interrupted to check she was referring to the infamous Salem witch trials in Massachusetts in the 1690s.
>
> Ms Harris then replied: 'A little bit. She is a very dramatic and iconic figure and there was that drama with the inquiry. She turned up with her mass of red hair, wearing a black outfit with a white collar and white cuffs.'
>
> The unflattering description was followed up by another guest, who described Mrs Brooks's appearance as 'Puritan chic'.
>
> He said the look was 'straight out of Arthur Miller's *The Crucible*', referring to the well-known dramatisation of the witch trials written by the celebrated American playwright...

The cue was speedily taken up by Guido Fawkes (aka Paul Staines, the Conservative political blogger): 'Guido can't help but notice Rebekah Brooks has gone for the classic Salem Show Trial chic for her turn on the stand...' (Fawkes 2012).

And numerous others soon followed, as the witch image, along with 'Medusa', speedily went viral. The cover of *Private Eye* – that reliable barometer of the British media climate – of 31 May featured Brooks in the notorious dress, with the caption:

THE STORY SO FAR: It is new England in the Year of Our Lord 2012, and diabolical goings-on have led to the Witchfinder-General being called in to determine who is guilty of bewitching whom. A simple girl, Rebekah, confesses to being a disciple of the Devil, known to all as Murdoch…

Brooks was also involved in spinning the story herself and with her husband Charlie claimed angrily that a 'witch hunt' was being perpetrated (*Mail on Sunday*, 2012), a claim that Charlie Brooks also made when they were arrested.

Why the Witch?

Apart from the joys of pure mischief, what was the attraction of the witch image? And what was involved in constructing it? Following Brooks's arrest, and appearance in court on 12 May, key elements were mortared into position. Rebekah Brooks's background was described as somewhat mysterious, with an evasive *Who's Who* entry masking 'umble origins, a tugboat-man father and an identity speedily nailed by *Daily Mail* journalists, courtesy of innumerable Victorian novels, as a sharp-elbowed social climber, a 21st century Becky Sharp. 'She never introduced us to people from her past' an informant told *Vanity Fair*. 'That was a little creepy, as if there was no past.' (*Vanity Fair* 2012) Not for her the traditional English (male) networks – school, university, clubs – but an adroit use of the dark (feminine) arts. According to one her more assiduous pursuers, Geoffrey Levy in the *Daily Mail*, her:

> … remarkably swift rise in the company was due not so much to her talents as a journalist but to her single-minded ruthlessness and her dazzling, feline ability to charm (Levy 2011).

Her alleged mysterious hold on powerful men, we are nudgingly told, involves an attempt to substitute for their natural daughters. 'I wouldn't think Rupert stood a chance,' one of her 'oldest acquaintances' told Levy (Levy 2012).The formation of the witching identity draws on some ancient myths and theories. For instance:

- the witch's background is mysterious – sired perhaps by the devil;
- witches breach natural relations;
- witches emanate malevolence – notably in the form of Medusa whose stare paralyses;
- she gets access to the powerful in a mysterious way, using wiles, charms and the power of prophecy;
- she threatens patriarchal systems with her special abilities;
- she is in touch at a mysterious level with the community – through gossip, the passing on of remedies, and the practice of old skills;
- other women look to her skills e.g. for abortions, female maladies, child illnesses, contraception, impotence cures;

- men can't compete with her intuitive qualities: she is in touch with the pre-Christian pagan self, and knows how to captivate, and capture male attention.

The longest, most sustained analysis of her mysterious powers appeared in *Vanity Fair* in February 2012:

'She'd get you to do things,' says another former *News of the World* reporter. 'She had this charisma, this magnetic attraction,' he says. 'She would praise to high heaven, make you feel like you were on top of the world. It was only afterwards that you realised you were manipulated.' In a largely male tabloid world – a business in which Brooks was once asked at a corporate golf gathering to sew a senior executive's button back on his shirt, which she did – perceptions counted for a lot (Andrews 2012).

Utilising her femininity?

For the BBC's Edward Stourton, Brooks utilises her femininity in an extraordinary, upfront way, combining self-confidence with a magical quality:

Colleagues at her first serious job in journalism remember her appearing as suddenly and mysteriously as a genie from a lamp. Graham Ball was the features editor on Eddie Shah's famously short-lived *Post* newspaper when the 20-year-old Rebekah approached him in its Warrington offices. 'She came up to me and said: "I am going to come and work with you on the features desk as the features secretary or administrator." I said: "I'm afraid that's not going to be possible because next week I'm going to London," and I thought nothing more of it. The following Monday, I got to our new office in London, and there she was,' he said. 'She did everything with great finesse, she was very clever' (Stourton 2012).

Edward Stourton's tale celebrates her mystery and seemingly superhuman cleverness. Not, of course, conventional intelligence – her 'childhood friend' Louise Weir describes Rebekah Brooks as more emotionally intelligent than academic.

She's been very charming and she's always been able to get what she wants out of people, even if they don't really like her. 'She is a typical Gemini; she's got her lovely fluffy side and then her angry side,' Louise recalls' (ibid).

How appropriate the horoscope should be deployed for a tabloid editor. A chap like Stourton can't compete with that, with a clear, above-board CV which shows he's gone to the right educational establishments, touched all the right journalistic bases…is one of us (and a bit more top drawer than most…):

- born 1957, Lagos Nigeria;
- educated Ampleforth and Trinity College, Cambridge;
- BA English Literature;

- graduate trainee ITN;
- founder member Channel 4 News;
- 1983 reported from Beirut;
- 1986 Channel 4's Washington correspondent;
- 1988 BBC Paris correspondent;
- 1990 ITN diplomatic editor;
- 1993 BBC *One O'Clock News*;
- 1999-2009 *Today* programme.

Of course, what is played with some nuance and sensitivity by Edward Stourton turns into an exercise in the bleedin' obvious in the coarser tones of the *Daily Mail*:

Rebekah Brooks, the schmoozer hated by Murdoch's wife and daughter

Who would have imagined when Lewis Carroll wrote *Alice's adventures in wonderland* in 1865 that the Cheshire village of Daresbury where he lived would one day produce its own real-life Alice? Her name was Rebekah Wade (now Brooks) and her tugboat-man father could have had no idea when his only child was born in 1968 that she would step – or rather schmooze – into a world of princes, prime ministers and proprietors, every bit as hazardous as Alice's. This was the media wonderland run by Rupert Murdoch, and until yesterday he made sure that no harm would come to the girl he has virtually treated as another daughter (he has four real daughters, from three marriages) (Levy 2011).

And then there's wee Peter Mackay, also of the *Daily Mail*, the journalist as frustrated screenwriter:

As a story, it has everything – larger-than-life characters, seedy villains, bewitching women, protesting celebrities who feel ill done-by, and a thrice-married, 80-year-old billionaire media mogul who said his chief aim was to stand by his Medusa-haired chief executive, who rose from the typing pool to the boardroom (Mackay 2011).

Imagine 'Medusa-haired George Entwistle…' Medusa, of course, a celebrated classical witch, is usually described as 'having the face of a hideous human female with living venomous snakes in place of hair. Gazing directly upon her would turn onlookers to stone…' *The Guardian*'s Simon Hoggart was captured playing the same game, in a radio interview about the *News of the World*, angering at least one female listener:

Nothing struck me until Hoggart brought up News International chief executive Rebekah Brooks, describing her as having 'curly red hair, rather like Medusa'. That's almost all he said about her. Maybe I'm overreacting, but that description rubbed me the wrong way. Powerful women are too often stereotyped in unflattering ways. Even though [she] may allegedly have overseen a hacking scandal [which she denies] couldn't Hoggart have stuck to the allegations rather than critiquing Brooks's appearance by comparing her to a monster of Greek myth? (Milne-Tyte 2012).

The Modern Medusa?

Harmless tabloid mischief? Maybe. A defining feature of British tabloid culture is its tendency to create objects of hatred by a process of de-humanisation and the routine invocation of 'evil' as an explanatory tool. As I have argued elsewhere (Tulloch 2009), this essentially Manichean view of the world deploys monsters and saints, angels and devils, and witches. In these moral fables of villainy, the demonisation and public execution of women has a special place.

No less a figure than Paul Dacre, editor of the *Daily Mail*, publicly embraced this role, when he told the Society of Editors in November 2008: 'Since time immemorial public shaming has been a vital element in defending what are considered acceptable standards of social behaviour ... For hundreds of years, the press has played a vital role in that process' (Dacre 2008).

Dacre's analysis shows this process is no mere populist reflex but a deliberate strategy. Circulations are built, and maintained, by creating the most powerful of Northcliffean 'talking points' – human evil (Tulloch 2000). Naming and blaming the guilty (wo)men is the oldest and most reliable strategy available to the popular press, and Brooks and her male colleagues are now a convenient receptacle for a big portion of the blame in the aftermath of the omni-scandals of News International. It would be a pity if this deflected attention away from the culture embodied by Dacre – well described in the words of the comedian Steve Coogan, quoted in Lord Justice Leveson's profound critique as characterized by:

> dispassionate sociopathic act[s] by those who operate in an amoral universe where they are never accountable (*Leveson Inquiry* Vol 2 para 2.26, p.593)

References

Andrews, Suzanna (2012) Untangling Rebekah Brooks, *Vanity Fair*, February. Available online at http://www.vanityfair.com/business/2012/02/rebekah-brooks-201202, accessed on 8 December 2012

Dacre, Paul (2008) Speech at Society of Editors Annual Conference, 9 November 2008. Available online at http://image.guardian.co.uk/sys-files/Media/documents/2008/11/07/DacreSpeech.pdf, accessed on 18 December 2008

Fawkes, Guido (aka Paul Staines) (2012) Guido Fawkes: Brooks (sic) at Leveson edition. Available online at http://order-order.com/2012/05/11/guidos-fashion-tips-brooks-at-leveson-edition/, accessed on 8 December 2012

HMSO (2012) *The Leveson Inquiry*, November, London: The Stationery Office. Available for download at www.official-documents.gov.uk

Levy, Geoffrey (2011) 'Rebekah Brooks, the schmoozer hated by Murdoch's wife and daughter', *Daily Mail*, 17 July. Available online at http://www.dailymail.co.uk/femail/article-2015257/Rebekah-Brooks-hated-Rupert-Murdochs-wife-Wendi-daughter-Elisabeth.html, accessed on 8 December 2012

Mail Online (2012) Rebekah Brooks compared to witch by hacking lawyer…. Available online at http://www.dailymail.co.uk/news/article-2143599/Rebekah-Brooks-compared-witch-phone-hacking-lawyer-Charlotte-Harris.html, accessed on 8 December 2012

Mail on Sunday (2012) It's a witch hunt: Rebekah Brooks and husband Charlie lash out after they are charged with perverting the course of justice in phone-hacking scandal, 12 May. Available online at http://www.dailymail.co.uk/news/article-2144615/Phone-hacking-Rebekah-Brooks-husband-Charlie-charged-perverting-course-justice.html, accessed on 8 December 2012

McKay, Peter (2011) Sucking up to the Sun King is a sign of *The Times*, Mail Online, 18 July. Available online at http://www.dailymail.co.uk/debate/article-2015816/Phone-hacking-scandal-Sucking-Rupert-Murdoch-Sun-King.html, accessed on 8 December 2012

Milne-Tyte, Ashley (2011) Rebekah Brooks –Medusa-like?, 12 July. Available online at http://www.ashleymilnetyte.com/ashleymilne-tyte/2011/07/rebekah-brooks-medusa-like.html, accessed on 8 December 2012

Private Eye (2012) Salem witch trial Day 94. Available online at http://www.private-eye.co.uk/covers.php?showme=1314, accessed on 8 December 2012

Stourton, Edward (2012) Profile: Rebekah Brooks, ex-News International chief, BBC News. Available online at http://www.bbc.co.uk/news/uk-politics-13117456, accessed on 8 December 2012

Tulloch, John (2000) The eternal recurrence of the New Journalism, Sparks, Colin and Tulloch, John (eds) *Tabloid Tales*, Boston and London, Rowman and Littlefield pp 131-146

Tulloch, John (2009) Printing devils: Reflections on the British press, the problem of 'evil' and fables of social disease, *Ethical Space: The International Journal of Communication Ethics*. Vol. 6, No. 1 pp 17-25

Note on the contributor

John Tulloch is Professor of Journalism at the University of Lincoln. He is co-director of the Centre for Journalism Research (CRJ). Previously (1995-2003) he was Head of the Department of Journalism and Mass Communication, University of Westminster and until 2012 Head of the Lincoln School of Journalism. Edited books include *Tabloid tales* (2000) (edited with Colin Sparks) *Peace journalism, war and conflict resolution* (2010) (edited with Richard Lance Keeble and Florian Zollmann), and *Global literary journalism* (edited with Richard Lance Keeble, 2012). He has also written recently on extraordinary rendition and on the journalism of Charles Dickens, Gitta Sereny, Gordon Burn and Geoffrey Moorhouse.

Leveson: Bonfire of the vanities for the chattering classes?

Professor Peter Cole has had two distinguished careers. In journalism, he edited *The Sunday Correspondent* and was Deputy Editor of *The Guardian*. In academia, he headed the journalism departments at UCLAN and Sheffield University. In the battle for action post-Leveson, he is firmly anti-statutory and pro-independent

It is not over yet. After 86 days of public hearings and 474 witnesses, at a cost that will probably reach £6m, the findings and recommendations were delivered. The urgency following the publication on 29 November 2012 of Lord Justice Leveson's four volume, near 2000 page, million word report on 'the culture, practices and ethics of the press' – statements and debates in Parliament, editors summoned to Downing Street and told they had days to produce detailed regulatory plans consistent with the Leveson recommendations, further editors meetings – did not last. Christmas and the New Year – when this was being written – left the situation as it has been for a while. There is acceptance that there has to be change in press culture, practices and ethics, and in the regulation of the press. There is division among politicians, editors, victims of shameful treatment by sections of the press, campaigners for reform, journalists and media academics about the precise nature of any reforms to be introduced, crucially whether or not they require legislation and whether that is acceptable in terms of cherished press freedoms that have existed for more than 300 years. There will be an outcome. Meanwhile, some observations on the process, content and people involved in Leveson, as The Leveson Inquiry: Culture, Practices and Ethics of the Press has come to be known.

Editors meet

There is no regular forum for national newspaper editors to meet. They bump into each other at press awards functions, but usually sit at separate tables with their own colleagues from their own newspapers. They did not meet at the Leveson Inquiry, attending to give their own evidence, not to chat in a waiting room to their peers there for the same purpose. There are one or two friendships between editors, but not many. They may encounter each other at state occasions to which they have all been invited, at the occasional drinks party at 10 Downing Street or other government departments. But they see surprisingly little of each other, and certainly not at any established or organised meetings. There is the Society of Editors which represents national, regional and local newspaper editors as well as senior journalists in broadcast editorial management. It has a representative role, campaigns for press freedoms, seeks to influence relevant legislation and controls over the media. It has a prestigious annual conference where national newspaper editors regularly speak, sometimes more than one of them on the same platform. But as for sitting round a table with fellow editors to discuss matters of mutual interest, that happens very seldom, not least because the main matter of mutual interest is competition.

The importance of outside influence, control over the conduct of journalistic inquiry, challenge to press freedom, government interference, regulation, prior restraint on publication, any of these is the one thing that can bring them together, make them accept that, to coin a phrase much used by the present government, they are 'all in it together'. Not that it has much seemed like that during the Leveson Inquiry.

My own experience of sitting down with the national editors occurred in 1990 when I was editing the (short-lived) *Sunday Correspondent*. The press had behaved in a scandalous way, sending a reporter and photographer masquerading as medics into a hospital (Charing Cross in London) to interview and photograph a TV actor called Gorden Kaye who was on life-support after suffering a serious head injury. The offending newspaper was the *Sunday Sport*, not recognised by any of the established nationals as 'one of them'. Its editor did not attend (probably was not invited) the meeting of editors at the Tower Hotel in London. It was chaired (nobody seemed to know why or how he had 'emerged') by Andreas Whittam Smith, editor of *The Independent*, then still independent, yet to be four years old, highly fashionable and admired.

After the furore brought about by the *Sunday Sport*'s behaviour, and a series of intrusions into the privacy of younger royals, the government set up an inquiry into press standards chaired by a lawyer, David Calcutt QC. His committee found the existing regulatory body, the Press Council (set up in 1953 as the General Council of the Press after the 1947 Royal Commission on the Press) unfit for purpose. Calcutt suggested one last chance for the press, 18 months of a new self-regulatory body but if no improvement in press standards in that period the threat of statutory regulation and a privacy law. It was these threats hanging over the press that brought the editors together in the Tower Hotel. It was clear then that there were two cultures represented by the editors in the room: the so-called quality or broadsheet press, whose editors were ignorant of the sometimes dark arts practised by the popular or tabloid newspapers, whose editors feared abandoning these arts might make it harder for them to acquire the stories that sold millions of copies.

However, the threats were considered real enough by all the editors, who gave their support to the setting up of a new body, the Press Complaints Commission, funded by the newspaper and magazine industry and administering and enforcing a code of practice developed by the editors themselves. Despite a review of the new system by Calcutt after the probationary period he had set, which found the new PCC wanting and recommended its replacement with a form of statutory complaints tribunal, a proposal rejected by the then Conservative government, the PCC continues to operate pending its replacement as recommended by Leveson.

The similarities between 1990 and Calcutt and 2012 and Leveson are considerable, a point recognised by Sir Brian Leveson who remarked frequently during his inquiry hearings that he was determined that his report should not suffer the fate of its predecessors: requiring a further inquiry into the press at some point in the future. Both Calcutt and Leveson looked broadly at press ethics, standards and practices but were provoked by (probably would not have happened without) a single press action which particularly shocked and appalled the public. In the case of Calcutt it was Gorden Kaye; in Leveson it was the hacking of Milly Dowler's mobile telephone. In both cases the existing self-regulatory body (Press Council for Calcutt, PCC for Leveson) was pilloried and it was accepted at an early stage of the Inquiry it would have to be replaced. In both cases national newspaper editors were drawn together to seek ways of resisting threatened legislation. In both cases, at least initially in the present case, a Conservative Prime Minister was reluctant to support legislation.

Cameron surprises

David Cameron's contributions to the Leveson debate have been inconsistent and at times surprising. He featured in the Inquiry into the relationships between national newspapers and politicians as a result of his friendship and social contact with Rebekah Brooks, former editor of the *Sun* and chief executive of News International, who has been arrested and charged in connection with the hacking allegations and allied matters. Cameron would have been relieved to read in the Leveson report that relations between politicians and the press were "in robust good health and performing the vital public interest functions of a free press in a vigorous democracy. Close relationships, including personal friendships, are very much part and parcel of all this and not in themselves any cause for surprise or concern." (Report 2012a)

After *The Guardian*'s Dowler phone hacking revelations in July 2011Cameron lost no time in setting up the Leveson Inquiry. Nothing unusual in that; PMs need to be seen to react to strong public feeling, and the Inquiry is a useful way of doing something while postponing substantive action. What was unusual in this case were Cameron's public declarations on matters he was asking a judge to explore. He said, at a Downing Street briefing on 8 July 2011, that the PCC lacked public confidence, was ineffective and lacking in rigour. A new system entirely was needed. The PCC should be replaced with a body independent of the press and politicians, he said. (Cameron 2011). Then later he said he would be in favour of implementing the Leveson report's recommendations unless they were "bonkers" (Cameron 2012a). However, after publication of the report the Prime Minister came out strongly against its call for statutory underpinning and verification of a new regulatory body. He told the Commons on November 29 (Cameron 2012b) he had "serious concerns and misgivings" in principle to any statutory interference. "It would mean for the first time we have crossed the Rubicon of writing elements of press regulation into the law of the land. We should think very, very carefully before crossing this line. We should be wary of any legislation that has the potential to infringe free speech and the free press."

This was more of a surprise than anything in the report. Cameron's coalition deputy Nick Clegg and Labour leader Ed Miliband had both supported the statutory elements of Leveson, citing their duty to the victims of reprehensible press behaviour. Nobody, however, assumed this would be Cameron's last word on the subject. He summoned the editors to Downing Street five days after the report was published and told them they had two days to agree a reformed regulatory structure which had to follow Leveson line by line, apart from the statute insistence. Statute or no statute, however independent of government the press is, prime ministers show no reticence in sending for editors, expecting them to turn up and telling them what to do.

Although some of the editors were not entirely opposed to statutory insistence on regulation and verification of its form, by the time they were together in Downing Street they seemed of one mind now they appeared to have the Prime Minister's too. The editor of *The Times*, James Harding, 'emerged' as the chair of the editors' group, but within a few days was removed from the editorship by his proprietor Rupert Murdoch. Another complication in this ever-moving situation.

The final few weeks before publication of the report saw much lobbying in print against statutory regulation. James Harding, then still editor of *The Times*, wrote powerfully against any form of statutory regulation on November 27 under the headline 'Don't force the press into politicians' arms.' *The Guardian* (November 26) expressed its doubts about Lord Hunt chairing a new regulatory body and sought much greater independence. The *Mail* suddenly produced a 12-page investigation into Leveson expert advisor Sir David Bell, former chairman of the *Financial Times*, who it described as 'an elitist liberal'. (Bell 2012a, Bell 2012b). The *Mail* also ran a somewhat hysterical leader on October 11 (Savile 2012) weaving together Leveson, the BBC and the Jimmy Savile scandal, on all of which the *Mail* has views. Its final sentence catches the flavour: "In what kind of moral universe is it more important to investigate the complaints of the likes of Steve Coogan, Max Mosley and Hugh Grant than it is to obtain justice for young women whose lives were destroyed by sexual predators shielded by a state-funded body?"

There were signs here of the tabloids getting back to confident form from the tone adopted during the public hearings of the Inquiry, when they seemed more constrained than usual, as though self-conscious about the tawdry picture being painted of them in the High Court. The coincidence of the Jimmy Savile revelations and inquiries into the BBC handling of the affair, and the new expenses allegations against Maria Miller, the culture secretary, who was also at the Downing Street meeting, perhaps led editors to think they could move off the back foot.

'Independent self-regulation'?

Or is that an oxymoron? Leveson's own recommendation described "independent regulation, organised by the press itself, with a statutory underpinning and verification." Self-regulation implies the press regulating itself, whereas independence suggests that cannot be so. The PCC, responsible for press regulation since 1991, is funded by the newspaper industry, through the Press Standards Board of Finance (Pressbof). Its chairman is Lord Black, executive director of the Telegraph Media Group and a former director of the PCC itself. Pressbof's board is entirely made up of senior executives from the newspaper and magazine industries. It appoints the chair of the Press Complaints Commission, which has 17 members, 10 of them (including the chairman) lay or public members with no connection to the newspaper and magazine industry, the other seven serving editors. The Editors' Code of Practice Committee, responsible for developing and amending the code regulating journalists' standards, at present comprises 13 editors plus the PCC chairman and director. The code committee, chaired by Paul Dacre, editor-in-chief of the *Mail*, has already responded to the Leveson recommendations by proposing to reduce the number of editors to 10 and adding five lay full members, including the chairman and director. This will not satisfy Leveson who recommended a code committee on which "serving editors (would) have an important part to play although not one that is decisive." The code committee would advise the new regulatory body which itself would take ultimate responsibility for its content and promulgation. (Report 2012b)

So how 'independent' does that leave the PCC? Throughout the Leveson hearings one common (and, as it turned out, complacent) presumption was that Lord Justice Leveson's report would recommend 'PCC-2', a strengthened version of the original model, more independent, more proactive, with investigatory powers and the right to impose large fines as sanctions. When Baroness Buscombe, a Conservative peer, resigned as chair of the PCC in 2011, having incurred criticism for her peremptory dismissal of the *Guardian's* hacking stories, Lord Black, another Conservative peer, was responsible for the appointment of Lord Hunt, also a Conservative peer, as her successor. In fact three of the PCC's five chairs have been Conservative peers, Lord Wakeham being the other. The other two were Lord McGregor, academic, Labour life peer, crossbencher in the Lords, and Sir Christopher Meyer, former British ambassador in Washington.

As soon as Lord Hunt took over, he said the PCC would have to be replaced and he took the necessary steps for it to be turned into a transitional body, while working with Black on the design of the revised PCC. He presented these developing plans in evidence to Leveson, and has continued to do so since. They included contracts between publishers and the new regulator, which would have the increased powers mentioned above. He must have been disappointed when the Leveson report said that the Hunt-Black proposals did not "come close" to true independent regulation (Report 2012c) However Hunt-Black is a tenacious partnership with strong experience of regulation and will be expected to make any changes to their model short of statute to hold on to the regulatory role. It seems unlikely, though, that the same chair of the regulator and the same chair of the funding body would represent sufficient change or sufficient independence.

It would seem likely that the present PCC infrastructure – its able staff dealing with the arbitration of complaints – would be kept on. That side of the PCC's activities is widely held to have been effective. The question is can you bolt on the investigative components that would make it an effective regulator, and convince the public and the verifying body that it is independent as well? All this without statute, the antithesis of independence. Leveson has suggested the verifying body should be Ofcom (Report 2012d). The editors are unenthusiastic about this, noting that the head of Ofcom is appointed by government. Alternatives have come from the then *Times* editor, James Harding, who suggested a panel appointed by the Lord Chief Justice. *The Guardian*'s editor, Alan Rusbridger, suggests a great-and-good-but-without-serving-lawyers threesome of, say, Igor Judge, the retiring Lord Chief Justice and consistent champion of a free (of government intervention) press, Shami Chakrabarti of Liberty, and Stuart Purvis, former ITN editor in chief. Would this convince the sceptics?

Understanding the popular press
The one newspaper closed by the hacking scandal (by its owner Rupert Murdoch within days of the Milly Dowler hacking revelation) was the *News of the World*, the paper with the largest circulation in Britain, about 2.7 million copies a week (Audit Bureau of Circulations, ABC). In the 1960s and early 1970s it was selling more than six million. This was the paper on which the hacking allegations focused, and thus was central to the Leveson Inquiry. However, since the police were investigating allegations of criminal activity by the News of the World in terms of phone hacking Leveson was unable to explore the specifics of the allegations. Part two of the Leveson Inquiry (if it ever happens) is charged with doing that.

So in its taking of evidence and examining of witnesses the inquiry had to keep away from the specifics of what caused it to be set up in the first place, the hacking of Milly Dowler's mobile telephone. Instead it worked to hugely broad terms of reference, allowing for every aspect of press culture and practice, including relations with politicians and the police, which received relatively little attention in the report compared with the issue of press regulation.

The Inquiry became about a series of other stories where press behaviour had been questionable or much worse. Some of these involved celebrities like Hugh Grant and Steve Coogan who as a result became not only witnesses but campaigners. Others involved those who had suffered heart-rending tragedies like a murdered child (the Dowlers) or a missing child (the McCanns). By front-loading the inquiry so that stark and dramatic victim stories came first Lord Justice Leveson set the tone. It was almost as though he was using tabloid techniques to shock the public at the outset of the Inquiry. The choreography did not always work.

Max Mosley is not a victim of the same order as Bob and Sally Dowler; Hugh Grant has not suffered like Gerry and Kate McCann. There seemed little understanding in the court of the difference between popular and serious newspapers. Sitting there you had the strong feeling that nobody in court 73 had ever read the *Sun* or the *Mirror*, few the *Daily Mail*. It was clear from the expressions on the faces of the lawyers and assistants that they knew little about the content of the mass selling tabloids (The *Sun* six times the sale of the *Times*; The *Daily Mail* 10 times the *Guardian* – ABC figures) and the techniques used to get their stories. Sir Brian Leveson himself seemed quite incredulous about some of the answers he heard from tabloid witnesses, not those about criminal activities like hacking but the legal investigative techniques employed to reveal corruption. It showed too in the choice of special advisors to the inquiry. The three journalists appointed came from the *Financial Times*, the *Telegraph* and *Channel 4 News*. Two of them had spent most of their careers working in Parliament as political correspondents. None of them had worked for a tabloid paper, in spite of the fact that the focus of the inquiry would almost certainly be the activities of the tabloid press. Only Paul Dacre, *Mail* editor-in-chief, spoke up consistently for the popular press, but that was mainly in the early days of the Inquiry (see below).

Victims do not make good law

Some of the celebrity victims embraced the inquiry to a much greater extent than giving their evidence, telling their stories of hacking, harassment and privacy invasion. Hugh Grant, Steve Coogan, Charlotte Church and Max Mosley, among others, became campaigners, available for radio and television interviews, signing up as the star members of the Hacked Off campaign for statutory regulation of the press. Hacked Off ran a very effective campaign of public meetings, letters to newspapers, and regular reactive quotes throughout and after the Leveson Inquiry hearing. These celebrity victims had frequent access to senior politicians. Reports would appear of meetings between Charlotte Church and the Prime Minister during the Conservative Party conference, and others put forward by Hacked Off meeting other party leaders. When current affairs programmes like *Newsnight* required an advocate for much tougher, even statutory, regulation of the press it was usually the Hacked Off representative that was chosen. The first person to be interviewed on BBC television after Sir Brian Leveson's presentation of his report on November 29 was Max Mosley, the former Formula 1 boss who successfully sued the *News of the World* for breach of his privacy after it ran a story about his sexual inclinations.

Brian Cathcart, one of the founders of Hacked Off, was a *Reuters* and *Independent* journalist and is now Professor of Journalism at Kingston University. He skillfully created an umbrella organisation for the victims and campaigners on their behalf, somehow persuading the politicians that it was in their interests to be seen to be listening to their advice first hand rather than digesting evidence from the Inquiry. It is no disrespect to those who suffered grievously at the hands of the press to suggest that while evidence of their experiences was vital their views on regulation and reform should have carried no greater weight than others. It was a point made by Tom Mockridge, then chief executive of News International on the BBC Today programme on 28 November, and quoted in a *Times* feature article by Matthey Syed on December 1 (Syed 2012). Mockridge was asked whether the Dowler family should have the power of veto over proposals on press regulation. He replied: "(Their status) doesn't mean they get to determine the legislation of the State that governs the principle of free speech." Syed, in the same article, suggests that "the crimes of the press (serious though they are) have been conflated with the death of an innocent schoolgirl. Sympathy at the Dowlers' loss alchemised into a tidal wave of revulsion at press intrusion. And from there we have seamlessly moved to the prospect of statutory underpinning which will affect all newspapers. Freedom of the press is simply too important to be hijacked like this."

'Hackademics' like to keep their hands clean

From the moment the Leveson Inquiry was set up there emerged a small industry of journalist navel-gazers, media pundits, columnists, broadcasters and reporters, editors with a reputation for playing a part in wider media debates, media lawyers and the journalism lecturers and researchers, with and without a professional journalism past (known as the 'hackademics'!). Whither journalism? debates were held up and down the land. It started with 'The Press We Deserve – a conversation with Sir Harry Evans' at the Banqueting Hall in Whitehall in September 2011. Jim Naughtie roved with the 'mike'. The editors of the *Times*, *Guardian* and *Financial Times*, the director general of the BBC, other luminaries and of course Sir Harry himself, took to the high ground and climbed further. Then came meetings set up by Lord Justice Leveson, to inform his Inquiry on the issues arising from its terms of reference and to hear views from many interested quarters. At this stage of the Inquiry, before its hearings started, Paul Dacre, editor in chief of the *Mail* and chair of the PCC's editors' code committee, was very visible and very active. A leading editor who was famous for shunning publicity and the public stage, he grabbed the challenge of Leveson and came out with a series of proposals before the Inquiry had started taking evidence. They involved the appointment of a single press ombudsman, lay representation on the code committee, and more prominence for corrections. It soon became clear from court 73 that this relatively minor tinkering with the PCC, which would continue in face-lifted form, would be nothing like enough. Dacre lowered his profile.

There followed very many meetings organised by campaigning groups and university media and journalism departments. There were meetings of major media figures (some requiring payment from the public to attend), which tended to feature a regular repertory company of pundits some of whom appeared on a succession of platforms.

The meetings were frequently lofty, seldom including representation (of advocates or views) from the popular press which was at the heart of the Leveson inquiry. The 'hackademics' seemed often to be the most detached from the real commercial world, some giving the impression that all would be well if the *Guardian* was the only newspaper on sale, distaste for the *Daily Mail* and all things Murdoch seemingly a badge of office. While there was an impressive core at the heart of the repertory company, mostly of former senior media executives (journalists and lawyers) who had had experience of and thought seriously about regulation and press freedom, too often those who spoke up in the debates appeared to have a low opinion of journalism in general rather than a respect for its watchdog role and its achievements in flushing out the corrupt and the abusers of power, not always the most straightforward or squeaky clean activity. And they did not like to pollute their idealism with commercial considerations, like the fact that newspapers need to make money to exist.

Too often the emphasis at these meetings was *doing something* about the popular press rather than preserving the freedoms of all the press. After all, if the police investigations had uncovered the extent of illegal phone hacking when it was first brought to their attention there would have been no need for Leveson. As it is, those areas of the press that have behaved disreputably and despicably have been so shamed by the evidence given to the Inquiry that such behaviour should not recur.

References

Bell 2012a: http://www.dailymail.co.uk/debate/article-2233709/Sir-David-Bell-publics-right-know.html

Bell 2012b: http://www.independent.co.uk/news/media/press/daily-mail-targets-sir-david-bell-in-preemptive-strike-8324256.html

Cameron 2011: http://www.guardian.co.uk/politics/2011/jul/08/david-cameron-speech-phone-hacking

Cameron 2012a: http://news.bbc.co.uk/1/shared/bsp/hi/pdfs/0710122.pdf

http://www.guardian.co.uk/media/2012/oct/07/david-cameron-denies-mind-leveson

Cameron 2012b: http://www.guardian.co.uk/media/2012/nov/29/david-cameron-refuses-to-write-press-law

Report 2012a: http://www.official-documents.gov.uk/document/hc1213/hc07/0779/0779.pdf

Executive summary, summary of recommendations, para 111, page 25

Report 2012b: http://www.official-documents.gov.uk/document/hc1213/hc07/0779/0779.pdf

Executive summary, para 60, p15

Report 2012c: http://www.official-documents.gov.uk/document/hc1213/hc07/0779/0779.pdf

Executive summary, paras 52-55, page 14

Report 2012d: http://www.officialdocuments.gov.uk/document/hc1213/hc07/0779/0779.pdf

Executive summary, summary of recommendations, para 31, page 36

Savile 2012: http://www.dailymail.co.uk/debate/article-2215946/Jimmy-Savile-BBC-inquiry-Lord-Leveson-look-cesspit.html

Syed 2012: *The Times*. December 1, 2012. Page 14. *The victims cannot choose the punishment*

Note on the contributor

Peter Cole was editor of *The Sunday Correspondent*, deputy editor, news editor and reporter on *The Guardian*, News Review editor of *The Sunday Times*, Londoner's Diary editor of the *Evening Standard*, and New York correspondent, features and diary writer on the *London Evening News*. Since 1993 he has worked in journalism education, heading the journalism departments first at the University of Central Lancashire and then the University of Sheffield. He is now Emeritus Professor of Journalism at Sheffield. He is the author, with Tony Harcup, of *Newspaper Journalism* (Sage, 2010).

Section B. So, will anything change?

John Mair

Raymond Snoddy has had forty years at the reporting media front-line. He has seen Royal Commissions come and go. Ray is a very firm Leveson sceptic though on mature reflection and more drilling down he is able to find something he thinks salvageable from the Leveson Report.

Professor Richard Sambrook is more positive. He signed the 'hackademics' letter to the *Guardian* calling for Leveson to be considered before instant rejection. Sambrook is a former very senior BBC Executive-Director of News, Global News and Sport at various times who has just taken over as Director of the very prestigious Cardiff University Centre for Journalism. His solution? Time to professionalise, follow the Americans and confine Nick Tomalin's aphorism about 'rat-like cunning, a plausible manner and a little literary ability' as the ideal type for a journalist into the bin of history

Bernard Clark invented 'Watchdog' inside BBC's '*Nationwide*' three decades ago. He then went on to make the first TV series to properly examine the press on a regular basis – Channel Four's '*Hard News*'. In his chapter he presents a rather dystopic view of the future of journalism on and off the internet. According to him, by looking at the press, Lord Justice Leveson was looking the wrong way, looking backward at a disappearing problem. Leveson should have been looking forward at the burgeoning and scary art of *Information Terrorism* especially on the internet where virtual mobs rule cyberspace and reputations are shredded in a thrice and with three clicks. Counter-intuitively he lists Sir Jimmy Savile as a victim of this.

Contrastingly and from a firm feminist perspective Deirdre O'Neill of Leeds Trinity University is hoping that the post-Leveson world will see the end of what she considers to be sexist reporting which objectifies women and leads to sexual crimes.

That's the trouble with Leveson the process, Leveson the report and post Leveson. It is like a societal kaleidoscope, with everybody looking into it is seeking and finding a different picture. Not all of them will get the right picture in the end.

Mature reflections on Leveson

Raymond Snoddy well deserves the moniker 'doyen' of the British media analysts. He has written about it for nearly four decades as Media Editor of the *Financial Times* and the *Times*. He also presented three of the very few TV analysis programmes of the press – *Hard News* on Channel Four *Media Monthly* on Sky and *Newswatch* on the BBC News Channel (2004-2012)

In my view, the only sane message to flow from Leveson and all his works is that it is time for the newspaper industry to move on and create a new journalism that is more consistently accurate, fair and responsive to both the needs of the public and the needs of society.

That is not to argue that all the recommendations of Lord Justice Leveson should be accepted wholesale as Ed Miliband, the Labour leader did so unwisely in his initial reactions.

A number are misguided, some are dangerous and should be opposed vigorously.

It is however an inescapable fact that journalists, or to be more precise some journalistic sub-cultures, have been guilty, apart from illegality, of unacceptable casual cruelties, inaccuracy and down-right unfairness, often in pursuit of stories that really didn't matter very much.

Lord Justice Leveson was at least prepared to accept a press that is "irreverent, unruly and opinionated." But he is surely right when he argues that some of the press, some of the time have been guilty of persistence that verges on harassment, and have shown, if the story is big enough, "significant and reckless disregard for accuracy."

Nothing could ever begin to justify, or even adequately explain, how Christopher Jeffries, the initial "suspect" in the Joanna Yeates murder case, or the McCann family were treated by the press.

Some of the complaints from actors, comics, footballers and former television presenters are, to say the least, more arguable.

But Leveson's castigations of papers, which stray into "sustained misrepresentation of groups in society, hidden conflicts of interest and irresponsible science scares," are all matters that should give all serious journalists pause for thought.

We should not have to accept a journalism of malice or ignorance.

In the light of some of the evidence given to Lord Justice Leveson, best practice must be re-defined and ways found of encouraging that to be observed throughout the industry by invigorated codes backed up by real sanctions.

Virtue brings its reward-respect and sales

The irony is that virtue, though neither blandness nor pomposity, could in future, increasingly bring its own rewards for the established media. A reputation for fairness, openness, accuracy and honesty is particularly important in the age of the internet – a development that Sir Brian had so very little to say about.

Earning and retaining the trust of the public could actually turn out to be good business, a trump card in the battle for survival of the existing, professional media. It could be a key differentiator from the endless tidal waves of unverified and sometimes poisonous information on the internet.

The need for reform that has flowed from the Leveson Inquiry should be accepted and even welcomed even though it is still necessary to register the political errors of Prime Minister David Cameron that led to the setting up of such a flawed, open-ended inquiry in the first place which could have had a much more damaging outcome. Instead of dealing with outrageous, blatant illegality on a small number of national newspapers, illegality that could and should have been dealt with by existing law, Cameron saddled the entire newspaper industry, innocent and guilty, with an inquiry "into the culture, practices and ethics of the press."

The most toxic fuel that propelled the creation of the Leveson Inquiry, that *News of the World* journalists had deleted messages on the phone of the murdered teenager Milly Dowler, interfering with police inquiries and, above all else giving her unfortunate parents false hope that she might still be alive, was almost certainly untrue. We will never know whether the hacking of Milly Dowler's phone alone would have been enough to trigger such a comprehensive inquiry.

Footnote 11 in Lord Justice Leveson's 2,000-page report is worth noting. "On the issue of deletion of messages, during the course of the Inquiry, considerable further work by Surrey Police has revealed that it is unlikely that the News of the World had, in fact, caused a moment of false hope: I proceed on that basis," Leveson concedes.

He adds that he entirely rejects "the suggestions that this error has undermined the basis for the Inquiry which, in the light of all the evidence I have heard, was and remains more than amply justified."

There is however a sense that Leveson, is, at least in part, relying on evidence, subsequently obtained, to justify the rationale for his Inquiry?

PCC gets a bad press. Deservedly?

The Press Complaints Commission (PCC), condemned by the Prime Minister and many others as a "failed organisation" actually dealt well and independently with thousands of complaints on behalf of members of the public and intervened with editors to prevent errors being published.

It is now however widely accepted that it was a complaints handling body rather than a regulator and certainly not one equipped to investigate large scale corrupt practices such as bribing police for information or industrial scale phone-hacking.

They are other guilty institutions too.

Before we move on it should also be emphasised just how unusual it was that the press alone should be singled out from among the miscreants in many of the UK's major social institutions, ranging from MPs and bankers to Britain's much heralded pharmaceutical industry, for a full judicial inquiry.

The actions of a surprisingly large number of MPs on their expenses is well known, less so the transgressions of the much-lauded pharmaceutical industry. GlaxoSmithKline was ordered in July 2012 to pay $3 billion in fines in the US for promoting anti-depressant drugs for unauthorised use for children, promotions backed up by generous jollies for doctors. Western Pharma companies have also been accused of involvement in more than 2,000 deaths in India linked to trials of new drugs where questionable consent had been obtained in the first place from the poorest of the earth and minimal compensation has been paid for those who have died of side-effects.

The largest banks colluded in the illegal manipulation for years of Libor, the London inter-bank lending rate. The $1.5 US billion penalty levied on UBS was exceeded only by the $1.9 billion HSBC agreed to pay to settle US charges in connection with separate allegations over the laundering of drug cartel money. There have been no sign of prosecutions in the UK, let alone any interest in setting up a judicial inquiry on the banks.

There is relevance in these comparisons with the ethics of other industries or professions in one respect – to highlight the fact that it is the press alone, which has been singled out for such special treatment not just from Leveson but also, eventually from the police. Over 90 journalists and newspaper executives have now been arrested, often in unnecessarily dramatic fashion in dawn raids worthy of a Third World dictatorship.

Rather like phone-hacking, the libellous attacks on Jefferies and the McCanns were against the existing law and both received hundreds of thousands of pounds in compensation. Their suffering should not, however, entitle them to disproportionate influence in calling for limits to press freedom – legal changes that would affect all citizens.

Leveson report to end up on 'journalism professor's bookshelf?'

We are however where we are and it is time to move on from the mud-slinging of self-serving opinion polls, the dissembling of some publishers and the rabid, if effective campaigning of small pressure groups such as Hacked Off. The campaigning group is probably correct from its point of view that the Government "can't be trusted" to implement the full Leveson proposals.

Will history show that despite Lord Justice Leveson's leaden report its legacy will be much more than the media textbook footnote and place on a journalism professor's bookshelf that he feared?

Sir Brian has at least stimulated a debate on media standards that will be cited round the world and will be argued over for years. Even though Leveson probably still does not realise it, his greatest enduring impact will come from the seemingly endless public evidence sessions rather than his 92 recommendations.

To that extent it was the Inquiry itself which provided the catharsis for all involved, with the report something of an anti-climax.

Newspaper industry willing to accept all bar one

Most of its main findings, save one, had already, at least in embryonic form, been conceded almost from the outset by the industry when the new PCC chairman Lord Hunt started from a blank sheet of paper to imagine a new more effective regulatory body. There should be, he concluded rapidly, a new body and it should be more independent from the industry, be properly financed and have the power to investigate systemic faults and levy fines of up to £1 million on persistent offenders.

The "Desmond problem" – a publisher such as Richard Desmond, owner of the *Daily Express* and *Daily Star* who pulled his papers out of the PCC – could be dealt with by rolling five-year contracts obliging membership and adherence to codes of practice under existing civil law.

The main newspaper publishers made it clear they would agree to such a regime in principle and the proposals were refined with the help of another peer Lord Black of Brentwood, executive director of the *Telegraph* Media Group.

Such proposals were rejected by Leveson as not nearly enough, mainly because there was no mechanism to ensure that all major publishers participated on a permanent basis, and no way of verifying that a new independent press regulator was doing its job effectively and that the industry was adhering to its principles and promises.

At least on a first superficial look Lord Justice Leveson has come up with a balanced and at times ingenuous package of press reform. He rejected what many had argued for, that the press should be brought under something similar to broadcasting regulation. After all, the argument went, broadcasters are not prevented from serious investigative reporting by being subject to statutory regulation under Ofcom, the communications regulator. Leveson though accepted that the history and role of the press, and therefore its mode of regulation, should be different to that of broadcasting where controls have their origin in spectrum scarcity.

Instead he has crafted a system of incentives and disincentives for the press. For the first time the Government would have a legal duty to recognise in law the freedom of the press.

In an interesting development Leveson also wants to see the creation of an arbitration service on libel and privacy complaints, which could reduce the cost of civil proceedings for both public and press.

Any publisher who refused to join the new self-regulatory body, which would have an independent appointments panel to choose its members, could face exemplary damages if successfully sued in court.

Unwrapping the Leveson package. Add in a 'dab' of statute

In what he accepts as his most controversial proposal Leveson argues it is essential that there should be legislation to give effect both to the incentives and to underpin the independent self-regulatory system "and facilitate its recognition in legal processes."

Whatever his opponents will say, Leveson insists this does not amount to statutory regulation of the press. "What is proposed here is independent self-regulation of the press organised by the press, with a statutory verification process to ensure that the required levels of independence and effectiveness are met by the system in order for publishers to take advantage of the benefits arising as a result of membership," is how Leveson puts it.

Ofcom should be responsible for the "recognition" of the new independent body and by this act of recognition Ofcom would "validate its standards code and the arbitral system sufficient to justify the benefits in law that would flow to those who subscribed." As for those who refuse to join the new system Ofcom would be the backstop regulator.

It is a rational and subtle confection and Lord Justice Leveson should be congratulated on the mental dexterity involved in trying to bridge the seemingly impossible gulfs between the positions of all the interests involved.

In return for escaping direct statutory regulation, which many want, plus real benefits in principle and kind, all you have to do is accept a modest degree of statutory underpinning. What could be more reasonable, modest even, given what newspapers have got up to in recent years?

Surely those who would argue against such a carefully crafted version of statutory verification are indulging in something akin to debates on medieval theology?

Dispute in the academe

Media academics, some of them former journalists some not, tend to be in favour of statutory underpinning although there are vociferous exceptions such as Tim Luckhurst, Professor of journalism at the University of Kent. The same applies to many journalists and producers who come from a broadcasting tradition.

Why are newspapers kicking up so much of a fuss? While most newspapers editors oppose any flirtation with statute even here views are not unanimous.

One of the greatest and bravest of them all Sir Harold Evans, former legendary editor of *The Sunday Times* said on the *Today* programme the day after publication of the Leveson Report (November 30th 2012) that he did not see much wrong with the Leveson recommendations. This sounded slightly strange given that Sir Harold has spent most of his recent years working in the US, the land of the First Amendment. (See Sir Harold's Cudlipp lecture on p 8 of this volume)

It is difficult to argue that free expression and the entire democratic process will collapse merely because the replacement body to the PCC should be recognised and underpinned by statute. Though it is difficult, and even appears curmudgeonly to oppose Lord Leveson, the effort has to be made. Statutory underpinning should be robustly rejected on grounds of history, principle, the dangers of mission creep, perception and political realities.

In fact the closer you look the more it becomes apparent there is more than a little statutory intervention in the Leveson package. Ofcom would not only be responsible for recognising the new body but for validating its standards code enough to justify the legal benefits. What does that mean in practice?

Ofcom, a statutory regulator, could in effect therefore be involved in the details of how editors and journalists do their job and make their professional choices. Leveson also wants to see greater clarity between broadsheets and tabloids on definitions of what constitutes public interest. Would that refinement too be subject to Ofcom validation?

The arbitration service would need to be recognised in law, according to Leveson, and provisions for exemplary damages, and exemplary costs for those complainants who ignored the low-cost arbitration route would also require legislation. Data protection laws would also have to be changed to meet Leveson proposals.

Giving the government a duty to protect the freedom of the press would require legislation although without a written constitution it would not be easy to give legal meaning to such a broad concept.

Suddenly it becomes apparent that a web of legislation would have to be created to implement the heart of the Leveson proposals – legislation that could easily be amended in an adverse direction for the press by any future government.

History of the 'free press'
The history on this issue is eloquent. Licensing of newspapers in the UK was abolished in 1695 – the date most newspaper historians chose to mark the arrival of a free press.

You could also choose 1855, if you want to, the date when the crippling per copy tax on newspaper advertising making newspapers too expensive for most citizens to buy, finally ended.

Since then, and despite seven previous inquiries into the press, some into standards and privacy others into the economics of the industry, no UK

Government of any political hue has seriously planned to introduce special legislation on the press.

The newspaper industry should continue to operate under the existing general laws of the land like any other business.

There is an important point of principle at stake, which is not lessened by the fact that statutory underpinning is a tangential form of the species.

David Cameron, the Oxford PPE graduate, made up for his initial error in setting up such an open-ended inquiry by rising in the House of Commons following the publication of the Leveson report to express "serious misgivings" about statutory intervention.

"It would mean for the first time we have crossed the Rubicon of writing elements of press regulation into law of the land. We should think very carefully about crossing this line," said the Prime Minister on the day of publication (November 29th 2012)

Better across the Pond?
He was right and most American journalists would be horrified if he changed his mind now or gave way to Coalition government partner Nick Clegg who, along with Labour, favours statutory underpinning.

The US is a very different society with a very different history to the UK but a British journalist can be forgiven for sometimes looking a little enviously at the American cousins and their First Amendment which states simply, economically and unambiguously that anything "abridging the freedom of speech, infringing on the freedom of the press" is prohibited.

The leading American newspapers even rejected the setting up of voluntary press councils WHEN as an unacceptable restraint on their freedoms.

The effects of the First Amendment were dramatically extended in 1964 in the libel case of the *New York Times v Sullivan* when the US Supreme Court ruled that actual malice, rather than mere inaccuracy, had to be proved before public officials or public figures could succeed in libel actions. Lord Justice Leveson and his work would not last very long in front of the US Supreme Court.

Newspapers around the world from the New Commonwealth to the Old have expressed concern at the terrible example that would be set if the UK press were to become ensnared in special statutory obligations for the first time in more than 300 years. It may sound like paranoia but once legislation is in place, however apparently benign, there is the possibility of a slippery slope taking the press further into the arms of government and control in future.

It is also a decidedly odd spectacle to see calls for greater controls on the press, an industry facing growing economic problems, at the same time as an ever expanding expanse of totally unregulated information on the internet.

However shrill the Hacked Off campaign gets, the political realities suggest a deal will be done by David Cameron, with the support of senior Cabinet ministers such as Education secretary Michael Gove, Foreign Secretary William Hague and the press barons.

Clearly a number of ideas are being explored for a non-statutory form of recognition and verification. One from the newspaper industry would see a panel chaired by the retiring Lord Chief Justice Lord Judge – a mechanism that would have considerable public moral persuasion over the operation of the new independent regulator.

Cabinet Office Minister Oliver Letwin has alternatively suggested that such a body could be established under Royal Charter, rather like the BBC. It is an idea worth exploring but the chairman of the BBC Trust Lord Patten is appointed by the Queen, which of course means the Government, and a Royal Charter would have to be enshrined in legislation.

Finding a non-statutory mechanism to ensure that the independent press regulator is fit for purpose will not be easy but should not be beyond the wit of man or woman as long as there is a will in the newspaper industry to reach a solution.

If they fall into their old ways and begin bickering again it will be very difficult to oppose statutory intervention and that would be an avoidable tragedy.

Certainly Lord Hunt, by profession a legal specialist in regulation, believes it is possible to produce the Leveson incentives, including a low-cost arbitration service, under existing civil procedures. So, it is more than possible that a post-Leveson package can be put together that does not breach historical precedents going back more than 300 years or 158 years depending on your starting point.

Unwrapping Leveson – the rest of the package

As for other parts of the Leveson's recommendations there are both good and bad. He correctly identifies the relative powerlessness of individual journalists when confronted with strong, and sometimes bullying, newsroom cultures. This is particularly important for young journalists often desperate to establish themselves in a difficult employment market, yet finding themselves being asked to breach code rules in pursuit of a story in complete contravention to what they have been taught even a few months earlier in their media courses at university.

The Leveson suggestion that the new regulatory body should set up a 'whistleblowing' hotline for journalists who feel they are being asked to do things contrary to the code should be welcomed.

The report also suggests that the newspaper industry and the regulatory body should consider requiring its members to include in employment or service contracts a clause protecting journalists from disciplinary action as a result of refusing to do things counter to that code.

Does Lord Justice Leveson not 'get it'?

Other Leveson recommendations serve to suggest that the judge even after as much as sixteen months of solid tuition still has not got a firm grasp on how the press sometimes has to work in informal ways.

Senior police officers, he suggests for instance, should always be accompanied by a press officer and all contacts with the press should be recorded and that record made available publicly.

For some reason Leveson wants the term "off-the-record briefing" to be replaced by the phrase "non-reportable briefing."

Much more serious are the Lord Justice's views on data.

He wants journalists to lose some existing rights under data protection legislation. Leveson, for example, would like to see data protection legislation amended so that subjects of news stories could have access to information journalists held about them.

Steve Panter, a former crime reporter, now a director of the National Council for the Training of Journalists has warned that under Leveson recommendations journalists could also be jailed unless they could show there was a public interest in obtaining personal data. And what constitutes the public interest is a notoriously difficult concept to define.

It gets worse. The language seems obscure but Leveson also called on the Home Office to amend the 1984 Police and Criminal Evidence Act to require journalists to show that information held in confidence was "subject to an enforceable or lawful undertaking, restriction or obligation." Panter told *The Times* this could force reporters to seek written agreements from sources something that is not to likely to happen in the real world.

Mark Stephens, the media lawyer, who for a time represented Wikileaks founder Julian Assange, believes that Leveson's data recommendations are "incredibly worrying" and if implemented would weaken some of the bulwarks needed for investigative journalism.

In a formal response to the Leveson Report, The Information Commissioner Christopher Graham expressed concern that Lord Justice Leveson's proposals for tougher data protection laws could have a chilling effect on investigative journalism.

"The significance of the proposed changes should not be underestimated," said Graham who added that the Leveson recommendations would turn the Information Commissioner's Office into an active regulator of the press something he would actively oppose.

"The ICO is not actively seeking a wider role in relation to the regulation of the press and does not underestimate the challenges it would bring," Graham said.

Meanwhile Hacked Off produced its own post-Leveson "Bill" with provisions requiring news organisations to pay all the costs of libel and privacy actions – even if they won – if they refused to join a new regulatory body recognised by statute.

One large issue for the future, which Lord Justice Leveson barely addressed at all, is how you regulate material on the internet. The judge described the matter as "problematical."

As convergence increases one day governments will have to look again at how all media is regulated. Those are arguments for another day once the battle to protect the press from statutory recognition and validation has been won.

For now the challenge is how to find a way to run lively and often raucous newspapers within the code of practice agreed by those very newspapers.

Training is part of it and more explicit debate on ethical issues should be built into training courses alongside conventional basic training on shorthand or feature writing. Ethics, where the issue is dealt with at all, is largely an afterthought.

Papers should also reinstate ombudsmen or reader's editors where matters of fairness and accuracy can be discussed in a regular and sustained way. There was a rash of ombudsmen appointments in the 1980's following the last great moral panic about newspaper standards but most subsequently fell by the wayside.

More editorial and moral lead

Above all else newsroom cultures have in many cases to change and editors have to give a greater moral lead. Following Nick Pollard's investigations at the BBC into the *Newsnight* debacle that led to the dropping of the investigation into Sir Jimmy Savile, the former head of *Sky News* set out a journalist's take on what should happen next, on how *BBC News* should be run.

It amounted to 'Pollard's Manifesto'. In part he said:

- hire good journalists and have faith in them
- gather credible evidence and rely on it
- have editorial executives who inspire confidence and loyalty in programme staff
- insist on mature and open discussions about the strength of stories
- don't let a poisonous atmosphere develop on programme teams.

Pollard was talking about the very different world of television news but maybe the time has come to produce a best practice manifesto for all newspapers – though mainly national newspapers where the pressures are greatest.

But first the established newspaper industry has to see off the threats of statutory intervention, establish a credible independent regulator with teeth, which can sustain itself indefinitely and subject to voluntary, though meaningful, recognition and validation.

This time the press really is drinking in former Broadcasting Minister David Mellor's Last Chance Saloon and drinking up time is rapidly running out unless prompt action is taken.

Note on the contributor

Born in Larne, County Antrim, Northern Ireland, Snoddy was educated at Larne Grammar School, and Queen's University in Belfast. After university he worked on local and regional newspapers, before joining The Times in 1971. He later moved to the Financial Times, joining in 1976 and reporting on media issues for the paper before returning to *The Times* as media editor in 1995. Snoddy presented *NewsWatch* from its inception in 2004 to 2012. The programme was launched as a response to the Hutton Inquiry, as part of an initiative to make BBC News more accountable. His other television work has included presenting Channel 4's award winning series *Hard News*, which covered the press, and Sky News' *Media Monthly*. Snoddy is the author of a biography of the media tycoon Michael Green, *The Good, The Bad and The Ugly*, about ethics in the newspaper industry, and other books. Snoddy was awarded an OBE for his services to journalism in 2000.

"Rat-like cunning, a plausible manner and little literary ability" Time to prove Nick Tomalin Wrong?

Richard Sambrook is a senior editor turned academic. He scaled the peaks of BBC News (and Sport) management, now he heads the elite Cardiff University Centre for Journalism. He says Leveson offers British journalism a chance to build professionalism, train properly, and consign the Tomalin tendency to the past

When *Sunday Times'* journalist Nicholas Tomalin coined his now well-worn aphorism about the only qualities essential for real success in newspapers he captured something particular about the culture of British journalism. It has always revelled in a romantic notion of amateurism and has leaned towards a literary tradition, rather than technocratic professionalism.

With the revelations and criticisms of The Leveson Report, still debated against a backdrop of low trust and economic decline, it is worth reviewing how well this culture currently serves British journalism, or the British public, and what a different culture might entail.

Tomalin's article in 1969 was a celebration of a tradition which eschewed formal training in favour of talent and initiative; which, as he put it, rejects the notion of "facts" in favour of the "creation of interest", which raised a flag on behalf of "a collection of wayward anarchistic talents responding to and usually opposing the society they are supposed to report" against those who treat news as "a service industry, shovelling out perishable facts and names just as the United Diaries deliver milk."[1]

There are many luminous names from the past who have made the same argument – from James Cameron to Cyril Connolly, William Rees-Mogg and more. It is a notion of glorious amateurism which has informed the literary myths of British journalism, from Evelyn Waugh's *Scoop*, to Michael Frayn's *Towards the End of the Morning* or Murray Sayle's *A Crooked Sixpence* – all celebrating the same approach.

It may have been an approach fit for the time. The media was less pervasive than it is today, print was dominant and owners and editors wielded great and often arbitrary influence. It was a time to prize flair over process.

Profession or rough trade?

Most leaders of the print industry still insist journalism is a trade not a profession – largely in order to reject any form of regulation, licence or imposed standards and to ensure it remains open to talent from any quarter. But of course the context in which they operate has changed utterly.

The requirements which are accepted in other professions would, in the eyes of most print owners and editors, amount to an unwarranted intrusion into the freedom of the press by holding them to account against externally set standards. So it is still possible to start working in a newsroom with no formal training in media law, public administration, ethics, or best practice in reporting and editing.

Of course there are training programmes – notably from the National Council for the Training of Journalists (NCTJ) – and other industry led courses based around the Press Complaints Commission (PCC) Editors Code of Conduct. But these have always been inconsistently applied. Although NCTJ training is high standard and has been an expectation for entry into newspapers for many decades, in practice it has been a porous standard unequally applied. In comparison with other professions – like the law, medicine or teaching – there have never been enforced entry qualifications, or any ongoing personal development programmes or requirements for continuous or updated training. Furthermore, increasing economic pressures have undermined some employers' commitment to training with most pre-entry instruction delegated to universities and colleges.

Proposals to "professionalise" journalism are often rejected as middle class elitism which resents or fails to understand the anarchic appeal of the pugnacious, mischievous tabloid press and seeks to impose its' own standards on others.

But beyond the need to avoid undue interference, it is hard to argue that the editorial qualities and culture appropriate fifty years ago should still hold sway over an industry so transformed in scale and ambition and which faces the current array of economic and technological challenges. Indeed a lack of professional standards or a professional framework seems likely to have contributed to the current low standing and low morale of British newspaper journalism and may yet hold it back from success in an all-digital future.

Trust and self – image

A regular YouGov poll[2] on trust among professions consistently shows journalists on 'red-top' newspapers at the bottom. In March 2003, 14% of those polled trusted tabloid journalists, against 93% who trusted doctors, 88% teachers and 82% local police officers. Broadcast journalists, working in a regulated environment, fair better at just over 80%, and journalists on mid-market newspapers 36%.

In the following nine years there has been a downward drift in trust overall, but in Nov 2012 the figures were doctors 82%, teachers 74%, 69% local police, broadcasters 44%, mid-market journalists 18% and 'red-top' journalists just 10%.

One of the things this underlines is the extent to which the British press is not really one business – and that is recognised by the public. Inconveniently for those seeking reform, it is the 'red-top', tabloid market – the least trusted – which makes the most money. The serious upmarket newspapers – the most trusted – tend to lose money.

So while the public may speak one way about trust, they say something different. when they choose what to buy.

However, journalists themselves are becoming more concerned. The preliminary results from an NCTJ sponsored survey into journalists at work[3] – presented at the NCTJ's 2012 Skills Conference – show significant changes in attitude among working journalists compared to a similar survey ten years ago.

This shows that although UK journalists are highly qualified (88% have a degree or higher qualification against 38% in the UK workforce as a whole) less than two thirds (63%) have a journalism qualification. Journalism qualifications are seen as increasingly important in getting work as a journalist (80% up from 72% a decade ago) and increasingly relevant to their work as a journalist (89% – up from 82% in 2002)

Although the majority have undertaken some learning in the previous 12 months (71%) most of this has been informal and self-taught, more likely to be paid for by the individual or free than paid for by an employer.

All those surveyed felt that changes in the last ten years have led to lower job satisfaction, feeling the job has been deskilled (40%) and they produce a lower quality of work (38%). Only half would recommend a young person to become a journalist – 48% would not.

This is a damning verdict from those currently working in British newsrooms.

Trust in journalists is at a ten year low, and journalists themselves are more pessimistic about the profession than they were a decade ago. The increasing casualisation of journalism – fewer staff jobs and greater use of freelances – is further undermining standards in the "trade" in ways which practitioners at least are recognising.

Ethics? A County East of London?
A separate study for the NCTJ, conducted by Phil Harding, found a range of further concerns. Interviews with senior editors from almost all the UK media groups revealed a shared concern that the Leveson revelations had "dented their own personal integrity and that of their profession as a whole. Most agreed that there needed to be changes and that ethical issues in journalism had to be given a much higher priority."[4] (See p 230 of this volume)

Others feared the report would lead to the suppression of good journalism and that important stories would go unreported. As one interviewee put it: "There is a big danger that the chattering classes will seek to impose their own values on this process and that they will seek to eliminate what they see as "tawdry" labelling it as unethical."

Over the last decade, criticism of poor journalism has come not just from the "chattering classes" outside journalism but from within its ranks as well.

Leading figures from the profession have launched their own attacks – and not simply the revelations about phone hacking from Nick Davies in *The Guardian*. His investigation was prefigured by his book *Flat Earth News* which in 2009 which laid out a damning indictment of British journalism: too much unfiltered PR, or "Churnalism", opting for safe facts, cheap stories and lowest common denominator journalism to satisfy public appetites and allow owners to make a profit:

> "…national newspapers and broadcasters across the developed world have been taken over by a new generation of corporate owners, who have cut their staffing and increased their output, heavily restricting the time available for journalists to check the truth of what they write. I found the same owners have caused the disintegration of the old network of local, front-line reporters, in domestic and foreign coverage, heavily restricting the flow of raw information to these hard-pressed national newsrooms."[5]

Malcolm Dean, also from *The Guardian*, in his book *Democracy Under Attack*, outlines seven deadly media sins: distortion, group think, being too adversarial, dumbing down, too readily duped, emphasising politics over policy and, of course, relentless negativity. Clearly from his analysis, they damage the democratic process that freedom of the press is meant to support. His critique is built upon the British journalistic culture distorting any attempts at serious or proportional analysis of social policy.

Before them, John Lloyd, in his book *What the Media are doing to our Politics* set out a similarly critical and polemical account of a cynical media prioritizing impact over the public interest in its coverage of politics.

So we have a catalogue of unethical behaviour revealed in a public inquiry, trust in the profession at a ten year low, journalists themselves more pessimistic about the future of their trade than a decade ago, and leading newspaper journalists kicking back at their profession for damaging practices and culture.

So, time for reform?
The newspaper industry is stubbornly dug in against reform. Rather as the pro-gun lobby in the US uses the Constitution's second amendment to block even a modest level of reform, the UK newspaper industry finds it hard to conceive of any significant change that might not undermine its freedom and independence. This is usually expressed in refusal to countenance any statutory underpinning to press regulation – a clear point of principle for the industry – but extends

further into refusal to seriously consider a firm commitment to qualifications, standards, public accountability or training.

It gives the appearance of an industry in denial – about the parlous state it has reached in terms of public trust and morale, and about the responsibilities the public require to accompany its influence. As Kevin Marsh wrote in a previous volume in this series: "As a society we have the right and the duty to expect of this powerful institution exactly what we demand of others. To determine how they should exercise that power. To insist they're accountable to us for the way they use their power."[6]

The press, swift to call others to account, seem unprepared to meet the same external standards they demand of other sectors. In all the debate about regulatory frameworks, there has been little discussion about changing cultural attitudes which may not be serving the industry well.

Media today inculcates all aspects of our lives. We are bombarded with messages every day; newsrooms have to serve the real time demands of the internet in a vastly more competitive environment. News cycles are now measured in minutes, not even hours, let alone days. The technology of newsgathering and production is increasingly sophisticated. The impact of the media on public debate and policy is substantial; political and corporate press officers now outnumber the staffs of major newsrooms. Is this any environment for even a gifted amateur or tradesman?

What is a professional?
Clearly it is true that journalists are not professionals in any objective sense. They do not stand comparison with true professions such as medicine or the law. Journalists, although more highly qualified than most of the country, do not require a formal education in their craft, and should not require a licence to practise. There have of course been attempts to establish the press card as a badge of legitimacy – most recently by some within the industry proposing a new form of self -regulation. But the need for independence has prevailed. Nor do journalists adhere to any universal or enforceable code of conduct. The PCC had a good Editors Code of Practice but, as Leveson revealed, it was not adhered to and the PCC was unable to enforce it in any meaningful way. Individual organisations may write and enforce their own codes or value statements but, as yet, there's no universally accepted set of professional values backed up by a governing body with the power to censure journalists who deviate from the code.

The only reason for journalism not to become a profession is the fundamental question of independence. Externally set standards and accountabilities, especially if set in statute, are clearly unacceptable to the industry – and it's a view shared by many politicians and large sections of the public who recognise the importance of "non-interference."

So could any framework of a profession be put in place without statute or externally imposed standards and would there be value in doing so?

Is education the answer?

Would formalizing journalism education make individual journalists or editors more effective? How would creating a professional pool of consistently trained journalists affect the entrepreneurial flair that drives editorial success? Can a new Editors code establish a set of common standards that would be enforceable? Can employers be persuaded to support career-long development of their staff?

Professionals in other sectors typically undergo a postgraduate programme. On qualifying, they then have to obtain a formal licence to practice by passing a comprehensive exam designed to test their mastery of their subject. Once they pass this test, they have to invest in a certain amount of continuing education to stay abreast of evolving knowledge. In some fields, licensed professionals must periodically pass further exams in order to re-certify their licenses.

Journalists don't face such challenges. Although increasing numbers now have university training, and those entering newspapers may sit the NCTJ exams, there is no formal requirement for entry – let alone that they stay current in their field.

As Phil Harding suggests, there is a growing need for consistent entry level training – but also for journalist training at mid career and senior levels. "There seems to be a substantial need for a programme of continuous professional development across journalism...such a programme could be part of a larger package of mid-career development which could also include refreshers on changes in the law such as the Bribery Act; new developments in social media and technology; latest market and readership trends; updates on recent compliance and regulatory issues; as well as leadership and management issues."[7]

Professions and Society

Society has an implicit contract with true professions—we grant them privileges because we trust them to self-govern. They are not always upheld, but they do establish a higher expectation than in a non-professional setting, and a higher degree of censure when those expectations are broken. If journalism were to be seen as a profession, supported by a transparent approach to training and development and qualification, public expectations and the expectations of journalists themselves would rise. It might be the start of strengthening trust and improving morale.

For that to happen, the industry would need to agree, and abide by, a consistent standard for entry to the profession – accredited independently by the NCTJ or others – and invest in a recognized programme of continuous personal development (CPD) for editorial staff. Currently there is little incentive for them to do so – and culturally little recognition of the need or advantages of doing so.

The American model

There is a parallel with the "professionalisation" of American journalism a century ago. In the 1920's there was a long and heated debate about press standards and purposes – following the yellow journalism of the press wars between Pulitzer and Hearst and the so called jazz age sensational journalism.

Michael Schudson suggests this debate led to a conscious decision on the part of American journalists to move towards a set of professional standards. A move which was also in response to the rapid growth of PR. In the US, they developed the first ethical codes of practice and the concept of objectivity as a core journalistic value took hold. Pulitzer also endowed Columbia School of Journalism in the belief journalism was important enough to require professional training. It was a view that did not cross the Atlantic.

> "Continental journalists already understood themselves in a publicly successful way – as high literary creators and cosmopolitan political thinkers. They did not have the down-and-dirty sense of themselves as laborers whose standing in the world required upgrading as American – and British – journalists did. If there was to be an upgrading, in any event, it was to a literary rather than professional ideal."[8]

Britain, as ever, was caught between Europe and the US. It aspired to the amateur literary journalistic tradition, but also – in broadcasting at least – adopted the objective/impartial ideal.

Through most of the last century this professional approach to newspaper journalism in the US has produced high quality, ethically sound, reporting. Critics would say it has also been less innovative or creative than British journalism and has not protected US journalism from some of its own scandals (e.g. Jayson Blair at the New York Times).[9] In addition, the digital age has undermined the value of such professional norms as objectivity which, in the US more than the UK, is now widely discredited as an impossible and therefore unhelpful standard to which to aspire.

Establishing professional norms in the US worked in the middle of the last century at a time when owners wanted to restore trust and build media empires based on scarcity of resource and distribution. In an era of digital plenty, and economic challenge, it is less clear that the same approach is relevant anymore. However, this shouldn't be confused with a lack of relevance of any professional standard.

If the norms of objectivity and impartiality are breaking down, what is to distinguish the professional journalist from anyone with access to social media or a blog? In an era when we are engulfed in information – much of it of poor quality, uncertain provenance or just wrong – there should be a premium on professional assessment, analysis and presentation of information of public interest. Trust in a professional approach requires transparency about standards, methods and motivations – and a culture which prizes accuracy and a positive relationship with the public rather than the cynical exploitation of them as revealed in the Leveson Inquiry.

There is of course a great deal of outstanding high quality journalism delivered every day by British newspapers. In many ways, we are lucky to have the range and quality that we enjoy given the economic circumstances. But in its approach to training and development, and the culture it nurtures, the industry is overly attached to the past.

Culture and Transparency

Lord Justice Leveson talks more about culture than about training or development in his report – while making clear that they are closely linked. He says no code of practice can turn an unethical organisation into an ethical one. However such codes can help ethical organisations to set standards. He quotes the evidence of Professor Christopher Megone, who, he says, has worked extensively with industry bodies (mainly in finance and engineering) on issues of workplace ethics:

> "… even more critical to the existence of an ethical media organisation is culture…. If there is an unhealthy culture then an organisation can have an ethical code but it will have little influence. Members of the organisation can undergo 'ethics training' but it will have little effect. As soon as they return from the training to their desk or office, the pervasive culture will dominate their decision-making. The culture brings to bear all sorts of 'accepted norms' which an afternoon's training will be relatively powerless to affect."[10]

Culture therefore becomes the core issue. As any manager will testify cultural change, even when recognised as needed, is hugely difficult to implement.

The example of business

In a curious and little commented upon digression, considering the tools a new regulatory system might use to change culture, Lord Justice Leveson turns to another witness, former government lawyer Donald Macrae. In paragraphs which could have come out of a business school handbook, he offers a four part analysis of bringing about cultural and behaviour change across the industry based on four principles: enable, encourage, engage and exemplify.

What is striking about this passage on cultural change is the extent to which Leveson believes those outside the industry are key to ensuring an environment which will stimulate and support a different media culture. The relationship between the media and society is of course crucial. If there is a lucrative market in unethical journalism, it will continue. If the public really want a more accountable media, they have to continue to demand it. At the heart of this relationship, as Leveson notes, sits transparency:

> "Transparency… could work in two ways. It can take the form of transparency of action (e.g. requiring all stories to run under the byline of a real person; requiring transparency on the sources of quotes, requiring transparency on the method by which any story has been obtained). It can also take the form of transparency of compliance (e.g. requiring visible corrections, publishing accuracy league tables, publishing data on compliance with regulatory standards)."

He also recommends the six principles of transparency offered by Baroness Onora O'Neill:

"Baroness O'Neill's suggested 'six principles of openness' for identifying ethical journalism which seem to me to have much to recommend them:

(a) openness about payments from others

(b) openness about payments to others

(c) openness about the interests (financial or otherwise) of owners, editors, programme- makers and journalists

(d) openness about errors

(e) openness about (most) sources, with an adequately drawn test of the public interest to allow sources to be kept secret, for specific reasons and in particular situations

(f) openness about comments from members of the public."

Ethics and transparency are about the media's relationship with the public. Adopting a framework of transparency of this kind – within whatever regulatory model emerges from the current political debate – would be a first step in strengthening that relationship, providing a basic level of accountability and rebuilding trust. It would also be a first step towards a more professional footing for journalism which could be built upon, without infringing independence or freedom of the press, with a serious and consistent approach to training and continuous personal development of staff.

It doesn't require statute to implement – merely a shift in perspective about newspapers' responsibilities towards the public and a recognition by employers about their responsibility towards a well-trained staff.

Some argue that the light and air brought to bear on the worst excesses of tabloid behaviour have reformed them in any case. I am less convinced. An industry which is quick to decry any fall in standards in others is overly defensive of its own position and in denial about what the collapse of trust and morale means for its future.

In rejecting the notion of "professionalism" along with statutory regulation newspapers may do themselves a disservice. 'Rat-like cunning a plausible manner and a little literary ability' may have been sufficient fifty years ago. Today's media, transformed in scale reach and influence, requires a different approach. A 24 hour global, converged media, undergoing rapid change, dealing with a constant deluge of information, and exerting huge influence over all our lives, should not be hesitant about calling itself a profession. It requires consistent editorial discipline and skills supported by industry-focused training and continuous development – to raise standards, establish an ethical culture, build public trust and raise morale. And perhaps in so doing, to secure a stronger long-term future.

Notes
[1] Tomalin, Nicholas (1975)"Reporting" Andre Deutsch, p77

[2] YouGov Trust Tracker poll available at
http://cdn.yougov.com/cumulus_uploads/document/syrhatyofp/Trust_trends_Nov_2012.pdf

[3] NCTJ Journalists at Work survey to be published in 2013 available at
http://www.nctj.com/about-us/research (Preliminary results given at 2012 NCTJ Skills Conference)

[4] Harding, Phil "It's time to take ethics seriously" British Journalism Review Vol 23 No 4 pp29-34(see also Harding in this volume p 230)

[5] Davies, Nick (2009)"Flat Earth News" Vintage p153

[6] Marsh, Kevin "…But what comes after?" Keeble & Mair, (2012) The Phone hacking Scandal: journalism on trial, Abramis, p84

[7] ibid (BJR Vol 23 No 4)

[8] Schudson, Michael, 2006, "Why Democracies Need an Unlovable Press" Polity p34

[9] See American Journalism Review for background, available at
http://ajr.org/article.asp?id=3019

[10] The Leveson Report available at http://www.levesoninquiry.org.uk/wp-content/uploads/2012/07/Witness-Statement-of- Professor-Christopher-Megone.pdf

[10] The Leveson Report p 1745

[10] The Leveson Report p88

References

Broesma, Marcel & Peters, Chris (2012) *Rethinking Journalism*, London, Routledge

Davies, Nick (2009) *Flat Earth News*, London, Vintage

Dean, Malcolm (2011) *Democracy Under Attack*, London, Policy Press

Keeble, Richard & Mair, John (Eds) (2012)*The Phone Hacking Scandal – Journalism on Trial?*, Abramis

Kovach, Bill & Rosentiel, Tom (2001) *The Elements of Journalism*, New York, Crown

Lloyd, John, (2004) *What the Media is Doing to Our Politics*, London, Constable

Schudson, Michael (2006) *Why Democracies Need an Unlovable Press*, Cambridge, Polity

Tomalin, Nicholas (1975) *Reporting*, London, Deutsch

Note on the contributor
Richard Sambrook is Professor and Director of the Centre for Journalism at Cardiff University. He started his career on local newspapers in South Wales before joining the BBC where he worked as a producer and editor for 30 years, culminating in ten years on the board as Director of Sport, Director of News and finally Director of Global News and the World Service. He is also a Visiting Fellow at the Reuters Institute for the Study of Journalism at the University of Oxford.

Welcome to the future –'Information Terrorism'

Bernard Clark is an entrepreneur in journalism. He invented 'Watchdog' inside BBC's '*Nationwide*' three decades ago. He then went on to make the first TV series to properly examine the press on a regular basis – Channel Four's '*Hard News*'. Here he presents a rather dystopic view of the future of journalism on and off the internet. According to him, by looking at the press, Lord Justice Leveson was looking the wrong way, looking backward at a disappearing problem. Leveson should have been looking forward at the burgeoning and scary art of *Information Terrorism*

A couple of decades ago, it took days for a political scandal, or a personal disgrace, to unfold across the media. A few puffs of smoke, say a diary item, would spark a column on page nine, then a flame as the growing 'scoop' moved to page one, until the firestorm would properly ignite when the bandwagon of 'exclusives' widened from the popular press into radio and TV. By the end of a week or two, questions may be asked in Parliament, or Lord Fluster's drawing room, with perhaps a few days later a bland but regretful statement. With the fire now raging, it was time to damp it down with a quiet resignation, or personal apology for appalling behaviour, or an admission through a solicitor of a shameful lapse of honesty.

Not so now.

Today, all of the above happen simultaneously in a nanosecond, often manipulated by *agent provocateurs* and stoked by a thousand grinding axes. There's no smoke, sparks, embers, or even flames – these days stories explode like massive bombs, destroying in an instant not just reputations, but any chance of the truth. And the cynical hands behind these bombs, using the inscrutable internet as their fuel and fuse, might be in 10 Downing Street, a Trade Union, shadowy groups or secret organisations, or just be ordinary folk who are minded by prejudice or malice.

These are the new terrorists in what has become an information war. Unregulated, unaccountable.

Back in History: 1991

It was just before Christmas in 1991 that David Mellor, the then Minister at the Home Office in charge of media, said to Ray Snoddy on the Channel 4 programme *Hard News*, that 'the press is drinking at the bar of the last chance saloon.' This was the first time I had heard that particular phrase, but the sentiment had been around. He meant, of course, that if the press did not sort themselves out, John Major's Government would do it for them. There were no hollow laughs from the newspapers, this was an explicit threat, with the Calcutt Commission investigating whether to regulate the press – but it was followed by bluster, farce, prevarication, the shelving of Calcutt's recommendations, and finally 'the same old nowt'.

With one exception.

A year later, the grubby sheets of the tabloids showed the grubby sheets of the unfortunate Mr Mellor across their front pages, the married Minister having been caught consorting with Spanish model/actress Antonia De Sancha while wearing, it was mischievously alleged, a Chelsea (his team of choice)football shirt.

Now the hollow laughs did ring out. Next time the Sheriff goes on his rounds, maybe he should give the 'last chance saloon' a miss. Calcutt, Mellor and good, but naïve, intentions were railroaded out of town by the hard drinking saloon clientele, for another decade or two.

History repeats itself

That was twenty years ago, now we are back in a similar place: For Calcutt substitute Leveson, for Major write Cameron: And Calcutt's recommendation, that the press be given eighteen months to put their own house in order, failing which there would be legislation, resounds like the most déjà of déjà vus.

So are we in for the same again? Will the press use yet another crony commission to repel the now more urgent sheriffs of accountability and regulation for the next twenty years? Very unlikely. Because there won't be much of a press left to regulate. But before we begin cheering from the i-space rooftops, the implications may be worse than we could possibly imagine. Newspapers did at least create a kind of order within their amoral invincibility; the vacuum left with their passing could herald the darkest of black holes because, regulation or not, for the last few centuries we've actually known very well where we are with matters of information, even if some proprietors and editors acted like renegades and thieves.

With their passing, we're entering a brave, or probably, not so brave, new world – in military terms like the move from all-out, but surprisingly honourable army style war, into the nasty, interminably tortuous world of terrorism. *Information terrorism*, in which generally unidentifiable forces, motivated by what they believe is principle but may in fact be malice, will use every known dark art against their resented target or imagined foe.

These will be informal groups, banded together by a common social, economic or political purpose, or, increasingly, through an arbitrary but unswerving belief in the evil of their quarry, and their own rectitude. The signs are already there.

Let's for a moment contrast this to the traditional structure most of us have been involved with over the years, of the constant war, albeit often gentlemanly, between politics, the law and the press. Without the press, it will be as if one leg of a stool has fallen off; though initially pleased to be unfettered, the law and the government will lose a particular edge, along with the little trust of the public they still enjoy. This is not because newspapers are especially good arbiters of power and justice – they often aren't – but because they have 'scale' and are predictable 'communities', as identifiable as a forthright uncle or strangely liberal sister, with whom we may not agree, but we understand where their opinions come from. Usually we respect their standards, and if they are not marching on Downing Street, then everyday life can't be that bad.

The *Daily Mail* is the most obvious, but the *Sun*, *Telegraph*, the more recent *Times* and sometimes even the *Guardian* has a view, a 'truth' even, in a way you would not expect or find on TV or Radio, except in the US, not least because in the UK they are required by law to be 'impartial' and are regulated. Ironically, much of this regulation was eagerly supported by the press at the time it was brought in, mainly out of a desire to hobble competitors, and it still is: when Ofcom, or the BBC Trust comes out with a particularly inane judgment – a not uncommon occurrence – most of the press leaps on the bandwagon, using what should be their natural enemy to attack what, in journalistic terms at least, should be their friend. It certainly will be fascinating if statutory regulation does eventually come in and The Mail finds itself under the yolk of OFFPRESS or the like; I think poor Mr Dacre might manage a treble 'C'. Bless him.

However, although a law could, in theory, require newspapers to observe a set of standards, there never could be legislation that would require them to be impartial – an independence that is the greatest value the press bring to our daily life. Love 'em or hate 'em, within the bounds of libel, they can, and do, say exactly what they want, when they want, and for that we should be eternally thankful.

This matters because, however much large sectors of the population may disagree with an editor or proprietor's partiality, their 'blood and thunder,' we all instinctively know that there are limits beyond which mass newspapers won't allow the government, of any hue or association, to go. Which gives them a power that is crucial to our democracy, and maybe even our freedom, and is an aspect of our lives that we will fight, fight and fight again, to retain.

Not so the internet, which is neutral to the point of irresponsibility, especially the mass-communication or 'scale' parts like *Google*, *Facebook*, *Twitter* or *You – Tube*, who frankly, my dear, don't give a damn. Not to content, political affiliation, investigation, fairness, or holding governments to account. Can you imagine Rupert Murdoch, even in his most commercial guise, turning such a blind eye? Or the dreaded Mr Dacre? However questionable their controlling instincts, however much they may bluster and occasionally bully, we do know they have a view, will fight for their truth, they will engage.

Into the abyss?
This is the nub of where we're really heading post-Leveson, not questions of self-regulation, or statutory codes, or deregulation. We're heading into a future of no regulation, and even worse, an inscrutable world of 'look the other way'. The world of 'i's' as in internet, irresponsible. Or i don't care?

This is not the same as powerlessness or being without influence. The internet monoliths will have plenty of clout, pretty well unfettered by democratic national governments (but not totalitarian ones, like China), which will be used to censor when it suits their commercial purposes. Beyond that they will turn a blind eye, because to them content doesn't matter, so long as editorial issues do not interfere with the off-shore bottom line.

Citing 'freedom of expression', which like motherhood and apple pie is impossible to attack, they will host their anonymous 'contributors'' bullying, lies, smears, breath-taking invasions of privacies and reputation-destroying carnage, while refusing all responsibility for what they host. And I know this from first hand.

The experience of a work colleague at the hands of *Facebook* was so alarming in the context of information misuse that it's worth recounting. He came to see me because someone, he did not know who, had taken his name and set up a *Facebook* page purporting to be his, along with a photo and several intimate details, some true, some false. The entry included enough facts and recent events to be both credible and distressing, and was playing havoc with his personal life and relationships. This created in his mind a sense of being stalked, as if someone had stolen his very being.

On my advice he contacted *Facebook* but they more-or-less didn't want to know. Pointing out that they had very few staff to look into such matters, their unconcerned operator put the whole onus on him to both prove he was in fact the named person, and also to demonstrate personal harm. And that was when we could get through – *Facebook*'s whole system seemed to be geared to discouraging any contact with their members (or in this case non-member) and ultimately he gave up. Eventually, we bluffed his anonymous character kidnapper – we still don't know who it was – into believing they would be exposed, so they finally they stopped, but not before he had suffered several weeks of shame and embarrassment.

Even in their most public-dismissing phases, the Press Council or the Press Complaints Commission would not dare to be so cavalier about what was clearly an outrageous denial of responsibility. Yet this was probably only one single crazy weirdo making someone else's life a misery, presumably for a laugh:

What's coming in the future could be far more deadly, involving widespread smears, character assassinations and the destruction of companies and maybe even institutions. And by then we may not have a vigorous press to bring it to account.

The strange case of John Leslie

To help illustrate this let's begin with the story of John Leslie, an ex *Blue Peter* presenter, who went onto host ITV's *This Morning*. He was not even named in the book by Ulrika Jonnson that led to his downfall, nor at first, in the press. Newspapers well knew that apart from a million pounds in libel damages, their reputation would be seriously harmed if they recklessly accused an individual of rape without cast-iron evidence. But others were not so careful. A few mentions on the net, a billowing of innuendo, eventually led to him being 'inadvertently' named on a low rated TV show, at which point his name, and the unproven accusation, went worldwide, web viral. Next, he lost his job, then a couple of dozen women came forward with unrelated, historical stories of sexual maltreatment by him, which led finally to the police bringing two cases of indecent assault. Later with his career utterly destroyed, the police subsequently, and quietly, dropped all charges by offering no evidence. And to this day not one sexual accusation stands against him.

As that scourge of our time, a 'TV personality', John Leslie always appeared a tad self-satisfied. It may be that jealousy, public dislike of a man who seemed like the cat that got the cream, or that well known British sport of resenting success, brought him down, but there was no clear organisation, no identifiable campaign, no 'Destroy Leslie' committee. It was worse than that. There was a gossipy interview to promote a celebrity book that produced some prurient curiosity, and then a few embers of misinformation ignited a firestorm of random indignation, until a large group of people became that ugliest of all things – a lynch mob. An electronic lynch mob. That swept truth, decency, fair play, the law and John Leslie before them.

This is the pattern of *information terrorism* : A trap is set, then a little spark, a cacophony of internet innuendo, reaching a crescendo, until one person 'inadvertently' mutters 'THE NAME', then the Twitter-and-friends worldwide web mob create an electronic doorstep, followed by ten, or twenty, or fifty, or a hundred new shrieking accusers, until the police arrive at dawn in ironed uniforms to escort the shocked and unshaven 'xx-year old man' to the police station. This is justice as Punch and Judy theatre, a kind of 'he's a celebrity, get him out of here', and while the images and restrained 'tut-tuts' loop on 24-hour news, a hitherto highly respected man, and it nearly always is a man, wonders whether the cops have taken the MBE in the large plastic bags along with his personal files, to test for 30-year-old DNA.

Sometimes this seems like the perverse price of long-term fame, as exacted by an electronic hangman, internet style, aided and abetted by police who enjoy turning the tables on celebrities rather more that ridding our cities of street crime.

While it's true to say the newspapers did belatedly hound Leslie too, for over a week the story, quite possibly entirely untrue, was fanned by the internet in such a way that Leslie could do nothing about it. He is now working as an estate agent, destroyed by smear, innuendo and mob rule.

How *information terrorism* works

That is the classic way *information terrorism* works: A single, seemingly innocent line in a celebrity book by one individual acts like a fuse to ignite an explosive mixture of internet gossip, to blow apart a reputation, a career, a life. And though the newspapers have committed the most heinous calumnies themselves over the years, at least they are accountable, if only to the law and to their readers. Not so, the internet.

The thousands, or even hundreds of thousands, of internet users who fan the flames, who widen the smear, sometimes for sheer fun, are accountable to nothing and no one, because the true publishers of their barbs have found a way of looking the other way – the Pontius Pilates of the information age. That's what Leveson needed to examine, the way reputations are traduced by a mass of accusation, images and innuendo, before the evidence is produced.

But doesn't this sound very familiar?

Jimmy Savile – the VICTIM?

In my view, controversial and possibly abhorrent to some people, much of the reputational damage that has followed the Jimmy Savile allegations falls into that same category of *information terrorism*, or certainly *information assault*. Again, as in the John Leslie story, the Police eventually take centre stage.

Post-Savile, family men, often with lives of unblemished public success, have been suddenly traduced by anonymous, out-of-the-blue allegations from twenty, thirty or forty years ago. For why? Because of completely unrelated media stories, about completely unrelated people, mainly completely unrelated circumstances, and unrelated crimes – inspired absolutely and only by a pass-the-parcel, 'it happened to me, too' accusation culture, fed by the never-sleeping information machine. Based on untested, historical information, presumably without a scrap of forensics or contemporaneous medical examinations, the distinctly excitable police – to the delight of the conveniently present photographers and gawping neighbours – arrest first and ask questions later.

Whether it's meant to terrify, it certainly has that effect. There are even a few men I've worked with over the years who are concerned about the battering ram on the door at five am, who have inspected their files to be on the safe side, who have had 'middle-of-night phone number' conversations with their solicitors. Though it's not Nazi Germany, for some this has reached that stage where a fear about something long forgotten, nags away in the small hours: "Did I once brush against a secretary's bottom, her breast, did I once go to kiss a cheek, and touch lips instead?"

Mea Culpa?

As a BBC presenter during the 1970s, some of this comes close to me, too.

I worked with Jimmy Savile in 1978, we co-presented the *Nationwide Skateboard Contest* ; from memory he was a highly professional, pleasant but wily man, the life and soul of the crowd that tucked itself around him for autographs. I also presented with another arrestee, the Disc Jockey Dave Lee Travis, who was less professional but more approachable, the *Nationwide Disco Doubles*, on which the main judge was Jonathan King – should I put my solicitor on standby?

You think I jest, but a couple of the people who have been frogmarched away are, if not friends, past acquaintances and, though their reputations are seemingly in terminal tatters, they remain uncharged, and therefore in theory, innocent. But to them, it doesn't seem that way; the first few pages of Google under their name now churn with words like 'paedophile', 'indecent assault' and 'Savile' – such is the power of the all-pervading, all-knowing search engines, they feel condemned until proven innocent.

While on the subject of Savile and the madnesses of *Newsnight*, I felt mildly concerned when watching the later ITV '*Exposure*' programme, that the ITV lawyers may have been uncomfortable at passing the investigation if Savile had still been alive, especially if Jimmy had the services of a Maxwellesque lawyer. Given that they would have had to put the evidence to him in advance, and the Police had previously been reluctant to proceed, it would have required a robust effort to get 'errors and omission' insurance as generally required by ITV. But, of course, none of that matters now that the pack of historical accusers has past the five hundred mark – it surely must be true, mustn't it? Equally, I'm sure it's completely coincidental that, according to one of the lawyers of a claimant I heard on Radio 4, Jimmy's estate of £4.3 million has not been disbursed yet.

Pleb or Plebgate?

Next, in this litany of how the stories of disinformation or defamation, whether justified or not, have moved from the newspapers to the baying internet mob, is the tale of Andrew Mitchell, until October 2012, a Tory Cabinet Minister and the Chief Whip. The Mitchell saga is a classic of its kind, and a clear harbinger of the future. Apparently, non-associated individuals with supposedly no axe to grind spontaneously put forward the same story, producing a web that Houdini would have been hard pressed to escape. The fact that it was a piece of excellent TV journalism by Michael Crick on Channel 4 that eventually exposed what really happened, is almost a miracle, and leads me to wonder how many other reputations will be destroyed through seemingly coordinated misinformation. With a little expert knowledge, by leaks and even an impromptu press conference, a semi-public body, the Police Federation, created a media blitzkrieg, which left even a Minister of the Crown so powerless that he had to be destroyed. *Information terrorism* might be a little harsh to describe Andrew

Mitchell's downfall, but the misinformation bomb that went off under his bike was designed to be as deadly and untraceable as Semtex.

The Savile story, John Leslie, the 59, 63, 69 year old men from Dorset or Timbuktu, and Andrew Mitchell, all have one thing in common. Being investigated by the Police, often for somewhat questionable reasons, which usually have been stimulated and amplified by the web. In misunderstanding the way the internet, journalism and electronic media combine to reinforce innuendo, the Police often seem naïve to the point of stupidity. Perhaps we should sympathise, because many detectives, and even more alarmingly, prosecutors, don't understand what the internet is, nor do they appreciate the way 'dark powers' swap unproven denunciations to attack, terrify and eventually destroy. But the forces of law and order need to wise up, or leave it alone, rather than follow the twists and turns of cyberspace, and then blunder in while almost entirely missing the point.

Julian Assange : the refugee from *information terrorism*?

A classic case of this can be found today languishing in the Ecuadorian Embassy in the body and increasingly crazed mind of Julian Assange. If *Information Terrorism* is a manipulation of half-truths to pick on defenceless individuals, Assange and Wikileaks produced the exact opposite because, not only was the target the most powerful military machine in history, the information was true. What followed, whether farce or deliberate plot, became such a convoluted story of condoms, 'consensual rape' or sex-while-asleep, that the leaked pictures of a helicopter gunship massacring a couple of dozen innocent Iraqis, including a Reuters journalist, palled in comparison. That was exactly what the US military wanted. Who cares about the message if you can character assassinate the messenger. And effectively lock him up to boot. Perhaps there is no conspiracy against Assange, perhaps he was just unfortunate in his choice of bed mates, but the suspicion remains that an unscrupulous super power have punished and eliminated an embarrassing critic for revealing uncomfortable truths. Wait a second: Governments wouldn't get involved in *information terrorism*, surely not?

One important observation on Assange. If he had been working for a newspaper, say investigations editor of the *Guardian*, which carried so much of the Wikileaks material, there would have been no question of him being extradited to the US for what the Right there say is spying, rape charges in Sweden or not. His vulnerability specifically stems from his status as individual internet whistle-blower. In the constant information war that will mark so much of our world in the coming decades, governments, whether those with freedom of the press in their constitutional hearts or not, will seek to distinguish between publications and media, and the internet, partly to undermine real investigations. This protection for individuals who, though not specifically whistle-blowers, but who operate in the public interest, is yet another issue that the end-game post-Leveson should embrace.

These days, when I look across the whole panorama of the way information disseminates – and I use that as an objective adverb on purpose – I see the destruction of people, companies and even governments accelerating, partly because the hunting pack can rip targets apart with random ease, and partly because transgressions which are often trivial can be blown out of all proportion by clever web-'spinners'. (Perhaps they will come to be called 'spiders")

When I was editing *Watchdog*, there were hundreds of stories of how a slipshod plumber had wrecked an old lady's heating system, or a teacher who had shouted and maybe lashed out at pupils, or a caterers who through rank incompetence ruined wedding receptions, leaving brides in eternal tears, but I would say to the sometimes outraged production team, 'this isn't a story, let's move on'. When pressed I would explain: "We can't destroy a person's reputation, in front of everyone they've ever known, everyone who loves them, because they've been incompetent – and yes, then covered up. Because we all do that. It would be disproportionate to shame them in front of 10 million BBC 1 viewers." Incompetence, then cover up, just wasn't a story for me – they had to be villains, not idiots.

My team would shake their heads, but inside they agreed, because the power we wielded through producing mass TV required us to be proportionate and worldly, a worldliness I've seen at first hand from the editor of every newspaper I've encountered. This used to be part of law enforcement before the Police's initiative was taken away by the maiden aunt attitudes of so many overseers. To me, worldly proportionality must be re-established, instead of decisions being made by naïve managers or lawyers who believe that the victim is the anonymous person who may have been touched/insulted or disrespected thirty years ago, rather than the person whose reputation, peace and whole life could be destroyed in a 24-hour global media firestorm. And that worldliness needs to inform our attitudes to every part of the new global media landscape, and not just the wise owl, aging press.

While it's true that the speed of the 'decline of print' may be exaggerated, with its printing presses, trucks and paperboys there's scale below which a newspaper can't go, and most of our dailies are bumping up against that commercial reality already. In the world of dog eat dog, there will be amalgamations and takeovers on the journey to newsprint oblivion, but the destination is already set – the all-embracing internet.

Personally, I am not as pessimistic as this essay seems to suggest because the real guts of the newspapers, the journalism will somehow survive; it's part of the human condition to want expose the truth, for us to read and to want to write stories. Equally, there will always be someone who needs both to encourage and control this, so we may even see a couple of Dacres and Murdochs of the 2030's continuing to shepherd writers and readers to their will.

In my more optimistic moments, I see a benign convergence of the *Huffington Post*, *Twitter* and *Wikipedia*, with an instant rebuttal unit, armed with the cyber equivalent of a Taser, a sort of a naughty step for truth transgressors – the converse of the lynch mob – with journalistic marshals riding to the rescue, although how that would be financed is anyone's guess.

Over the next decade or two we will look back with astonishment at the whole edifice of Leveson, and wonder how so many people took so much time and used so much money to produce a report of relevance to so few. We will say 'a whole year, zillions of pounds, to produce a massive and perfectly wise report --- on the press! That old bunch of renegades, who were on their last legs anyway. Blimey! Didn't the noble Lord know about cyberspace? Surely he must have seen that's the real story: surely he must have realised that it is no longer reasonable for the big players, the *Googles*, *Facebooks*, *You – Tubes* and *Twitters* to say, 'nothing to do with us, Guv, we only provide the pipes. What goes through them, that's up to the folk who put it there.'

When a new dimension, like the internet, is added to a world of goodies and baddies, there is bound to be an upside and a downside, so as the landscape changes it's possible to be both thrilled and terrified. The terror is now clear to see – that the internet is the nuclear equivalent of truths being 'twisted by knaves to make a trap for fools'. However, it also has within its power a bright new dawn of freeing journalism and storytellers from the editorial and political tyrannies of the past. But it does need regulation, not least so that to its power will be added reliability and credibility.

By looking backwards at a world now receding in the rear-view mirror, Lord Justice Leveson did not do that. It was a big opportunity missed. But maybe it's not too late to take the fussy but eternal principles in his report, make them more worldly, and craft a new set of ideologies, rules and disciplines for a converged and electronic future.

But that's probably old ink thinking. As the newsprint machines fall silent, and the trucks no longer race through the night, an entirely new information world will rise in a grey and foggy world, a world in which each of us can be readers and editors, contributors and subscribers, and maybe even proprietors, at the same time.

Hark, was that a nightingale I heard? Or a bomb?

Note on the contributor

Bernard Clark is now Chairman of TVT. He joined the BBC in 1968 working as a BBC Correspondent, reporting for *Nationwide* and originating *Watchdog* and *Bookmark*. In 1985 he set up Clark TV, an independent production company. Bernard has been the Executive Producer of hundreds of documentaries and series, including many award winners. He helped establish TVT in 1994, which has grown to be one of the UK's largest versioning and translation companies. In 2009, Harper Collins published his best selling book, '*A Mother Like Alex*'.

Will Leveson see off sexist coverage in the press?

Deirdre O'Neill asks whether Lord Justice Leveson asked enough and the right questions about the portrayal of women in the National Press. Did he miss a trick?

By 12 December 2012, the number of victims claimed to have been abused by Jimmy Savile had reached 450. Along with his celebrity status and charity work, the culture of the 1970s, when most of the assaults took place, contributed in no small part to Savile being able to prey with impunity on vulnerable young women; a culture where others turned a blind eye to his predilections; where sexist and predatory behaviour were routine and normalized.

Read many of our national newspapers or their websites and you could be forgiven for thinking we were still living in that age, where women are still regarded as little more than the sum of their tits or bums. The same papers that have article after article declaiming Savile in tones of moral outrage continue to carry content that denigrates and objectifies women. On the days before Leveson reported, there were 14 pictures of semi-naked women in the *Daily Star* (28th November 2012). Click on the *Star*'s website and you are invited to give topless women a 'Babe Score' out of 10.

The anachronistic and hypocritical nature of this type of content was neatly encapsulated in a message on a giant card delivered to the editor of *The Sun* on the 42nd birthday of Page 3: "Still stuck in the sexist, Savile-loving 70s, Dominic?" asked one (Cochrane, 28th November 2012, *The Guardian*).

Too often critics are dismissed or silenced with insults; women who speak out against these images are portrayed as po-faced or worse. In his report, Lord Justice Leveson noted: "When Clare Short MP campaigned against Page 3 in the 1980s she was described by *The Sun* as 'fat', 'ugly' and 'jealous of beautiful women'. When the Rt Hon Harriet Harman proposed legislation to ban Page 3 in 2010, she was described as a 'harridan' and a 'feminist fanatic' on a 'furious rant'. Similarly, when ex-Equalities Minister Lynne Featherstone MP raised the issue in Government, she was described as a 'battleaxe'." (2012: Vol. 2: 642).

For those inured to sexist and salacious coverage of women, it can be salutary to reverse the gender roles: imagine opening your paper and there's Sean or Freddie revealing their bare bottoms, with a caption about how they love cleaning and "scrub up nicely" (see "Mel" on page 3 in the *Daily Star* on 28th November 2012). And imagine a constant stream of this type of coverage, belittling, undermining and humiliating men.

A broad alliance of groups that campaign for women – Eaves (which supports vulnerable women), End Violence Against Women, Equality Now and Object – found just this happening to women when they carried out research into sexism in UK newspapers. Their report, "Just the Women" (2012)[1], recorded 1,300 examples of sexist coverage in 11 newspapers over two weeks (*The Sun, The Daily Mirror, The Daily Star, The Sport, The Daily Mail, The Daily Express, The Times, The Financial Times, The Guardian, The Independent* and *The Telegraph*). The campaign groups' report found that sexism was systematic across the British press, appearing in various guises that negatively affected women's access to justice, safety and equality (2012: 7).

Selective and de-contextualised coverage meant that women and their lives were consistently misrepresented and stereotyped; women were excessively objectified as sexual commodities; in the worst examples, myths about victims and the perpetrators of violence were reinforced, with the potential to impact on the judicial system and access to justice (2012: 7).

Celebrity (sexist) coverage?

The Leveson Inquiry took evidence from representatives of these women's campaign groups. His report acknowledges that sexist objectification of women extends beyond Page 3 type photos, influencing the way that other women, including celebrities, are portrayed (2012, Vol. 2: 663).

On the one hand, idealized and unattainable airbrushed versions of womanhood are promoted in celebrity stories, presenting artifice, in the form of silicone breasts and hair extensions, as normality. On the other hand, there is critical focus on women's appearance and behaviour that implicitly and explicitly reinforces narrow, stereotyped definitions of acceptable femininity. Female celebrities are scrutinized in a way that no men would be. Journalist and feminist Caitlin Moran "argues that coverage of women is 'hugely reductionist and damaging': a female celebrity only has to be photographed without makeup, in a 'bad' dress or having changed body shape to be pilloried. 'I've read more about Oprah Winfrey's arse than I have about the rise of China as an economic superpower.'"(Moran, 2011, in O'Neill, 2012: 38).

It took just two minutes on the Mail's website on 17 December 2012 to find three examples of coverage criticising the appearance of female celebrities. Actress Selma Blair displayed her "incredibly bony chest-plate"[2] while out with her small son. This wasn't her only crime: she "also looked extremely tired – her make-up free complexion only serving to draw attention to the heavy bags under her eyes". Gwyneth Paltrow[3] got similar treatment for not wearing makeup, while Rebecca Adlington[4] was criticised for not being able to carry off a fashionable dress because her "over-developed shoulders" and "muscular thighs" tend to make her look "slightly butch and uncomfortable".

Nor is the quality press immune to the siren call of celebrity. Research has shown it is on the increase across *all* newspapers (Pugh, 17th Oct 2011, *Press Gazette*), and it is pushing out other news, limiting the ability of the press to act as a fourth estate (O'Neill, 2012). The sheer volume of celebrity news means it is inescapable, rather like the nuisance drunk at the party. For example, in a snapshot of newspaper coverage the day before Leveson reported (28th November 2012), 60% of all articles in the *Daily Star* were based on celebrity, while around a quarter of articles in *The Sun*, *The Mirror* and the *Daily Express* were about celebrities. It would be possible to shrug off isolated examples of sexist celebrity culture, but it is so all-pervading that its pernicious effects are cumulative.

On the same day, just 7% of stories in *The Sun* and *Daily Express* were related to politics, and some of these stories were arguably more related to crime (Cyril Smith) or para-celebrity (Nadine Dorries in the TV programme '*I'm A Celebrity*').

Research by the Hansard Society found that the public believe the media have influence but it is not providing them with enough information, particularly about issues relating to politics.[5] The bombardment of readers with vacuous or sexist celebrity coverage is leading to a democratic deficit.

Women's self – image

How women are depicted *does* matter. Newspapers both reflect and contribute to our wider culture and clearly have the power to influence attitudes about society, gendered relations and how women see themselves. A recent study led by the University of Durham confirmed that the images women see plays a strong role in how they view their bodies.[6] Lead author Dr Lynda Boothroyd, from Durham University's Department of Psychology, said: "There is evidence that being constantly surrounded through the media by celebrities and models who are very thin contributes to girls and women having an unhealthy attitude to their bodies." (*ibid*).

The "Just the Women" report (2012: 20) highlights research that shows "66% of teenage girls would consider plastic surgery[7]; that of the 1.6 million people in the UK suffering from an eating disorder, around 89% are female[8], and that pressures to become sexualised have led to girls across all social strata reporting mental disorders at a rate of 44%, making them the most depressed section of the population[9]. Furthermore, research conducted by the Future Foundation think tank (April, 2012) found that one in four girls has low self-esteem."[10]

As a university lecturer, female students often tell me how some newspaper coverage makes them feel. One 20-year-old student said: "I start to feel uncomfortable if I'm next to someone who has *The Sun* open on Page 3."

Another 19-year-old said: "I know I shouldn't allow it [sexist celebrity coverage] to affect me, but I also know it does. We are bombarded with coverage that says we should look a certain way, be a certain size. It definitely affects my self-esteem and, in the past, has coloured my attitudes to eating." A first-year student added: "I have one friend who has an unhealthy relationship with food…always dieting and obsessing about her weight. And she is always reading celebrity stories, and this seems to fuel her insecurities, which is really sad. What's more, the tone of a lot of these articles is quite nasty, with negative comments about how women look. When my friend is reading these articles, she starts to adopt the same type of tone, criticising the weight of other women. It's just depressing."

Attitudes to violence against women

Even more depressing are attitudes about violence towards women highlighted in "Just the Women" (2012: 5): "Violence against women and girls cannot be prevented unless the attitudes that excuse and normalise violence are changed. These include: 36% of people believe that a woman should be held wholly or partly responsible for being sexually assaulted or raped if she was drunk, and 26% if she was in public wearing sexy or revealing clothes[11]. One in five people think it would be acceptable in certain circumstances for a man to hit or slap his female partner in response to her being dressed in sexy or revealing clothing in public."[12]

The latest figures on sexual crimes from a survey by the Ministry of Justice, Home Office and Office for National Statistics reveal the serious and shocking scale of the problem: one in twenty women is raped or undergoes a serious sexual assault by the age of 60, and 85,000 women are raped a year. Of the 500,000 victims of sex crimes every year (the vast majority of whom are women), only a small minority report the crimes and few such reports end in convictions. These findings are based on interviews with 47,000 adults (Ford, *The Times*, 11th January 2013: 1).

The sexualisation of children

While schools are repeatedly told by governments that they are required to raise the achievements and aspirations of pupils, the same pupils are deluged by a media culture seen at its worst in sections of the British press – a culture that places a premium on looks, which commoditises women's bodies, and exposes our children to an inappropriate sexual culture, including the sexualisation of children. The day before Leveson reported (28th November 2012) the *Daily Star* carried a story of the 6-year-old daughter of "tragic" model Anna Nicole Smith doing a "fashion shoot", complete with pictures of the little girl dressed and posing like an adult. This is not an isolated example; the "Just the Women" research found repeated sexualised coverage of young girls, including toddlers. (2012: 15).

This is an issue increasingly worrying parents[13], so much so that Mother's Union chief Reg Bailey[14] was commissioned to look into this, producing recommendations in a 2011 review that The Prime Minister and the Department of Education are currently looking into. The Department of Education website states, "The Government made a commitment to take action to protect children from excessive commercialisation and premature sexualisation to address parents' concerns that children are being pressured into growing up too quickly."[15] The government would do well to take note of the "Just the Women" recommendations to take newspapers into consideration as part of this process, and to consider positioning of newspapers at the point of sale so they are not on view at a child's eye level (2012: 32).

Discrimination at work

Meanwhile, women remain disempowered and discriminated against in other ways. They still do not have the same earning power as men; the 2011 Annual Survey of Hours and Earnings found that for men, average full-time earnings a week were £539, compared with £445 for women (Office of National Statistics, November 2011)[16]. Only four out of 87 chief executives appointed by Britain's 100 biggest firms in the past two years were female. (Brown, 12th August 2012, *Daily Mail*). And women have to fight protracted struggles for equal pay; in a recent landmark case the Supreme Court has allowed 170 former Birmingham City Council female workers to claim compensation because, the women argued, the local authority had denied them payments and benefits that were given to men doing the same level of work. Most of these women were cooks, cleaners and care assistants, traditional women's roles that society continues to undervalue. (Butler, 24th October 2012, *The Guardian*). It is against the background of all these factors that women's lives are being played out daily. In its portrayal of half the population, the national press has to take some responsibility for contributing to these stark realities, by pumping out coverage that contributes to undermining, demeaning and restricting women.

Women at the journalism coal – face?

The dearth of women in top jobs is reflected within print journalism itself. A study monitoring the media over a 15-year period (the Global Media Monitoring Project, set up in 1995 and reporting every five years since) found that in the UK that, while more women are entering journalism and while more are now in senior posts, they still lag behind men in terms of career progression and salary (Ross and Carter, 2011). A recent Women in Journalism report examining the front pages of newspapers found women wrote just 22% of front page articles (Martinson *et al*, 2012). Another pilot study into journalism workplaces found that ageism is rife, with 71% of the survey of 100 women anxious about being forced out of their careers as they reach their 40s and 50s, and 70% seeing older men outnumbering older women at every level. (Campbell, accessed 18th December 2012).

The silent woman?

Employment patterns within journalism may go some way towards explaining the relative lack of women's voices in the news. Over the 15-year time period of the GMMP, the visibility of women as producers and subjects of news media has improved steadily, but relative visibility of women to men remains at a ratio of 1:3 (Ross and Carter, 2011). And men's voices are generally privileged as being more authoritative when it comes to being used as "expert" sources.

In certain categories of stories women were even scarcer. Male views were heard in 75% of stories about domestic politics; 100% of stories about national defence; 90% of stories about war; 87% of stories about sport and 83% of stories about the legal system. Women's voices, views and expertise are restricted; it was only in stories about peace, education, accidents/disasters and consumer affairs that they were heard more (*ibid*). These 2011 findings seem to be borne out by the Women in Journalism report (Martinson *et al*, 2012) which found that women account for just 16% of those mentioned or quoted in lead stories on the front pages of newspapers and three quarters of "expert" voices were male.

Nor is this under-representation confined to the front pages. Brookes (2002: 128) claims that in general terms, studies on gendered sports coverage shows that coverage of women's sport "routinely amounts to less than 10 per cent of the total available". Preliminary findings of a current study into women's sports coverage in the press paints an even bleaker picture, with coverage in early 2012 and 10 years earlier averaging around 2% when references to big events like the Olympics are removed (O'Neill, current research project).

Lord Justice Leveson's response: enough?

Introducing a discussion about Leveson's response to the representation of women, *Woman's Hour* presenter Jenni Murray pointed out, "You have to dig hard to find it" (BBC R4, 30th November 2012). While Leveson's report states, "There is credible evidence that [sexist coverage] has a broader impact on the perception and role of women in society, and the sexualisation of society generally", he shirks the issue by saying that the Inquiry is not the place to analyse or draw conclusions (Vol. 2: 665) and that issues of taste and decency were not within his remit. However, on the same *Woman's Hour* programme, Jackie Hunt of Equality Now broadly welcomed what Leveson had to say: that some sections of the press "often failed to show consistent respect for the dignity and equality of women generally, and that there was a tendency to sexualise and demean women"; that this goes beyond Page 3 images; that there is hypocrisy in newspapers condemning paedophilia while continuing to provide coverage that sexualises young women; and, in particular, that any new regulator should have the power to take complaints from representative groups. (Vol. 2: 662-665). This final point is significant in that under the previous regulatory system, the PCC would only allow complaints from individuals involved in a story, which resulted in many complaints falling at the first hurdle by being inadmissible.

Overall, Lord Justice Leveson's response could hardly be said to be robust. With so few recommendations, a mere acknowledgement of many of the problems will have little impact. It is hard to understand why issues of taste and decency are omitted. Ofcom, which regulates broadcasting, has regulations about this and there is a watershed for certain content to protect young children. Why are certain images, language and views, that would not be acceptable in a workplace and on certain websites, allowed to be freely plastered over much of our press and displayed in shops and supermarkets? The irony is that the very examples of sexism submitted to the Leveson Inquiry were deemed sufficiently inappropriate to be censored, while Facebook took down an image of the Page 3 protest birthday card because the images violated Facebook's terms (Cochrane, 28th November 2012, *The Guardian*).

Whatever the complexion and remit of any new regulator, a Code alone will not change coverage; what is needed is a wider cultural change in the attitudes of the press, an indigenous culture that promotes standards and responsibilities rather than an externally imposed framework that encourages journalists to push the limits of the rules: "Instead of asking whether some action is [within the Code or] legal, we should ask whether it is right. It's a different test, to do with treating people as we might have them treat us." (Fletcher, 2012:4).

Teaching anti-sexism early?

Representation and equality issues should be part of journalism training, and schools encouraged to explore critical thinking and education about the media; the press industry needs to encourage women to take up senior posts in the print media; and the public, academics and campaign groups should insist that any new regulator does indeed act on Leveson's recommendation to take complaints from third parties. In responding to the latest worrying figures about sexual crime, Holly Dustin of End Violence Against Women said, "We need to look at the broader culture in which this type of behaviour happens" and that public awareness campaigns to change attitudes were urgently needed (Ford, *The Times*, 11th January 2013: 6). Any change in culture will need media and press attitudes and coverage to change. The work of campaign groups like End Violence Against Women, No More Page 3 and Object is far from over.

Notes

[1] Just the Women report, November 2012, http://i2.cmsfiles.com/eaves/2012/12/Just-the-Women-Final-e59e46.pdf

[2] http://www.dailymail.co.uk/tvshowbiz/article-2249340/Shockingly-Selma-Blair-displays-skeletal-figure-takes-son-Arthur-park.html#ixzz2FK6JOeY0

[3] http://www.dailymail.co.uk/tvshowbiz/article-2249415/Gwyneth-Paltrow-loses-Hollywood-glow-steps-make-free-prepares-fly-home.html#ixzz2FK7ICw2K

[4] http://www.dailymail.co.uk/femail/article-2249229/Sports-Personality-Year-Liz-Jones-gives-verdict-sports-stars-outfits.html-

[5] Audit of Political Engagement 9, The 2012 Report: Part Two, The media and politics
http://www.hansardsociety.org.uk/files/folders/3395/download.aspx

[6] http://www.medicalnewstoday.com/releases/252527.php

[7] mykindaplace.comsurvey of 1,800 teenage girls, 2005

[8] The National Institute of Health and Clinical Excellence, referenced by Beat:
http://www.b-eat.co.uk/aboutbeat/media-centre/facts-and-figures/

[9] Sweeting H, Young R, West P. GHQ increases among Scottish 15 year olds 1987-2006.
Social Psychiatry and Psychiatric Epidemiology 2009; 44:579-86

[10] http://www.independent.co.uk/life-style/health-and-families/health-news/girls-
interrupted-revealed--the-truecost-of-low-selfesteem-7606258.html

[11] Home Office (2005) http://www.homeoffice.gov.uk/publications/crime/call-end-
violence-women-girls/vawg-paper?view=Binary

[12] Home Office (2009) http://www.homeoffice.gov.uk/publications/crime/call-end-
violence-women-girls/vawg-paper?view=Binary

[13] Let Girls Be Girls Mumsnet Campaign, launched 2010
http://www.mumsnet.com/campaigns/let-girls-be-girls

[14] Letting Children be Children – Report of an Independent Review of the
Commercialisation and Sexualisation of Childhood, June 2011
https://www.education.gov.uk/publications/standard/publicationDetail/Page1/CM%2
08078

[15] Review of commercialisation and sexualisation of children, 6th December 2010
http://www.education.gov.uk/inthenews/inthenews/a0069862/review-of-
commercialisation-and-sexualisation-of-children

[16] Office of National Statistics, November 2011,
http://www.ons.gov.uk/ons/rel/ashe/annual-survey-of-hours-and-earnings/ashe-
results-2011/ashe-statistical-bulletin-2011.html)

References

Brookes, Rod (2002) *Representing Sport*, London: Arnold

Brown, Laura (12th August 2012) The new glass ceiling, *The Daily Mail*
http://www.dailymail.co.uk/news/article-2194610/The-new-glass-ceiling-How-
companies-keeping-women-senior-positions.html#ixzz2FPZjYc5E)

Butler, Patrick (24th October 2012) Birmingham equal pay victory for women may
impact City of London, *The Guardian*

Campbell, Alexandra (accessed 18th December 2012) *The Lady Vanishes – At 45*,
Women in Journalism http://womeninjournalism.co.uk/the-lady-vanishes-at-45/

Cochrane, Lisa (28th November 2012) Turning the page, *The Guardian G2*, p.6

Eaves, End Violence Against Women Coalition, Equality Now, OBJECT (November
2012) *Just the Women*
http://www.endviolenceagainstwomen.org.uk/data/files/resources/51/Just-the-
Women-Nov-2012.pdf

Fletcher, Kim (2012) A Question of Trust? *British Journalism Review*, Volume 23, Number
3, pp.3-4.

Ford, Richard (11th January 2013) Scale of rape revealed in national sex crime survey, *The Times*

Hutchinson, Tom, (28th November 2012) Danni: My Tribute to Mum Anna, *Daily Star*

Leveson Report (23rd November 2012), Ch. 6, Vol. 2. http://www.official-documents.gov.uk/document/hc1213/hc07/0780/0780.asp.

Martinson, Jane, Cochrane, Kira, Ryan, Sue, Corrigan, Tracey and Bawdon, Fiona (15th October 2012) *Seen But Not Heard: How Women Make Front Page News*, Women in Journalism
http://womeninjournalism.co.uk/wpcontent/uploads/2012/10/Seen_but_not_heard.pdf

Moran, Caitlin (2011) *How To Be a Woman*, London: Ebury Press

O'Neill, Deirdre (2012) No cause for celebration: The rise of celebrity news values in the British quality press, *Journalism Education*, Vol. 1, No. 2, pp.26-44. http://journalism-education.org/2012/11/no-cause-for-celebration/

Pugh, Andrew (17th October 2011) Study: 'Tabloid –broadsheet divide has blurred', *Press Gazette*
(http://www.pressgazette.co.uk/story.asp?sectioncode=1&storycode=48054&c=1)

Ross, Karen and Carter, Cynthia (2011)'Women and news: A long and winding road', *Media, Culture and Society*, 33 (8), pp.1148-1165

Note on the contributor

Deirdre O'Neill is Associate Principal Lecturer in Journalism at Leeds Trinity University. Before coming into education she worked as a journalist on magazines and as a press officer. She has undertaken and published research on news values in the UK national press, news sources in the local press, trade union coverage and media-relations, and celebrity press coverage. She is currently working on research into women and sports coverage.

Section C. Lap dogs and lamp-posts? The Press and Politicians

John Mair

David Cameron set up the Leveson Inquiry in July 2011 with support from almost the entire House of Commons, revulsed at the Milly Dowler phone-hacking. Lord Justice Leveson took as party of the three legged stool of his investigation 'the relationship between the Press and Politicians'. A succession of present and former Prime Ministers – Cameron himself, Gordon Brown, Tony Blair and John Major stepped into the witness box. Media moguls galore too or their presences on this Earth – Rupert Murdoch, son and then presumed heir James, Lord Rothemere, Richard Desmond, a Barclay progeny, a Lebedev plus 'their' editors of all the national newspapers to explore and confirm/deny their closeness (or not).

It was an unedifying spectacle.

So who, in H. L. Mencken's famous metaphor, came out of the Report the better the dog (the press) or the lamp-post (politicians) or vice versa according to your view?

Nick Jones the scourge of spin-meisters and political manipulators thinks LJL missed the target altogether. He got the wrong answers in Nick's view because his leading counsel the Gnomic wordsmith Robert Jay QC simply asked the wrong questions. Leveson for him showed a lack of curiosity about the Press/Politicians 'collusion'. Jones labels the exercise a 'charade'

Au contraire, Professor Ivor Gaber of City University London is surprisingly positive. He asks for 'two and a half cheers for Leveson!' having read all 359 pages of the report on the matter he thinks Leveson has got it right in his recommendations. Nearly.

Professor Mick Temple of Staffordshire University has made the politician-press nexus the oeuvre of his career. He looks at Leveson in the light of the six or seven previous big ticket official inquiries in the last half century into the behaviour of the press. All of them have failed to generate any lasting statute. Temple thinks history will repeat itself.

The lamp-post will still be standing firm as the dog goes off to relieve itself elsewhere. One up to the watchdogs of the national press?

A meaningless charade? Rules to prevent ministers colluding with the media likely to be ineffective

Lord Justice Leveson turned a blind eye to the black arts of political propaganda and paid the penalty; the judge was upstaged by the press proprietors' spin. Nicholas Jones deplores Leveson's lack of curiosity about the tricks of the trade of what the judge dismissed as the 'day to day business' of political journalism and he laments the Inquiry's failure to get to grips with the collusion surrounding the trade in political exclusives and newspaper endorsements

Lord Justice Leveson had the misfortune to find himself outmanoeuvred and outgunned by a pre-emptive strike by the newspaper proprietors during the long build-up to the publication of his report and recommendations. In the end the judge had no alternative but to accept that he was virtually powerless to respond when the owners' front organisation, the Free Speech Network, engaged in the kind of political collusion and media manipulation which he and his legal team had so pointedly refused to investigate with any thoroughness during the eight months that his Inquiry took evidence. Leveson considered that 'a number of issues..."spin", so-called anonymous briefings and the practice of "feeding" favoured journalists with stories in return for an expectation of a certain type of treatment' were not 'central to the work of the Inquiry'.[1] Yet these were the very same techniques which the proprietors, editors and Conservative politicians used with such devastating effect to spin the line that the judge intended to turn Britain back three hundred years to what the *Daily Mail* predicted would be the 'new dark age' of a licensed press.[2]

His lofty declaration that the Inquiry was not 'directed at the relationships of everyday political journalism'[3] became a central flaw in his recommendations regarding one of the duties set out in the Inquiry's original terms of reference, to examine 'the future conduct of relations between politicians and the press.' He concentrated instead on what he believed was 'most directly relevant' to the public interest, namely:

'the question of a closeness which may have, or appear to have, impacted on the willingness or ability of the politicians to decide matters of public policy about the media, and specifically of policy on press standards.'[4]

Leveson could hardly be faulted on the broad sweep of the Inquiry's investigation into the controversies surrounding Rupert Murdoch's ownership of four leading British newspapers and News Corporation's aborted bid to take total control of BSkyB but by turning his back on the issue of press standards and ethics as they applied to political journalism, the judge failed to inquire into, let alone appeared to show any understanding of, what after all has been the covert daily currency of 'relations between politicians and the press.' Proprietors and politicians have always been careful to avoid scrutiny of their two-way trade in favourable press reporting in return for a sympathetic approach towards media ownership and regulation. Therefore the very occasional insight into this hitherto hidden relationship could be all the more revealing.

What did the judge think David Cameron had in mind when he gave the Inquiry his explanation for the October 2009 text message from Rebekah Brooks saying that 'professionally we're definitely in this together!'?[5] Cameron told the judge it meant that he as future Prime Minister and she as the newly-appointed CEO of News International 'were going to be pushing the same political agenda'.[6] Neither Leveson nor the Inquiry's leading counsel Robert Jay QC thought it worth asking either Cameron or Brooks how delivery of this shared 'political agenda' had worked out in practice during the first year of his Premiership, namely in the period before revelations about the phone hacking scandal forced the closure of the *News of the World* in July 2011 and then the withdrawal of News Corporation's attempt to take total control of BSkyB. The evidence was there for the asking. Under her editorship (and later as News International's chief executive) the *Sun* delivered unquestioning support to Cameron's campaigns and initiatives both before and in the twelve months immediately following the 2010 general election; the propaganda advantage this gave the Conservatives could not be divorced from the mood music surrounding the almost instant imposition of a six-year freeze in the BBC licence fee in October 2010 or the about-to-be-signed-off bid for total ownership of BSkyB the following July.

Woefully inadequate strengthening of Ministerial Code

When the Free Speech Network, representing publishers, editors and other media groups, unleashed its co-ordinated campaign to pre-empt and then to thwart Leveson's over-riding conclusion that independent press regulation would require the backing of legislation, the opportunity for pertinent questions had passed; the report makes clear that the judge's mindset all along was that his chosen path was correct, that he believed he was right to have concentrated on the way the newspaper owners had tried to lobby ministers in person about media policy and press standards rather than get sidetracked by 'everyday political journalism' and the role of newspaper campaigns. But had he missed a rare opportunity to question proprietors, editors and also leading politicians about the ways in which the daily papers could be used to twist the news agenda to their own commercial and political advantage?

Leveson was adamant this was not his terrain; he reminded readers of his report that he had 'already put beyond doubt that I emphatically do not see any case at all for interference in the day to day business of the interaction between journalist and politician.'[7] But the contradictions and missed opportunities were highlighted by the plaintive line, repeated at his launch news conference, that even before he had concluded his report the newspapers had 'started using their considerable megaphones for their own purposes'.[8] If the judge had taken a greater interest in the mechanics of political campaigning by the press – and its relevance to the government of the day – he could well have anticipated the Free Speech Network's propaganda offensive and he might perhaps have been able to take evasive action. His muddled thinking also resulted in a woefully inadequate attempt to strengthen the Ministerial Code as it related to 'meetings with media proprietors, editors and senior executives at which their commercial interests are discussed'.[9]

Perhaps not surprisingly in view of his narrow focus and his conclusion that 'only very limited steps'[10] were needed to 'enhance' the Ministerial Code, my own evidence to the Inquiry did not see the light of day. I had set out proposals for a far more transparent code of conduct designed to keep track of collusion between politicians and the press, a requirement which hopefully would have exposed any hidden dealings over the 'considerable megaphones' which were subsequently directed at the judge. Ministers would have had to disclose their contact with groups such as the Press Complaints Commission, the Press Standards Board of Finance and the Free Speech Network and also any ministerial link-ups with those newspapers which campaigned so vociferously on the industry's behalf against state interference.

Dazzled by Blair's news management but a lack of interest in Cameron's spin routines

Leveson rarely held back when offering his opinions on the state of 'everyday political journalism'. He found nothing which 'gave rise to any legitimate concern' about the way information flows from the state to the press; he thought the interaction between politicians and newspapers was in 'robust good health'.[11] But the judge's pronouncements had clearly not been thought through because he repeatedly tripped himself up when offering his reflections on the impact of government news management over the last thirty to thirty-five years. He contradicted his initial assertion about the robustness of the 'free-flowing interaction between politicians and the press' by concluding later in the report, that politicians had been conducting themselves in a way which had not served the public interest, so as:

> 'to seek to control (if not manipulate) the supply of news and information to the public in return for expected or hoped-for favourable treatment by

sections of the press beyond that which is appropriate or an inevitable by product of politics in a 24-7 media age, but to a degree and by means other than the fair and reasonable partisan conduct of public debate'.[12]

No evidence was quoted by the judge to support this conclusion, not least because there had been no concerted attempt during the Inquiry to test his opinions. Nonetheless he did accept that the extent to which politicians attempted to manipulate press coverage was 'a thread running through a quantity of the evidence' and it did offer the prospect of an insight into 'where power lies'.[13] Indeed Leveson and his counsel Robert Jay QC had seemed in awe of the news management techniques exercised by Tony Blair's government. Leveson quoted at length from the evidence of Lord (Peter) Mandelson and Alastair Campbell; the judge acknowledged that Campbell's role was certainly one that 'trod new ground' but he concluded that New Labour became 'a victim of its own success, and resulted in diminishing public confidence in political communications'.[14]

Given his acknowledgement of the lengths to which politicians had gone in previous years to manage the news agenda, Leveson's failure to follow through the lasting impact of New Labour's 'spin' routines was all the more surprising. He appeared oblivious to the fact that many of the news management techniques of the Blair era had become entrenched in Whitehall; the judge certainly gave every impression of having pulled his punches when assessing the media strategies adopted by David Cameron and the Coalition government. Andy Coulson's appointment in May 2007 as the Conservative Party's head of communications reflected the fact that Cameron had been as desperate as Blair had been to hire a media technician who understood the mindset of the tabloid newspapers and who could withstand the pressures of the 24-7 news agenda. Coulson transformed Cameron's ability to connect with the national press as effectively as Campbell had done a decade earlier for Blair but the significance of Coulson's achievements both before the 2010 general election and then in government seemed to have passed Leveson by.

The sure touch of the former *News of the World* editor in guiding the Conservatives' media offensive was acknowledged in October 2008 when he was named public relations professional of the year by *PR Week*. Danny Rogers, the editor, considered Coulson's main strength was his capacity for damage limitation; time and again he 'gained control of a story by responding quickly and decisively'. Coulson remained in close contact with former colleagues at News International, especially Rebekah Brooks, then editor of the *Sun*, and during his three years as the Conservative Party's top spin doctor, the breadth of his experience of campaigning journalism was soon being reflected in the pages of the Murdoch press.

Cameron was quick to exploit the *Sun*'s campaign for greater support for 'Our Boys' serving in Iraq and Afghanistan; he became the only party leader to endorse with a signed article the *Sun*'s petition for the dismissal of the social workers who were said to have failed 'Baby P', a campaign which attracted 1.2 million signatures and resulted in the dismissal of Sharon Shoesmith, head of children's services for the London Borough of Haringey. Under Coulson's guidance Cameron gained favourable headlines to the disadvantage of the then Prime Minister Gordon Brown when in May 2009 the *Daily Telegraph* began publishing its highly-acclaimed run of exclusive stories exposing the scandal of MPs' expenses.

Leveson's lack of curiosity and failure to explore Cameron's dependence on Coulson's expertise was all too apparent when the Prime Minister and his former director of communications gave evidence to the Inquiry. In the eight months Coulson served in Downing Street as the government's media chief, the Cameron-Coulson-Brooks partnership became highly effective in 'pushing the same political agenda' in support of the newly-elected Premier. Two *Sun* campaigns in the first few months of the new administration, which were both endorsed with his signed articles, were a graphic illustration of Brooks' 2009 text message to Cameron that 'professionally we're definitely in this together'. Here was the country's biggest selling newspaper providing favourable and sustained political propaganda on behalf of the Prime Minister just as the Coalition government was about to take critical decisions on the future of both the BBC and BSkyB. But the behind-the-scenes negotiations which must have preceded publication of these endorsements were not mentioned in Cameron's quarterly declaration of his meetings with 'newspaper and other media proprietors, senior editors and executives'; nor would the contact which must have taken place been picked up by the enhancements to the Ministerial Code which were proposed by Lord Justice Leveson. On the other hand the draft code of conduct which I had submitted to the Inquiry as part of my evidence would have demanded far greater transparency:

> 'Full declaration is also required of negotiations aimed at securing party political promotions in newspapers and other media outlets e.g. signed articles by Prime Ministers, party or government endorsements and exclusive interviews to promote press campaigns'.[15]

The shared 'political agenda' of Cameron and Brooks as delivered by the *Sun*

A *Sun* campaign to cut the bill for welfare payments by exposing 'benefit scroungers' was a tailor-made illustration of the shared 'political agenda' of Cameron and Brooks – and also of Coulson's ability to provide the impetus for delivering it by crafting headline-grabbing coverage. In August 2010, within weeks of the Coalition's post-election emergency budget, the paper launched a hotline for readers to expose 'feckless benefit claimants'. A two-page spread under the banner headline 'Help us stop £1.5 billion benefit scroungers',[16] featured a prominent signed article by the Prime Minister in which he promised that 'people will not get away with fraud':

'You know the people I mean. You walk down the road on your way to work and you see the curtains drawn in their house.'[17]

Cameron's phrase about 'curtains drawn' would become part of the government's mantra when justifying the measures being taken to tackle benefit abuse; the Chancellor of the Exchequer, George Osborne, used the image repeatedly although occasionally he tweaked the phraseology. In his speech at the 2012 Conservative Party conference he referred to the 'shift worker, leaving home in the dark hours of the early morning, who looks up at the closed blinds of their next door neighbour sleeping off a life on benefits', a description he repeated almost word for word when delivering his 2012 Autumn statement.

Few media strategists would doubt the long-term impact and effectiveness of the *Sun*'s 'scroungers' campaign. Week after week, following tip-offs from neighbours, the paper exposed 'disabled spongers cheating the benefit system'; stories exposing benefit fraud also became the regular fare of other tabloid newspapers. A study published by the University of Kent[18] into the stigma attached to claiming benefits included a word search of 6,612 newspaper articles published between 1995 and 2011. It revealed an increasingly negative vocabulary. The *Sun* was way out in front: 78 per cent of its stories used negative words, followed by the *Daily Express* (68 per cent) and *Daily Mail* (67 per cent). The report said the shift in language and 'the rise in a scrounger discourse is a genuine phenomenon', a tribute if one was needed to the *Sun*'s pursuit of the Cameron-Brooks' political agenda.

'We are all in this together?'

Cameron's declaration of his meetings with senior media representatives failed to make any mention of another well-planned but ultimately ineffectual propaganda offensive by the *Sun* to re-launch the Conservative Party's 'Big Society' initiative. A signed article by the Prime Minister was spread across two pages and offered him a valuable platform to promote a concept in which he had already invested considerable political capital: 'Yes, my Big Society plan is ambitious but I make no apology for that...'[19]

Leveson's reflections on the media strategy which Cameron had adopted both before and after the 2010 General Election could hardly have been any shallower but were only to be expected given the simplistic and rather inept level of questioning. George Osborne, who recommended that the Conservative Party should appoint Andy Coulson as its 'spin doctor in chief', told the Inquiry that he did not think there was 'a particular strategy for *The Sun*'[20] but at no point was he asked why it was, as my evidence had illustrated, that Cameron had supplied many more signed articles to the *Sun* than to any other national newspaper. Osborne acknowledged that Coulson did advise Cameron on how 'to talk to proprietors and editors and so on'[21] but at no point was the Chancellor of the Exchequer challenged on the fact that the Murdoch press had provided such a regular and extensive platform for Cameron both as Conservative Party leader and then Prime Minister. Leveson concluded that ultimately Rebekah Brooks' text message saying 'we're definitely in this together' did seem to be more a question of 'News International being "in it together" with Cameron, and seeking to get his messages across for him'.[22] But the judge had not inquired either about the mechanics involved or sought to establish how many 'messages' the *Sun* had published on the Prime Minister's behalf. Similarly when Cameron told the Inquiry that his meeting with Rupert Murdoch in Downing Street in May 2010, within days of the Coalition government taking office, was an opportunity to 'thank him for his support'[23] there was no follow-up interrogation as to why the backing of the News International titles had been so important. When Rupert Murdoch was asked about his visit to the Prime Minister, he recalled Cameron having thanked him 'for the support of our papers'[24] but again there was no attempt to probe the significance of the backing Murdoch's newspapers had given to the Conservatives. Rather than tackle the real substance of a press proprietor's political patronage the judge's report reproduced chapter and verse of Robert Jay's amusing but fatuous grandstanding with Murdoch about why he went through the back door of No 10 rather the front door in Downing Street.

Other absurdities peppered the report: Leveson thought it noteworthy to mention that despite the pre-election support afforded to Cameron by the Murdoch press there had been 'noticeably critical coverage'[25] in the News International titles since the phone hacking scandal reached its apex. Detecting a shift in the tone of the *Sun*'s reportage once the Inquiry began taking evidence was perhaps only to be expected; what was of far greater significance was their support for Cameron which continued in the months immediately after the 2010 election, a factor which seemed to have completely escaped the attention of the Inquiry's legal team.

In the judge's assessment the 'language of trades and deals' was 'far too crude' when trying to get the measure of ministers' relationships with Rupert Murdoch; sometimes the 'very greatest power' was exercised without having to ask and Murdoch's editors knew the basic ground-rules, so did the politicians. Nonetheless Leveson concluded that a case by case examination of the policies introduced over a long period, failed to demonstrate that 'politicians compromised themselves or their policies to favour Murdoch's business interests directly'.[26]

Cameron's amendments to Ministerial Code made a mockery of the need for transparency

In my evidence to the Inquiry I said the absence of any mention of the way the Prime Minister had worked hand in glove with the *Sun* on campaigns such as 'benefits scroungers' and the 'Big Society' demonstrated the 'sheer inadequacy' of the additional declarations which Cameron had asked all ministers to make in July 2011 as part of his response to the phone hacking scandal and the appointment of Lord Justice Leveson. An immediate amendment to the Ministerial Code required ministers to 'record all meetings with newspaper and other media proprietors, senior editors and executives – regardless of the nature of the meeting'.

Within a matter of days Cameron, the Deputy Prime Minister Nick Clegg, the Chancellor of the Exchequer, George Osborne, and the leader of the Labour Party, Ed Miliband, listed their meetings since taking office. But their declarations made a mockery of the need for greater transparency because except for identifying who, when and where they met the lists gave no hint as to either the purpose or the outcome of their deliberations. Cameron used the catch-all term 'general discussion' alongside eight of the entries for meetings with Rupert or James Murdoch or one or other of their News International editors. There was no indication of the topics which had been discussed nor was there any clue as to what transpired during Rebekah Brooks' visits to Chequers or the Prime Minister's social engagements with James Murdoch and other News International executives.

Negotiations with the *Sun*'s editorial team over the Prime Minister's two signed articles might have been brokered by Andy Coulson or could have been conducted by the Downing Street team of politically-appointed special advisers but the point remained: politicians and their 'spin doctors' socialised with media proprietors, editors and executives for a purpose and the outcome needed to be declared. I said in my evidence that any recommendations which Leveson made about the 'future conduct of relations between politicians and the press' would have to require greater transparency. If such contact was to be policed effectively, then Leveson had to insist that ministers could no longer hide behind terms like 'general discussion'.

In the event the judge focussed almost entirely on what he said was the 'limited nature of the problem...the arena within which decisions about public policy relating to the media are lobbied about and, ultimately, taken'.[27] Politicians had spent 'too much time and effort on the press' and had risked 'actual or potential conflict of interest' and had done so 'in dealing with sources of influence which are, in themselves, powerful and unaccountable'. Given the strength of Leveson's strictures about relationships having for some years been 'too close to give sufficient grounds for confidence that fear or favour have not been operative factors',[28] his conclusion that he did not need to concern himself with the 'day to day business' of political journalism was inexplicable. His conclusion was all the more confusing because he acknowledged there was an 'inevitable "trading" element' to the relationship because politicians could offer journalists 'exclusive news and exclusive relationships'.[29]

Having failed to take on board why Cameron's declarations amounted to an empty gesture, the judge's template for an enhanced Ministerial Code lacked the teeth to deliver a new era of openness. Leveson ignored my call for greater clarity about the purpose and outcome of discussions which had taken place on either formal or social occasions and without an explanation about the nature of such contact, and the outlawing of such euphemisms as 'general discussion', the declarations would remain a meaningless charade. While Leveson was to be applauded for recommending greater transparency about the frequency and intensity of such dialogue he had skirted round the elephant in the room: newspaper endorsements and favourable press propaganda were at the heart of the relationship between proprietors and politicians and deserved far greater attention than a few passing mentions in the judge's report and recommendations.

Paying the penalty for turning a blind eye to impact of newspaper campaigns

As a first step towards 'more transparent relationships' Leveson suggested that one way to build on the Ministerial Code would be for all the political leaders to face up to the erosion in public confidence. He recommended they should:

> 'Reflect constructively on the merits of publishing on behalf of their party a statement setting out, for the public, an explanation of the approach they propose to take as a matter of party policy in conducting relationships with the press'.[30]

Leveson believed the value of such an approach was that it would force the party leaders to recognise the potential pitfalls of such relationships and require them to set out the rules by which they expected to be judged when it came to 'safeguarding a free and responsible press'. Leveson offered no explanation as to why he had singled out the press rather than make a recommendation which would have applied to the media at large and required political parties to publish a statement of intent regarding their approach not only to the press but also to radio and television, as well today's burgeoning on-line output. Any political party which was tempted to follow his suggestion would have no alternative but to promise an even handed approach in their dealings with all media organisations and journalists otherwise it would lack credibility and, in such a highly-competitive market place, only cause division between the press and other news outlets.

When it came to his proposals for extending the scope of the Ministerial Code, the judge thought there was a real risk of a blurring of the boundaries between 'political or private activities' on the one hand and the 'conduct of government business' on the other. Amendments to the code introduced by David Cameron in July 2011 did not provide sufficient clarity about the difference between 'party' or 'private' time and he urged senior politicians to give 'very serious consideration' to providing 'a more rounded picture'.[31] Future obligations for greater transparency should also apply to the leader and front bench of the Official Opposition and to opposition parties which aspired to holding a balance of executive power; Leveson welcomed the commitment by the Labour Party leader Ed Miliband to accept similar standards. To ensure that senior politicians respected public perceptions 'fairly and squarely' party leaders, ministers and front bench Opposition spokesman should also consider publishing the 'simple fact of long term relationships with media proprietors, newspaper editors or senior executives'.[32] In order to prevent the circumvention of transparency by third-party agents or 'back channels', he recommended that the interaction of the respective agents of senior politicians and proprietors, editors and senior executives should also be declared, such as:

> 'junior political colleagues, special advisers and civil servants on the political side, and representatives and professional lobbyists on the press side'. [33]

A further improvement in the visibility of such relationships could be achieved through specific guidelines for contact other than by face to face meetings, by introducing a transparency obligation to cover correspondence, phone, text and e-mail. Exhaustive new requirements would be impractical, unnecessary and counter-productive but Leveson did not consider it need be:

> 'either intrusive or burdensome for politicians to indicate on a quarterly basis, in relation to any individual senior principal within the press (or their agents), by way of general estimate, something about the frequency or density of such interactions...I do not suggest there is any case for descending into detail or content'.[34]

By restricting his remit simply to cover lobbying about the commercial interests of the press, his recommendations were limited to requiring a declaration of the 'general nature of any discussion of media policy issues' at meetings; the same requirement applied to other contact:

> 'A fair and reasonably complete picture by way of general estimate only, of the frequency or density of other interaction (including correspondence, phone, text and email) but not necessarily including content'.[35]

But unless there was some clue as to the purpose or content of meetings other than those solely related to the business interests of media companies or issues relating to press standards, a simple calculation of the 'frequency or density' of such contact was hardly likely to throw any light on the hidden trade in political endorsements by the press, the deliberate leaking of government announcements or the supply of exclusive stories, privileged access and signed articles.

Leveson and his team had failed to pick up on the inadequacy of the declaration procedure within the existing Ministerial Code. In their daily round of engagements on government or political business, or at social occasions, ministers might have all kind of conversations or contact with media representatives; a minister's quarterly declaration should at least give some hint of the topics discussed. By allowing the continued use of terms such as 'general discussion' Leveson had ignored the reality of the 'everyday' discourse between politicians and the press and I considered his recommendations for 'a moderate, achievable move in the direction of further transparency' were hardly likely to produce the improvement in public confidence which he thought was needed.

Free Speech by Proprietors?

Despite having missed his own opportunity to probe and reflect on the potential impact of newspaper campaigns, and having fallen well short of providing a framework which might have succeeded in exposing the propaganda value of collusion between politicians and the press, Leveson did not let the proprietors' offensive against him pass entirely without comment. He had clearly been irritated by a barrage of negative publicity in the weeks leading up to the publication of his conclusions and recommendations. He made no direct reference to the effectiveness of the Free Speech Network in marshalling a united front against him among newspaper and magazine editors or its success in orchestrating a timely run of exclusive interviews and signed articles from sympathetic Conservative politicians which urged the government to safeguard the freedom of the press. Nevertheless the judge's annoyance was all too obvious notwithstanding his convoluted phraseology. He emphasised the 'immediate need' for politicians to reflect on his suggestions for greater transparency about meetings and contacts, not least in relation to 'interactions' relevant to contents of his report:

> 'I encourage politicians to reflect on the legitimate public interest in understanding at least something about the interactions they have had with the press (whether direct or indirect) on the subject matter of the Inquiry. It is clear from all that has been put into the public domain that the press and the politicians have been closely engaged on this and doubtless will continue to be. The opportunity for transparency is obvious.'[36]

'Don't even think about regulating Britain's free press'[37] was the clarion call of the Mayor of London, Boris Johnson, as the campaign by the Free Speech Network reached its crescendo in the weeks before Leveson published his recommendations. Conservative politicians lined up with interviews and articles to support full page advertisements in the national dailies which painted a lurid picture of how state regulation of newspapers would turn the clock back more three hundred years to the days of a licensed press. 'If the press was shackled would any of this ever have happened?'[38] was the bold question over reproductions of front-page exclusive stories which illustrated how successive British politicians had been held to account. Another advertisement featured photographs of dictators around the world who did 'believe in state control of the press'[39], a point echoed by William Hague, the Foreign Secretary, in his declaration that Britain should 'Stand firm for a free press'.[40] John Whittingdale, Conservative chairman of the House of Commons Culture, Media and Sport Committee, feared the judge was about to send 'a very dangerous message' that needed to be challenged: 'State controls on press would be a green light to tyrants'.[41] Journalists from around the world provided supportive commentary: 'Shackle UK press and world suffers', said the Pakistani journalist Afzal Butt:[42] 'Your press is envy of the world because it's free,'[43] was the verdict of Jurgen Kronig, German head of the Foreign Press Association in London.

Given the way Conservative-supporting newspapers had mobilised their campaign against state regulation, David Cameron inevitably had newspaper editors and many political commentators singing his praises after he told MPs it would be a dereliction of their duty to the House of Commons, which had 'stood up for freedom and a free press year after year, century after century, to cross the Rubicon by legislating on the press without thinking about it carefully first'. His warning that the press had a 'limited period of time' to accept Leveson's proposals for a regulator independent of editors heralded the start of detailed negotiations. But the call by the judge for politicians to reflect on the 'immediate need' for greater transparency about their 'interactions' in the weeks leading up to the publication of his report seemed a vain hope.

The networking that had gone on behind the scenes involving press proprietors, editors and sympathetic Conservative politicians was precisely the kind of 'interaction' which was well below the radar of the existing Ministerial Code and the enhanced regime proposed by Leveson. When the judge had the opportunity to probe the collusive relationships that help sustain Britain's politicised free press he turned a blind eye and as a result paid the penalty. Having failed to explore how newspaper owners could collude with the government of the day to promote and sustain a shared 'political agenda', Leveson was hardly in a position to complain if he found his own objectivity was being questioned and the Prime Minister was signalling his intention to side step the full force of the Inquiry's recommendations well before they had even been published.

Notes

[1] Leveson Report, Vol. III, page 1430

[2] *Daily Mail* (3 November 2012) 'The New Dark Age'

[3] Leveson Report, Vol.III, page 1118

[4] Leveson Report, Vol.III, page 1118

[5] Leveson Report, Vol. III, page 1194

[6] Leveson Report, Vol. III, page 1195

[7] Leveson Report, Vol.III, page 1450

[8] Leveson Report, Vol.III, page 1458

[9] Leveson Report, Vol. III, page 1213

[10] Leveson Report, executive summary, page 29

[11] Leveson Report, executive summary, page 25

[12] Leveson Report, Vol.III, page 1439

[13] Leveson Report, Vol.III, page 1156

[14] Leveson Report, Vol.III, page1161

[15] Jones, Nicholas, unpublished evidence submitted to Leveson Inquiry April 2012

[16] *Sun* (12 August 2010) 'Help us stop £1.5 billion benefit scroungers'

[17] Cameron, David, article, *Sun* (12 August 2010) 'People will not get away with fraud'

[18] Elizabeth Finn Care/University of Kent (2012), *Benefits Stigma in Britain*

[19] *Sun* (8 October 2010) Britain's verdict on PM's vision

[20] Leveson Report, Vol.III, page 1179

[21] Leveson Report, Vol.III, page 1182

[22] Leveson Report, Vol.III, page 1195

[23] Leveson Report, Vol.III, page 1216

[24] Leveson Report, Vol.III, page 1216

[25] Leveson Report, Vol.III, page 1217

[26] Leveson Report, Vol.III, page 1432

[27] Leveson Report, Vol.III, page 1450

[28] Leveson Report, Vol.III, page 1119

[29] Leveson Report, Vol.III, page 1446

[30] Leveson Report, Vol.III, page 1452

[31] Leveson Report, Vol.III, page 1454

[32] Leveson Report, Vol.III, page 1457

[33] Leveson Report, Vol.III, page 1454

[34] Leveson Report, Vol.III, page 1456

[35] Leveson Report, Vol.III, page 1457

[36] Leveson Report, Vol.III, page 1459

[37] *Daily Mail* (22 November 2012)

[38] *The Mail on Sunday* (25 November 2012)

[39] *Sun* (22 November 2012)

[40] *Daily Mail* (26 November 2012)

[41] *Daily Mail* (18 November 2012)

[42] *Sun* (27 November 2012)

[43] *Daily Mirror* (26 November 2012)

Note on the contributor

Nick Jones was a BBC Industrial and Political Correspondent for thirty years. He has written many books on the culture of 'spin' under New Labour, the rise and fall of the Labour Correspondent and the General Election of 2010.He is the brother of George Jones, one of Lord Justice Leveson's expert assessors.

Two and a Half Cheers for Leveson!

Professor Ivor Gaber is a long time student of the politician/press/proprietors ménage a trois. He has published widely on it. Reading Lord Justice Leveson's 359 pages on the matter gives him cause for optimism. Almost

In his chapter in this volume (p 143), Professor Mick Temple begins with H. L. Mencken's dogs and lamp posts analogy about the relationship between politicians and journalists. My Leveson starting point is also a canine one but derives, not from Mencken but from Sir Arthur Conan Doyle and Sherlock Holmes' famous dog that didn't bark. This particular mutt is the relationship, not between politicians and journalists as such, but that between politicians and proprietors – a far more poisonous one and one far more toxic to the body politic.

Many people have had much to say about the Leveson Report, most of it pretty negative, but in his very broad sweep of the relationship between the press and politicians, all 359 pages of it, the good judge gets more right than wrong and merits at least two and a half cheers.

He begins, and then reaffirms on a number of occasions, that there is a clear distinction to be made between those contacts between journalists and politicians that are fundamentally editorial and those that are in essence about media policy or the corporate interests of the press. His view is unambiguous:

> "... relations between politicians and the press on a day to day basis are in robust good health and performing the vital public interest functions of a free press in a vigorous democracy, providing an open forum for public debate, enabling a free flow of information and challenge and holding power to account."[1]

It could be argued, indeed should be argued, that this is somewhat of a rose-tinted view of the current state of relations between journalists and politicians at

Westminster. But it does convey an essential historical truth, a truth revealed by Leveson's own very comprehensive recounting of the last 30 years of this relationship and that is that we are (returning to the canine mode) neither living through a period of the lapdog journalism of the early years of the Thatcher and Blair governments (Barnett & Gaber and Jones 1995, 1991 & 2001), nor the attack-dog mode that began with Bernard Ingham, Mrs Thatcher's in-house Rottweiler, and was perfected by Alastair Campbell under Tony Blair (Barnett & Gaber, Harris and Jones 1995, 1991 & 2001).

Relations between the two sides are not perfect, nor should they be, but they are tolerable; and they function, more or less, in the way outlined by Lord Justice Leveson. However, what is far from perfect, and represents a real threat to the body politic, is the relationship that exists between politicians and media proprietors, executives and editors. This came into stark focus when, as a result of the phone hacking scandal, David Cameron was forced to amend the Ministerial Code and reveal the full extent of contacts between him, his ministers and media owners, executives and editors. As outlined elsewhere (see Nicholas Jones, p 119 in this volume) that relationship was far more intense than most outside observers had realised; in the year following the 2010 General Election an average of one meeting every fortnight was taking place between senior members of the Coalition government and senior executives of News International (although significantly only Conservative ministers were involved!). (Gaber 2012)

During the course of his Inquiry Sir Brian Leveson heard from a wide range of politicians, editors and proprietors. His conclusions, for the most part sound, have to be read bearing in mind that they have been written by a senior judge used to making finely honed judgements, and with large spaces left between the lines for alternative readings. He begins his analysis with the observation that:

> "The pattern which emerges is one in which senior press/political relationships have been too close to give sufficient grounds for confidence that fear or favour have not been operative factors in the determination and implementation of media policy."[2]

He starts with the relationship between Rupert Murdoch and Margaret Thatcher in 1981, when News International was trying to acquire *The Times* and the *Sunday Times* and did not want the matter referred to the Monopolies and Mergers Commission (MMC). Despite the fact that only in 2012 was it revealed that a 'secret meeting' had taken place between Thatcher and Murdoch to discuss the deal, which Leveson describes as "troubling in its lack of transparency"[3]. He says – somewhat surprisingly – that the decision not to refer the bid to the MMC "does not appear to me to be directly attributable to personal influence."[4] Less convincingly he goes on to say, "The Prime Minister was not in any event the decision maker."[5] This statement surely has to be taken with a large pinch of salt in the light of the memoirs of Thatcher's former Cabinet colleagues who speak of the extent to which she dominated her government (Lawson and Howe). And Leveson, in an apparent contradiction of his conclusion, goes on to indicate that he is unconvinced by the protestations of innocence that surrounded the *Times* bid:

> "Why then did Mr Murdoch seek an invitation to Chequers? The prospective deal was plainly of great importance to him. He no doubt believed that there was real value in meeting the Prime Minister face-to-face, to inform her of his bid and his plans in the event that it was successful, and importantly, to form a personal connection…"[6]

He continues:

> "I have carefully considered what conclusions (whether as to fact or credibility), if any, I should draw from Mr Murdoch's inability to recall the meeting either when interviewed for the *History of The Times* or when he appeared before the Inquiry. It is perhaps a little surprising that he does not remember a visit to a place as memorable as Chequers, in the context of a bid as important as that which he made for *Times Newspapers*. However, perhaps that is all I need to say."[7]

With which the riposte "say no more" comes to mind.

If Leveson had been in any doubt about the extent of Murdoch's influence over Thatcher, and the sequence above appears to demonstrate that he wasn't, then the evidence to the Inquiry from one of her former ministers, David Mellor, should have laid any further doubts to rest:

> *"… he was used to Ministers doing his bidding, rather than the other way around. He was personally charming to deal with, but he was one of the few people, apart from Heads of State, I, as a minister, had to visit at his premises rather than him having to schlepp over to the Home Office."*[8]

Although Murdoch did not establish the same rapport with Mrs Thatcher's successor as he did with the 'Iron Lady', John Major's evidence indicated to Leveson that Murdoch expected the same rights of policy veto that he had exercised, or had sought to exercise, under Mrs Thatcher. Lord Justice Leveson quotes Major thus:

> *""It is not very often someone sits in front of a Prime Minister and says to a Prime Minister. "I would like you to change your policy, and if you don't change your policy, my organisation cannot support you".*[9]

Under Major's successor, Tony Blair, those rights seemed to get re-established as the new Labour leader offered, as a sacrifice to Murdoch, those Labour's polices that might have impacted on the growth and influence of News International. Leveson says of Blair

"... he readily accepted that had he maintained the old [media] policy then: *"it would definitely have been a problem with the Murdoch media group in particular ..."*[10]

Leveson notes:

"Shortly before the 1997 election, Mr Blair wrote two articles in The *Sun*... Mr Campbell recalled that it had been made clear to him by the editor of The *Sun* that, if Mr Blair were to emphasise the point in these articles that there would be no entry into the Euro without a specific referendum on the issue, and that he understood people's fears about a so-called European super-state, this was likely to be the final piece of the jigsaw before Mr Murdoch agreed that the paper would back the Labour Party at the election."[11]

The above makes an interesting juxtaposition with Mr Murdoch's repeated declarations that he did not seek to influence the political stance taken by his newspapers (Gaber 2013).

And Leveson makes plain his view that no formal agreement would have had to be put in place to secure Murdoch's support for Blair: "The evidence does not support an inference of an agreement between Mr Murdoch and Mr Blair."[12] – but what he doesn't need to add is that these things are never formally written down.

One of the key moments in the Blair/Murdoch affair was Blair's intervention with the Romano Prodi, then Italian Prime Minister, following Murdoch's 'request' that Blair should seek clarification if Sky's bid for the Italian commercial TV network Mediaset, would be blocked by the Italian Government. Both Murdoch and Blair initially denied that any such intervention had taken place, until even Mr Murdoch's own newspaper was reporting that such a request had indeed been made:

"Despite a number of ambiguous statements from Downing Street spokesmen over the past few days it is now clear that last week Mr Murdoch rang the Prime Minister to see if he would find out what the political reaction might be."[13]

The 'ambiguous statements' was a reference to attempts by Alastair Campbell to throw a smokescreen over the affair by saying that Blair had never made the call to Prodi on Murdoch's behalf. In fact the truth of the matter was that the subject came up during a call initiated by Prodi who had called Blair on another matter. Leveson was unimpressed, dismissing the issue of who called whom as unimportant but noting:

"... what may be more important is what can be inferred from the fact that Mr Murdoch was able to ask the Prime Minister to make the enquiry in the first place."[14]

Leveson is equally sceptical when discussing Murdoch's support for the US/UK invasion of Iraq in 2003 , and the fact that Blair had time to take three calls from Murdoch in the weeks prior to it , he writes:

> "Although Mr Blair did not have a clear recollection of the precise content of these calls (and nor did Mr Murdoch when asked about them), it is interesting that he made time to discuss these issues with a newspaper proprietor speaking from the USA. It is also interesting that Mr Murdoch's 173 newspapers worldwide all supported the war."[15]

In dealing with Gordon Brown, Blair's successor, Lord Justice Leveson notes how before the latter moved into Downing Street, Murdoch had an even closer relationship with him than with Blair, but one which soured soon after Brown became Prime Minister. In broad terms Leveson appears to accept Brown's version of the souring, rather than Murdoch's but he does express some scepticism about Brown's own denials that his 'spin doctors'– Charlie Whelan and Damien McBride – ever undertook anonymous negative briefings saying that such briefings had not occurred or that if they had, it was without his knowledge or sanction. One can almost see the judge's eyebrows arch as he writes: "Many political commentators have expressed surprise at this evidence."[16]

When it comes to the Murdoch/Cameron relationship Leveson's focus was, inevitably, News International's attempt to take over BSkyB and the neutrality, or lack of it, displayed by the Cameron Government, and in particular the Culture Secretary Jeremy Hunt. But what is surprising is how Leveson lists all manner of events which appeared to display a clear lack of impartiality by Hunt's office, and then gives the Minister a clean bill of health – thus earning Leveson the two and a half, rather three cheers, he almost merited.

Leveson is in no doubt that leaving the principal role in the negotiations between News International and the Government to a Special Adviser, as opposed to a senior civil servant or even a junior minister, "...was, in my judgment, unwise"[17] and he goes on to explain why,

> "That is not because of any question about his integrity or calibre, but because he had a pre-existing and amicable relationship with Mr Michel, News International's public affairs adviser, which Mr Michel was able to exploit to engineer contact that was inappropriate in volume and in some cases in tone."[18]

Voluminous these contacts most certainly were; during the time when the BSkyB bid was being considered by Hunt's office, no fewer than 690 text messages passed between News International's lobbyist Frederick Michel and Hunt's Special Adviser, Adam Smith.[19] Leveson draws attention to the dangers of such 'informal' contacts,

" .. the fact that such practices have a side-effect (**I say no more than that**) (emphasis added) of placing the conduct of public policy issues outside the mechanisms of transparency, accountability and public record cannot but give rise to perceptions and questions which are corrosive to public trust and confidence."[20]

He adds that this "...was a risk which was, or should have been, obvious from the outset"[21] and he has no doubt as to where blame should be attributed:

"The consequential risks were then compounded by the cumulative effects of the lack of explicit clarity in Mr Smith's role, the lack of sufficient express instruction that it was clear he fully understood, and a lack of supervision. They are all matters for which Mr Hunt was responsible, although they might have been prevented had Mr Hunt fully appreciated the extent to which meticulous attention had to be paid to every aspect of the conduct of quasi-judicial procedure."[22]

So despite the fact that Leveson castigates Hunt for failing to supervise Smith's contacts with News International, and failing to appreciate how important it was not just to be impartial but to appear to be impartial, he concludes that there was no "credible evidence of actual bias on the part of Mr Hunt."[23] This is an odd conclusion given that Leveson has consistently pointed to the fact that when it came to alleged 'deals' between the press and politicians, nothing was set down on paper, nothing specific was probably even said; but, as he consistently makes clear, in this world no such undertakings are ever formally given, all business is conducted on an informal 'understood' basis. The evidence overwhelmingly suggests that this was what happened with regard to Hunt's overseeing of the BSkyB bid, and yet Leveson finds him 'not guilty' – perhaps he meant to say 'not proven'?

Lord Justice Leveson also refers to this lack of any formal evidence when discussing the broader issue of Murdoch's influence over successive British Prime Ministers. He notes that

"He (Murdoch) denied on several occasions that he made any express deals with politicians, and the available evidence does not prove that he ever did. **This, however, is not the end of the story.**"[24](emphasis added)

He goes on:

"If Mr Murdoch made no express deals with politicians within government, the question which arises is whether he made any implied deals or reached tacit understandings with those who engaged with him."[25]

And he notes that:

"All the politicians who gave evidence before the Inquiry said that Mr Murdoch exercised immense power and that this was almost palpable in their relations with him. ...This is not to say that Mr Murdoch set out to wield power or that his personal manner was other than amicable and respectful in his dealings with politicians. But it is to say that he must have been aware of how he was being perceived by his interlocutors; to suggest otherwise would be to suggest that Mr Murdoch knows little about human nature and lacks basic insight, **which could not, of course, be further from the truth**."[26] (emphasis added)

Noting that since Murdoch made no secret of his views on any particular topic he did not need to give his editors specific instructions about the political line to take, Leveson observes that this enabled Murdoch to exercise power, by remote control so-to-speak, over both his editors and those politicians seeking his favour:

"Sometimes the very greatest power is exercised without having to ask, because to ask would be to state the blindingly obvious and thereby diminish the very power which is being displayed. Just as Mr Murdoch's editors knew the basic ground-rules, so did politicians. The language of trades and deals is far too crude in this context."[27]

Leveson observes that,

"... politicians were well aware that 'taking on' Mr Murdoch would be likely to lead to a rupture in support, a metaphorical declaration of war on his titles with the inevitable backlash that would follow."[28]

Perhaps more importantly (in terms of the Inquiry's central concern i.e. press regulation) was that this could lead to politicians having,

".. an appreciation of the consequences both of disturbing the status quo as regards the regulation of the press and, more broadly speaking, of adopting policies which would damage Mr Murdoch's commercial interests."[29]

This leads Sir Brian to the crucial point that "...**the influence exercised by Mr Murdoch is more about what did not happen than what did**."[30] (emphasis added) Murdoch, he notes,

"... fully understood the value of personal interactions, the value of the face-to-face meeting. ...Suffice to say, Mr Murdoch well understands the value of 'less is more'."[31]

Turning his attention to the overall relations between press proprietors, executives and editors and politicians in general, he is unambiguous:

"In my view, the evidence clearly demonstrates that the political parties of UK national government and of UK official opposition have had or developed too close a relationship with the press.... I do not believe this has been in the public interest."[32]

And he specifies his principal concerns:

- Politicians have devoted too much time and attention to these relationships
- Appropriate boundaries between the conduct of public affairs and their private or personal interests have not always been maintained and
- The relationships have not been conducted with sufficient transparency and accountability from the point of view of the public.

From this he concludes that politicians have not been acting in what he describes as the "public interest"[33]. He makes this charge because they have

"...risked becoming vulnerable to unaccountable influences in a manner which was, at least, potentially in conflict with their responsibilities in relation to the conduct of public affairs"[34].

They have also missed,

"...a number of clear opportunities decisively to address (and persistently fail to respond more generally to) public concern about, the culture practices and ethics of the press"[35]

and finally they have sought

"... to control (if not manipulate) the supply of news and information to the public in return for expected or hoped-for favourable treatment by sections of the press".[36]

Leveson is particularly concerned when press interests use their 'special relationship' with politicians to lobby for their own commercial interests. He says that responsibility for policing this lobbying lies with the politicians not the press although he has noted, with some concern, how when, listening to the evidence of media executives, "the rhetoric of public interest tends to become elided with the self-interest of the press."[37] But what particularly concerns him in this relationship is that the conversation between media executives and politicians tend not to simply be about governmental matters but frequently elide into discussions about party and private business. This, he says, makes press regulation particularly problematic:

"The impression is given of decisions being taken about matters of media policy in the context of close, personal relationships (and friendships); there is then a legitimate concern that the public will be in the dark on matters of legitimate interest to them and accountability will be lost."[38]

In 2011, in the wake of establishing the Leveson Inquiry, Cameron announced changes in the Ministerial Code which sought to make relations between press proprietors and politicians more transparent. Leveson does not believe that these changes went far enough. He recommends that the Code should be extended as follows:

- That meetings between press executives and politicians that cover not just governmental business, but also those classified as party political and private, should all come within the Code.
- That transparency should be extended from meetings with ministers to meetings with other political colleagues, special advisers and civil servants; and that it should cover opposition parties as well,
- That publishing the fact that such meetings have taken place (which is the current position) is not sufficient but also the details of the discussions should also be made public and
- That the code should apply, not just to face-to-face meetings but to phone conversations emails and text messages.

These proposals should be welcomed. Indeed Leveson is particularly keen to ensure that they are put into place urgently so that they cover meetings between the press and politicians about his own report. To no one's surprise this has not happened and instead, the old regime of confidential meetings between ministers and press executives has been the order of the day in an attempt to stitch up a post-Leveson deal.

Lord Justice Leveson's conclusion to his section on relations between the politicians and the press is brief, and to the point. In his final flourish he writes,

> "...the press has to be accountable to the public in whose interests it claims to be acting and must show respect for the rights of others to such extent as legitimate public interest does not justify otherwise. It should not be acceptable that it uses its voice, power and authority to undermine the ability of society to require that regulation is not a free for all, to be ignored with impunity. The answer to the question who guards the guardians should not be 'no-one'.[39]

Alas at the time of writing (January 2013) the guardians remain unguarded, no doubt much to the relief of News International and all the other press proprietors.

Notes
[1] Leveson Vol. 3 p.1117

[2] Leveson Vol 3 p.1119

[3] Leveson Vol 3 p.1245)

[4] Leveson Vol 3 p.1122)

[5] Ibid

[6] Leveson Vol 3 p.1245

[7] Ibid

[8] Leveson Vol. 3 p.1123

[9] Leveson Vol. 3 p.1131

[10] Leveson Vol. 3 p.1137

[11] Leveson Vol. 3 p.1142

[12] Leveson Vol. 3 p.1298

[13] *The Times* March 27, 1998, "Friday Call halted Murdoch deal" by Raymond Snoddy

[14] Leveson Vol. 3 p.1148

[15] Leveson Vol. 3 p.1148

[16] Leveson Vol. 3 p.1155

[17] Leveson Vol. 3 p.1406

[18] Ibid

[19] Leveson Vol. 3 p.1380

[20] Leveson Vol. 3 p.1405

[21] Leveson Vol. 3 p.1406

[22] Ibid

[23] Leveson Vol. 3 p.1407

[24] Leveson Vol. 3 p.1431

[25] Ibid

[26] Ibid

[27] Ibid

[28] Leveson Vol. 3 p.1432

[29] Ibid

[30] Ibid

[31] Ibid

[32] Leveson Vol. 3 p.1438

[33] Leveson Vol. 3 p.1439

[34] Ibid

[35] Ibid

[36] Ibid

[37] Leveson Vol. 3 p.1442

[38] Leveson Vol. 3 p.1446

[39] Leveson Vol. 3 p.1460

References

Barnett, S. and Gaber, Ivor. *Westminster Tales: The 21st Century Crisis in Political Journalism*. London: Continuum, 2001.

Fowler N. *A Political Suicide: the Conservatives' Voyage into the Political Wilderness*. London, Methuen 2010

Gaber I. 'Moment of Truth: What "Hackgate" Tells us About the Changing Relations Between the Media and Politics.' in *The Phone Hacking Scandal: Journalism on Trial*. Ed. R. Keeble and J. Mair. Bury St. Edmunds: Arima publishing 2012

Gaber I. 'The many faces of Rupert Murdoch as revealed by his evidence to the UK's Leveson Inquiry into the Cultures. Ethics and Practices of the Press' in Gordon J. & Rowinski P. *Br(e)aking the News*, Oxford, Peter Lang 2013

Harris R. *Good and Faithful Servant: the Unauthorized Biography of Bernard Ingham*, London, Faber & Faber 1990

Howe G *Conflict of Loyalty*, London, Methuen 2007

Jones, N. *Soundbites and Spin Doctors: How Politicians Manipulate the Media and Vice Versa*. London: Indigo, 1995.

Jones N. *Sultans of Spin: The Media and the New Labour Government*. London: Victor Gollancz, 1999.

Jones N. *The Control Freaks: How New Labour Gets Its Own Way*. London: Politcos 2001.

Lawson N. *The View from No 11: Memoirs of a Tory Radical*, London, Bantam 1992

Leveson B. *An inquiry into the culture, practices and ethics of the press* Volume III London: The Stationery Office, 2012

Note on the contributor

Ivor Gaber is Professor of Political Journalism at City University London and Research Professor in Media and Politics at the University of Bedfordshire. Formerly he was a political journalist with BBC TV and Radio, ITN and Sky News. He has published widely on relations between the media and politicians.

The dog and lamp-post: why Leveson won't change the relationship

Professor Mick Temple, a long-time academic observer of the British media/politics interface, looks at the Leveson Report in the light of the six previous investigations into the power of the press and the need for regulation. All have failed

"Journalism is to politician as dog is to lamp-post", H.L. Mencken, *The Oxford Dictionary of Literary Quotations*.

Does the dog need the lamp-post?

Mencken's famous analogy is amusing but unhelpful. Whether or not journalists are the dog and politicians are the lamp-post, the nature of their relationship has contributed not only to a public sphere in which reliable information about politics is all too rare but also to the increasingly negative image the public have of both professions. Lord Justice Leveson may have produced a decidedly "mediocre" report (*The Economist*, 8 December, 2012) filled with vague and essentially unworkable recommendations, but his central message is clear and indisputable. The relationship between British politicians and journalists needs to change. Senior politicians have for too long responded like Pavlov's dogs to the temporary obsessions of newspapers like the *Sun* and *Daily Mail*, and are so afraid of powerful press barons like Rupert Murdoch that they openly court their approval and support in return for policy pay-offs. On the other hand, many political journalists have become too reliant upon and too close personally to senior politicians and their spinners. The result? The evidence presented to Leveson shows a relationship corrupted by mutual suspicion and cynicism in which the public have been the chief losers.

In a democracy, the exchange of information between journalists and politicians is both necessary and inevitable. But they must be careful to strike the right balance. Politicians have lived in fear of the urinating (or even worse) reporter – but political reporters have come to dread the splash-back from a legion of Alastair Campbell clones. Of course, the relationship is also frequently

143

collusive. As Ivor Gaber presciently pointed out in his examination of the first year of Tony Blair's premiership, a latter-day Mencken would have characterised the dogs in his analogy as both the media and politicians – with the people "reduced to the role of the much-abused lamp-posts" (1998: 65). The process preceded Blair, but there's little doubt of the acceleration of the close ties between leading politicians and journalists during and after the Blair years, to the detriment of the public interest.

If we believe that an informed population is essential to democracy, then public trust in our press is crucial. That trust has been damaged by the picture emerging from the Leveson Inquiry. If the electorate's perception of both the press and politics is predominantly of worlds inhabited by the devious, ill-informed, corrupt or incompetent, they are unlikely to believe political news reporting and far less likely to engage in any meaningful political activity. Declining electoral participation rates, falling party memberships and unprecedently low levels of public trust in both politicians and journalists (Ipsos MORI 2011) do not suggest a thriving political public sphere. Although our newspapers are only one factor, they have contributed to the decline.

Let us explore the potential impact of Leveson's recommendations on the three-way relationship between the press, politicians and the public.

Control of the press: a long history of failure

Ever since William Caxton set up Britain's first printing press in 1476 the powerful have attempted direct control of the flow of information, but there is space here only to briefly outline some key post-war governmental attempts to rein in the press. Labour's landslide election success in 1945 reflected a new ideological environment in which greater control of the press could be considered. In 1946, the National Union of Journalists initiated a House of Commons motion calling for a Royal Commission to inquire into the finance, control, management and ownership of the press. The impact on newspaper practices of that Royal Commission report in 1949, as with those of 1962 and 1977, was minimal. The first report is notable for Lord Beaverbrook's typically candid admission to the Commission that he owned his newspapers "purely for propaganda and with no other purpose" (Temple 2008: 55-6). None of the three Royal Commissions led to strong government action or to any effective control of perceived newspaper excesses: in particular, the anodyne McGregor report of 1977 made almost no impact (Lacey & Longman 1997: 25). Neither did the 1972 Younger Report on privacy. The fourth estate rhetoric prevailed and it would have been a brave government that risked introducing legislation curtailing 'press freedom'.

The Conservative government set up the Calcutt Commission (1990) to examine privacy and related matters, which recommended the Press Complaints Commission (PCC), to replace the moribund Press Council in January 1991. Following a series of intrusive stories, Calcutt's second review recommended legislation on privacy and a compulsory system of press controls under an official Press Tribunal, although he was not hopeful the press would be willing to make "fundamental changes" (Calcutt 1993: Para 5.30). Editors and their newspapers responded with fury and John Major's weak Conservative administration capitulated, illustrating an old rule of politics: "no government wants to fight against a united press" (Tunstall 1996: 403). Implementing Leveson's recommendations in similar conditions will be equally problematic.

The journalist-politician relationship

The often sordid informal relationship between politician and journalists uncovered by Lord Justice Leveson is not new. From almost the very start of the British press, governments wanted newspapers to present their policies in a positive way to the public. Every politician had journalists he could persuade by various means to publish favourable material. Rather than continually attempting to suppress unhelpful information, governments started to develop ways of managing the news. So did individual politicians such as Benjamin Disraeli, who often rehearsed his speeches privately in front of *The Times'* parliamentary reporter. The 19th century campaigning journalist W. T. Stead asserted that there could be no doubt that "the influence of the press upon the decision of Cabinets is much greater than that wielded by the House of Commons" (Temple 2008: 22-7), a view that still resonates. And as voting rights grew, Lord Northcliffe was to note that "every extension of the franchise renders more powerful the newspaper and less powerful the politician" (Koss 1990: 450), an acute and accurate observation that reveals his awareness of the potential power of newspapers in a mass democracy.

That power arguably reached its peak during the mid-to-late 20th century. The recent relationship has been heavily weighted in the press's favour, as politicians sought to ingratiate themselves with the perceived 'king-makers' of the popular press. It may or may not have been *The Sun* 'wot won it' for the Conservatives in 1992 but the perception remains. Rupert Murdoch was at pains to deny this in his evidence to Leveson, saying he'd given "a terrible bollocking" to Kelvin MacKenzie for making the claim (Bagehot, 2012b), but both sides of the relationship have acted as if this representation of press power was true (see also Barnett & Gaber 2001: 28-9).

A decline in deference?

Savagery by the British press towards the rich and the powerful "taps into an ancient British tradition", one characterised by an "instinctive derision" for the 'strutting politician' (Bagehot 2012a). Most politicians accept this as part of the essential scrutiny of their activities which democracy demands, but the decline of deference which characterises the post-war years has led to coverage which often concentrates on issues outside of the 'public interest' – and fails to act in the interests of the public.

The press treatment of John Major offers a graphic example of this decline in deference. For most of his seven years in office, we saw the unedifying spectacle of a Conservative prime minister vilified almost daily in the Conservative-supporting press. Following the economic disaster of Black Wednesday in September 1991, leading to sterling being withdrawn from the European exchange rate mechanism, Major called *Sun* editor Kelvin MacKenzie to ask how his paper was going to report the story. "Let me put it this way", said MacKenzie. "I have two buckets of shit on my desk and tomorrow morning I am going to empty both of them over your head" (Temple 2008: 71). Clearly, the normal courtesies "shown to elected power by print power" had all but disappeared (Marr 2005: 187).

More sympathetic accounts of the politician-journalist relationship place them both as victims of their environment (Davis 2010 pp 65-6). Both find themselves squeezed by constituents or audiences, public opinion or advertisers, parties or editors in a highly pressurised environment which is not of their making. While newspaper journalists were once able to take the lead by presenting the implications of an event the following day, technology is denying newspapers their former role of producing more considered analysis. This leaves them little opportunity to give real insight to stories. Instead, stories increasingly focus on sensational aspects, leading to allegations of dumbing down even in the 'quality' press (O'Neill 2012) and raising further questions about the contribution of journalism to democracy (Lilleker & Temple 2013).

The democratic functions of the press

Observers have frequently noted the democratic importance of the press. Barnett & Gaber (2001: 12-13) pointed out three crucial contributions that good political journalism can make to democracy. Firstly, by acting as "tribunes of the people", they can represent the views of the "multitude" to political representatives. Secondly, the media can convey "accurate, intelligible and comprehensive knowledge" to allow citizens to formulate their own responses to political events and thereby participate in the political process. Thirdly, they can contribute to that process of public opinion formation by providing a forum in which citizens can share their views and allow "a collective view to evolve".

The evidence to the Leveson Inquiry clearly showed the inadequacy of much of the press in those essential roles. The close relationship between politicians, media owners and political journalists – with fear being the key driving factor behind politicians' compliance – means that, too often, the views of the public are crudely manipulated and misrepresented. Indeed, far from "accurate, intelligible and comprehensive knowledge" being presented to the public, political spin and proprietorial preferences have dominated. Newspapers may frequently claim to be speaking for their readers. *The Sun Says* uses phrases such as 'us' to refer to itself and its readers, who are represented as sharing the same preferences and opinions – but the role of a newspaper is largely to present the 'common-sense' world view of their owner, a common-sense that on inspection tends to fit the commercial and ideological ends of multi-national companies (Temple 2008). The views of readers are useful only when supporting the paper's current line on any controversial issue.

Aeron Davis argues that the politician-journalist relationship has become "institutionalised, intense and reflexive" with the danger both that journalistic independence is compromised and that "politicians may be setting agendas, choosing and promoting policy solutions and party representatives" based on the preferences of media owners (see Davis 2009: 215). The replacement of Vince Cable by Jeremy Hunt as the Minister with the responsibility for the BSkyB bid in December 2010 certainly supports that belief. Unlike Cable, Hunt's appointment fitted the needs of the Murdoch empire, whose employees' close personal links with David Cameron's administration were the object of much of Lord Justice Leveson's criticism.

Leveson looked much wider than the reporting of politics – the majority of illegal activity concerned celebrities – but one aspect of modern day political journalism, the focus on the private lives of politicians, is an area where (unlike most celebrity intrusions) detailing such private activity can have a public interest defence. At its best, modern political coverage includes greater scrutiny of the activities of elected representatives and their staff: however, there is also a greater willingness to carry negative and highly personal stories by the media. If, after Leveson, journalists have to be more transparent about their sources, such stories may be less likely to appear, perhaps to the detriment of the public sphere. The need for journalists to produce ever-increasing copy at speed facilitates politicans controlling access to information in the hope of favourable coverage. This has negative consequences for the democratic ideal of an informed public (Lilleker & Temple, 2013).

Post-Leveson: changes in the relationship?

Astonishingly, Leveson argues that the day-to-day relationship between journalists and politicians is in "robust good health and performing the vital public interest functions in a vigorous democracy" (Leveson 2012b: 6). Members of the Westminster lobby, in particular those who were frozen out of the loop during the Blair years because of their unwillingness to toe the line, might disagree with Leveson's assessment, which also contradicts the bulk of evidence to his Inquiry. In addition to his condemnation of much journalistic practice, Leveson makes a number of specific allegations against senior politicians: there has been a lack of transparency in their relationship with senior media figures; "appropriate boundaries" have not always been maintained; and politicians have spent "a surprisingly large amount of time, attention and resource on this relationship ... at the expense of other legitimate claims in relation to their conduct of public affairs" (Leveson 2012a: 26). In short, the relationship between politicians and journalists is "too close" (Leveson 2012a: 3)

How likely is there to be any change in the "too close" relationship following Leveson's report? The Guardian's veteran political reporter Michael White maintains:

"politicians and the press have always been locked in a love/hate relationship. It is one of cheerful loathing, mitigated by drink, grudging respect and the shackles of mutual dependency: information traded overtly and covertly for publicity".

White's analysis of the potential for change concludes by noting that, following Leveson's report, MPs and political reporters "muttered in Westminster's dark corners as usual" (2012). Indeed, Leveson's recommendation that senior politicians should publish all the details of their meetings with senior journalists may well lead to even more of a clandestine relationship between politicians and journalists, as meetings become more off–the-record or carried out by proxy.

Life after Leveson on the political street?
It also appears unlikely that Leveson's main recommendation of a regulatory code of conduct underpinned by statute will be implemented, at least in the near future. David Cameron told the House of Commons on November 30th 2012 that he had "serious concerns and misgivings" about any legislation that has "the potential to impinge free speech and a free press". Labour's initial rush to accept every one of Leveson's reforms has now been tempered and the press continue to lobby forcefully against any statutory underpinning. But after Leveson and the frequently disgusting and indefensible practices unearthed, newspapers are anxious to appear willing to change. However, at the time of writing, editors have yet to agree on their promised quick response to Leveson. The wish to avoid statutory legislation by producing a more robust voluntary system has floundered in debates about the detail, with "suspicion and conflict" characterising their relationship with government (Sabbagh 2012). It is starting to sound all too familiar.

And the actions of some politicians are also contributing to growing concern as the potential repercussions of some form of state control become increasingly apparent. Even as national newspaper editors were meeting with the Prime Minister to discuss reform, senior government advisers were warning the *Daily Telegraph*'s editor to drop a story examining the Culture Secretary Maria Miller's expenses claim, reminding him that Miller was currently considering press regulation. The paper claims the threat shows "the potential dangers of politicians being given a role in overseeing press regulation" (*Daily Telegraph*, 12 December 2012), with observers noting "the chilling effect the threat of Government involvement in regulation of the press is already having" (Pugh 2012).

Lord Justice Leveson himself noted that his was the seventh such inquiry into the press commissioned by government during the post-war years. The six previous failed to have much effect and the sceptical among us suspect that Leveson's impact will be similarly impotent. It is not just that editors (and the prime minister) are resistant to statutory regulation, or that defining what is or is not a 'newspaper' is extraordinarily difficult, especially online. Leveson's solution fails to deal with the realities of regulating 'the press' in the 21st century. Emily Bell (2012), discussing Twitter and Google, notes that "effectively the two most powerful platforms for news (and gossip) dissemination in the world are already outside jurisdiction". It seems that both Leveson and the supporters of statutory regulation such as the Hacked Off campaign have failed to comprehend that the world has changed. The printed newspaper is on its last legs and attempting statutory control of online and effectively global newspapers will be way beyond the scope of any British government.

And what of the dog and lamp-post relationship? It is difficult to disagree with Michael White's assessment that the "historic mutual dependency and cheerful loathing" between politicians and journalists will endure and that "nothing in Lord Justice Leveson's report will change that" (White 2012). In an age of mediated politics, politicians are unlikely ever to gain the upper hand and they will need to beware the approaching Rottweilers for some time to come. The public needs a vigorous free press and whatever the many flaws of our newspapers, press freedom is too valuable to sacrifice on the recommendation of a mediocre and ill-considered report.

References

Bagehot (2012a) 'Politicians and the press: are British newspapers a menace to democracy?' *The Economist*, 26 April, available online at http://www.economist.com/blogs/bagehot/2012/04/politicians-and-press, accessed 12 May 2012

Bagehot (2012b) 'The pen is mightier: why the British press holds such sway over politicians', *The Economist* 28 April, available online at http://www.economist.com/node/21553472, accessed 12 December 2012

Barnett, Steven and Gaber, Ivor (2001) *Westminster Tales: the twenty-first century crisis in political journalism.* London: Continuum Press

Bell, Emily (2012) 'The Leveson inquiry is irrelevant to 21st-century journalism', *The Guardian*, 28 November

Calcutt. David (1993) *Review of Press Self-Regulation.* London: HMSO Cm. 1102

Davis, Aeron (2009) 'Journalist-source relations: mediated reflexivity and the politics of politics', *Journalism Education*, Vol. 10 (2), pp.204-219

Davis, Aeron (2010) *Political Information and Social Theory.* Abingdon: Routledge

The Economist (2012) 'Hacked to pieces', leader column, 8 December

Gaber, Ivor (1998) 'The new world of dogs and lamp-posts', *British Journalism Review*, Vol. 9 (2), pp.59-65

Ipsos MORI (2011) *Trust in Professions.* Available online at http://www.ipsos-mori.com/researchpublications/researcharchive/2818/Doctors-are-most-trusted-profession-politicians-least-trusted.aspx, accessed 28 November 2012

Jones, Jonathan (2012) 'Prising politicians away from the press', *The Spectator*, 29 November

Koss, Stephen (1990) *The Rise and Fall of the Political Press in Britain.* London: Fontana

Lacey, Colin and Longman, David (1997) *The Press as Public Educator: Cultures of understanding, cultures of ignorance.* Luton: University of Luton Press

Leveson, Lord Justice (2012a) *An Inquiry into the Culture, Practices and Ethics of the Press: Executive Summary*. London: The Stationery Office. Available online at http://www.official-documents.gov.uk/document/hc1213/hc07/0779/0779.pdf, accessed on 4 December 2012

Leveson, Lord Justice (2012b) *A Report into the Culture, Practices and Ethics of the Press: Remarks by Lord Justice Leveson*. Available online at http://www.levesoninquiry.org.uk/wp-content/uploads/2012/11/Remarks-by-Lord-Justice-Leveson-29-November-2012.pdf, accessed on 8 December 2012

Lilleker, Darren and Temple, Mick. (2013) 'Reporting politics: enlightening citizens or undermining democracy?' in S. Allan & K. Fowler-Watt (eds.) *Journalism: New Challenges* (Pearson)

Marr, Andrew (2005) *My Trade: A short history of British journalism*. London: Pan Macmillan

O'Neill, Deirdre (2012) 'No cause for celebration: the rise of celebrity news values in the British quality press', *Journalism Education*, Vol. 1 (2), pp.26-44

Pugh, Andrew (2012) 'Telegraph reveals Leveson 'menaces' of Government adviser over Maria Miller expenses story', *Press Gazette*, 12 December. Available online at http://www.pressgazette.co.uk/telegraph-reveals-leveson-menaces-government-adviser-over-maria-miller-expenses-story, accessed on 19 December 2012

Sabbagh, Dan (2012) 'Fleet Street's harmonious response to Leveson falls apart', *The Guardian*, 12 December

Temple, Mick (2008) *The British Press*. Maidenhead, Open University Press

Temple, Mick (2012) 'In defence of a free press', *Journalism Education*, Vol. 1 (2), pp.93-5

Tunstall, Jeremy (1996) *Newspaper Power: the new national press in Britain*. Oxford: Oxford University Press

White, Michael (2012) 'Press and politicians? Leveson's report will not change these uneasy bedfellows', *The Guardian*, 29 November

Note on the contributor

Mick Temple is Professor of Journalism & Politics at Staffordshire University. His books include The British Press (2008), Blair (2006) and How Britain Works: From Ideology to Output Politics (2000). He is the author of many academic journal articles in political science, the media and journalism studies, and comments regularly on current affairs in the local and national media. He is co-editor of the Association for Journalism Education's academic journal, Journalism Education, and a co-convenor of the Political Studies Association's Media and Politics group.

Section D. Regulation before and after the good lord

To regulate or not that was the major question facing Lord Justice Leveson. Self-regulation of the press had patently failed. Something needed to be done. The British press had fought off any regulation by statute many times before; this time the artillery and megaphones started long before Sir Brian Leveson reported on November 29th 2012. He plumped for a self-regulated system backed up with a 'dab' of statute – not the Ofcom option the megaphone diplomats would have us believed.

Dorothy Byrne deals with a regulator – Ofcom – day to day as a broadcaster. She looks at the rough and smooth of this marriage. She has always operated under the 'yoke' of regulation from Ofcom or before that the ITC. It has not stopped her commissioning and making some superb revelatory shows like 'Sri Lanka's Killing Fields'. But defending them ex post facto to a regulator can prove costly and time consuming as she demonstrates. Dorothy is now the longest serving commissioner of news and current affairs at Channel Four and indeed in British broadcasting and is one of the major sponsors of good investigative journalism in the UK through her *Dispatches* and *Unreported World* Strands as well as the nightly *Channel Four News*.

My life with the regulators. The smooth and the rough

Dorothy Byrne, now the longest serving commissioner of news and current affairs at Channel Four and indeed in British broadcasting, is one of the major sponsors of good investigative journalism in the UK through her Dispatches and Unreported World Strands as well as the Nightly Channel Four News. She has always operated under the 'yoke' of regulation from Ofcom or before that the ITC. It has not stopped her commissioning and making some superb revelatory shows like 'Sri Lanka's Killing Fields'. But defending them ex post facto to a regulator can prove costly and time consuming.

I have never been married but I have a relationship with an entity which bears many of the hallmarks of a marriage. For example, were I to sing to it, the words, "You are always in my mind," would be appropriate. Indeed, I know the opinions of this entity so well that I could almost say they are not just in my mind, they are imprinted on it. I can chant them from memory as others recite The Bible.

The entity is, of course, Ofcom, the Office of Communications which regulates broadcasters. It's not for me to say whether newspapers should enter into such a relationship with Ofcom or another regulator and, if they did, I doubt it would be on precisely the same terms as television journalists, just as all marriages are different. However, I think it's useful for me to say a little about what it's like to live with Ofcom. In particular, newspaper journalists fear that a legally-binding regulator stifles difficult and important journalism. My experience is that it does not but that those under investigation will sometimes attempt to use the regulator in every way they can to hinder journalism. Defending that journalism against such attacks can be extremely expensive and immensely time-consuming.

Rules are rules...

There may be people who do not know Rule 4.6 "Improperly exploit...." Susceptibilities" or Rule 5.7 "Due Weight" or who have even managed to live a full and satisfying life without truly understanding rule 3.1 "Material likely to encourage crime or lead to disorder." Were I to hand the Ofcom Broadcasting Code to some passing hacks, they might find it daunting but the first issue is whether the rules and the guidance contained within it represent reasonable practice to which a good journalist should want to adhere anyway.

Section Eight on Privacy Guidance is one that some newspapers journalists would benefit from reading. Some of it is obvious. The guidance, "Privacy is least likely to be infringed in a public place," might be stating the obvious. But there is then an interesting discussion on whether a railway station or a shop, while being both technically privately owned and accessible to the public might be places where someone could expect a degree of privacy and sometimes not.

Good points are also made about the need to be aware that "innocent" bystanders can be caught inadvertently in secret filming. This is followed by a discussion of some of the factors a broadcaster should consider when broadcasting footage of accident victims. I think a reasonable person who was also sufficiently deranged to want to sit down and read through all this stuff would think that it made a great deal of sense. However, it is extremely detailed and it's hard to picture a free press being regulated so tightly.

Rules and extra rules

But here is the strange thing; broadcasters and television news organisations all have their own rules and guidelines which they have devised in addition to what Ofcom says. Open the Compliance Manual of ITN, the organisation which produces news for Channel Four, ITV and Channel Five and everything in that seems jolly sensible too. In fact, it is a wise document. Section 5.9 reminds people not to use patronising references such as "confined to a wheelchair" or "stricken down with" and to ensure reference is made to a person's religion, race, colour, sexuality or disability only if there is editorial justification. Section 5.13 might cause some papers difficulty; it advises that images of nudity or the discussion of sexual issues should be presented carefully, especially before 9pm. That might put paid to a few pages of our morning papers. Reports about health scares should not "cause public fear and alarm". That would be a few more pages of our newspapers gone. Journalists should avoid unsourced speculation. Also, "We must avoid invading private grief or dwelling on pictures of people in distress". The manual also reminds people against hacking or "encouraging others to carry out such acts". The whole thing runs to 133 pages and every employee has to sign a statement that they have read it all and will abide by it.

Sanctions for breaking the rules

Of course, broadcasters' additional rules and guidelines do not carry the potential sanctions which a breach of the Ofcom code can bring. Fines are rare but a finding that one is in breach is damaging to a broadcaster's reputation.

Newspapers sometimes have a field day with such rulings and if the subject of an investigation wins a complaint they may take out a prominent advert in a newspaper. Questions can be asked in Parliament. We have to broadcast any significant finding against us in a slot as prominent as the breach and those are a few minutes of wretched humiliation for television journalists. All of which is why the rules are not just imprinted on my brain but also engraved on my heart and tattooed up my arms.

So, why not Ofcom for newspapers?

Now if I worked on a newspaper I might feel I don't need a regulator to tell me what to think about in a railway station or indeed to inform me as does section 8.22 of Ofcom's guidance notes that, "A child of five has a very different view and understanding of the world around it than a 15 year old teenager has."

This sort of stuff might be all very well for broadcasters who have the special privilege of entering people's living rooms uninvited but do the tone and the detail quite fit with the notion of a free press? If I worked on a newspaper, I would be especially worried about whether all these rules would be manipulated to prevent me revealing wrongdoing.

In my experience, organisations with the money often do attempt to use the regulations, as opposed to the law of the land, to intimidate one into dropping all or parts of investigations. Knowing in advance that they are likely to do this, we must go to ever greater efforts to ensure from the very beginning of an investigation that we do nothing wrong.

Do the rules have a 'chilling effect'?

A newspaper journalist might begin enquiries into a potential investigation by making a few calls. In television, we often have to decide from a very early stage precisely how we are going to describe the project we are working on so that no person telephoned can say, months in the future, they were 'misled'. We agree with Channel Four's lawyers a description of the project and the circumstances in which it will be acceptable not to be completely open with some of those we contact. Before we even consider any form of secret recording we prepare documents which may run to tens of pages justifying any potential invasion of privacy. If our plans vary slightly for some practical reason, a new document is, time permitting, prepared before proceeding. A lawyer and a commissioning editor have to agree each detail and I have to sign it off as the head of news and current affairs.

Rights to reply and others

Further down the line, a whole new document must be prepared before the transmission of such a recording. We also work out very precisely how to frame the request for a right to reply from each person or organisation criticised, even if they are not the major feature of the programme. Again, lawyers are involved, as they are in the decision as to precisely how many days we will give people to respond.

Now we always did this sort of thing in some form but, even compared with three years ago, we have to be extraordinarily punctilious because, when we receive the responses from the lawyers of the organisation being investigated, more often than not, they will include only some vague reference to potential defamation but the main body of the letters consists of a detailed recital of Ofcom regulations with a series of claims we must surely be in breach of them. They also quote alleged rights their clients have under these rules.

When I say "letters" in the plural, we might receive several of these in one day, including letters which are obviously sent deliberately very late on, including on the day of transmission. They dance on the pinhead of the rules! One favourite is to claim we have breached the privacy of some poor innocent employee who is now living in terrible fear and distress. Another is to claim they have been given hardly any time to deal with the allegations rather than to answer them. Always they cite the Ofcom rules on fairness. Again, lawyers have to be involved in all these responses.

Complaining sorts

Sometimes the organisation makes a public statement about potential legal action but generally, if they do anything, it is to make a complaint to Ofcom. These complaints are sometimes of immense length including huge numbers of small points. One presumes they hope they might win at least one very small point they can then publicise. Of course, individual members of the public do sometimes go to Ofcom about a mistake they think we made. But the majority of the work I end up doing with regard to Ofcom is not about the protection of the reputation of a maligned ordinary individual but about a powerful organisation. Of course, this may be because the Ofcom regulations preclude us from attacking individuals unfairly even should we wish to do so.

Sri Lanka; a faraway place but making plenty of noise

The greatest amount of time that I have had to spend on complaints to Ofcom has not concerned anything which happened in this country but events which took place far away in Sri Lanka. Responding to complaints about our investigations into alleged war crimes and crimes against humanity committed by the Sri Lankan Government has cost Channel Four many hundreds of hours of lawyers' and my own time. The total cost to Channel Four I do not know but it must be many tens of thousands of pounds. As we are a public service broadcaster, ultimately owned by the people of Britain, one wonders if this is a good use of our money. Dealing with the complaints must also have cost Ofcom a great deal of money. Yet most people would think that a regulator was there to deal with matters pertaining to potentially wronged people in this country.

Our investigations began on *Channel Four News* where the team revealed evidence of terrible crimes committed near the end of the civil war in Sri Lanka in 2009. The Channel Four news team demonstrated clear evidence of the abuse of the civilian Tamil population and execution of Tamil Tiger rebels by government forces.

The Sri Lankan Government complained anonymously to Ofcom. ITN, which makes *Channel Four News*, insisted that the complainant was identified and then asked for this complaint to be dismissed on the very proper point that a country who would not be permitted to sue for libel should not have the right to complain to Ofcom as, if they were permitted to do so when criticised, it would be a clear restriction on freedom of expression. ITN had to pay for expensive legal advice. Before Ofcom decided the point the Government of Sri Lanka's lawyers withdrew their complaint. But this was just the beginning.

From News to Current Affairs

We then decided that the material which the news team had gathered was so important that we should make a one hour current affairs documentary *Sri Lanka's Killing Fields*. As our news is pre-watershed we had been unable to show much of the horrifying footage they had obtained. It showed, among other things, bound men being shot in the head at close range and naked, murdered women, their hands tied behind their backs, who appeared to have been raped before they were murdered.

All of this footage was authenticated carefully by technical experts and forensic pathologists. We demonstrated how tens of thousands of innocent civilians had been killed as the government advanced to crush the Tamil Tigers once and for all. Hospitals appeared to have been targeted and huge numbers died in alleged 'no fire zones' set up by the government. We were clear that the Tigers also showed great brutality and were themselves a cruel force often conscripting child soldiers and pioneering the use of suicide bombing.

We offered the Sri Lankan Government a right of reply. The film, transmitted in June 2011, caused a great stir internationally and has won many awards but the Sri Lankan Government hated it. Their representatives claimed that we had acted with sinister motives and the Sri Lankan Defence Secretary claimed that either Channel Four or ITN had received money to make the film from the Tamil Tigers themselves. They organised a major campaign against the programme, even making an entire film *Lies Agreed Upon* to rebut it as well as organising demonstrations and publishing a whole magazine condemning the film which was delivered to every Parliamentarian and leading journalists. I even received one myself.

No country but 118 individuals!

But you will remember that the Sri Lankan Government knew we would object strenuously if they made a complaint to Ofcom, as had happened when they complained about the news reports. However, this time 118 other people complained about a range of issues including impartiality, offensiveness and the broadcast of misleading material. You might like to know who those people were. I would like to know but I don't and even if I did, I couldn't tell you. They were and are anonymous.

These complainants seemed to be a very well informed lot about both events in Sri Lanka and Ofcom rules. We had to spend a lot of time answering them in detail. 118 is a lot of complaints and vastly more than even highly controversial films about Britain generally get. Ofcom then had to spend a lot of time considering both sides. In their ruling of October 2011 they stated, "It is important to note that the broadcasting of highly critical comments concerning the policies and actions of any state or government (such as happened here concerning the Sri Lankan Government's military forces) is not in itself a breach of the Code. It is, in fact, essential that current affairs programmes are able to explore and examine such issues and take a position even if that position is highly critical".

That, of course, was why the Sri Lankan Government couldn't complain. Lucky for them then that 118 other people, who remain anonymous, decided to complain. However, unluckily for them, Ofcom rejected all 118 complaints, stating "Channel 4 has a unique public service remit to provide programming that is challenging, diverse and likely to provoke debate. Consequently, the broadcaster has a history of broadcasting very challenging material from war zones (including graphic footage) and seeking out the voices and views of those who may not be represented. The images included in this programme, whilst brutal and shocking, would not have exceeded the expectations of the audience for this Channel 4 documentary scheduled well after the watershed with very clear warnings about the nature of the content". Phew!

Follow that

But more was to follow. We obtained more information and decided to make a further documentary *Sri Lanka's Killing Fields: War Crimes Unpunished* transmitted in March 2012. New evidence of alleged war crimes demonstrated the chain of command. The film looked at four key events during the war including decisions made by Sri Lankan Government forces to shoot into a 'no fire zone', the withholding of food and medicines from civilians and the torture and execution of captured prisoners.

'Complainant A'

This time there were only 20 complaints. But one of those complaints from a person identified by Ofcom in its report only as "Complainant A" was 141 pages long plus extensive appendices which included very detailed "evidence". Interesting to us was the fact that this complaint, although it cannot have come from the Sri Lankan Government bore an uncanny resemblance to all the criticisms made by the Sri Lankan Government.

We raised with Ofcom that two of the complainants, including Complainant A with his massive report, had a political interest in Sri Lanka and were not genuine viewers at all. The whole idea of the Ofcom complaints system, as most people have understood it, is that it is supposed to be for genuine viewers. However, Ofcom said it had to follow its procedures which made clear that it is the issues in a complaint which matter rather than the identity of the complainant.

They expressed appreciation for the problems caused to us by the huge length of the complaints. They wrote in November 2012 "It is not Ofcom's intention to place a disproportionate burden on broadcasters by asking them to comment in unnecessary detail on very lengthy complaints, especially when there is a risk that by doing so the broadcaster might be discouraged from producing controversial programmes." But remember, if a finding is made against us, it damages our reputation so of course we had to answer the detailed complaint in great detail. We even had to employ a barrister to assist so the rest of us could get on with our normal work.

Phew! Once more…

So, follow that

At the end of it all, this complaint was not upheld either. All these complaints were rejected and did not stop our investigations. As I write, we are preparing a further, feature length documentary film. However, we are a well-funded broadcaster, thanks to our revenue from television adverts and sponsorship, so we can afford the staff, the time and the money to defend our journalism against what has honestly felt like an onslaught. I have no complaint against Ofcom but it is worth newspapers being aware of what can be involved when you have a legally binding system of regulation. The organisations you will be investigating certainly know all about it and will be waiting for you.

Note on the contributor

Dorothy Byrne began her television career at Granada Television on *Granada Reports*, moving to *Union World* and then *World In Action*. She became the deputy editor and then editor of *The Big Story* on ITV before moving to Channel Four in 1998 as Commissioning Editor of *Dispatches*.

Why Leveson won't Work!

Peter Preston the former and very distinguished Editor of the *Guardian* for two decades has been here before. He knows a press enquiry when he sees one. He is very sceptical of the 'Leveson Effect'- chilling or not

The problem with the whole Leveson debate – before and as it continues – is that it's personal. It's personal for MPs with old scores to settle. It's personal for Downing Street with those LOL emails and for Scotland Yard who only managed to lots of inertia to begin with. It's personal for many media academics who don't want to teach a grimy, despised non-subject to their students and for many quality paper journalists who think the pall of the tabloids sullies their own self-image. It's personal for specialist media legal lawyers who see cash, briefs and their futures at stake. It's personal for celebrities who want to live a quieter, but maybe wilder, life. And, if I'm honest, it's personal for me as well.

40 Years experience

I first burrowed deep into the entrails of press regulation nearly 40 years ago, sitting beside the then editor of The *Guardian* as we gave evidence to the third Royal Commission on the Press. Sir Morris Finer, yet another barrister and judge, should have been running that show, but he was suddenly dead and Professor Oliver McGregor from the LSE had taken over. McGregor – like David Ross, the chairman of the 1947 Royal Commission – was a philosopher, and he had a puckish sense of humour. There were heavy issues of codes and compliance to discuss; but there was also the light touch of human understanding. The Professor seemed to understand what newspapers were about.

Which is why, a decade-and-a-half later, he was called to the rescue as the Press Council collapsed and a Press Complaints Commission, as recommended by Calcutt Mark One had to be set up in its place. We, the press under pressure, couldn't put another lawyer in charge. Sir Louis Blom-Cooper, the sixth stop on this legal regulatory branch line, had struggled valiantly to save the Council from extinction: but it couldn't truly be re-launched with conviction. The owners who paid the bills, the editors who had ceased to offer support, and a public still required to believe had all run out of patience. A welter of third-party complaints and a dragging weight of legal delay had finally drawn a line under this venture in self-regulation – especially, the critics said, because the Council couldn't play champion of a free press and, simultaneously, its invigilator.

The evidence of what was needed seemed clear enough. It was an inability to tackle complaints fast and decisively that had caused most public dismay. When Sir Frank Rogers at the Newspaper Publishers Association called for McGregor, he wanted something that responded to the mood, something entirely different. By then, Oliver McGregor was boss of the Advertising Standards Authority, a notably successful industry regulator (as it is to this day). Observers saw how smoothly and consensually it operated, and a natural symmetry with press complaints seemed to take easy shape. McGregor and his able young assistant, Mark Bolland, moved over to found the Press Complaints Commission: Matty Alderson, director of the ASA, would later sit on the commission as well – and, tout ça change, Lord Chris Smith from the ASA currently finds himself roped in as one of the three wise, independent men advising Lord Hunt on what comes after the PCC.

Was McGregor prescient?

Examine the discredited luggage McGregor jettisoned at transformation time. He ruled that there would be no lawyers on the new commission. He decided that complaints would be handled expertly and fast by a keen, non-legal team of complaints handlers. He set reconciliation of complaints as the first, prime task of these handlers. Better to get a correction or apology published within a few days rather than a few months. He demanded that editors themselves, rather than their deputies' long-suffering deputies, serve in rotation on the commission, because their involvement would register the importance of abiding by PCC rules in their own newsrooms.

McGregor scrapped any thought of championing the freedom of the press. That was not PCC business: too confusing. And he insisted that, quite separately, editors themselves should own the code the PCC policed, because they would draw it up themselves. The editor of the *News of the World*, Patsy Chapman, was the driving force and first chairman of the code committee. When most people, including Lord Justice Leveson, praise the reach and common sense of that code, they're really praising Patsy.

Dabbling in souls and bad information

I served on the commission early on (once Max Hastings at the *Telegraph* had done his stint). I sat on the code committee too – that bit about observing the code "in the spirit as well as the letter" is mine. I suggested the first hotline for readers to call and get something urgent done. In short, I was pretty engaged without the whole enterprise, spending countless Sundays at home with complaints for the next meeting spread out on the kitchen table.

What did I learn along the way? That editors – say Brian Hitchen of the *Daily Star* – were far more caustic in their comments and decisions than any of the lay members. Proper poachers became proper gamekeepers in an instant. That the most lugubrious cases usually began with an unwanted solicitor's letter from Peter Carter-Ruck or one of his legal brethren. And that the really perilous moments for the Commission came when Oliver McGregor, caught bleary-eyed at home by a TV camera crew, lurched into action without consulting the media professionals first. There was Mac on television condemning journalists for "dabbling in people's souls" (the people in question being Diana and Charles); and here, it transpired, was Andrew Morton, sitting quietly on Diana's sofa, taking notes.

Is Leveson just Mcgregor Mark Two?

Now, let's take every one of those points, of those lessons learned by hard experience, and put them to the Leveson test.

A role in championing press freedom? It's back. A commission with editors on board? They're off. A commission with active and senior journalists in close contact, briefing against pitfalls and pratfalls of the Di variety? Only retired and therefore prospectively out-of-touch hacks need apply. Lawyers? Back with a vengeance. The editors' own code? No: here come lay committee members.

This is all completely circular. Save for £1 million fines for outrageous behaviour and a supposedly cheap, quick tribunal to resolve complaints that might otherwise go to trial, this is back to the future. And anyone who truly supposes that the heirs and successors of P. Carter-Ruck won't argue, successfully, that clients need their expertise once a light touch tribunal is up and running have surely got heavy disappointment coming.

So you sense, perhaps, the cause of my personal gloom? We're all for progress, for moving forward, for seeking new solutions and scaling new mountains. But this is the old valley of despond from 22 years ago revisited. This is circular reform that gets us right back where we started from. And that very circularity sends out its own claps of doom.

Freedom to be right – and wrong

Press freedom, with inexorable logic, is the right to publish stories I disapprove of just as much as stories I wholly endorse. Press freedom operates inside a very broad church. And the kind of press freedom we see in almost every democratic nation – as monitored by the Reuters Institute – works with that grain of common sense. When something is wrong, it offers a complaints mechanism and the opportunity to correct or apologise. It does not fine or ban (unless the law is involved). It concedes, in short, that there is no perfection.

Self-regulation expects slippages, because that is absolutely in the instant, ultra-competitive nature of journalism. And the moving finger always twitches on, taking every fresh incident or outrage and adjusting the governing code to try to encompass it in true This-must-never-happen-again mode.

Go through the code we have now and, time and again, you can chart these shifts along the journey. There is no final, definitive set of rules. (See how even Lord Justice Leveson now permits some payments for information and compare that with past denunciations of cheque book journalism).

There is no final definition of the public interest. There is only a pragmatic series of changes in the light of events. And that, in its flexibility, isn't the nature of law – any more than it is the nature of courtroom decision-making. Thus, I increasingly feel, the entire search for some strict regulatory parameter that can be enforced by some mechanism the public can be deemed to "trust" is wholly misguided.

Whether or not the rules are underpinned, contracted or pavilioned in statute, they will always be broken by some newspaper or other in a situation that hasn't been visualised. And then what happens next? More sound and fury; more code tightenings; more clauses and allegations of bad faith; the whole rigmarole we know and don't much love. But, because it's the press, because clichés about' last chance saloons' haunt newsrooms, our freedom to investigate and report will become ever more circumscribed.

Views can't trump good information

There is a ratchet, and you can see it working in Leveson. Should police and reporters be able to meet and talk off the record? No. Can newspaper executives have freewheeling conversations with politicians any longer? Don't bank on it; and don't bring the proprietor when you come calling.

Is an investigation in its early stages in "the public interest"? Ask the advisory board of the new commission and expect the answer "No" if the story has clear risks attached – because no regulator is going to put his job in jeopardy without exercising legal caution. Must an extensive audit trail be organised, even in the early stages? Of course. Leveson, and the kind of regulation he recommends, sees journalism as an exercise in providing cases for courts to examine. He deals in the finished article, not the trek for truth. And there is absolutely no doubt that implementing all these regulations, and more, will have a chilling effect on getting stories in the first place.

Sir Brian Leveson may believe in a free press as passionately as he vows. He may welcome – or at least not frown too fiercely on – raucous, vituperative leader columns. But he doesn't understand where stories come from, or the lets, hindrances and perils that digging them out entails. Yet there's no point in freedom to publish if the facts that need to be revealed are stuck in the legal mud (even before changes to Freedom of Information access and the new Bribery Act chip in). And just in case you blithely assume that only the tabloids chasing Sienna Miller afresh will be hampered in their hunt, I've gone through some of the old cases the *Guardian* took up in my day and wanly concluded that many of them wouldn't have happened. Jonathan Aitken? Probably Lord Aitken of Smith Square by now, living out a blameless and well-heeled existence.

Lessons of the Tisdall Affair

But now I'm getting personal again, for the story of a life in journalism is, inevitably, the story of reports you've prised out and run, tales that have made a difference. The story of my life in journalism – at least for the last quarter century – is of watching, admiring and trying to help journalists overseas for whom their work is a constant, dangerous struggle. That became a preoccupation in the mid-eighties after I'd made a mistake that haunted me – and haunts me still.

Some of you may remember the case of Sarah Tisdall, the Foreign Office clerk who went to prison because she leaked details of US impending cruise missile installations to the *Guardian*. Most will remember the document in the case that ought to have been shredded on day two, not copied and distributed so that it couldn't be destroyed in short order if Special Branch came calling. My mistake.

But examine that saga now in two different lights. How does Leveson see the fate of MoD papers marked Top Secret along his audit trail? Is it in his version of the public interest to destroy stolen paper-work that describes how the Government of the day will slide the details of deployment through Parliament much like a three card trick?

One judge (the brilliant Richard Scott) asked to decide, found that we had the right not to hand over the document. That was his morning's work. But three appeal judges, sitting in the court next door that afternoon, reached a diametrically different conclusion. Their interpretation of the public interest shifted 180 degrees in 40 yards and 40 minutes (though I'm sure they'd all say that they believed in the freedom of the press).

And thus – we're onto that second light now – asks how you feel when you've fought and lost a high profile case with some pretty brutal consequences? You feel sick, but you also feel alone: which is when I signed up to work and raise funds for the International Press Institute in Vienna, whose business is helping to banish that loneliness, to make journalists in trouble understand they are part of a wider community.

And the abiding point there is discovering that we are indeed a community. Only ignorance divides journalists in the wise, well-fed sheep of the First World and the goats of the Third World. In fact, as you discover the moment you go out into the one world of journalism, everything connects. The friends in one world who suffer the most.

My journo friends world-wide

So I have friends in this connected world. Friends in Sri Lanka where a press council erected on PCC lines is one frail defence against government interference. Friends in South Africa, where the whole Leveson process is viewed with manifest distress by editors who really do stand on the front lines of freedom – and know that the ANC is watching. Friends in the West Indies, where Professor Pinker of the Press Complaints Commission took his travelling models for newspaper regulation. Friends in Zambia like Fred M'membe of the *Post* whose experiences of an editor's life in and out of prison are now helping write a PhD on the history of journalism's struggle for freedom in post-colonial Africa – a history that weirdly echoes the self- same arguments beloved of Prime Ministers in Downing Street and judges in the Strand. A pseudo royal charter in downtown Lusaka? Rule nothing out because the politicians who put secrecy and sycophancy first are always watching and waiting.

And that, in a way, is grimmest story of the lot – of the havoc we here at home, have wrought by letting a few cowboys run loose; of the damage we inflict on my friends – my friends – abroad when we do.

Days of Hope?

It's a sad tale of myopia and insularity. It's also a challenge to look both wider and deeper. So lock the supposed culprits up if they're guilty, by all means: that's what the law is for. But don't make it easier for the next generation of crooks and shysters to get away with it, because that would be pure tragedy.

If you view the essential interface as one where the press intrudes or overshoots and the object of their endeavours are victims, then the debilitating debate can never end – because journalism that's doing its job will always throw up messy conundrums. Statute or the threat of statute will always be invoked. But that's not the real world we live in – a world where, largely unremarked, the Legal Services Ombudsman is spurred into action over 7,000 times a year, chivvying slow-moving, incompetent or rapacious solicitors. In this world, we expect no perfection.

Our lone best hope is a steady, tolerable state. Our aim is to keep things under control rather than spiralling away. That's the reality before, during and after Leveson. It's the one that fits the press rather than mires it in constant confrontation with higher authority, a war waged in the name of a public which seems more tolerant than you'd expect, because it keeps buying the papers. And, personally, it's the one I embrace.

Note on the contributor

Peter Preston is a columnist for the *Guardian* and the *Observer*. He was previously editor of the *Guardian* for 20 years, from 1975 to 1995, a member of the Scott Trust from 1979 to 2003, Chairman of the International Press Institute from 1995 to 1997, and Chairman of the Association of British Press Editors. He has written two books, *Bess* (1999) and *The 51st State* (1998).

Ireland's Press Regulation: An Irish Solution to a British Problem?

Tom Felle a journalist turned 'Hackademic' at the University of Limerick looks at the Irish experience of a Press Council and Press Ombudsman, which seems to work and asks whether the press over the Irish Sea could learn lessons in light touch regulation from their Celtic cousins

The proliferation of UK newspapers, as well as all UK television, in the Irish Republic has had an indelible impact on Irish popular culture. The *Daily Mail, Sun, Mirror, Daily Star* and the *Sunday Times* all have Irish editions, which are heavily influenced by their Fleet Street parents, as well as including a significant amount of the main UK editions' content. While intrusions of privacy have not extended as far as law breaking and phone tapping in Ireland, all Irish newspapers have made mistakes, and some have been guilty of gross errors. The fallout from Leveson in the UK is likely to have an impact in Ireland because of the close cultural links between the two islands, and their connected media landscapes. But even without Lord Justice Leveson's much anticipated report, the publication by the *Irish Daily Star* in September 2012 of topless pictures of Kate Middleton (pictures that were not published in the UK edition) has seen a backlash by the public, the British co-owner threatening to close down the newspaper, the editor resigned and the Irish government warn it would introduce tough new privacy laws.

Circulation and the tightening market
Any discussion about the Irish newspaper market would be pointless without at least a passing reference to newspaper circulation since the end of the 'Celtic Tiger', and subsequent economic collapse of the Irish economy from 2007 onward. Figures from the Audit Bureau of Circulation (ABC, 2000-2012)[1] indicate that Irish newspaper sales, despite a major increase in population (CSO, 2007; CSO, 2011), remained relatively static during the first six years of the 2000s, and have collapsed by a quarter since then. Table 1 below details

aggregated figures for all daily and Sunday titles sold in Ireland between 2000 and 2012 (ABC, 2000 – 2012).

Table 1: Irish Newspaper Circulation (Jan-Jun figures used for comparison)

	2000	2006	2012	decline 2006-12
Tabloid daily	266,616	287,999	205,259	-29%
Broadsheet daily	374,522	418,469	326,502	-22%
Total daily	641,138	706,468	531,761	-25%
Tabloid Sunday	577,548	583,540	405,664	-30%
Broadsheet Sunday	635,423	677,217	509,046	-25%
Total Sunday	1,212,971	1,260,757	914,710	-27.5%

The tabloids have fared worst, and have been falling for longer. The market for tabloids peaked in the early 2000s and had been falling slowly until 2007, when sales of all newspapers began to free-fall. In 2005, 'red tops' represented 45 per cent of all daily newspapers sold in Ireland. By 2012, that figure had dropped to 39 per cent of an already significantly depressed market (Doyle, 2012). Irish editions of British 'red tops' including the *Irish Daily Star*, the *Irish Daily Mirror* and the *Irish Sun* fared among the worst, with declines of 33, 35 and 38 per cent respectively from their peaks (ABC, 2000-2012). The *Daily Mail* only entered the Irish market in 2006. In October 2012 the *Irish Sun* (72,500 daily sales) announced the departure of Irish editor Michael McNiffe and a re-structuring of its Irish operation to put more of what it termed the "DNA" of the *Sun* into its Irish edition in difficult economic circumstances (Halliday, 2012). Richard Desmond's – the co-owner of the *Irish Daily Star* (75,000 daily sales) – intentions are unclear in Ireland. Given tiny sales compared to their UK parents', these newspapers, along with the *Irish Daily Mirror* (57,000) and the *Irish Daily Mail* (51,000) cannot continue in perpetuity in Ireland if sales continue to slide.

The reasons the tabloids are suffering worst are of course worthy of their own book-length explanation, and cannot be examined in any great detail here, but the internet; pressure from other media (entertainment news is the bread and butter of a plethora of magazines and websites); perhaps the insubstantial nature of the product; and the demographics of its audience are all likely factors in their continued circulation demise. If the current rate of decline in Irish tabloid newspaper circulation of about 5 per cent per year continues, the total Irish market for tabloids will be less than 100,000 daily sales within 10 years.

The pressure to regulate

To suggest that the Irish press voluntarily decided en masse to regulate itself is a fallacy; the industry was forced to do so by the Irish government in the mid-2000s after a very real threat by the then Irish Justice Minister to introduce statutory press regulation, and a far-reaching (some might argue draconian) privacy law, to regulate the media. The Irish newspaper landscape had operated not dissimilarly to the British one for most of the previous 100 years, though Irish newspapers were in the main relatively tame compared to their British counterparts. Scandalised tales of the erotic activities of vicars and divorcees, or the paid-for stories of murder accused that were the stock and trade of Fleet St hacks in the 1950s (Hennessy, 2011) never made it into print in Ireland, and in the main political corruption remained unreported. Regulation of the press was anathema to journalists, who saw it as an attempt to censor a free press.

But Irish society opened up considerably in the later decades of the last century. A number of major Irish political corruption scandals lead to calls for the introduction of a raft of open government and transparency legislation (Felle and Adshead, 2009: 10). Laws including the *Freedom of Information Act* lead to a much more aggressive and investigative media. Increasing pressure on circulation from British tabloids, with a concurrent adoption by practically all Irish tabloid newspapers of a British tabloid 'model' of entertainment and celebrity news, and human-interest stories, also led to complaints by politicians (in some cases legitimately, in other cases out of concern for themselves) of media intrusions of privacy. To blame it all on the media is of course naïve in the extreme, Irish society changed, the public were interested in celebrity and entertainment stories, and the tabloids satisfied that demand. It is also important to note that celebrities were, and are still, often complicit with Irish tabloids' stories regarding their private lives, and supposed 'papped' pictures were often posed. A lot of good was also done by reporters: Irish investigative journalism in the public interest exposed corrupt practices of politicians such the *Irish Independent* journalist Sam Smyth's reporting of politician Michael Lowry's tax affairs (Smyth, 1997); and the various journalists including then *Sunday Tribune* political correspondent Geraldine Kennedy (later editor of *The Irish Times*); Frank Connolly of the *Sunday Business Post*; RTE journalists Charlie Bird and George Lee; and *The Irish Times'* Colm Keena, who reported stories of political corruption.

But along with the prize-winning scoops, there were also mistakes, and in some cases gross intrusions of privacy by the media. The media reportage of the mugging of the 14-year-old son of the then Irish Justice Minister Michael McDowell after the incident was reported to the police led to accusations of media invasion of his family by McDowell (Ruddock, 2006). However the fact that the son of the Justice Minister was mugged, it can be argued, was in the public interest given the minister was in charge of policing. In 2003 an expert committee set up by McDowell recommended statutory regulation of the press (Mohan, 2003). McDowell also proposed privacy legislation to outlaw intrusion by the media (Ruddock, 2006), however the Irish government held off after intense lobbying by newspapers. The promise by the press to introduce an independent council to regulate itself was a compromise. The Press Council was established in 2007, with the first Ombudsman, a former journalist and academic Prof John Horgan appointed in August that year. Prof Horgan, as noted by Leveson (vol 4 p1708-09) suggested the Council was introduced against the background of a very real threat of imposing statutory regulation if the industry did not introduce better standards. The 2009 Defamation Act, which updated Ireland's draconian libel laws, and the shelving of the Privacy Bill by the then government was a *quid pro quo* for introducing the Irish Press Council according to Prof Horgan (interview with the author, December 2012).

The Irish Press Ombudsman and Press Council

The Irish system is not unique in that the press is regulated voluntarily by a Press Ombudsman, and a Press Council – common to many jurisdictions. However the Irish system is unique in how it operates. The regulatory body, while recognised in legislation, is not a statutory regulator, and newspapers are free to sign up, or not (though all national newspapers are members, as well as virtually every regional newspaper). While the press in Ireland cannot be said to be controlled by statutory regulation, and the body that regulates the press in Ireland – the Press Council – is entirely independent, the Council is recognised explicitly in Irish law in the 2009 Defamation Act.

The 2009 Act does regulate the press, or impose regulation; it merely enshrines in law what the press itself agreed to do by setting up the Press Council and Ombudsman's office. The Act, in a schedule dealing with the Press Council, recognises the body and stipulates its membership and general functions, including protection of freedom of expression; protecting the public interest by ensuring ethical, accurate and truthful reporting; maintaining certain minimum ethical and professional standards and ensuring that the privacy and dignity of the individual is protected (*Defamation Act, 2009*, schedule 2.1). The legislation stipulates the independence of the Council, from both the State and from the press, with a majority of independent members representing the public interest. Membership totals 13, with seven independent members, five members representing the interests of media owners, and one member representing the interests of journalists. The chair must be an independent member. The Act also lays down three broad based criteria for the Press Council's code of practice, namely:

(a) ethical standards and practices,

(b) rules and standards intended to ensure the accuracy of reporting where a person's reputation is likely to be affected, and

(c) rules and standards intended to ensure that intimidation and harassment of persons does not occur and that the privacy, integrity and dignity of the person is respected (ibid, 2.4-2.7).

It is via this code of conduct that complaints to the Ombudsman's office are determined. All British newspapers with Irish editions subscribe to the code. Lord Justice Leveson noted this, suggesting "they do not appear to allow any principled objections to statutory underpinning of press self-regulation to get in the way of constructive and willing participation in this system" (vol 3, p1713).

Since 2008, the Ombudsman's office has received on average more than 300 complaints per year, though a large percentage are not valid for various reasons. Most complaints the office deals with are settled informally through informal discussion, and it is only in a small minority of cases that the Ombudsman makes a ruling. A sizeable number of these have been then appealed to the Press Council, or referred to the Council by the Ombudsman for a decision. Figures from the Irish Press Council's 2011 annual report shows that of 42 decisions by the Ombudsman, 22 were appealed, seven by newspapers and 15 by complainants, though none were allowed (Irish Press Council, 2011: 7). Other Irish Press Council figures show that on average about one third of complaints concern the truth and accuracy of reports, while privacy, respect for rights, comment and prejudice also feature prominently in complaints (Irish Press Council, 2008-2011).

The Irish Press Ombudsman has said his office has had a beneficial impact since it began its work. Irish newspapers initially had some reluctance in accepting they were wrong, but after four years editors are much better at engaging with his office, Prof Horgan has suggested (interview with the author, December 2012). There was also a cultural problem on the part of complainants, "when people feel they have been hard done by they want to find someone who is powerful and will hit the offender over the head, so when they come to me they wanted me to condemn," (ibid). In general, Irish news organisations also believe the Ombudsman and Council have worked well, according to *The Irish Times* managing editor and Irish Press Council member Eoin McVey.

> "The office has irritated a lot of newspapers, there are decisions newspapers don't always agree with, but by and large it generally seems to be working well. If anybody thinks there's money in it, they still go to the courts. We didn't expect it would reduce our legal bill, and it hasn't," (interview with the author, December 2012).

The powers of the Irish Press Ombudsman are limited however. The office has no power to initiate inquiries of its own volition, and can only act on receipt of a complaint. The only sanction is a finding against the newspaper, which the newspaper must publish with due prominence, and the office cannot impose a fine. The Ombudsman also has no power to act against a publication that has not signed up to the code.

Privacy and the Irish tabloids

The Irish press has not been involved to the same extent in breaches of journalism ethics, gross intrusions of privacy, or the scandalous law breaking in which some UK media organisations engaged. The systemic allegations of intrusions of privacy, bribery and criminality uncovered at the *News of the World* did not occur in Ireland. However Irish newspapers are not without sin, and have pushed ethical boundaries in search of an exclusive, and in some cases engaging in nefarious activities in the pursuit of a scoop. One former Justice Minister has accused the tabloid media in Ireland of paying police for tip-offs. He claimed the practice was covered up through the expenses system (Ryan, 2012). There have been allegations that some news organisations were involved in buying the social welfare records of a lottery winner (Healy, 2009). Pop guru Louis Walsh successfully sued the *Irish Sun* following its reporting of a complaint of his alleged sexual assault to Irish police. The complainant was subsequently charged and jailed for making a false complaint, and Walsh received €500,000 damages from the newspaper (O'Carroll, 2012). Walsh's lawyer Paul Tweed specifically pointed to Leveson when he criticised the newspaper for failing to check the story before running it:

> "This is a prime example of what we would look to see come out of Leveson. We are not trying to gag the press or stop investigations, but if there was a strong body that we could have rung before to get them to stop the story for 24 hours, we could have provided proof that Louis wasn't even in the place at the time and all this would have been avoided. They gave us just a few hours, they were determined to run it. Louis didn't get an apology then and we were hurtling towards court. It is only through this settlement we have got the apology. We need some sort of regulator that could act to pre-empt false stories getting in the paper, otherwise I think we are going to go back to square one" (ibid).

The largest libel damages in the history of the Irish state of €1.9m were awarded against Independent News and Media in 2009 after it published a series of articles about a PR consultant in 2004 in its' *Evening Herald* newspaper. She claimed the newspaper made false allegations that she got public contracts as a PR consultant because she was having an extra-marital affair with the then Environment Minister Martin Cullen (RTE, 2009).

The Duchess, the Irish tabloid, and those pictures
There are many other examples of such behaviour, but it was the publication of topless pictures of the Kate Middleton by the *Irish Daily Star* in September 2012 that drew the most recent criticisms of the Irish tabloid media. Initially, the then editor of the newspaper Michael O'Kane sought to defend the publication, suggesting the story was a legitimate one. "She's not our Queen, she won't rule over us at any stage, and they're just very good pics," he told the Irish state broadcaster RTE (2012a) however he was suspended from his post after the British co-owner of the paper media tycoon Richard Desmond (of Northern and Shell) threatened to close it. His Irish partner, Independent News and Media, described the threat as an over-reaction initially, however some weeks later it announced that O'Kane had resigned (RTE, 2012b). News of the resignation of an editor of an Irish newspaper with sales not even into six figures would not normally make headlines, but the announcement was reported

worldwide (ABC, 2012) perhaps underlining the seriousness of the breach and the interest in the story. Months earlier the *Irish Daily Star* had published nude photos of Prince Harry, boasting at the time that it was the only paper to do so, under the headline "FLASH HARRY: Playboy Brit prince bares crown jewels" (Casey, 2012). The move by Desmond to threaten closure may have been aimed more at protecting his interests in the UK, nevertheless *Star* editor O'Kane clearly misread the appetite in Ireland for publication, and the implicit impact Lord Justice Leveson was already having, before his report had even been published. It is arguable that had the pictures been published at any period prior to the Leveson Inquiry, O'Kane might still have a job.

A new Privacy Act?
Following the Kate Middleton saga the Irish Justice Minister Alan Shatter announced his intention to revisit the idea of introducing privacy laws in Ireland, saying he wanted to put an end to "creepy keyhole journalism" (McEnroe, 2012) and re-activate the bill his predecessor Michael McDowell had tried to introduce in 2006. The National Union of Journalists (NUJ) described Shatter's announcement as a "knee jerk reaction" to the *Irish Daily Star*'s publication of the Middleton pictures (Sheahan, 2012). All major Irish newspapers editorialised on the proposed privacy law, criticising the idea. *The Irish Times* (2012) described it as a "serious attack on the freedom of the press". Any move to introduce privacy legislation would be met with fierce opposition from the newspaper industry. In doing so, they may well point to Ireland's existing Press Council code, which includes protection for a right to privacy. Legal experts have argued that publication of the Kate Middleton pictures was already outlawed under Irish law (O'Dell, 2012).

However the minister is not alone in voicing concern about media intrusion. Influential barrister and newspaper columnist Noel Whelan argued that there was a need to protect ordinary citizens' right to privacy (2012a). He highlighted what he said were media intrusions into private grieving, especially in cases where journalists approached bereaved relatives seeking photographs and interviews, known in newsrooms as the 'death knock'. He claimed new privacy legislation was needed as the Press Council was "neutered" by virtue of the fact that it could not initiate its own investigations (Whelan, 2012b). While Whelan's point is valid, is also important to note that the reportage of tragic events is, in many cases, in the public interest. Some families want to talk to the media, and have their stories told.

The Irish Justice Minister may be well intentioned in his attempt to protect citizens from gross intrusions by the media, but the problem with privacy laws – particularly gagging orders – is that very often it is not ordinary citizens they protect, despite the best intentions of the legislators. Newspapers rightly argue that it is those with the means to hire teams of expensive lawyers, and use privacy legislation to gag newspapers from reporting on issues that are legitimately in the public interest, that will benefit the most from them. The issue will likely rest for the moment, but the Irish government will most certainly have one eye on Whitehall, and the fallout from Leveson, as well as the conduct of the Irish press, when deciding on future action. What is certain is that the newspapers, particularly the tabloids, are the authors of their own collective destinies on this issue.

Lord Justice Leveson's report and its' impact in Ireland

What Leveson has proposed – an independent, statutory body to regulate the press with the power to launch investigations and fine offenders for breaches – is significantly more far-reaching than what is in operation in Ireland, though it is arguable Leveson was inspired, at least in part, by the Irish system. Ironically, given the close cultural connections between the two islands, and the cross proliferation of media from the UK to the Irish Republic, it is undoubtedly the case that his report will also have consequences in Ireland. The Irish Communications Minister and political heavyweight Pat Rabbitte, who is responsible for planned new media mergers legislation, has suggested as much, saying the report "would be important for us all" (Slattery, 2012). Other cabinet ministers have also suggested changes (Edwards, 2011).

Leaving aside the thorny issue of statutory regulation, there are three substantial differences between what Leveson has proposed, and what is in operation in Ireland, that might indicate where future changes to the Irish model may occur. Firstly, Leveson recommends no more than one serving editor should sit on a press council. The Irish Press Council includes a substantial minority (five of 13 members) who represent Irish media organisations. Secondly, unlike what is proposed in Leveson's report, the Press Ombudsman's office can neither initiate its own investigations (it can only act on receipt of a complaint) nor receive complaints from third parties. Thirdly, Leveson recommends a system of fines for the press of up to 1 per cent of turnover or a maximum of £1m, whereas the Irish Press Council is unable to impose fines for breaches of its code (Leveson vol 4, p1803-1806).

Given the fact that the Irish system is generally perceived to be working well, it is unlikely that, any time soon, the Press Council or Press Ombudsman's terms of reference will be altered – though the "noxious twin" (*The Irish Times*, 2012) – privacy legislation – is a distinct possibility. Statutory regulation would quite simply be unacceptable in any democracy, including Ireland, and would be a direct challenge to a free press. A system of fines may be an issue of discussion in time, but as Ombudsman Horgan notes, the Irish system is delicately balanced, and may lead to newspapers withdrawing if fines became onerous (interview with the author, 2012). Tougher sanctions against the media, especially a system of fines, may have unintended consequences such as self-censorship or hesitance in conducting investigations (which, by their nature are risky ventures) for fear of the costs of mistakes. Equally, Horgan notes that a finding by his office against a newspaper, and the subsequent publication of that finding, is something "newspapers take extremely seriously… it's a major embarrassment, they do like going there if they can possibly avoid it" (ibid).

No system of press regulation can account for a news organisation that decides to be reckless, or wilfully break the law. Equally, in future pressures on newspapers to tighten budgets and cut corners might lead to, as the former *The Irish Times* editor and retired Garda Ombudsman Conor Brady argues, "lapses, errors and tendencies toward sensationalism" (Brady, 2012). The Irish Press Council is not the perfect system, but despite its shortcomings it is finely balanced, culturally sensitive and country specific, essentially an exercise in soft power, and arguably the right fit for Ireland.

It is worth noting that one of the biggest media scandals in Ireland in recent years was caused by the actions not of a newspaper but by the State-owned, taxpayer funded, national public service broadcaster Raidió Teilifís Éireann (RTE). It wrongly accused a Catholic priest of raping a minor and fathering a child while he served as a missionary in Africa in the 1980s (Cullen and McGreevy, 2011). The resulting furore saw the RTE managing director of news retire, other senior editorial staff moved, and the journalist responsible resign. A damning report into the culture and practices in operation at RTE's *'Prime Time Investigates'* unit concluded there were inadequate editorial controls, the methods used to investigate encroached on the priest's right to privacy and "group think" was in operation, which lead to inadequate fact checking (Carragher, 2011). The victim, Fr Kevin Reynolds, subsequently sued and was awarded substantial undisclosed damages, while the state broadcaster was fined €200,000 (RTE, 2011) by a Broadcasting Authority of Ireland (BAI) investigation.

The BAI is a statutory body, and it regulates broadcasters. The Irish Press Council is not a statutory body, though the system is anchored in legislation – an important distinction. This allows the press itself to remain uncensored, but with a self-regulating body to police abuses. However the BAI has the power to initiate its own investigations, and to impose fines. If the ability to launch independent investigations and impose fines is in existence for Irish broadcasters and is introduced in the UK for the press following Lord Justice Leveson's report, it may be hard to argue against such a system for the press in Ireland.

Notes

[1] While the original data is compiled by the Audit Bureau of Circulation, much credit is due to media marketing consultant and web analyst Conor Doyle of iLevel.ie, who collated much of the Irish national newspaper circulation data used in this article.

References

Audit Bureau of Circulations 'Island of Ireland' reports, 2000-2012. ABC: Hertfordshire.

Audit Bureau of Circulations 'National Newspapers' reports, 2000-2012. ABC: Hertfordshire

Brady, Conor (2012) 'Ireland does not need Leveson-type structures' in *The Irish Times*, December 4, 2012

Carragher, Anna (2012) *Report Pursuant to Section 53 of the Broadcasting Act 2009 in respect of the programme 'Prime Time Investigates – Mission to Prey' broadcast on 23 May 2011*. Dublin: Broadcast Authority of Ireland.

Casey, Colin (2012) Flash Harry: Playboy Brit prince bares crown jewels' in *Irish Daily Star*, August 22, 2012

Central Statistics Office (2007) Census of Population 2006. Dublin: Central Statistics Office

Central Statistics Office (2011) *Census of Population 2011: Preliminary Results*. Dublin: Central Statistics Office

Cullen, Paul and McGreevy, Ronan (2012) 'RTE shelves investigative series and concedes '"grave mistakes"' in *The Irish Times*, November 23, 2011

Doyle, Conor (2012) 'Media blog' various postings available at www.ilevel.ie/media-blog/print accessed December 26, 2012

Edwards, Elaine (2012) 'Varadkar hints at media legislation' in *The Irish Times*, July 26, 2012

Felle, Tom and Adshead, Maura (2009) *Democracy and the Right to Know. Proceedings of a conference marking the 10th anniversary of the Freedom of Information Act in Ireland 1998-2008.* Limerick: University of Limerick Papers in Politics and Public Administration, 2009/4

Government of Ireland (2009) *Defamation Act 2009*. Dublin: Government Publications Sales Office

Halliday, Josh (2012) 'Irish Sun's editor exits in strategic review' in *Media Guardian* online http://www.guardian.co.uk/media/2012/oct/16/irish-sun-editor-exits accessed December 23, 2012

Healy, Alison (2009) Civil servants warned on access to records' in *The Irish Times*, September 7, 2009

Hennessy, Mark (2011) in Before Murdoch, Fleet St was all about murder in *The Irish Times*, July 30, 2011

Hennessy, Mark (2012) 'Irish Press Council's autonomy vital, Leveson told' in *The Irish Times*, July 14, 2012

Leveson, Lord Justice Brian (2012) *An inquiry into the culture, practice and ethics of the press*, Vols 1-4. London: The Stationary Office

McEnroe, Juno (2012) 'Shatter vows to put end to "creepy keyhole journalism"' in *Irish Examiner*, September 19, 2012

Mohan, Hugh (2003) *Report of the Legal Advisory Group on Defamation*. Department of Justice, Equality and Law Reform (Ireland) 2003. Unpublished.

Newcomb, Alyssa, 2012 'Tabloid editor resigns over topless Kate Middleton pics' in ABC News online http://abcnews.go.com/blogs/entertainment/2012/11/tabloid-editor-resigns-over-topless-kate-middleton-pictures/ accessed December 9, 2012

O'Carroll, Lisa (2012) 'Walsh received €500,000 in damages from the *Sun*' in the *Guardian*, November 28, 2012

O'Dell, Eoin (2012) 'Flawed privacy bill offers us no protection' in *Irish Examiner*, September 19, 2012

Press Council of Ireland (2008-2011) *Annual Reports*. Dublin: Press Council of Ireland

Raidió Teilifís Éireann (2009) 'Leech awarded €1.9m in libel damages' in RTE News online http://www.rte.ie/news/2009/0624/leechm.html accessed December 17, 2012

Raidió Teilifís Éireann (2011) 'Fr Kevin Reynolds, RTE defamation case settled' in' in RTE News online http://www.rte.ie/news/2011/1117/reynoldsk.html access December 20, 2012.

Raidió Teilifís Éireann (2012a) 'Marian Finucane Show' Podcast September 15, 2012 http://www.rte.ie/radio1/marianfinucane/2012-09-15.html accessed on December 9, 2012

Raidió Teilifís Éireann (2012b) 'Editor of Irish Daily Star Michael O'Kane resigns' in RTE News online http://www.rte.ie/news/2012/1124/irish-daily-star-editor-.html accessed December 17, 2012

Ruddock, Alan (2006) 'Shameful privacy bill degrades McDowell' in *Sunday Independent*, July 9, 2006

Ryan, Philip (2012) 'Harney wanted PD merger with Fine Gael' in *Sunday Independent*, November 4, 2012

Sheahan, Fionnan (2012) 'Shatter solo run on photo row sparks Cabinet rift' in *Irish Independent* September 18, 2012

Slattery, Laura 'What lessons will be take from Leveson?' in *The Irish Times*, May 31, 2012

Smyth, Sam (1997) *Thanks a Million Big Fella*. Dublin: Blackwater Press.

The Irish Times (2012) 'A discredited bill' editorial, September 19, 2012

Whelan, Noel (2012a) 'Media's silence on privacy makes case for Shatter's law' in *The Irish Times*, September 22, 2012

Whelan, Noel (2012b) 'Leveson model a stronger system of press regulation' in *The Irish Times*, December 1, 2012

Note on the contributor

Tom Felle is a former Independent News and Media journalist and has worked as the *Irish Independent*'s Midlands correspondent. He has worked as a journalist in Europe, Australia and in the Middle East and has contributed to a wide range of international publications on foreign affairs and political issues. In 2006 and 2007 he was Beirut Bureau Chief of the Lebanon News Agency. He teaches newspaper reporting at the University of Limerick, Ireland. His research interests include FOI and open government; media and democracy; social media; and data journalism.

Newspaper ombudsmen and other internal accountability mechanisms

Damian Carney of Portsmouth University looks beyond the question of statute and asks whether the way to better journalism is better internal ethical policing in newsrooms by ombudsmen

Most commentary on the Leveson Report has focussed upon the form and powers of any new press regulator. This is not surprising given the widespread belief that the Press Complaints Commission had failed in ensuring the press acted ethically and lawfully in the past. However, what has often been overlooked in the discussion of Lord Justice Leveson's recommendations is that it also requires a strengthening of the internal controls within newspapers. It is this aspect of the proposals which will be examined in this chapter, and in doing so the chapter suggests that many (but not all) of the internal controls could be performed by a newspaper ombudsman.

The need for more 'robust' internal controls

The Leveson Inquiry was triggered in part by concerns about the unethical / unlawful behaviour of journalists and newspapers. In particular, there were worries about the widespread use of phone-hacking and other means of interception of communications used by the press to obtain stories. The conviction of Royal Editor Clive Goodman in January 2007 for conspiracy to intercept communications led to three inquiries at *The News of the World* ('NOW') (Culture Media and Sport Select Committee 2012: para 18) which all failed to identify any other example of wrongdoing. Yet by December 2012, Operation Weeting (phone-hacking), Operation Elveden (corrupt payments to police officers) and Operation Tuleta (email and computer hacking) had led to the arrest of seventeen former *NOW* employees with seven being charged with criminal offences. This suggested that the mechanisms used to prevent and detect unethical and/or unlawful activities within the newspaper industry (or at least certain sections of it) were inadequate.

The Leveson Report also examined the response of the *NOW* to Goodman's conviction and particularly the assertion of Colin Myler who became *NOW*'s editor soon after that conviction, that he had improved the internal protocols and systems at *NOW* and he had made it

> "...abundantly clear that the employee understands and accepts that failure to comply with the requirement, which was PCC, criminal law, will lead to disciplinary proceedings, which may result in summary dismissal." (Leveson 2012a: Volume II, 496)

However, Leveson found that during Myler's period as editor (from 2007 to 2011) only one verbal and one written warning had been given to *NOW* journalists despite at least five upheld PCC complaints, and 19 defamation actions (including 12 settled) since 2005 (ibid: 503) which must be evidence of unethical and in some cases unlawful activities. The lack of disciplinary action during this period was, according to the report reflective of

> "it ... not [being] possible to ascertain who, if anyone, had senior responsibility for ensuring legal and ethical compliance within the organisation." (ibid: 528).

Indeed in giving evidence to the Inquiry the senior management all had different views as to which of them were responsible for ensuring the ethical behaviour of their journalists, with none of them accepting it was their own responsibility (ibid: 529). This suggested that management were not really concerned about their reporters maintaining ethical standards, and the clear reference to compliance with the PCC Code and criminal law in journalists (and third party contracts) was little more than window dressing. A culture had grown up in the paper in which the industry code of ethics and the criminal law were not taken seriously.

The need for a proper and fair internal complaints system
The Leveson Report also examined how newspapers treated complaints from the subject-matter of stories and the general public. It noted that a number of newspapers had adopted clarification and correction columns (including one announced by the *Daily Mail* in October 2011 in the early days of the Inquiry), and complimented those publications using a newspaper ombudsman on how they dealt with complaints (ibid: 709). However, the Report also found,

> "... there was also substantial evidence of poor practice, showing first, that the complaints process can be (sometimes, it was thought, deliberately) protracted, complicated and expensive; second that there is a strong reluctance in parts of the press to apologise even when it is not in dispute that a story was incorrect; and third, that apologies, retractions and corrections are frequently given substantially less prominence than the offending article and therefore fail to satisfy those who are aggrieved." (ibid)

The Report examined in particular the treatment of the parents of Madeline McCann who had been subjected to prolonged and defamatory press coverage. Meetings with newspaper editors to stop these articles proved to be to no avail; when legal action was threatened against papers in the Express newspaper group the response was not to publish an apology but to get a journalistic advantage, namely to allow the McCanns to give an exclusive to *OK! Magazine* (a magazine owned by the same publisher) (ibid: 709 – 710). Refusals to apologise or place the apology in the same place within the paper as the original (inaccurate) article were common (ibid: 710, 714 – 715), and it seemed that many newspapers would only apologise, or retract the original article, if the complainant proved to be willing to pursue libel actions. Newspapers frequently delayed addressing the complaint, sometimes ignoring the initial complaint, at other times making the process deliberately complicated and drawn out. Several newspapers adopted a 'give an inch at a time approach' which seemed comprised of denial of the inaccuracy; then apologise but refuse to print the apology or retraction, then agree to an apology but not in terms acceptable to the complainant; or if it was acceptable it was in a less prominent place than the offending article; and then after an agreement had seemingly be made either unilaterally alter the terms or seek to renegotiate. One thing was clear, namely that in the majority of newspapers and other print publication there was a lack of a transparent, fair and consistent mechanism to deal with complaints.

Lord Justice Leveson's recommendations on internal controls in newspapers

The Report concluded,

> "It is abundantly clear from this that [the] current [system] of ... internal governance in some parts of the press... [has] not worked and are not working." (Leveson 2012a: Volume IV, 1748)

And with this in mind it made the following recommendations:

- That regulated publications should have "appropriate internal governance processes, transparency on what governance processes they have in place", and give the regulator "notice of any failures in compliance, together with details of steps taken to deal with failures in compliance" (Leveson 2012b: Recommendation 10)

- "that newspapers publish compliance reports in their own pages to ensure that their readers have easy access to the information" (ibid Recommendation 34(a))

- "that a named senior individual within each title should have responsibility for compliance and standards" (ibid Recommendation 34(b))

- Complaints should have "adequate (and timely) processes in place for dealing with complaints from readers and members of the public about breach of standards" with this process being the first port of call which had to be exhausted before a complaint to the regulator could be made (Leveson 2012a: 1764)

- There should be annual reports by publications on how they dealt with complaints and complied with the regulator's code. (ibid)

The newspaper ombudsman: an introduction
Leveson commented that readers' editors or newspaper ombudsmen had proven to be an effective system of dealing with complaints (Leveson 2012a: 709) and noted that the MediaWise Trust recommended that any publication with a circulation above a certain level should be required to appoint such an individual (Leveson 2012a: 1687). This suggests that in the future many more newspaper or newspaper groups will adopt this mechanism as its' internal complaints process.

The newspaper ombudsman concept originated in the United States in the 1960s, albeit with Japanese precursors in the 1920s and 1930s (Maezawa 1999). The original ombudsman was established by the *Louisville Courier-Journal* in 1967, and the post holder here investigated and adjudicated upon complaints by readers as to the accuracy of stories and journalistic standards, but it was not until the 1980s that the paper followed the trend in other North American news organisations and used a regular column in the newspaper to, inter alia, report on his judgments.

Newspaper ombudsmen in the United Kingdom
In 1985 *The Mirror* newspapers appointed Sir William Wood (a retired civil servant) as the first newspaper ombudsman in this country (Lycett, 1988). Most national newspapers created readers' editors around the time of the Calcutt Inquiry in 1989/1990 but most had fallen into abeyance by the early 1990s, although they re-appeared again in many national newspapers in the late 1990s. Today, the *Guardian, Observer,* both *Independent* titles, and more recently *The Sun* have appointed ombudsmen, whilst in the regional press *The Belfast Telegraph, The Scotsman* and *The Ipswich Evening Post* all have such a position in their paper.

A cynic may argue that most national newspapers have only shown an interest in the concept of an ombudsman when their ethics have been called into question and more regulation was threatened. It could also be argued that the majority of newspapers when they have had such positions have not tended to give a great deal of publicity to the posts and functions beyond their launch and consequently can justify their abandonment on grounds that they are unnecessary, or too costly, for the benefits they bestow on the readership. However, in the post-Leveson era, if his recommendations of robust and transparent internal complaints procedures are to be complied with a newspaper ombudsman would be a perfect mechanism to perform this role.

The newspaper ombudsman – a contested role
The label of 'reader's editors' often given to newspaper ombudsmen, reveals a frequently articulated view in North American newspaper that they were to "represent the public," (Starck & Eisele 1999) or be the "readers' advocate" (van

Dalen & Deuze 2006). The Organisation of Newspaper Ombudsmen suggests that "[a]n ombudsman is there to explain how and why the news organization operates and to hold it to account" (Dvorkin 2010: 8) and "a powerful commitment to making journalism better by letting the public insider the process of information gathering, editing and distribution"(ibid: 7). Others are more critical labelling such positions as a 'public relations' gimmick (Ettema & Glasser 1987), or portraying the holders as the 'newspaper's ambassador' (van Dalen & Deuze 2006) a consequence of many being either part-time ombudsmen performing other journalistic and editorial roles for the newspaper and/or being seasoned journalists at that organ.

The newspaper ombudsman: a complaints mechanism

If the newspaper ombudsman is to perform his complaints function adequately he must be clearly independent and equipped with both adequate powers of investigation. Independence may be guaranteed by fixed term 'no fire, no re-hire' type contracts, or the appointment of outsiders (Dvorkin 2010: 12). The ombudsman's independence must also be clearly demonstrated in relation to both any newspaper column he possesses and any recommendation or decision he makes as to the remedy that the complainant has. The new regulatory background (if it is based on Leveson's recommendations) should strengthen this. The Report recommends that the new Board should have the power to "direct the nature, extent and placement of apologies" (Leveson 2012a: 1767) and this should ultimately be something which the newspaper ombudsman decides when he has concluded there is a need to publish an apology. Although the Leveson Report envisages the publication and complainant negotiating on this, if there is a time frame which is given for resolution then the ombudsman must have the ultimate power within the internal complaints mechanism to decide what form the apology should take. If the complainant is unhappy with this he can ultimately complain to the new board.

In terms of investigatory powers an example may illustrate what is required. If for example, a complaint is made that a reporter has obtained information unethically, the ombudsman must be able to question or seek the views of the journalist concerned and look at whatever notes he has made on the story. He must be able to have the ear (and support) of the editor to deal with uncooperative employees. Suspicion of newspaper ombudsmen have on occasions led to conflict with both editors, and suspicions by reporters of their role, and in the post-Leveson era their likely backing by the new regulator could result in the development of the same type of resentment which internal affairs officers' experience within the police. The extent of such opposition is likely to be dependent upon the attitude taken by the senior editors to the role of the ombudsman, and the approach taken by the ombudsman to resolve complaints. The 'questioning' approach is investigatory in nature, whilst 'seeking the views' of journalists may suggest that the role of ombudsman is more of a mediator between complainant and journalist/newspaper. The latter is less confrontational and more likely to get the co-operation of the journalists investigated, but unless properly managed may have the negative effect of undermining the trust of complainants.

One way in which this can be overcome is by making it clear to the complainant as to what the process is, what the powers of investigation are, and what remedies the ombudsman has within his powers. This is necessary to meet the transparency obligation suggested by the Leveson Report and would be a major step, even for those UK newspapers that currently have ombudsmen. None as far as can be seen, explain to the complainant the time frame in which complaints will be made, and all could benefit from explaining the process and remedies.

The newspaper ombudsman: compliance with ethics

Dvorkin clearly envisages that newspaper ombudsman also has an important role in ensuring the maintenance of journalistic standards (Dvorkin 2010: 7-8). Any time a complaint is reported upon in a newspaper, the journalist concerned and other staff will have an indication of the boundaries of acceptable journalistic behaviour. In many ombudsmen's columns the content is often about broad issues of newsgathering and journalism, not only within the organ in which it appears but also more generally. The ombudsman is therefore identifying the standards expected. However, it has been claimed that newspaper ombudsmen have had little effect upon the journalists within the organ in which they operate (Pritchard 1993: 79 and 85). Meyers suggests that to be effective in this aspect of their position, the newspaper ombudsman must create an "ethical climate in the newsroom" which considers both internal values (such as accuracy and scoops) and external principles (such as concerns about privacy) (Meyers 2000: 252).

Meyers suggests that the ombudsman must be able achieve this by making recommendations in regards to the discipline and reward of individual journalists. Although the sanction would be imposed by the editor of the newspaper, this power would have a degree of impact in the post-Leveson regulatory world as it bound to be something which needed to be referred to in the annual compliance reports. An editor's regular failure to follow his newspaper ombudsman's recommendations that a journalist be sanctioned, and he is not, may call into question the adequacy of the internal controls.

Meyers' suggestion whilst welcomed envisages a rather limited role in relations to ethics compliance for the ombudsman. As essentially someone who is trying to ensure journalistic standards he should be expected to take on a role not only as the complaints mediator or resolver, but as a guardian of ethics. His role would be to demonstrate, teach and guide journalists as to what is ethical or not. In this capacity he could (and perhaps should) also act as the confidante for those journalists wishing to whistleblow or raise concerns about the newsgathering / reporting of that news organ is performed.

Annual compliance reports and other internal mechanisms

Leveson's recommendation that each publication, or publication group, publishes an annual compliance report is an innovative and necessary requirement to demonstrate the effectiveness and transparency of the internal controls. It should require clear data about the number of complaints, how they were resolved and if necessary any sanction imposed upon company's employees for ethical breaches. However, there must also be a requirement that this report is prepared by the newspaper ombudsman rather than editorial staff or others in the company. This would fit into the general role that the ombudsman would have, and would be written by an individual who was involved in the process, who is independent of the publication, and who is committed to ensuring ethical compliance. The report could include additional information about ethics training or issues which have not been the source of complaint.

Conclusion

Leveson's recommendations require UK newspapers to put in place strong internal mechanisms to ensure ethical behaviour and an adequate system to deal with complaints. Properly implemented they will require complainants and the general public to know that ethics and complaints are taken seriously. Though other mechanisms could be created to perform these tasks, a strongly equipped newspaper ombudsman is capable of performing most of these inter-related functions. The position has other benefits. Although it might seem an expensive option, and economic considerations have often been a justification in the past to cut such positions in the past, there is evidence that the existence of this position at The *Guardian* has saved litigation costs and it is one of the cheapest of options for a newspaper to resolve disputes. It can, if properly operated, also offer speedy resolution to problems. Finally, as it is a concept that has been around both in the United Kingdom and elsewhere for some time, it means newspapers can adopt and adapt something which already exists within the industry, rather than try to create some new mechanism from scratch.

References

House of Commons Select Committee on Culture Media and Sport, (2012) 11th Report – News International & Phone-Hacking (HC 903-I), London: Stationary Office

Dvorkin, Jeffrey (2010), 'The Modern newspaper ombudsman: a user's guide,' Place of publication unknown: Organisation of News Ombudsmen

Ettema, James S. & Glasser, Theodore L. (1987), 'Public accountability or public relations? Newspaper ombudsmen define their role', Vol. 64 No.1 Journalism Quarterly pp3-12

Leveson Inquiry (2011) Terms of reference, available online http://www.levesoninquiry.org.uk/about/terms-of-reference/ accessed 23 December 2012

Leveson, Lord Justice (2012a), An inquiry into the culture, practices and ethics of the press report. (HC 780), London: Stationery Office

Leveson, Lord Justice (2012b), An inquiry into the culture, practices and ethics of the press report: executive summary (HC 779), London: Stationery Office

Lycett, Andrew 'US Scribers like their sheriffs – The ombudsman system spreading among newspapers in America would please John Birt', The Times, 8 April 1988 available on Nexis accessed 23 December 2012

Maezawa, Takeshi (1999) 'The controversy over the origins or functions of ombudsmanship', Organisation of Newspaper Ombudsman, 23 November 1999. Available online at http://newsombudsmen.org/category/articles/origins accessed 23 December 2012

Pritchard, Stephen (1993) 'The impact of newspaper ombudsmen on journalists' attitudes' Vol. 70 No. 1 Journalism Quarterly pp 77-86

Starck, K. and J. Eisele (1999) 'Newspaper Ombudsmanship as viewed by ombudsmen and their editors', Vol. 31 No.4 Newspaper Research Journal pp37–49

Unknown, 'The Guardian's Readers Editor'. Date unknown. Available online at http://www.guardian.co.uk/theguardian/page/readerseditor accessed 23 December 2012.

van Dalen, Arjen & Deuze, Mark (2006) 'Readers' advocates or newspaper ambassadors: newspaper ombudsmen in the Netherlands', Vol. 21 Issue 4 European Journal of Communications pp 457- 475

Note on the contributor

Dr Damian Carney is a Principal Lecturer in the School of Law at the University of Portsmouth. He is currently writing a monograph on the protection of journalists' confidential sources and is preparing a bid for research to look into the historical and future role of newspaper ombudsmen in the United Kingdom.

Who regulates the regulator?

Professor Chris Frost, author of a standard journalistic tome of ethics, takes a step back from the fray, rises above the heat of debate and asks the question '*Quis custodiet ipsos custodes?* in the post-Leveson world

Lord Justice Leveson's report was always going to be controversial as he himself recognised. The various vested interests: the press, obviously, but also parliament and the police as well as a number of organisation representing sections of the public including the victims would ensure that his words would be carefully perused, but not always so carefully reported.

As these various interests combed through Leveson's two thousand pages of evidence and recommendations seeking comments that would support their campaign's viewpoint, battle has raged around relatively few contentious points.

There is general acceptance, even within the press, that the present system of self regulation is broken beyond repair. The Press Complaints Commission is closing down and Prime Minister David Cameron has started the search for a new regulator by welcoming most of the Leveson report's recommendations in the House of Commons.

A free press at risk?

Whilst Leveson LJ, many politicians and most of the public believe we need a regulator with teeth and one that has universal writ, there are some, particularly those working in journalism, who believe that any regulation of the press risks damaging the concept of a free press. If a few publishers want to agree a code of conduct and come together to police that, then of course that is their choice, they say, but to insist that all should be obliged to stand by a regulator is unacceptable.

Journalists are trained from an early age to be sceptical to the point of cynicism about the different agendas people bring to the business of the media and they are well aware that the desire of many people to limit the press's power to publish is often driven by the basest of motives so it is hardly surprising that journalists should be particularly suspicious of anything that has the stated intention of improving standards with its clear implication of control. But wanting to prevent those with base motives from covering their tracks is not, of itself, a good enough reason to demand to be able to write anything you want when you want. I have yet to meet anyone who thinks one should be allowed to write a lie about someone and publish it as journalism. Nor is the press itself immune to base motives. As Baroness O'Neill Professor of Philosophy at Cambridge told the Inquiry: "I've noticed a lot of misuse of the phrase "independent regulation" for what is actually self-interested regulation. So what we need first to do is to get away from that…" Leveson (2012: 1758)

The individual's right to free expression, the right to free opinion and the right to receive information are vitally important in a democratic, free society but none of these is under any threat from a press regulator however constituted. Individuals will still be able to express themselves face to face, in letters, emails, publications, blogs tweets and elsewhere exactly as they do now.

Identifying press freedom

Press freedom is generally taken to mean the freedom of newspapers and magazines to write what they like restrained only by the law of the land (itself a regulation, of course). Any publications, books, leaflets or pamphlets all qualify for freedom of the press because they are one manifestation of the right to free expression of any citizen. The big differences between free expression, whether face to face or on the internet or elsewhere and newspaper freedom to publish, is both the huge power a newspaper has to push its views to millions of people as a regular whisper in one's ear and the limited ownership of newspapers that leads to tight control of the range of views people receive whether about individual stories or wider issues. Many giving evidence to the Leveson Inquiry were concerned that one of the biggest impediments to a free and pluralistic press in the UK is ownership. A commercially driven press, answerable to its shareholders, puts just as many limitations on a free press as any government is capable of in a mature democracy.

Much has been made in the debate about press freedom that surrounded the Leveson Inquiry that we are returning to the days of John Milton and press licensing. However, the idea that Leveson's backstop regulator risks following in the footsteps of the 1644 government that Milton thwarted is fantasist nonsense. Milton wrote the Areopagitica as an appeal to Parliament to rescind the Licensing Order of 1643. This would have brought publishing under government control by restoring the printing monopoly of the Stationer's Company thus ensuring an official censor would need to approve a writer's work before it could be published. No such order has been either suggested or considered by Leveson or anyone else.

It seems redundant to reproduce here Milton's arguments about censorship limiting the discussion of both good and bad ideas and the fear of officially sanctioned thought, vital thought they are. No one reading this text is likely to oppose them but then neither is anyone suggesting pre-publication censorship or prior approval in any suggested regulatory system. The only potential for limitation in such circumstances is the alleged 'chilling effect' that would come from having to follow an accepted code of practice even though I don't recall anyone previously condemning the PCCs code of practice as chilling free expression.

Some people seem to argue that press freedom is so important that the press should be allowed a licence available to no one else. I can see no good argument for this – the press should be allowed exactly the same right of free expression as anyone else, neither more nor less. It is no longer the sole outlet for public debate and the presentation of news to support comment and opinion is a commercial activity that should require adherence to understood and shared standards. To do otherwise is to invite governments to legislate as they have done with the right to reputation, fair trial and (to a lesser extent) privacy.

All or nothing?

The big divide in the debate about press freedom is twofold:

Should the press be able to publish what it likes?

Are there consequences that may or should follow that?

Leveson leaves the first unchanged and all newspapers will still be able to publish what they like. However he does propose that publishers should take responsibility for ensuring their newspapers follow generally agreed norms of journalistic behaviour. We already accept that the law says what publishers must do in order to protect individual rights. The state already has a battery of laws that interfere with press freedom in order to prevent harm or the breach of individual human rights. Those who oppose the need for tougher self-regulation should be wary for it would be but a small step for the law to develop incrementally to support higher standards in a way that would be far more dangerous to press freedom than a regulator. It is clear that the public is no longer prepared to leave those decisions in the hands of a press that is either unwilling (for fear this may be a breach of free expression) or unable to regulate (for fear it will damage its commercial opportunities).

There is also a clear majority in the House of Commons for strong regulation: the Labour Party has published a Bill that mirrors Leveson's recommendations and the Liberal Democrats also favour some sort of legislative framework. In addition, more than 70 Conservatives, mainly MPs have signed letters to the press supporting statutory underpinning and several more have since publicly expressed their support. In these circumstances there seems little point (as some industry insiders want) in arguing about whether a statutory backstop is a step too far. If the industry delivers the goods on regulation, a backstop regulator as identified by Leveson will not be needed and if it doesn't the backstop regulator will be put in place. Either way, there is press regulation that will cover all the industry.

Statutory recognition?

Lord Justice Leveson of course has made it clear he would prefer not to use the big stick of a backstop regulator brought in if all else fails. He wants statutory underpinning so that rewards or incentives for membership could be recognised. Many witnesses to the Inquiry suggested forms of incentives from tax-breaks to offering some protection against civil claims for members who could show they upheld the regulator standards. All of these would require that the agency offering or controlling the incentive would be able to identify that a publisher was a member of a satisfactory regulator. The body itself need not be set up by statute, just a recognition of its existence and ability to provide satisfactory regulation. Such a system exists in Ireland where the Defamation Act obliges the courts to consider a defence of reasonable publication to newspapers that subscribe to the Irish Press Council and follow its code of practice. Frost (2010: 289). (See Felle, p 165 in this volume)

Lord Lester went the statutory recognition route, proposing the Independent Press Bill to the House of Lords to bring about recognition. It contains only three clauses: calling for the President of the Supreme Court to certify that a proposed Independent Press Council complies with requirements to promote and protect freedom of expression and freedom of the press; encourage and maintaining high professional; consider complaints of professional misconduct; and provide redress and impose sanctions for professional misconduct. There no criteria on membership.

Statutory underpinning?

Those championing statutory underpinning are adamant this is not statutory regulation, although opponents don't see it that way. Lord Black, representing the broad swathe of the publishers, told Lord Justice Leveson that press regulation should be free of statutory intervention:

> "I have always believed – and I believe it is a view across the bulk of the industry – that self-regulation is the guarantor of press freedom and interference (sic) from state control." Leveson (2012: 1673)… "statutory underpinning is simply a term of art for a form of statutory control. I don't believe there is a halfway house between them". (ibid. 1675)

Leveson LJ said that many of the proposals submitted advocated some form of statutory underpinning but Tim Suter [a media consultant and former Ofcom-the regulator for much of broadcast in the UK- Partner for Content and Standards] best explained the difference:

> "By state control I think everybody has set up this dangerous notion that the state would dictate what the press could do, would dictate the standards by which the press had to operate and would form judgments as to what was or was not acceptable. I see statutory underpinning as being further removed from that, or setting a framework within which the regulation happens, but where the regulation itself is carried out by

independent bodies dealing directly with the press and the regulated entities." (ibid. 1673)

So statutory underpinning would identify the body and its purpose and would lay down criteria, possibly including membership, which would need to be recognised in order for the regulator to fulfil the certification requirements. The Labour Opposition has proposed a Bill that fits into this model: It has six relatively short clauses and a longer schedule, calls for ministers to be obliged to uphold press freedom and sets up a 'recognition panel' of the High Court with the Lord Chief Justice sitting with other judges and 'such assessors, as the LCJ may nominate for that purpose'. All such assessors must possess sufficient independence and expertise. This panel must grant an application from a 'Press Standards Trust' if it meets the criteria. The Bill identifies criteria for this new body including:

- Membership must be independent of parliament and the press;
- Membership must cover all national papers and "substantially the totality" of the rest of the press;
- The body must be governed by a board independent of the executive and Parliament and a majority independent of the press;
- The body must have sufficient medium-term funding;
- It must have a standards code binding on every member of the body;
- The board must also issue guidance on the concept of public interest in relation to the code;
- Each member must have internal governance arrangements including a free system for receiving and resolving complaints from the public;
- The board must maintain a complaints scheme binding on the body's members;
- The body must establish and maintain an arbitration scheme for civil claims.

Statutory regulation?
Some Leveson witnesses wanted a statutory regulator. This would require the setting up of some sort of Commission or Tribunal. There were fewer supporters of this form of regulation at the Leveson Inquiry. Sir Louis Blom-Cooper called for a statutory commission and the Campaign for Press and Broadcasting Freedom wanted a Media Standards and Press Freedom Council while the Media Regulation Roundtable sought a Media Standards Authority. Statutory regulation of this type would move the ownership of press standards away from the industry to these new authorities.

This was not the first time this statutory regulation had been proposed. Sir David Calcutt was asked to review the PCC in 1992 and reported back in 1993 saying the PCC should be wound up and a statutory Press Complaints Tribunal put in its place. Frost (2010: 238). John Major's fear of a hostile press at a time of a small parliamentary majority was probably the report's doom leaving David Mellor, the cabinet minister responsible, to warn the press about their 'drinking in the last chance saloon'. The National Heritage Committee (predecessor of the Culture Media and Sport Select Committee) meanwhile recommended a Press Commission with the power to fine and order compensation and a statutory press ombudsman. (Ibid. 239)

A backstop regulator?

Despite this long history of 'drinking in the last chance saloon' Lord Justice Leveson was not minded to use the statutory option, at least not while the industry was prepared seriously to consider self-regulation:

> "I will say again, because it cannot be said too often, that the ideal outcome from my perspective is a satisfactory self -organised but independent regulatory body, established by the industry, that is able to secure the voluntary support and membership of the entire industry and thus able to command the support of the public." Leveson (2012: 1771)

However, he was willing to make it clear that if self-regulation failed it should be replaced by a statutory regulator. This was Leveson's warning about the key problem identified by most witnesses at the Inquiry. What happens if a major publisher refuses to join the new self -regulator? Can self-regulation then work? This is not an idle mind game. One of the reasons the PCC was seen as so weak was its need to play to the lowest common denominator. Its inability to persuade Northern and Shell (who publish the *Daily/Sunday Express* and the *Daily/Sunday Star*) to pay its subscriptions from 2008 was a serious threat to its existence well before Leveson. So he had no difficulty recommending that:

> "a new system of regulation should not be considered sufficiently effective if it does not cover all significant news publishers. The challenge, then, is to find a way of achieving that result." Leveson (2012: 1754)

Leveson LJ is far from alone in this view. The Lord Chief Justice, Judge LJ, speaking to a human rights conference in London picked up on the point even before his brother judge reported:

> "The new PCC – that is the new body currently in my contemplation in any new system of self-regulation – must be all inclusive. You might perhaps be willing to discount a news sheet circulated to about 25 people, but any national or regional paper would have to be included. In short any new PCC would require to have whatever authority is given to it over the entire newspaper industry, not on a self-selecting number of newspapers."[1]

Several publishers also admitted this was the case. The Joint owner of Independent Print Limited, Evgeny Lebedev, told the Inquiry, "I think everybody in the industry has to be part of this new future body in order for it to work." Aidan Barclay, Chairman of the Telegraph Media Group said, "I think it does need to include everybody." Leveson (2012: 1753)

So after sixteen months of hearings and scores of witnesses we come back to the problem we all had in the first place: should we have regulation or not, because a halfway house of self-regulation without some kind of backstop legislative support/recognition/underpinning or statutory regulation is simply not going to work?

The politics is now deeply involved. As well as Labour's Bill and Lord Lester's Bill in the Lords, the government is considering a Royal Charter as a way of incorporating a new press regulator. It also threatened to publish an alternative draft bill that is intended to show that press regulation by statute would not work, according to the *Guardian*.[2]

The Chairman of the current PCC, Lord Hunt is also pressing on with his plans for a new body with membership underpinned by civil contracts. He claims that no one had yet refused to join even though he accepted that his system was also underpinned by statute.

> "Hunt also said he had 'never been averse to statutory regulation', telling journalists that he had drawn up a list of all 27 UK statutes which refer to the press.
>
> 'When people say they don't want statutory underpinning, they ignore the fact that there are already all these statutes,' he said, adding: 'As Nicholas Philips reminded me this morning, to have a contract underpinning this new regulator means it is underpinned in law. Because civil law is law, whether it is by statute or by case law.'" Pugh (2012)

The debate will go on, but for the industry the way forward is stark: try to get a regulatory body, probably underpinned by statute, everyone can live with or get stuck with one that it doesn't want.

Notes

[1] (http://www.guardian.co.uk/media/2011/oct/19/lord-chief-justice-press-regulation). Accessed 21/12/12

[2] (http://www.guardian.co.uk/media/2012/dec/13/oliver-letwin-finalises-press-regulator?utm_medium=twitter&utm_source=twitterfeed). Accessed 21/12/12

References

Frost, Chris (2010) *Journalism Ethics and Regulation 3rd edtn* London: Pearson

Leveson LJ (2012) *An Inquiry into the Culture, Practices and Ethics of the Press* London: The Stationery Office

Pugh, Andrew (2012) *Industry to unveil draft contacts for new press watchdog* [sic] in Press Gazette available online at http://www.pressgazette.co.uk/industry-unveil-draft-contacts-new-press-watchdog accessed on 17/12/12

Note on the contributor
Professor Chris Frost is professor and head of Journalism at Liverpool John Moores University and has been a journalist, editor and journalism educator for more than 40 years. He is member of the National Executive Committee of the National Union of Journalists and a former President, chair of the union's Ethics Council and Chair of the Association for Journalism Education. He has written several books on Journalism as well as many book chapters and papers.

Section E. The Chilling Effect? Privacy and Investigative Journalism after Leveson

John Mair

When they were not bleating about the threats to 'Press Freedom', the newspaper barons were warning of the likely 'chilling effect' of any post-Leveson regulation on investigative journalism (which it is pertinent to observe very few newspapers now finance or practice. It was only diligent and obstructed-by other papers- work by the *Guardian*'s Nick Davies that led to the phone hacking scandal being finally exposed at all.)

But 'the great chill' on the journalism of upset was forecast by those from Cabinet Minister Michael Gove (a former news editor of the *Times*) downwards In this section, Eamonn O'Neill who teaches one of the tiny number of university courses in investigative journalism looks at the history of 'chilling' with especial reference to one of the other great pieces of investigative journalism -Woodward and Bernstein uncovering the secrets of Watergate and deposing President Richard 'Tricky Dicky' Nixon thirty years ago.

Much of the material for good investigations in journalism comes from aborted or live police investigations. They have the skills, the manpower and the resources to (usually) do it well-unless they are DAC Yates and the phone hacking bin bags he never opened. Journalists and policemen – 'cops' and 'hacks'-to each other are fellow travellers in the gutters of society. They live in the nether world and have done from the times of Charles Dickens. They have a long history of co-operation and crumbs falling off each others' tables to the advantage of both. A quick drink here and there never went amiss. I once obtained a whole series of British Rail internal audit reports for *Dispatches* on some dodgy deals for a regular pint or two with a senior BTP policeman at Paddington on his way home. No money, just a pint or two with shall we call him 'Vic'.

Could all of this be endangered by Lord Justice Leveson? In his witness box some remarkable stories of the closeness of the Press and the Police in other ways came out; the *News of the World* staff who flitted between Wapping and New Scotland Yard, The Metropolitan Commissioners who ran campaigns for 'office' aided by tabloid journalists 'spinning' for them plus the stunning evidence DAC Sue Akers on the extent of payment to public officials (including policemen) by newspapers. Part of the police triptych of investigations looking at phone hacking – Operation Eleveden is examining just that. As of January 2012, 54 (fifty four) have been arrested, journalists, army personnel, prison officers and policemen/women. One, DCI April Cashburn was convicted in January 2013 of 'misconduct in a public office' .With some irony, she tried to sell secrets of the Met Phone Hacking investigation to the *News of the World* – who shopped her to the police?

Duncan Campbell pounded the police and crime beat on The *Guardian* for many years. He looks at the history of the Cops/Hack relationship and uncovers some rather unconventional and probably now banned liaisons. Will Lord Justice Leveson (and the Filkin Report before him) end the police/journalism love in? Time for the 'big chill' there?

Finally, Natalie Peck who has gone from the Hacked Off hackette on the spot in Court 73 during Lord Justice Leveson's hearings to teaching journalism to wannabe hacks at South Bank University. She looks at the privacy implications for the British press post – Leveson. Will invasion of privacy now be just illegal and become history? Watch these newspaper spaces.

So the 'Big chill' on 'free and independent journalism' is part and parcel of the Leveson effect the sceptics and doubters say. Others that any regulation will not have as simplistic effect as some would like us to believe. Ultimately, time will tell.

Cops and Hacks: Is Leveson the end of a beautiful friendship?

Duncan Campbell is the just retired and very distinguished Crime Correspondent for the *Guardian*. Lord Justice Leveson has as part of his remit police/press relationships. He found them too close and in need of more formalization and clear blue water. Is this the end of a beautiful friendship?

Relations between the police and the media have always been fraught. That is how it should be. The dangers of too close a relationship are obvious. Percy Hoskins, the *Daily Express*'s crime correspondent in the fifties and president of the Crime Reporters Association (CRA), described that organisation then as "a group of professional journalists who are to Scotland Yard what lobby journalists are to the House of Commons – an elite body who can be trusted with confidential information to be used to mutual advantage."

Within that "mutual advantage" lay a trap. What would a member of the "elite body" do if they came across a story that gave no advantage to the police but, in fact, was very damaging to them? This was essentially what happened in the sixties and early seventies, when the detective branch of Scotland Yard was riddled with corruption but the crime correspondents of the time – much like the City reporters before the international financial crisis in 2008 – missed the story in front of their noses.

That failure to nail corruption at the Yard in those dirty days – until non-specialist journalists, notably at a pre-Murdoch *Times*, did so – was the disturbing downside of that cosy relationship between police and press. As the late Sir John Junor, the former crusty editor of the *Sunday Express*, suggested, journalists are not corrupted by power or money but by friendship. Now we have learned from the Leveson Inquiry that a different form of "mutual advantage" came into play over the last decade or so, with the Metropolitan Police and News International intertwined far too closely.

Leveson was critical of the Metropolitan police's failure to pursue the phone hacking inquiry and "the incredibly swift dismissal of the allegations in the

195

Guardian article...the continued defensive mindset over the months" and also the relationship between the former assistant commissioner, John Yates, and Neil Wallis (then deputy editor of the *News of the World*)." Even the Met appeared to have accepted that this was the case. Their counsel, Neil Garnham QC, said, in his closing statement to the Inquiry: "we frankly admit that there have been incidents which have led to a plain perception of cosiness between particular senior Metropolitan Police service officers and particular journalists [and we] also acknowledge that the decisions in July 2009 and September 2010 not to reopen the phone-hacking investigation were taken too quickly and with a defensive and closed mindset."

Is Lord Justice Leveson right?

So the police must have been relieved that Leveson's conclusion was that "the issue is about perception more than integrity." When plain Brian Leveson QC, as he then was, led the prosecution of Rosemary West, Britain's most notorious female serial killer, at Winchester Crown Court in 1995, he made it clear that her guilt required the most serious penalty available. In contrast, the police who were the subject of his detailed forensic inquiry in 2012 must feel that they have been let off with a conditional discharge.

Lord Justice Leveson was, of course, right to warn the police – and the Met in particular – against favouring particular media organisations and right to advise officers against accepting plum jobs in the media once they have retired from the service for at least a year. How you actually stop that happening is another matter. But Leveson has also called for records to be kept of meetings between senior police officers and the media, for police whistleblowers concerned about malpractice within the service not to go to the media but to an independent body, for "off the record briefings" to be replaced by "non-reportable briefings" and for caution to be used in accepting hospitality from and consuming alcohol with journalists.

Now if every contact between senior police officers and journalists were indeed to be noted and recorded, it would have a dangerously chilling effect on the news. And what if a detective is aware of corruption or malpractice amongst his or her superiors and wants to tell a journalist about it? Leveson suggests that they should not contact the media any more but seek out "confidential avenues in which they have faith." The police duly welcomed this recommendation that officers should not act as whistleblowers (wasn't blowing whistles once an essential part of a police officer's job?) Andy Trotter, the Chief Constable of the British Transport Police, who responded to the report on behalf of the Association of Chief Police Officers (ACPO), applauded Leveson for warning against such action. "Most whistle blowing is internal gossip and attempts to embarrass others in the organisation," he told Vikram Dodd of the *Guardian*.

But when the *Guardian* reported on a major corruption investigation into Stoke Newington police in the nineties – which led to the Police Federation's unsuccessful libel action against the paper on behalf of five officers – some of the initial information came from serving Metropolitan police officers who were disturbed about what was happening at the station. Would any officer now risk talking to a journalist about this? And would they really be confident about calling a proposed hotline instead? In fact, the big chill on relations between police and journalists had already started some months before the Leveson report was completed.

Wendy Cope, in her wonderful poem, How to Deal with the Press, advises "when tempted to confide, resist/ Never trust a journalist." (Every journalist should read it.) Dame Elizabeth Filkin appeared to have channelled the verse in her report, *The Ethical Issues Arising From Relations Between the Police and the Media*, which was commissioned in 2011 by the Home Secretary, Theresa May, and the then commissioner of the Metropolitan Police, Sir Paul Stephenson. This was carried out in the wake of the initial revelations about phone-hacking but before the Leveson Inquiry got underway. Filkin's report, published in 2012, suggested that officers watch out for "late-night carousing, long sessions, yet another bottle of wine at lunch – these are all long-standing media tactics to get you to spill the beans. Avoid."

The Leveson report echoed Filkin's conclusion that "mixing the media with alcohol is not banned but should be an uncommon event." She suggested that drinking with officers "may be seen as inappropriate hospitality". Officers should be encouraged to keep a note of any conversation they have with journalists, the report said.

Filkin also advised the police to "watch out" for reporters "flirting", which, she said, is designed to get officers to drop their defences. Much of the chatter about women reporters flirting for information was just malicious gossip spread by male reporters who had been scooped by their female rivals. Sylvia Jones, the former *Daily Mirror* crime correspondent and the first female chairman (she preferred that title to chair) of the Crime Reporters' Association, has recalled how, in the seventies, rivals talked behind her back to try and discredit her when she got good stories. "They spread rumours about me," she said in an interview with the *Guardian* in 2009, "that I was sleeping with people to get information."

The Filkin report received a warm welcome from the then newly-appointed Commissioner of the Metropolitan police, Sir Bernard Hogan-Howe. "There should be no more secret conversations," he said at the time of its publication. "There should be no more improper contact and by that what I mean is between the police and the media – that which is of a selfish, rather than a public interest. Meetings will no longer be enhanced by hospitality and alcohol. It doesn't mean to say there will never be an occasion when we take hospitality with journalists, but on the whole, we wouldn't expect to see it."

The worry over both the Leveson conclusions and the Filkin report is that officers who would once have had a quiet off-the-record chat at a crime scene, a coffee after a press conference or a couple of explanatory words outside a court will now button their lips. This is the price we will be paying for the coppers who pocketed a few quid for tipping off the press about a celebrity and for parts of the Met being too close to the Murdoch empire.

Leveson and Filkin wide of the Mark?

It is now more than 40 years since the former Met Commissioner, the late Sir Robert Mark, addressed a far greater scandal at the Yard – the widespread and cynical corruption involving hundreds of detectives, particularly in the areas of vice and drugs – not by closing down informal contact, but by encouraging it. This is what he said in his briefing on media relations at the time: "officers who act and speak in good faith may be assured of my support even if they make errors of judgment when deciding what information to disclose and what to withhold."

The key phrases Sir Robert used were "in good faith" and "even if they make errors of judgment." That makes it very clear that any gratuitous use of police information – a tip-off of when a celebrity is to be arrested or is the victim of a tragedy — should be avoided, as there is no way that that could be seen to be "in good faith" – despite the belief of some newspapers that the photo of a famous person in tears is "in the public interest." What Sir Robert realised was that sometimes an officer might try and flesh out a story for a reporter to explain why the police had acted – or not acted – in a particular way. If this has then been misrepresented in the media, then the officer would not be punished for a genuine mistake.

Detectives also, on occasion, use the media as part of their investigations. When the Oxford student, Rachel Maclean, disappeared in 1991, the prime suspect was her boyfriend, a New Zealander called John Tanner, a student at Nottingham University who claimed to have seen Rachel depart from Oxford station with a long-haired stranger. He even went on television to ask Rachel to get in touch and reassure her family that she was all right: "in my hearts of hearts I know she is still alive." The media was invited to a press conference at which Tanner would repeat this plea. It was made clear to those of us attending that conference that the police were already deeply suspicious of Tanner and were happy for us to ask any questions we wanted while they watched him to see how he reacted and whether his story changed. Tanner did not crack during the press conference but he eventually confessed after Rachel's body had been found under the floorboards in her lodgings. He received a life sentence and was released after serving twelve years.

The press may also be used in investigations in a different way: when the police have deep suspicions about someone but no clinching evidence, they may leak a detail to a newspaper, having installed a bug, which can be authorised by a judge, in the home of the suspect. They will then listen to see whether the news item has prompted a nervous phone-call from the suspect or an incriminating in-house conversation.

Coppers for sale?

Have police officers often sold stories to reporters? Of course. Many a well-known person who has contacted the emergency services over a tragedy or alarming incident has been surprised to discover that their call will presage the arrival not only of the police and the ambulance service but a member of the tabloid press. Often the contact with the media will not have been made directly by police but through a conduit. This may well be a former – and perhaps disgraced – officer who has found a new role for himself as the link between a newspaper with money for stories and police officers happy to take a few hundred pounds for anything from a bit of celebrity tittle-tattle to a real scoop. The point is that it has always been against the law for the police to take money for information and it has always been against the law for them to leak damaging information that disrupts an investigation or prejudices a trial.

It should not be forgotten that the press in the distant past behaved in ways that would have more than raised eyebrows at the Leveson Inquiry. The crime reporter of an era before mobile phones had to use his initiative in other ways. Stanley Firmin, the *Daily Telegraph*'s crime man in the post-war years, recalled that a colleague, bored with the lack of breaking news on a murder near the Blackwall Tunnel in London, cut his own finger, soaked a handkerchief in the blood and dumped the hankie in the tunnel. He then wrote a news story headlined 'The Clue of the Bloodstained Handkerchief'. Not that Firmin approved of this "indefensible" act of pre-DNA irresponsibility, of course, but he had to admit that it did "illustrate to some degree the quality of initiative and enterprise that the present-day crime men, have, so to speak, inherited". Indeed.

In 1958, the *Sunday Pictorial* splashed with the headline "I KILLED SETTY...AND GOT AWAY WITH MURDER." This was the "startling confession" of Donald Hume to the murder of Stanley Setty in Finchley, north London in 1949. Hume, a car thief, had stabbed Setty, a car dealer, to death at his flat. He had then cut up the body and disposed of it at sea. He was found not guilty of murder at his trial at the Old Bailey in 1950 but convicted of being an accessory for disposing of the body and jailed for twelve years. After his release, he sold his story, having secured an agreement from the *Pictorial* that they would not publish it until he had left the country. Under the old rules of double jeopardy, which were not changed until the Criminal Justice Act of 2003 allowed retrials in certain circumstances, Hume could not face a second trial. The paper supposedly paid Hume £2,000 – £150,000 today – according to the book, *Scenes of Murder Then and Now*. How would that have gone down today?

The Scotland Yard Lobby Correspondents?

Political correspondents need to talk to MPs and spend much of their time – sometimes, perhaps, too much – so doing. This is often how genuine news stories are broken, even if too often the anonymity is used to settle grudges, as "friends" of leading politicians unburden themselves to political correspondents. MPs are, like the police, public servants, paid for by the taxpayer and subject to the law in relation to the way they use their authority. How damaging it would be for the flow of information if politicians were told to make a note of every chat with a reporter and thus restricted themselves to press releases. In the same way, it should be possible for crime reporters to talk to police officers, just as it should be for any other specialist reporter to get information from the horse's mouth without having to hand out sugar lumps.

Currently, the official channel for information between the police and the media lies in the hands of the media offices attached to the various forces. As both the Leveson and the Filkin inquiries have found, some newspapers were favoured over others in terms of stories made available by the Metropolitan Police. No surprise there, perhaps, that papers seen as uncritically pro-police should be rewarded with special favours, while those seen as sceptical or hostile should be kept at arm's length. Smaller forces doubtless seek favourable coverage from their local press, television and radio stations by giving them advance notice on stories or special access. But too often a reporter seeking official information from the police is dependent on the ability and accessibility of the press officer concerned. Some police media officers around the country are helpful, pro-active and smart; others are lazy, obstructive and thick and seem to take a real pleasure in explaining that they can provide no information. How to rectify that if police officers are to be discouraged from engaging with the media or even talking to them?

Perhaps the greatest achievement of the Leveson Inquiry was to shine a light into the darker corners of police-media relations, regardless of what the conclusions were or which recommendations may ever be adopted. Now what happens? When Sir Robert Mark issued his police-media guidelines four decades earlier, he was most concerned about the level of corruption at the Met and said that his aim was to "make virtue fashionable." Not a bad motto for police officers and journalists alike on the rocky road ahead.

Bibliography

Cope, Wendy (2001). *If I Don't Know.* Faber & Faber

Firmin, Stanley (1950). *Crime Man.* Hutchinson

Ramsey, Winston (editor) (2012). *Scenes of Murder Then and Now.* After the Battle

Note on the contributor

Duncan Campbell is a former *Guardian* crime correspondent and former chairman of the Crime Reporters' Association. He is the author of *If It Bleeds*, a novel about crime reporting, and three non-fiction books on crime: *That Was Business, This Is Personal; The Underworld;* and *A Stranger and Afraid, the story of Caroline Beale.* He was previously news editor of *Time Out* and *City Limits.*

Public Figures, Press Victims and Private Lives: Some privacy implications of the Leveson Report

Natalie Peck was a first-hand observer of the Leveson Inquiry; she sat though much of it and reported it for the Hacked Off Campaign. Here she considers just what Lord Justice Leveson understood by privacy, the measures he proposed to protect it and how realistic they are

The discussion of privacy, as both a concept and a human right in relation to press intrusion, was a central element to the Leveson Inquiry's evidence hearings, as was the case during the formation of the two Calcutt reports[1]. Although the Inquiry was set up in order to investigate the 'culture, practice and ethics of the press' in broad terms, it was a single significant privacy invasion – the hacking of murdered teenager Milly Dowler's voicemail by the *News of the World* – and the resulting public outcry that acted as the catalyst for the government's decision to set up a judicial Inquiry in the first place.

In philosophical and legal literature, privacy has been likened to an "elusive status" (Inness, 1992)[2] and "murky conceptual waters" (Marx, 2001)[3]. Many academics, journalists, legal writers, lawyers and judges have tried to pin down privacy in definitional terms and although many have gone some way in understanding how the concept could be categorised and dealt with in law, no single definition or way of dealing with potential and actual privacy invasions by journalists and photographers has been arrived at.[4] The Press Complaints Commission, floundering even before the Leveson Inquiry was set up, was rendered obsolete over the course of the Leveson hearings as all but one of its previous commissioners giving evidence admitted it never really acted as a regulator.

While the nature of regulation was heatedly debated during the Inquiry, and continues to be so in the pages of our national newspapers, it was largely agreed that a new form of regulation was needed, the PCC (as was) would not cut it this time. And most agreed: the new regulator would have to at least attempt to mediate privacy complaints, along with others such as defamation, to address some of the time-worn concerns about press intrusion.

With such a topical hot potato in his hand, Lord Justice Leveson navigated the course of the Inquiry in practical terms – examining but never lingering on the definitional problems of privacy.[5] The judge's focus lay in uncovering and understanding the "dark arts" of journalism , including, but not exclusively, phone hacking, blagging, covert surveillance, harassment and deception, and hearing the evidence of those who had been affected by press intrusion, while seeking to understand the process from the point of view of journalists and editors.

As was made clear during proceedings, the Leveson Report steers clear of recommending the extension of the civil law to protect individual privacy[6] – a point that has been tossed around and largely disregarded either during or following previous inquiries.[7] Rather, the action centres around the formation of a new press regulator which could include an adjudications arm to deal with complaints instead of, or pre-ceding, legal action.

Former Prime Minister Gordon Brown put it succulently during his evidence to the Inquiry: "[The Dowler family] would support, I have no doubt, the freedom of the press, but they're worried about the threat that was made to their privacy as individuals, and I think Lord Justice Leveson put it: Who will guard the guardians? – was a question which he wanted to address. I will say: who will defend the defenceless? We have to provide answers in a situation where we have two freedoms that are competing with each other" (11 June 2012).

As Lord Justice Leveson made clear his desire to protect the freedom of the press while moving forward with a new, stronger regulatory system, so any recommendations involving privacy have had to balance the concerns of targeted individuals and the working practices of journalists.

Privacy problems at the Inquiry

Unlike the evidence presented during Calcutt twenty-two years before, hearings before Lord Justice Leveson in Court 73 in the High Court were heard in public and streamed live on the Inquiry's website, with videos of each hearing available online permanently. The judge himself made reference to the difficulties of this arrangement, noting that, while it was of utmost importance evidence should be made as accessible as possible, it posed the problem of exposing those who had already suffered privacy invasions to further scrutiny by the media, and the public.[8]

He told actress Sienna Miller, who was followed constantly by paparazzi photographers until a successful series of legal actions from the summer of 2008: "I'm very conscious that you have strong views about privacy and that the very act of coming to give evidence to me exposes you and means that you're talking about things which actually you're quite keen not to want to talk about" (24 November 2011).

Likewise, Christopher Jefferies, the landlord of murder victim Joanna Yeates, was told: "It must be singularly unpleasant to have to revisit the events through which you lived and then to have to recount them in public for all to hear, thereby giving further oxygen to the unpleasantness that you have suffered. I'm very grateful to you for having done so. I'm sure you appreciate the importance that I attach to trying to get to the issues that I have to resolve, but I do recognise the imposition of a breach of your privacy that it involves" (28 November 2011).

This paradox was demonstrated prior to the Inquiry by legal action bought by former FIA (Formula One) boss Max Mosley's against the *News of the World* in 2009. Mosley had to expose his private life to bring his claim (Rozenberg, 2009: 103). Many victims of press intrusion were collectively known as "core participant victims" or "CPVs" over the course of the Inquiry, and were represented by barrister David Sherborne.

The Leveson report: dividing the witnesses
After noting it would not serve the terms of the Inquiry to enter into a sprawling narrative of the evidence, Lord Justice Leveson divided the witnesses into four categories in the report itself: people with a public profile, victims of crime, innocent bystanders and those with links to the above (2: 446).

Individuals could be divided in alternate ways but the discussion of privacy and the press often revolves around vague understandings and concepts. To categorise the victims in broad terms, rather than by making value judgments on the legitimacy of types of reporting, seems sensible.

In relation to victims of press intrusion, also referred to as "the public" in the report, the judge sets out it would be wrong to see this group as homogenous or conclude the Inquiry had only heard complaints from the rich and famous. In his report Leveson continues: "The spectrum of people who claim to have been the victims of unethical or damaging behaviour by the press and have given their personal accounts to the Inquiry is broad" (2: 445).

Robert Jay QC, the Inquiry's lead barrister, mentioned in his opening statement that some individuals garnering press interest are public figures and others not, and suggested that the courting of celebrity should be taken into account by the Inquiry to consider "under the overall rubric of privacy" (14 November 2011).

People with a public profile
Lord Justice Leveson makes clear the nuances in this group, which could also be named "public figures" (as by Jay QC, above), by splitting individuals into a further three sub-categories. The first is "those who occupy positions of power and responsibility in our democracy", including politicians, corporation heads and possibly owners and editors of national newspapers. The second, those "famous as a consequence of their success in their chosen profession", is exemplified by many well-known faces who gave evidence to the Inquiry: the actors Hugh Grant, Steve Coogan and Sienna Miller, author JK Rowling and

singer Charlotte Church. The third and final sub-category is referred to as "those who are famous only for their celebrity" – reality television stars, for example.[9]

Victims of crime

This category includes the second majority of CPVs as represented by the Dowler, McCann and Watson families, those affected by criminal activity who had to deal with subsequent press intrusion. It also includes those wrongly accused of committing crimes like Chris Jefferies, who won libel damages against eight newspapers for the coverage of his personal life and alleged connection to the murder of Joanna Yeates, of which he was cleared completely by police.

Innocent bystanders

This group could also be considered those who could or would make third party complaints against the press, if the current Press Complaints Commission were to allow it. Lord Justice Leveson heard from many campaigning groups and charities on this matter including those representing women, ethnic minorities and transgender individuals. It is unclear whether complaints by such individuals will be considered by a new regulator.[10]

Those with links to the above

The Inquiry heard from, or about, several individuals who were affected in relation to other categories: the mother of Charlotte Church, the singer, the mother and grandmother of Hugh Grant's daughter, and Mary-Ellen Field, who became "collateral damage" and was dismissed from her employment by supermodel Elle MacPherson after private information was reported in the press (2: 449).

These distinctions were heard in one form or another over the course of the Inquiry. Lawyer Graham Shear referred to "different classes or groups" of individuals in relation to the public interest in revealing private information (21 November 2011). Paul Staines, the author of popular political blog *Guido Fawkes*, told the Inquiry: "I particularly don't think people in public life, people who are, you know, paid for by the taxpayers, or subject to the voters, should expect the same degree of privacy as a private citizen who has no public life can expect" (8 February 2011).

John Battle, head of legal services at ITN, told Leveson: "Everyone is entitled to some measure of privacy, even celebrities who put their private life into the public domain. However, whether an individual is a public figure, such as a politician or celebrity, who has placed their private life firmly in the public domain, or an ordinary member of the public who has not sought publicity may be relevant but not necessarily conclusive in considering a privacy issue" (23 January 2012).[11]

A way forward?

The categories listed in the report are guidelines for considering the evidence heard, and offer a potential way forward in deciding how to approach privacy concerns according to individual circumstances, a task already performed by judges in the courts of law. It is significant, however, just how the approach of the Leveson Report differs to previous attempts at reframing press regulation. Instead of engaging in debates about privacy and who should be entitled to it, the simple categorisation of individual victims of intrusion allows the evidence to speak for itself. The question then becomes about resolution rather than cause and effect, which features in the report in a largely historical context.[12]

In one of the stronger statements in his report, Lord Justice Leveson says: "There have been too many times when, chasing the story, parts of the press have acted as if its own code, which it wrote, simply did not exist. This has caused real hardship and, on occasion, wreaked havoc with the lives of innocent people whose rights and liberties have been disdained. This is not just the famous but ordinary members of the public, caught up in events (many of them, truly tragic) far larger than they could cope with but made much, much worse by press behaviour that, at times, can only be described as outrageous" (Executive Summary: 4).

Access to justice

While Lord Justice Leveson lays out extensive recommendations for a new regulator – holding with previous views that a tough and effective system of self-regulation will be best way of maintaining press freedom and protecting the privacy of every individual (Wakeham, 2002)[13] – it is the suggestion of an arbitration system that is the most relevant to questions of resolving disputes over privacy. The judge made it clear over the course of the Inquiry he was keen to find approaches through privacy, confidentiality and libel that could be accessed without the cost of legal proceedings.

The arbitration system would be recognised and taken into account by the courts in any legal proceedings that might follow an unsuccessful or continued resolution of a claim; would be overseen by retired judges or senior lawyers with a specialist knowledge of media law and paid for by the publisher in question to resolve privacy, defamation and other small claims and strike out invalid ones without wasting time and money during legal proceedings. By way of incentive, publishers who deprived claimants of access to the arbitration system could be prevented from recovering costs (even if successful). Publishers could also be liable for exemplary damages if they chose not to join up to the system (Executive summary: 16-17).

It is unclear at the present time how far the arbitration system will be considered in the formation of the new regulator. Lord Black, chairman of the Press Standards Board of Finance, suggested at the Inquiry it could be tacked on to a reformed system at a later date. Lord Justice Leveson was keen for it to be included from the germination of the new regulator, emphasising its importance in the post-phone-hacking system as a true alternative to the courts – providing a legally binding result or a vital first step to proceedings before a judge.

Privacy isn't 'just for paedos'...

Former *News of the World* reporter Paul McMullan caused a stir with the infamous utterance "privacy is for paedos", while giving evidence at the Inquiry (29 November 2011). His extreme view that privacy "is the space bad people need to do bad things in" was rejected by several other witnesses[14] and demonstrably Lord Justice Leveson held little weight with the notion of there being no difference between the public interest and what the public are interested in.

In many cases, the examples of press intrusion put before the Inquiry were not public interest journalism but rather damaging stories of little consequence to public life other than curiosity. On dubious press practice, in particular phone-hacking, Professor Brian Cathcart says: "The subject matter is almost never important – except to the victims, whose lives may be permanently blighted – and while a story may entertain, it does so only in the way that bear-baiting and public executions used to entertain." (2011: 36).

Now Lord Justice Leveson has put forward his recommendations, and the evidence is in the public domain, the decision on future regulation is now in the hands of the government. It remains to be seen whether an arbitration system will be included in the regulatory body the press must operate in accordance with.

It looks unlikely that the report will be adopted in its entirety, as the government tries to appease the ever-influential press and those who have been wronged in egregious privacy invasions. But it seems vital that the practical privacy recommendations of the Inquiry are taken seriously in to account, to allow easy access to justice for the public and a cheaper way to resolve claims for both claimants and newspapers.[15]

Notes

[1] The first Calcutt Report was published in 1990 with a second report ("Review of Press Self-Regulation") published in 1993. This is not exhaustive, there have been several inquiries including the 1947 Royal Commission and 1972 Younger Committee.

[2] Inness is one of several American academics, including Ruth Gavison, Anita L. Allen, Robert C. Post, Jeffrey Rosen and Daniel Solove, to tackle legal and philosophical privacy literature in order to reach a definition. While clearly the legal aspects differ from Leveson's remit, the philosophical debates remain relevant.

[3] In his paper, Marx discusses the problems with seeing the distinction between public and private as a "uni-dimensional, rigidly dichotomous and absolute, fixed and universal concept". This is relevant to what I have nicknamed the "exposure debate" aired at Leveson and elsewhere; the argument over how a right to privacy is diminished by the willing participation of an individual with the media.

[4] A helpful overview comes from Loughlan et al: "In a legal sense, the term 'privacy' has come to encompass a number of aspects of the state of being private or of keeping one's life, personality, property and activities free from interference by others" (2010: 101).

[5] *Private Eye* editor Ian Hislop told the Inquiry: "Privacy has become more of a problem than libel, or had become more of a problem than libel before the sort of explosion over

this -- the previous summer." He refers to the influx of super-injunctions taken out against members of the Press into the legal system during 2011. Similarly, Neville Thurlbeck, formerly of the *News of the World*, told the Inquiry (12 December 2011) that privacy had become a "huge matter" over the previous three years and said the kiss-and-tell stories were "largely dead as a genre". Horrie notes the danger of people using privacy law instead of libel to deter journalists (2000: 121).

[6] The Calcutt 1993 review attempted to address this following Press breaches post-Calcutt 1990 this, but was rejected by politicians.

[7] Most significantly, "HJK" was the only witness to give evidence anonymously and in private, with the live streaming turned off and a written transcript made available after the fact (see S19 Restriction Order HJK, 23 November, 2011). For more on this case see my interview with HJK available at: http://hackinginquiry.org/news/exclusive-anonymous-phone-hacking-victim-hjk-speaks-to-hacked-off/.

[8] In reference to HJK's evidence, Lord Justice Leveson told the inquiry on 23 November 2011: "HJK's concern is that in the anxiety of giving evidence, and I have no doubt there are some people in the room today who will understand that, that he will say something that he didn't mean to say and that would therefore compromise the privacy that he is seeking to protect." Film-maker Chris Atkins and undercover journalist Mazher Mahmood were also granted the right to give evidence with the court cameras switched off, due to the confidential nature of their work.

[9] In the report, Leveson notes: "Certainly in these cases, where the fame of the individual is linked to their exposure to the public through the Press and other media, the relationship between individual and the Press, and what is acceptable and what is unethical, is more nuanced. In such cases the public interest in what might otherwise be private matters may well be stronger and the nature of what can and cannot be considered private may be more difficult to determine" (2: 446).

[10] Such individuals are not covered by the current PCC system, which does not adjudicate third party complaints.

[11] It is perfectly reasonable for there to be further sub-categorisation. Focus groups in research carried out by Kieran et al (2000) held that sportsmen would have greater protection of privacy than film stars, who court publicity to promote films.

[12] Lord Justice Leveson selects case studies from evidence heard to illustrate Press malpractice, including the story of the Bowles family (see 2: 576).

[13] It is worth noting at the time of writing, Lord Wakeham was chairman of the Press Complaints Commission and advocated the body as an example of this, a position he later rejected when giving evidence before Leveson (15 May 2012).

[14] *Guardian* investigations editor David Leigh told the inquiry: "We all have not exactly skeletons in our cupboard, perhaps, but things about our private lives which are embarrassing, perhaps, or shameful perhaps, or just overly intimate or -- I mean, medical things, for example, and the whole question is whether you're entitled to bring these up. People aren't necessarily doing something wrong because, for example, they are now an MP but 25 years ago they had a brief affair with a woman not their wife, or a man not their husband. It doesn't follow, does it? So this line that privacy is for paedos was a very good *News of the World* headline, and I thought it was quite insupportable" (6 December 2011).

[15] As Lord Justice Leveson himself recognised when giving a lecture in Australia following the publication of his report, the growth of the internet has made effective enforcement of the civil law more difficult, in relation to privacy and defamation. The Press may not be allowed another drink in the last chance saloon but this may make no difference in the Wild West of the online world "without an effective sheriff or a Wyatt Earp to ride into town". Lord Justice Leveson speech to University of Melbourne, 12 December 2010: available at http://www.scribd.com/doc/116509654/Unimelb-Leveson-Speech.

References

Cathcart, Brian (2011) Code Breakers in Privacy is Dead, Long Live Privacy! Index on Censorship, Vol. 40, No. 2, pp. 34-45.

Horrie, Chris (2000) Investigative journalism and English law, de Burgh, Hugo (ed), Investigative Journalism, London: Routledge, second edition, pp. 114-129.

Inness, Julie C. (1992) Privacy, Intimacy and Isolation, London: Oxford University Press.

Kieran, Matthew, David E. Morrison and Michael Svennevig (2000) Privacy, the public and journalism, Journalism Vol. 1, No. 2, pp. 145-169.

Loughlan, Patricia, Barbara McDonald and Robert van Krieken (2010) Celebrity and the Law, Sydney: The Federation Press.

Marx, Gary T. (2001) Murky conceptual waters: The public and the private, Ethics and Information Technology, Vol 3, No. 3, pp: 57-169.

Rozenberg, Joshua (2009) Private Lives in The Big Chill, Index on Censorship, Vol 38, No. 2, pp. 98-107.

Wakeham, Lord (2002) Press, privacy, public interest and the Human Rights Act, Tambini, Damian and Clare Heyward (eds), Ruled by Recluses? Privacy, journalism and the media after the Human Rights Act, London: IPPR, pp. 23-39.

Note on the contributor

Natalie Peck is a journalist and lecturer at London South Bank University. Currently, she is researching privacy law and the portrayal of public figures in the press at the Centre for Law, Justice and Journalism, City University London. She previously worked for the Hacked Off campaign, reporting from the Leveson Inquiry hearings at the Royal Courts of Justice.

A New Chilling Effect? Could Leveson lead to less investigative journalism being undertaken in the UK?

Eamonn O'Neill analyses whether the Leveson Inquiry could bring about a period of chilling in the UK press regarding its attitude towards carrying out investigations

Introduction

The Leveson Inquiry's report mentioned the phrase 'chilling effect' several dozen times in its text. This red-flag usage suggested an acute awareness amongst all sectors of those giving evidence to Leveson of the possibility that any perceived restrictions on the ability of the British press in all its forms, to carry out investigative journalism could have a detrimental impact on democratic society, the public sphere's ability to examine itself and the quality of free speech. This is commonly referred to as the 'chilling effect'[1] and is almost exclusively used in connect with the genre of reporting known as 'investigative journalism', although it was mentioned more generally and perhaps most (in)famously by Education Secretary Michael Gove MP in February 2012 during a speech to journalists.

This chapter tests the possible outcomes for investigative journalism in the UK following the Leveson Inquiry's report against the multi-layered consequences which followed the Watergate investigation in the USA. The unpredictable nature of these events which played out across decades, indicate that McNair's 'Cultural Chaos'[2] theory is a useful concept to consider in relation to future events in the UK.

The Leveson Inquiry's relation to the 'Chilling Effect'

Lord Justice Leveson's Report[3] seemed intensely aware of the impact new press regulation might have on the UK press' ability to deliver robust investigative journalism above all else. The various participants in the Inquiry also seemed alert to this matter and throughout the hundreds of pages of the final report delivered their evidence. These individuals came in all shapes and forms, identifying themselves with different corners of the debate and using the phrase in varying ways. Examples of these included the 'publicist' Max Clifford who said in evidence that he felt the Inquiry was having such an effect as to have thwarted the publication of stories which felt would otherwise have been in the headlines.[4]

Clifford's evidence was interpreted broadly as a good thing, insofar as it was assumed he was referring to potentially harmful stories which would have had a negative impact on the reputation of the British press. Indeed Leveson summed up Clifford's contribution in warm terms. Implicit in these comments is the awareness that the Inquiry was even at a mid-stage of proceedings having an impact on 'investigations' although the scope and quality of them was not discussed in detail.

In February 2012 Education Secretary Michael Gove MP said "there is a chilling atmosphere towards freedom of expression which emanates from the debate around Leveson,"[5] He then went on to argue that the focus should be on policing current laws which were "central to making sure that this country remains free" and that existing laws should be "upheld" and "policed" vigorously. Leveson registered subsequent displeasure at the remarks by such a senior Cabinet member whilst the Inquiry was ongoing. This led to Prime Minister David Cameron, who appeared before the Inquiry later, to use the phrase himself to partially explain and express some inferred sympathy with Gove's remarks, ""Well, we have a slightly different view. I mean, Michael comes from a print press background[1]. He was news editor of *The Times*. I think he's right to make the point there is a danger if we don't get this right, that you could have a chilling effect. We don't want that. But we all put our points in our own way."[6]

The Inquiry also saw exchanges between News International lawyers and Leveson about the nature of the 'chilling effect' and theoretical implications of prison sentences handed down to those found to be breaking the law. The phrase was used out of its normal media context as first mentioned by Alex Jones in 1985 and instead applied in more broad and indeed less precise terms.[7] This usage suggested that a 'chilling effect' generally speaking was a positive outcome for society which discouraged illegal behaviour by individuals being used by the press for nefarious access to, for example, private records. The phrase was uttered, in different forms, by others including Sir Christopher Meyer and Harriet Harman MP in their evidence and a range of others too. The issue of disclosure of sources by journalists and the European Court of Human Rights' ruling referring to proportionality between the aim of the journalist and the matter being investigated was touched on also.[8] Additionally, the issue of prior notification and the ruling relating to the Mosley case, after his unsuccessful appeal to the ECHR, ruled that this was good practice but not a legal requirement since to make it such might have a 'chilling effect' on journalism.[9]

Leveson's recommendations included the phrase as a touchstone for what his proposals for statutory underpinning to a new independent regulatory body would *not* do:

> As for the challenge that this goes too far, I simply do not accept that these provisions will have a chilling effect on free speech or press freedom.[10]

Leveson went further and used the phrase again when referring in positive terms to the work done by Ofcom saying no-one suggested its work ever caused a chilling effect on broadcast investigations.[11]

In his recommendations for 'Voluntary Independent Self-Regulation' Leveson states emphatically that:

> It safeguards press freedoms, *will not chill investigative journalism* [emphasis mine] that is in the public interest, and can command public confidence.[12]

Investigative Journalism and the 'Chilling Effect'

Although the phrase 'chilling effect' was first used in relation to investigative journalism in the mid-1980s, its roots reach back a decade earlier.

The theoretical context for the usage of the term 'investigative journalism' is valuable for the contents of this discussion in relation to Leveson since different participants in the Inquiry used the term in diverse ways sometimes alluding to very unique interpretations. The straightforward 'administrative' classification of the genre assumes too much from the reader in terms of them understanding the internal and external at play for the practitioner. If no such drivers exist, then that in itself is of note and should be explicitly explained by the authors of such studies. This rarely occurs however. Yet in the author's experience, to undertake a practitioner role in investigative journalism requires professional stamina and a deeper understanding of the failures of most news provision. From the few available studies[13] it seems the driving forces behind forging a career in this genre of journalism includes deeply held personal beliefs that it can be effective in scrutinising the powerful, acting as a watchdog for the weakest, and, creating positive social change by exposing wrongdoing and laying out facts and hidden motives for examination by the public. Ettema and Glasser[14] provide a more comprehensive yet nuanced 'normative' theoretical backdrop between the practice cited in laudatory terms by Leveson and the examples cited here.[15] This author agrees with their thesis of a 'morally engaged voice'.[16]

The generally-accepted high watermark for this kind of investigative journalism was *The Washington Post*'s Watergate investigation by reporters Carl Bernstein and Bob Woodward during the 1972-74 timeframe. The comparison between the corruption within the Nixon administration and the actions accrued out by sections of Rupert Murdoch's staff from News International has not gone unnoticed by Bernstein who stated:

> For this reporter, it is impossible not to consider these facts through the prism of Watergate... All institutions have lapses, even great ones,

especially by individual rogue employees—famously in recent years at *The Washington Post*, *The New York Times*, and the three original TV networks. But can anyone who knows and understands the journalistic process imagine the kind of tactics regularly employed by the Murdoch press, especially at *News of the World*, being condoned at the *Post* or the *Times*?[17]

The Watergate reporting by the 'Woodstein' duo did not end neatly. The impact of their reporting does not have a neat linear upwards trajectory of positivity either. It could be argued that Watergate, in some ways, did more damage to investigative journalism in the long term than it did in providing a short term boost for the practice. The effect of Watergate in the three decades which followed its reporting by Woodward and Bernstein was to draw incoming fore from predictable (e.g. political opponents of the so-called 'Liberal' press personified in the eyes of enemies by JFK friend and *Post* Executive Editor, Ben Bradlee) and unpredictable (e.g. lawyers hired by the private sector who felt targeted by post-Watergate investigative reports) sources.

One of the 'myths' which Schudson addressed in 1992 was the argument that journalism as a profession received a boost and that "Watergate led to a permanently more powerful, more celebrated, and more aggressive press."[18] This has been challenged on several levels. Firstly, strong anecdotal evidence, laid out by Schudson[19] in his research, would seem to persuasively argue that the journalists who had covered the White House felt somewhat usurped by the investigative success of two, relatively-inexperienced reporters, in unravelling a top-level political story they'd apparently 'missed' despite it being under their noses. Secondly, as numerous authors have stated, the more aggressive reporting post- Watergate, tended to be only of surface-value, inasmuch as the 'aggressiveness' tone tended to be from on-screen reporters who often simply upped the volume level of their superficially aggressive shout-out questions (which often went unanswered) at press conferences.[20] Schudson[21] characterises the press coverage of President Carter as being 'devastating' since the entire White House press corps was on high alert for another Watergate. No such scandal on the scale of Watergate ever unfolded during Carter's term in office – apart from an alleged drugs scandal involving his Chief of Staff, Hamilton Jordan[22] – but Woodward maintained that the man who had run successfully for office promising the American people, "I'll never lie to you," had in fact "broke his most basic promise made when he campaigned for the presidency. He did not always tell the truth."

The subsequent post-Watergate Reagan era was, indeed, marked out by the relative well-behaved attitude of the press to the administration, and inspired the writing of a book about the phenomenon aptly titled *On Bended Knee*. Although there was a perceived high-point for investigative journalism after Watergate, in many ways, the picture is far from straightforward. Whilst Woodward and Bernstein's journalism pointed the way for investigations by congressional committees, it was the machinery of government which forced Nixon from office. If investigative journalism was temporarily emboldened, then evidence suggests that its targets were also ready to fight their corner. Libel cases and the awards given against media companies grew during the 1980-90s time-frame.[23] The outcome of this was a 'chilling effect' on the perceived post- Watergate aggressiveness of news organisations to investigative tough stories that had the potential to attract large libel lawsuits from their targets. Other issues also swarmed around investigative journalism too which might have further helped temperatures plummet. The cases of Cooke, Blair and Glass, would all feature in headlines down the decades. In all cases they were caught fabricating evidence in the course of their investigative journalism. Although the logic of 'the exception proves the rule' might be applied in all such cases, in reality, these instances are played out in the full view of public glare and wider scrutiny and the negative images stick in the collective psyche. This helped reinforce negative stereotypes that investigative journalism is an unreliable, under- scrutinized, under-resourced and even implausible form of journalism. When placed alongside the wholesale hacking which occurred under the auspices of the *News of the World* – and which Bernstein referred to in his own comparative analysis of the issue[24] – these simply pale. The future impact the revelations we already know about and those which criminal trials still to be held may yet deliver, is not quantifiable but suffice to project they will be largely negative.

The early 1980s saw something of a stagnation in the genre despite the glorification of the folk-hero model of the intrepid investigative journalist in films, books and TV series. One author has argued:

> In the post-Watergate years… the flaws of the press loomed larger because the power and the promise of a free press never seemed stronger. The press opened itself to renewed scorn among readers and listeners because of its arrogance and intractability.[25]

Some clear similarities with the 2013 situation in the UK media are obvious. Between polls taken in 1980 and 1997-8, which posed the question, 'How important do you think it is for the news to do this type of investigative reporting?' respondents who thought it was 'Very Important' fell from 77.1% in 1980 to 31.8% in 1997-8.[26] How the country and the industry will view the importance and need for investigative journalism in the UK post-Leveson is not clear but it's unlikely to fair much better than these figures indicate was the situation in the USA.

Opposition to post-Watergate investigative journalism
Additionally, threats and challenges to the investigative model which existed in the US pre-Watergate and immediately afterwards, emerged from interesting areas of society.

In just one example of hard-hitting post-Watergate journalism, ABC's *Prime Time Live* investigative programme sent undercover reporters to work at FoodLion stores. In the process they lied on the CVs and once *in situ* didn't actually do the jobs they were hired to do, but instead spent their time gathering journalistic evidence of wrongdoing including old fish being washed in bleach and re-sold; rancid meat being sloshed in barbecue sauce to disguise the stink and then being repackaged; and the selling of old cheese which had been gnawed by rats which had invaded the store. After the programme was broadcast on ABC, Food Lion responded aggressively with a lawsuit claiming the documentary had been horrifically damaging to its reputation. The producers felt secure in the professional belief they were protected by the US First Amendment. They also felt the programme had a definite public interest core to it and the public-at-large would be swayed by the vigorous investigation into accepting the infractions they committed during production constituted the breaching of minor laws on behalf of a greater good. Food Lion maintained that it lost some $230m+ in stock value because of the broadcast. It took ABC to court and asked for a settlement in the region of $52m-$1bn in compensatory and punitive damages. The jury went on to find in Food Lion's favour and decided the investigative current affairs show had committed 'fraud, trespass, and breach of the fiduciary duty…' during the making of its programme. The company was awarded $1,402.00 in compensatory damages and the sum of $5.5m in punitive damages (this was later reduced under appeal to $315,000). The judge's written comments in the court record were revealing and harsh. He stated that the purpose of *Prime Time Live* was to "capture the largest possible audience…" and that it wasn't a "straight news" programme but instead featured "undercover… investigative… and inside" stories which were "sensational" in nature and were designed to attract high advertising ratings and awards.

The judge focused narrowly on the fact ABC undercover reporters had obtained their jobs with the company by deceptive means; that they had selfish goals in mind (i.e. high ratings); and had essentially committed a break-in to the grocery- chain's places of work in order to gather their material for the show. In the judge's eyes, this allowed him to use an earlier judgement handed down by the Supreme Court which simply said that if this interpretation was applied, then the journalists in question were guilty of breaking general laws in the course of their investigations. The television station's lawyers argued that First Amendment rights of a free press meant that their clients were acting in the greater public interest were rejected and judged not to be superior than the other general laws being broken.

According to Winch in *Ethical Challenges for Investigative Journalism* there was a mixed reaction to this verdict. Some news professionals readily threw their hands up in horror and argued that the judgement meant that the 'messenger was being shot'. But a more interesting reaction, arguably, came from the foreman of the jury, who stated that the jury wanted the investigative journalists to play fair and use only legal means to obtain their information.

A further consequence of the Watergate scandal was the creation of the Office of the Independent Counsel (OIC) in the US. On October 26th 1978,

President Carter ushered in The Independent Counsel Act, thereby empowering the Attorney General of the US, to request an outside prosecutor be appointed in special cases involving high government officials 'where personal, financial, or political conflicts of interest' is too great. Over a score of investigations by successive counsels have followed in the decades since the office was brought into being and its status was confirmed in a Supreme Court ruling in 1988.[27] Yet the OIC came under enormous criticism for its perceived lacklustre and slow investigation under Lawrence E. Walsh into the Iran-Contra scandal, something the US press was itself criticized for missing in the first place. Walsh's investigation lasted seven years and his final report was delivered only days before the 1992 Presidential election, eliciting such heated controversy from both the Republicans and the Democrats that the law relating to the Office of Independent Counsel was allowed to lapse for the two years which then followed. However in 1994, the newly-elected Democratic President Bill Clinton, kick-started legislation which ended this 'lapse. Ironically, this raised even further the profile of the independent counsel who had already been appointed to examine the President and the First Lady's financial affairs, former judge Kenneth Starr in the so-called real-estate deal known as the 'Whitewater' inquiry during the same year.[28] This inquiry later expanded its remit and managed to uncover the sexual relations which occurred between Bill Clinton and an intern, Monica Lewinsky. The majority of the reporting on this scandal however, used sources emanating from the OIC in one shape or form, rather than Watergate-era style 'shoe-leather' investigative reporting.

Industry veteran Tom Brokaw stated:

> The difference between this [Clinton scandal reporting] and Watergate... is what I call the Big Bang Theory of Journalism. There's been a Big bang and the media have expanded exponentially... Back then, you had no *Nightline*, no weekend *Today* or *Good Morning America*, no Internet, no magazine shows [except *60 Minutes*], no *C-Span* no real talk radio, and no CNN pr MSNBC or Fox news doing news all day... As a result of all that, the news process has accelerated greatly...[29]

Post-Leveson Cultural Chaos
Regarding 'Cultural Chaos' McNair argues that:

> In chaos science – the study of systems in nature such as the weather and the movement of tectonic plates – everything is connected and small happenings have big consequences. From the gentle beat of the butterfly's wing grows the meteorological monster of Hurricane Katrina. This can be extended to today's media environment of turbulence and volatility, in which news travels faster and further than ever before... Its roots lie first in the destabilising impact of digital communication technologies.[30]

This concept may be applied to what will occur with investigative journalist in the UK post-Leveson. The events in the US post-Watergate, when the cultural omens looked good for the survival and growth of this kind of reporting underpin this assertion. The challenges to investigative reporting already looked at in this chapter (e.g. corporate; legal; government statute) could not and were not, predicted, even by experienced players like Bradlee at the centre of this national drama. Later, when they themselves were caught in the first wave of digital reporting (e.g. Drudge and Lewinsky-Clinton scandal) many by their own admission (e.g. Brokaw) produced low-quality reporting. All of this, created a prevailing culture amongst the public that this kind of reporting was not always welcome and a legal backdrop which ensured it was not always allowed to go unchallenged.

This equation produced the post-Watergate 'Chilling Effect' on investigative journalism in the USA.

The Leveson Inquiry's report seemed wary from the outset about the chilling effect which it may bring about. Such awareness could never fully ensure the outcome because there were too many variables at play. As McNair said, 'Everything is connected and small happenings have big consequences.'

Moreover, the Leveson's Inquiry's scant consideration of the role of the internet in its findings was commented on widely. Its omission of recommendations which took into account the fact that two of the world's largest digital information providers and information traffic sources – Google and Twitter – existed outside direct UK control was startling. Merely trying to ring-fence digital platforms as some kind of extension of existing media groups was equally surprising. The non-stop evolution of digital mechanisms and devices for shifting all kinds of information meant that Leveson's recommendations were, in some ways, being eroded and made redundant, before they'd even been implemented. It seems ridiculous that a scenario where a non-domestic organisation is able to use a digital platform uncontained by national borders, might team up with a digitally-based, philanthropically-funded group, to produce powerful investigative journalism (think: Wikileaks 2.0 *meets* a UK version of ProPublica) was not considered by Leveson as realistic. In fact, the component parts for such a scenario already exist. Whilst many of his recommendations are already respected and adhered to by important companies producing ethical investigations, the reality is that the black-hole of his report's conclusions on the internet does not address what the future may well bring. One example which gives traction to the Cultural Chaos concept is the recent BBC scandal involving an investigation in abuse by adults of children in care-homes.[31]

Conclusion

Leveson's report correctly identifies the excellent work done by Nick Davies from *The Guardian* and recognises his initially lonely role in kick-starting the investigations into phone-hacking activities amongst sections of the UK press.

Throughout the report it praises the past-work of investigative journalists like Davies and indicates repeatedly it wishes to encourage the continuance of such work. It recognised and identified various elements which might produce a so-called 'chilling effect' on this category of reporting and issued assurances that it did not foresee its recommendations bringing this about. The example of Watergate, perceived by most as a highpoint in investigative reporting, is instructive however in how difficult it is to predict what the fates have in store. This chapter has shown how it fell victim to the chilling effect in various forms through its own conduct and behaviour and also when it came under attack from various sources. Few who were core players in the process either saw these events coming or realised the long-term consequences they would have. This is particularly true of the Clinton-Lewinsky scandal where a Democrat President fell under the scrutiny of a judge appointed to the Office of Independent Counsel, a special position created in turn – ironically – because of the failures of Watergate and mistrust of the Executive's abilities to investigate itself.

McNair's thesis on 'Cultural Chaos becomes even more pertinent as digital platforms and devices to engage with them, develop at a rapid speed. Reports like Leveson's into press behaviour and ethics, whilst of huge significance, seem diminished by this evolution. The decision by him to not look at the matter of digital online issues related to his core brief, is regrettable. Recent examples, such as the BBC *Newsnight* scandal which led to the wrongful naming of an individual on the internet in relation to child abuse allegations, clearly indicate that Leveson's recommendations do not comprehensively address the digital world outside major media groups in the UK. It is therefore instructive but not convincing to argue that taking into account the post-Watergate 'Chilling Effect' during the Leveson Inquiry, is enough to even partially protect robust investigative journalism in the future. The technology, approaches, platforms, cross-border initiatives and devices are changing too fast to foretell the outcome one way or another. Add to the mix the complex behaviour of human beings who will be central to such projects and the picture becomes, if it were possible, even murkier.

Notes

[1] A phrase coined by Alex S. Jones, media reporter with *The New York Times* in January 1985.

[2] See shortened version:
http://www.guardian.co.uk/media/2006/may/01/mondaymediasection

[3] Executive Summary available here: http://www.official-documents.gov.uk/document/hc1213/hc07/0779/0779.pdf

[4] http://www.official-documents.gov.uk/document/hc1213/hc07/0780/0780_ii.pdf

[5] http://www.guardian.co.uk/media/2012/feb/21/leveson-chilling-freedom-speech-gove

[6] In the interests of full disclosure the author Eamonn O'Neill registers the fact that he worked alongside Michael Gove at Scottish TV during 1990-92 timeframe.

[7] http://www.guardian.co.uk/media/2012/jun/18/cameron-silences-ministers-leveson-inquiry

[8] See the exchanges on pp.1088-9 for example: http://www.official-documents.gov.uk/document/hc1213/hc07/0780/0780_iii.pdf

[9] See Appendice 2.68: http://www.official-documents.gov.uk/document/hc1213/hc07/0780/0780_iv.pdf

[10] See note 3.124: http://www.official-documents.gov.uk/document/hc1213/hc07/0780/0780_iv.pdf

[11] See Part K. 7.8: http://www.official-documents.gov.uk/document/hc1213/hc07/0780/0780_iv.pdf

[12] See Chapter 8. 5.3: http://www.official-documents.gov.uk/document/hc1213/hc07/0780/0780_iv.pdf

[13] See footnote 44: http://www.official-documents.gov.uk/document/hc1213/hc07/0780/0780_iv.pdf

[14] See, for example, De Burgh, (Ed) *Investigative Journalism* (Routledge, London & New York, 2008) 2nd Edition.

[15] See Ettema, James S. and Glasser, Theodore L. 'The Reporter's Craft as Moral Discourse' in *Custodians of Conscience: Investigative Journalism and Public Virtue* by (New York: Columbia University Press, 1998)

[16] His repeated praise of The Guardian's Nick Davies' early work on the phone-hacking scandal is an example of this. See, for example, 24. At: http://www.official documents.gov.uk/document/hc1213/hc07/0779/0779.pd

[17] See Ettema, James S. and Glasser, Theodore L. 'The Reporter's Craft as Moral *Discourse' in Custodians of Conscience: Investigative Journalism and Public Virtue* by (New York: Columbia University Press, 1998) P3.

[18] http://www.thedailybeast.com/newsweek/2011/07/10/murdoch-s-watergate.html

[19] See 'Watergate – A Study in Mythology' by Michael Schudson, in *Columbia Journalism Review*, May/June 1992 p2.

[20] Ibid.

[21] See, for example, 'Watergate – A Study in Mythology' by Michael Schudson, in *Columbia Journalism Review*, May/June 1992 p2. Schudson points out that the White House press corps was ill-behaved after Watergate. Len Downie, now Vice Executive Editor-at-Large for *The Washington Post* is also quoted in this article stating that heavily-controlled White House press conferences were not a good place to gather real news and to anything that's been discussed in the previous 24-hour news cycle relating to the Oval Office agenda. Ibid. Schudson cites the example of the Reagan Administration's 'Devear Rule' established by the White House Press aide of the same name who told the press – like a teacher to a roomful of noisy children – that they would not get their questions answered unless they sat in their chairs and raised their hands politely.

[22] This was as improbable as Presidential reporting gets: Hamilton Jordan, was alleged to have snorted cocaine at the infamous Studio 54 nightclub in New York. He denied it. The allegation – not entirely beyond the bounds of possibility to those who knew Jordan, although unproven – was actually part of a last-ditch attempt by the disco's owner, Steve Ruebell, to buy himself a deal with federal prosecutors. Hamilton was exonerated but his legal bills and damaged reputation hung around him for years. Carter,

publicly celebrated the verdict, but years later admitted to Bob Woodward that the impact of the drugs scandal involving his Chief of Staff had been 'serious'.

[23] Douglass K. Danielm, 'Best of Times, Worst of Times', *The Big Chill* (Iowa: (Iowa State University Press, 2000) p20. In the 1980s media juries awarded libel damages cases against media companies in figues varying from approximately $500,000 to $2m. In the 1990s, media companies lost 2 out of 3 of the cases against them and the amounts awarded by juries increased to an average of $4.5m. Even allowing for variables (cost of living increasing in a year and particularly egregious professional missteps by reporters, it's clear that something is happening and that journalists were no longer seen as the First Amendment 'good guys'.

[24] http://www.thedailybeast.com/newsweek/2011/07/10/murdoch-s-watergate.html

[25] Douglass K. Danielm, 'Best of Times, Worst of Times', *The Big Chill* (Iowa: (Iowa State University Press, 2000) p12.

[26] See 'Public Perception of Investigative reporting' by Susan K. Opt and Tomothy A. Delaney in *The Big Chill.* p89.

[27] *Morrison Vs Olson* Decided June 19th 1988. The Supreme Court of the USA decided by a ruling of 7 to 1 that the Independent Counsel Act was Constitutional.

[28] The Clintons were involved in a land deal involving a legal entity known as the Whitewater Development Corporation. Friends of the Clintons, Jim and Susan McDougal, handled some investments from the Clintons as early as 1977. The primary idea behind the venture was for the young Governor Clinton (of Arkansas) and his lawyer wife, to supplement their relatively modest incomes. It failed. By the 1980s they'd lost between $37,000-$69,000. Despite this loss, the 'Whitewater' 'scandal' entered the popular and political lexicon. Nothing on the scale, or even close, to wrongdoings in the Watergate case has ever been uncovered.

[29] 'Pressgate' by Steven Brill, *Brill's Content* July/August 1998. P147

[30] See shortened version:
http://www.guardian.co.uk/media/2006/may/01/mondaymediasection

[31] http://www.thebureauinvestigates.com/2012/11/25/a-report-by-the-bureaus-trustees/

References

Aucoin, James, L. (2005) The Evolution of American Investigative Journalism, (Missouri: University of Missouri)

De Burgh, Hugo (ed.) (2008) *Investigative Journalism*, (London: Routledge, second edition)

Ettema, James S. and Glasser, Theodore L. (1998) The Reporter's Craft as Moral Discourse, *Custodians of Conscience: Investigative Journalism and Public Virtue*, New York: (Columbia University Press)

Gaines, William C. (2008) *Investigative Journalism: Proven Strategies for Reporting the Story.* (Washington DC:CQ Press).

Mair, John & Keeble, Richard Lance (eds) (2011) *Investigative Journalism Dead or Alive* (Suffolk: Abramis).

McNair, Brian (2009) *News and Journalism in the UK* (London Routledge).

Spark, David (1999) *Investigative Reporting: A study in Technique.* (Oxford: Routledge).

Note on the contributor

Dr Eamonn O'Neill is a Lecturer in English & Journalism and Course Director of the MSc in Investigative Journalism at the University of Strathclyde, Glasgow. Over a career spanning 23 years he has been honoured internationally for his investigative journalism in both broadcast and print in, amongst others, the British press Awards, BAFTAs and the Paul Foot Award. In 2008, he became the first British recipient of an Investigative Reporters and Editors Award (Special category – Tom Renner Award) in one of the USA's premier peer-judged honours for his work investigating miscarriages of justice. In 2010, 2011 and 2012 he received honours in the Strathclyde Excellence in Teaching Awards following nominations by students. His work appears in broadsheets throughout the UK and he regularly broadcasts on BBC Scotland.

Section F. What do we tell the kids? Ethical Education

John Mair

Much of the alleged illegality that led to Leveson took place by hardened 'hacks' working in hardened and old established newsrooms where the culture too easily went off kilter. The 'for Neville' (Thurlbeck) email showed just how widespread phone-hacking was in the *News of the World*. It was not one 'rogue reporter' but one (and maybe more) 'rogue newsroom'. Moral relativism ruled there and getting the story-by whatever means – became paramount.

What of the next generation of journalists? Hundreds come out of university journalism schools (including mine) and from training schemes each and every year. Some are taught or pick up ethics along the way. Just how intrigued Lord Justice Leveson.

One certainty in the post-Leveson world of journalism training is that ethics will assume a central position on all courses. It has to.

Phil Harding has made a career latterly out of ethics. He was the last stop on ethical, moral, political and editorial decisions for the BBC as Controller Editorial Policy. Now he is a media consultant and has evolved a module on ethics for the courses run by the UK's biggest accreditation body – The National Council for the Training of Journalists. Here he outlines just how he and they will put ethical education centre stage

Bob Calver of Birmingham City University is at the education coal-face teaching wannabe journalists day to day. He looks at the new tool kit they will need to face difficult ethical decisions in their careers day by day, even hour by hour, minute by minute in the ever increasing pace of the modern news machine especially the broadcast version. En passant, he confesses to a series of ethical lapses in his own journalism career.

One big dilemma facing the journalists of the future is the 'inflated expectations' of foreign, especially war correspondents as war becomes increasingly 'live'. One of the modern war reporting greats – Stuart Ramsay of *Sky News* – pointed this out to my Brunel University students in late 2012. He was worried that broadcast news desks were expecting more and more and much more 'bang bang' from war corrs. He did not see these inflated expectation as ending any where but in danger or death.

Discuss the ethics of that kids...

Teaching ethics after Leveson

Bob Calver of Birmingham City University is a hack turned academic. He teaches ethics to his students but wonders if post-Leveson he and they need a new tool kit to understand the ethical dilemmas that will face them every day, every hour even?

During the Leveson Inquiry I found myself cast in the role of media commentator, being interviewed regularly on local radio and appearing on regional television news programmes about the Inquiry's progress, about key witnesses and – as the police investigations unfolded – even arrests.

The interviews continued in the immediate aftermath of publication of the four-volume epic in November 2012 and indeed expanded via Associated Press and even a couple of appearances on China Radio International. In each case I was billed as an academic – not as a former (and indeed still practising) journalist and yet during all those broadcasts I was asked only once about the teaching of ethics to journalism students in my university. Even then it was an almost insignificant element of the interview, amounting to little more than confirmation that our students did spend time pondering ethical issues.

In his report[1] Sir Brian Leveson says: "Finally I would like to add a word on journalism training. I have not sought to look at the adequacy of the training available to, or provided to, journalists. However, a number of Professors of journalism have given evidence to the Inquiry and it is apparent from their evidence that the schools of journalism are committed to offering high quality training in which ethical journalism plays a full part. Largely as a result of the financial pressures on parts of the press, journalism training is increasingly moving away from newsrooms and into the universities."

He goes on to stress the importance of ongoing in-house training including in relation to new laws and ethical compliance issues highlighted by particular cases and says: "It is clearly important that the industry generally and employers in particular should place a high priority on training to ensure, inter alia, that all journalists understand the legal and ethical context in which they work."

Any response from the Training Councils?

The brevity of that reference to journalism training moving into the universities perhaps hides the scale of the job we have to do because for those of us in journalism education, the post-Leveson world – whatever the regulatory regime that results from his recommendations and the ensuing political wrangling – does raise important questions about how we teach 'journalism ethics' or 'ethical behaviour'.

The NCTJ (National Council for the Training of Journalists) was quick off the mark to announce at its annual skills conference that a new ethics module will be included in its Diploma in Journalism. (see Phil Harding, p 230 in this volume)

The December 2012/January 2013 edition of *The Journalist* quotes Joanne Butcher, the NCTJ's Chief Executive, saying: "Following recent research and much soul searching we have concluded that far greater emphasis must be placed on ethics in the industry's journalism training and qualifications." She went on to say: " There is agreement across the industry that journalistic ethics matter a lot so that readers and audiences trust the information they are being given by the media."

The news release on the NCTJ website[2] describes how the conference debated the possible format of any such module and how it might be assessed. It reports NCTJ chair, Chris Elliott (The Readers' Editor of The Guardian in his day job...) as saying: 'it would be crazy for the NCTJ not to take cognisance of what has happened around Leveson.'

He added more structure as an assessment to a national standard was required as, according to an independent report commissioned by the NCTJ, current teaching was: "Patchy, random and implicit."'.

The release goes on to quote David Rowell, Johnston Press head of editorial learning and development and member of the NCTJ Journalism Qualifications Board. "Ethics has to be at the heart of journalism training and the new diploma structure does put much greater emphasis on this".

Later the release said: "The newest member of the NCTJ board and editor of the *Derby Telegraph*, Neil White, told delegates trainees needed to have the confidence to deal with ethical issues on a regular basis. 'Every single day my guys go out and they have to make decisions when they are doing death knocks, when they are covering inquests, on just how far to push people.' However some delegates questioned the effectiveness of an exam-based assessment to test students' knowledge of ethics, as it would be 'hard to write a model answer'."

My personal journey through the ethical minefield

The NCTJ is not alone in turning its attention to ethics teaching in the light of Leveson. Many of us will, no doubt, have examined our own practice in this area. We have probably even reflected on how we were taught (or more probably not taught) about such things and I cannot believe I am alone in having searched my mental archive to revisit my own journalistic behaviour.

We will each arrive at our own conclusions, but my own journey has led me to a couple of surprising places. My view before Leveson was that ethics, like all the other subject areas that make up a journalism curriculum, need to be taught in a practical context and the appearance of the 1,987 page report and the reaction to it has only strengthened that belief. Just as we teach interviewing by getting students to question real people involved in real news stories, or pass on radio package making skills by getting students to produce real pieces of broadcast-quality radio, so we must get them grappling with real topics and cases to hone their ethical thinking.

The dilemma of the deadline
In their book *Doing Ethics in Media*[3], Jay Black and Chris Roberts rightly point to the dilemma that sets "abstract concepts that for millennia have intrigued philosophers, historians, sociologists, psychologists, economists, political scientists and other thoughtful observers and policy makers' against journalism and media students being 'immersed in controversial current events while learning decision-making processes that may be applied daily – often on deadline."

For postgraduate broadcast journalism students like mine, of course, 'applied daily' can be replaced with 'applied hourly'. We would not, however, use the pressure of a deadline as an excuse for a badly-written voice piece or a jump cut in a television report so we cannot begin to think that it provides justification for falling below acceptable standards of behaviour.

Before going on to consider just how we might prepare young reporters for that world and educate a future generation of editors who will set the ethical tone of news organisations and outlets, we need to give some consideration to what areas of behaviour we are actually talking about.

Much of the debate during the Inquiry and since has been focussed on activity best covered by the heading 'Newsgathering'. That is hardly surprising since it was illegal phone hacking that set this hare running but references to 'doing death knocks' or 'covering inquests' have reinforced the suggestion that we need to focus almost exclusively on our pursuit of stories. It is clearly the area most likely to pose dilemmas for students and working journalists, particularly in the newspaper setting, but students also need to be open to issues of representation and diversity, how they present a story not just in the language they use but also in the selection of images, voices, faces and sounds. Overwhelmingly they need to recognise that accuracy is paramount in building the trust of the audience or readers.

My view before the report appeared and now (with great respect to the NCTJ who oversaw my own journalistic infancy) remains that we should resist a rush to create new Leveson-inspired modules or post-hacking Powerpoints and instead emphasise the fact that ethics are simply another element of professionalism, which should be, and I believe actually is, already at the heart of our teaching.

It was not an unethically motivated desire to blacken the name of Lord McAlpine that cost the BBC so dearly, it was the failure to follow some basic journalistic steps on the way to a 'story'. Simply showing a photograph or two to Steve Messham of his alleged abuser would have killed a lie before it became a libel. Putting the 'evidence' to the noble Lord would, at the very least, have raised enough doubts to ensure the story was pursued more rigorously before being screened.

Writing the above, reminds me of the first dawning of a sensation that led to the examination of my own teaching in this field. As academics (many of us might still prefer to be identified as journalists who teach) we must guard against a sense of self-righteousness, a finger-pointing stance highlighting the failings of others.

Bring on the bloated cow?

I became acutely aware of that danger when a colleague and I were discussing the whole issue of ethics with a group of international students. Focussing on that idea that high standards are an extension of journalistic professionalism we had used the example of the ITV *West Country* breakfast news bulletin that reported a polar bear having been washed up on a Cornish beach[4]. The programme reported: "A walker in Cornwall has caught an extraordinary sight on camera. A polar bear has washed up on a beach near Bude. The bear comes from the Arctic Circle and an investigation is under way as to how it could have ended up there."

As we probably all know by now the creature was in fact a cow that had become bloated during its time in the sea having fallen from a cliff. The point of using this example with students was to show how an untruth could be broadcast simply by not doing some simple things, like asking questions about the likelihood of such a story being true and making a few calls to locals in Bude or the Coastguard or a marine expert. What we were aiming at was to show students how easy it is to undermine the audience's trust in our output when our standards of professionalism drop.

They got the point but I decided to underline it by using an example from my own journalistic practice. I found myself telling them of the August Bank Holiday Monday in the late 1970s when I was called at home by my news desk to go to the scene of a 'probable drowning' close to Hadrian's Wall in rural Northumberland. I outlined how I spoke to people by the side of a former quarry and how one described how a group of young men, who had probably been drinking, were messing around in the cold, deep water when one of them disappeared. By the time I was there the Fire Service were on hand with inflatable boats and police divers were searching for the young man. I rushed home, filed my story and waited until the next morning when it appeared on the front page under my name.

There was a clear gasp from the students when I said: "And that news story was completely untrue". To my continuing embarrassment (perhaps even shame) I had failed to get a full address for my 'eye witness'. I had a name, a town and even his job but no amount of searching by the Coroner's Officer or my own careful scanning of Electoral Rolls could find him.

Instead, the investigation uncovered the story of a teenage boy whose day out with his family had ended in tragedy. It was a sunny August day and the young man was not alone in having been tempted into the water but he was certainly not part of any group of young men, drunken or otherwise. I will never know whether there was indeed a group of young men and my witness simply assumed the dead youngster was with them or whether he was just mistaken in what he thought he saw. The fact is that my failure to do a simple reporting task, getting the full details of my interviewee, meant it was impossible to go back to him to check his account. He gave me a 'good story' and I was satisfied but that failure on my part added to the family's pain and undermined their trust in my newspaper and, no doubt, in journalists in general.

That unprepared summary of my professional slip sparked a discussion that showed it had brought home the point to students that I was trying to make. Indeed, so effective did it seem to be that with future groups of students I've incorporated a picture of the scene, Crag Lough, into the presentation I use to explore ethical issues. It continues to surprise students and set them talking.

Like other institutions we use scenarios, including those developed by the BBC College of Journalism to examine the thorny area of 'the public interest' but real life examples seem to have much more impact. I share experiences of the 'death knocks' I did as a young newspaper reporter and tell my students how, as a local radio news editor, when all my team expressed their distaste for my decision to cover the funeral of a young murder victim I went myself. Their belief was that such coverage would be unduly intrusive and add nothing to the story. I hope a thoughtful voice piece and some affecting interviews proved them wrong.

In their work 'Exploring the Ethics of Death Reporting in the Social Media Age[5], published in *The Phone Hacking Scandal: Journalism on Trial*, Sallyanne Duncan and Jackie Newton, are clear that that the 'death knock', interviewing the bereaved following a tragedy is an important journalistic activity, even in this new digital age. Duncan and Newton have advocated more vigorous and ongoing training for journalists in this field. Many of us involved in journalism education would agree, particularly with the 'ongoing' element. Just as when our students are learning relevant areas of law we stress that their learning will be a career-long affair, so we need to make the point that ethics are not just an interesting area for classroom discussion but something they will have to deal with throughout their professional lives.

So, time for an ethical education toolkit?

The European Broadcasting Union has developed a useful toolkit[6] to help students and journalists examine how minorities are represented – and can be demonised – in radio and television reporting. It contains clips of real examples which are invaluable in teaching. The supporting documentation is divided into sections such as 'Checking the facts' and 'In the newsroom – good practice'. In the section on balanced representation it encourages students to ask if it is possible to be objective, or to avoid hidden messages and whether they are aware of the power of certain emotional words. It even questions, "To what extent do you use music and sounds to achieve a certain impact on the audience?"

The toolkit looks only at the issues of diversity but it is a model of what needs to be developed by journalism educators with the support of the industry to ensure we develop a practical approach to teaching ethics – call it applied ethics if you like.

Producing an EBU-style toolkit with real stories, TV footage and audio clips will be more challenging in this field, not least because the really interesting questions will be those that have gone on in the newsroom and in the journalists' own consciences before the decision to publish or broadcast has been taken. It will, then, need input from editors and working journalists prepared to talk openly not just about the dilemmas that can arise but about the occasions when they got it wrong. It will also be valuable to hear from reporters about the times when they have felt an editor has made a bad call, leaving them to make personal decisions on how they should behave.

In the meantime, let us involved in day-to-day teaching be brave in sharing the details of the times when we have slipped from the professional approach to the job that we want our students to demonstrate. Let us be frank, too, about the consequences of those actions in terms of shaping perceptions of journalists' behaviour. My own experience is that students respond well to such examples, perhaps because it allows them the freedom to discuss their concerns and move towards their own personal codes in an atmosphere free from any sense that they are required to measure up to some theoretical ideal that has no hope of survival in 'the real world'.

So, pending the creation of a useful tool kit I am happy to offer my shortcomings to anyone who might find them useful and I would be happy to hear other's examples that I could use with my students. Confession is not just good for the soul it can be an important teaching tool.

Notes

[1] Leveson Report Volume II Page 736 Point 2.79

[2] NCTJ announces compulsory ethics module for diploma students, November 30th 2012 WEB REF?

[3] Doing Ethics in Media Theories and practical applications (Jay Black and Chris Roberts) Routledge 2011

[4] 'ITV embarrassed by report of polar bear washed up on beach'. Daily Telegraph, September 21st 2010 WEB REF

5 'Exploring the Ethics of Death Reporting in the Social Media Age' (Sallyanne Duncan and Jackie Newton) in The Phone Hacking Scandal: Journalism on Trial' (ed John Mair and Richard Keeble)

[6] A Diversity Toolkit for factual programmes in public services television' a collaborative project developed under the Intercultural and Diversity Group (IDG) of the EBU (2008) WEB REF

Note on the contributor

Bob Calver is Senior Lecturer in Broadcast Journalism in the School of Media at Birmingham City University. He began work as a journalist in his native Norfolk before moving to the Newcastle Journal. He joined the BBC in 1979, working as a local radio reporter, producer and news editor and later as a Home Duty Editor for BBC Newsgathering nationally. He has worked part-time at BCU for almost 15 years while continuing his journalism. In early 2012 he launched a 'glossy 'magazine in Herefordshire which he describes as both a return to his local roots and a foolhardy vote of confidence in local print publishing. In addition to journalistic ethics, his academic interests include models of research through practice and their potential in the fields or journalism and media production.

Time to put ethics centre stage?

Phil Harding was the ethicist in chief at the BBC – the Controller of Editorial Policy. Since, he has advised worldwide on matters journalistic and ethical. Here he proposes putting the teaching of ethics at the core of the journalism curriculum. An earlier version of this chapter appeared in the British Journalism Review

The Leveson Inquiry Report into the "culture, practices and ethics" of the press has raised profound questions about how the ethics of journalism are taught, discussed and disseminated in this country. While most of the debate post-Leveson has focused on regulation, at least so far, the wider issues around the training of journalists and editors are crucial ones which will have to be faced by every major media organization in this country.

In the autumn of 2012 and prior to the publication of Leveson, I was asked by the National Council for the Training of Journalists (NCTJ) to look into some of these questions. I interviewed senior editors and executives from almost all of the main media groups (print and broadcast) as well as some of the main providers of journalistic training. This chapter is partly based on that research.

As a result of the report that I presented to the NCTJ, the organization has already announced some big changes in the way it organizes its training programme. I detail those changes later in this chapter.

Reactions to Leveson
Almost all the people I talked to felt ashamed about past events: "Every journalist in this country has to be touched by Leveson and by what's been revealed. Whether we've been directly involved or not, we are all in this together". They felt the revelations had seriously dented their own personal integrity and that of their profession as a whole. Most agreed that there needed to be changes and that ethical issues in journalism had to be given a much higher priority in the future.

A minority of respondents were more worried about where the debate on ethics could lead. They feared it would lead to the suppression of good journalism and that important stories would go unreported: 'There is a big danger that the chattering classes will seek to impose their own values on this process and that they will seek to eliminate what they see as 'tawdry' by labeling it 'unethical'.

Ethics do matter
There is a lot of unanimity in the journalism industry that ethics matters – and matters a lot. There is a vital compact between the reader and the journalist: 'You the reader put your trust in me, I will do my best to honour that trust by being as truthful and straightforward as possible.' There is also a keen appreciation of the harsh commercial reality that will follow if that bond of trust is broken – 'if readers no longer trust us then they will no longer buy the paper'. Though interestingly no one put forward the idea that at least some of the current decline in circulations might be because of any lessening of that feeling of trust.

The growing importance of social media in newsrooms and newsgathering has complicated existing ethical issues as well introducing new ones. It has made sourcing more complicated; it has blurred the boundaries between what is public space and what is private space.

The twenty four hour nature of media these days means that there is now very little time for any reflection, debate or questioning. Print deadlines and broadcast schedules which would once have offered at least a little time for consideration, now offer none.

Career Stages
In looking at what is currently on offer in terms of the ethical foundations of journalism there are two crucial career stages. The first is the training of those entering journalism as new joiners. The start of anyone's career is an important time in forming their professional mind-set.

The second is the provision for mid-career and senior journalists. There is a big gap here yet these are the people who play a crucial part in the management and editorial leadership of newsrooms on a day-to-day basis. In newspapers they will be the people leading the news desk or the foreign desk, giving assignments to and guiding reporters and correspondents; with broadcasters, they will be the people responsible for the output on a day-to-day basis. Yet often they will have received little or no training since they first joined the organization. They will be expected to have acquired the leadership, management and editorial skills necessary for their changed roles by osmosis. They are often the neglected and 'squeezed middle'.

Pre-Entry Training
There is a lot of teaching of regulation at the moment. There is a lot less teaching of media ethics. The words ethics and regulation often seem to be used

inter-changeably. But they are not the same. It is important to understand the difference. Ethics goes much wider and deeper than regulation.

Regulation is what you can and can't do; ethics is what you *should* do. There may well be a whole series of journalistic circumstances where there are ethical considerations which are not covered by regulation. Good journalists not only need to know *what* is right and wrong but they also need to understand *why*. It is quite possible to meet the considerations of a regulatory code without having much understanding of the reasoning behind the code. There is a world of difference between teaching the letter of the PCC Code and its spirit. It is the spirit which needs to be captured in any future programme of ethics.

Doctrine and belief

It is of course important that both the PCC Code (and whatever ultimately takes its place) and the Ofcom Code are integral parts of journalistic training. Entrants to the professions need to know about them. But teaching regulation without teaching ethics is a bit like preaching the Ten Commandments without giving any understanding of religion.

How much is done on ethics in pre-entry training, over and beyond the basics of the regulatory codes, does need to be seriously looked at. Most syllabuses don't give any impression that ethics is a crucial part of training. There is seldom a separate section on journalistic ethics in the programme of study. Indeed the very word 'ethics' or 'ethical' occurs rarely and when it does crop up it is usually peripheral. Ethics training needs to be given a higher profile in most syllabuses.

Time is clearly a big factor for many providers of training. All acknowledged the importance of ethics but many worried about how they were going to fit anything more into their already crowded timetables.

Everyone agreed that the teaching of journalistic ethics needed to be grounded in and based on real-life practical case-histories. One example of how this can be done is to be found in some of the current modules on journalism and society and the relationship between the two. They are rooted in practical journalism and include whole chunks on ethics based on real life case studies. At the end of the course there is a specific ethical question in the exam which looks not only at solutions but also the reasoning involved. This seems to me to offer something of a model for the future.

Raising the profile of ethics in training was a key recommendation of the report I submitted to the NCTJ. In November 2012 the organization announced that from 2013 onwards a new module on ethics is to be included in its Diploma in Journalism. The new module, to be called Practical Journalism Ethics, will have a one-hour written exam in which students will be judged not on right or wrong answers but on how well they identify the issues. At the same time, the NCTJ Diploma's Essential Media Law module will be revised to include a greater emphasis on regulation.

Mid-career and Senior Journalists

When I asked senior news executives about the training of senior and mid-career journalists the quotes were quite startling:

> *"The gap [in ethics] is really with senior editors."*

> *"If there is going to be a prompt change in the culture of journalism in this country then there has to be a re-education of editors – this has to start with the 'back-bench'"*

> *"Journalism must be one of the only professions or trades where the only place you do any training or development is at the beginning. After that you are just expected to pick this stuff up"*

> *"We've got some journalists, now working as editors, who were hired as brilliant writers twenty years ago and who have had no training ever since."*

> *"Senior journalists are just expected to pick it all up from reading the Media Guardian and the odd PA Law Report."*

These quotes sum up why I now think mid-career training is crucial. These are the journalists who often have to take the most sensitive ethical decisions. They are the ones briefing reporters before they leave the office; they are the ones junior colleagues come to with their dilemmas; they are the ones who watch over and approve the final copy. But most will have received little or no training since they first entered journalism. Most will have received no training for the job which they are now doing.

One shrewd editor remarked to me that at a senior level it's often about the questions you ask of those who are doing the reporting and that what newsgathering editors need most is training in 'ethics supervision'.

Newsrooms have always been places where fast decisions have to be made. There has never been much time to pause or reflect. That is even more the case today. Newsroom cuts have reduced the numbers; those who remain are taking more decisions faster than ever. There are fewer people around to ask. The pressures of twenty four news have speeded up the decision-making time scale even more. As one managing editor said to me with real feeling: 'Senior journalists are so busy they never have to time nowadays to pause and think about any of this stuff'

How much, if any, training senior journalists receive does vary from organization to organization. Most news organizations have organized some short legal refresher courses, some in response to the strictures of the Bribery Act. Some have organized sessions with the PCC to go over some recent cases.

The role of the PCC

In recent years the PCC has taken on an increasingly important role in journalism ethics training. It is not a role for which it was originally designed nor is it one for which it was funded.

The PCC has sent a speaker or a trainer to several Diploma level training courses to speak to entry-level students in order to introduce them to the essentials of the PCC Editors' Code.

At a more senior level, the PCC has offered news organizations update seminars on some of its recent adjudications and cases. These often took place in newsrooms, were open to all staff and usually lasted for an hour or an hour and a half. They were done on an ad-hoc basis, as and when requested and when someone was available. There have also been seminars on specific topics at the PCC Holborn headquarters for senior representatives from the main news groups.

When the PCC was in full flow doing workshops they were reaching some 100 newspapers a year, though this activity has dropped off with the Leveson uncertainty over the future shape of regulation.

If there is to be a programme of training and development in the future for senior editors and executives, the successor regulator to the PCC could have a crucial role to play.

Continuous Professional Development

Almost all professions now require their practitioners to undertake some form of continuous professional development (CPD) to ensure that everyone is up to date with current developments. Lawyers have to do it, so do doctors. Even plumbers have to be retrained to fit the latest boiler. The phrase 'continuous professional development' is a helpful one to use. It more accurately describes what is involved at a senior level than the word 'training'.

But apart from the odd refresher session or PCC seminar, there has been little training for senior staff in most newsrooms. Everyone claims to be too busy for there to be any explicit discussion of the various ethical issues that can arise. This is a big gap. Most of the people I interviewed thought something should be done about it. Views varied as to what and how.

There are some exceptions to this lack of senior training and development. In the wake of the phone-hacking revelations two media groups have launched new initiatives. One group started seminars last year for its senior editors; another is about to launch a series of workshops for its senior journalists called 'Ethics and Dilemmas'. Separately, in response to the Hutton Report in 2004, the BBC some years ago introduced a leadership course for journalists who are becoming editors for the first time and this includes some sections on ethical journalism ('what is journalism in the public interest?', 'what is impartiality?').

But so far these courses are the exceptions across the industry as a whole.

All these courses are being delivered by senior journalists or ex-journalists. A lot of respondents stressed to me how important it was for the credibility of the message that it was delivered by senior working journalists.

There seems to be a substantial need for a programme of continuous professional development across journalism. This need is likely to become even more urgent in the post-Leveson world. This is not a responsibility that can be farmed out to the lawyers or the HR department. Good, effective and credible ethics training has to be journalistically led and led by journalists. It is important that ethics is seen as something that journalists should worry about and that they should 'own' the issues.

Ethics could form a part of a larger package of mid-career development which could also include law refreshers, changes in the law such as the Bribery Act; as well as new developments in social media and technology, latest market and readership trends, updates on recent compliance and regulatory issues as well as leadership and management modules.

Professional development is probably going to be done by most organizations in-house but there is going to be a natural desire among all of them not to re-invent the wheel for every individual scheme. There could be a lot of content and case studies that could be shared across courses as part of a cross-industry initiative.

It won't be easy. This is new territory for journalism. Several people made the point to me that the lead needs to come from the top. If the Boards of the various media organizations and the editors-in-chief don't take this stuff seriously then no one else will. The three initiatives mentioned above all came originally from their respective boardrooms.

But if journalism is to regain its credibility and regain the trust of the public it is essential that it takes ethics very seriously – and is seen to do so – and that it creates the right professional forums and programmes where such issues can be discussed and best practice shared.

Note on the contributor
Phil Harding is a journalist, broadcaster and media consultant. He is a former Editor of the Today programme and Controller of Editorial Policy at the BBC. He is a Fellow of the Society of Editors. This chapter is based on the research he recently carried out for the National Council for the Training of Journalists.

Section G. Suffering for the sins of others; the regional and local press

John Mair

All wars injure innocent bystanders. The War for Lord Justice Leveson's Ear has its' fair share. The national broadsheet journalists and editors claim 'not us' and pin the tail of blame on the donkeys that are the British 'red-top' tabloids for bringing Leveson about through their outrageous (and illegal) behaviour.

The local and regional press in the UK also claim innocent bystander status. They were hardly called to Lord Justice Leveson's witness box. He said 'they have been much praised 'in his report but they are still likely to be subject to the same regulatory system-whatever emerges- as the nationals once the dust and debate have settled. Not a prospect to which they look forward.

Tor Clark is a regional newspaper journalist and editor turned 'hackademic'. He is not as despondent as his former colleagues in local journalism. He finds some grounds for hope in the post-Leveson world of journalism. Much more worrying for them is their seemingly inevitable and unremitting commercial decline they all face. Death by a thousand cuts. Many or most are in the intensive care ward waiting for the Grim Reaper to call.

Paul Marsden is a former local 'hack' too. He now studies and teaches 'hackery'. He has seen the locals suffering for the sins of the others who employed industrial scale phone hacking, open 'blagging' (importuning to obtain documents or information), bribery and corruption (to which we still have to attach the adjective 'alleged') and all the other 'dark arts', mostly illegal, of the latter day Fleet Street. In Blackpool, Bolton and Bradford though the 'dark arts' remained just that to the vast majority of journalists. Ethics was more than a 'county down South'.

The war set off by the closure of the *News of The World* in July 2011 has set off many other bush fires. Not only the guilty have been consumed in their flames.

Leveson: Four reasons to be cheerful for the regionals!

Tor Clark is a true 'hackademic', a former regional newspaper editor turned educator of wannabe journalists at De Montfort University in Leicester. He looks for some good news for the local press in Lord Justice Leveson's report, which has been painted into a very negative corner. He finds it. It may not suffer for the sins of others.

Gloom hung over the regional press as it anticipated the Leveson Report. Lord Justice Leveson had not been impressed by the antics of parts of the national press during his Inquiry and many in local journalism feared harsh regulation would be visited upon them by the sins of their national brethren.

But in the end, not only is the regional press likely to be able to live happily with a new independent self-regulation regime, but Leveson also served up a prominent vindication of the value, and timely warning about the financial state of the local press.

The headlines on publication of the Report were all about statutory underpinning of the new regulation regime, but careful reading of Leveson's voluminous content reveals reasons to be positive for the regional press.

Four main issues emerged for local newspapers.

Firstly, the regional press response to statutory regulation; secondly the experience of press regulation; thirdly the regional press having to suffer a harsher regulation regime for crimes which Leveson acknowledged they had not committed; and finally Leveson's sympathetic and heartfelt characterisation of the importance of the regional press to its communities and his warning of the danger to society if its current plight was ignored.

Regional voices against statutory regulation

Most of the press, regional and national, has united in its opposition to statutory regulation.[1] Legislation is as much an issue for the regional as the national press and is dealt with elsewhere in this book.

Speaking on behalf of the regional press, Adrian Jeakings, president of the Newspaper Society, said: "The Leveson Report made clear the criticisms of the British press over the past 18 months were not directed at our titles, indeed our contribution to the life of local life was 'truly without parallel'.

"However, like it or not, we are an important part of the press and any system of regulation will likely apply to us as much as to the national papers. It is therefore essential we work with them to quickly put in place a tough, effective and independent system of self-regulation without statutory underpinning."[2]

On the day of the Report, as regional editors sounded off against statutory regulation, Jeakings' immediate reaction was: "Local newspapers have always been vehemently opposed to any form of statutory involvement or underpinning in the regulation of the press, including the oversight by Ofcom proposed in the report. This would impose an unacceptable regulatory burden on the industry, potentially inhibiting freedom of speech and the freedom to publish."[3]

Legislation is a major issue and though the regional press has largely come out against a press law, a case could be made that statutory regulation of press, though not a desirable principle, is inevitable after 20 years in the 'Last Chance Saloon' and should not seriously affect the local press anyway because it is least likely to offend.

These are important areas, but it is more useful to dwell on more practical issues around the operation of the regional press.

The regional press experience with regulation

Leveson referred to the 70 years of attempts to regulate the press by various inquiries and regulatory regimes. The most recent, the Press Complaints Commission (PCC) was imposed on the press after a spate of high-profile transgressions by the national tabloids. Then, as now the regional press faces the same sanctions regime.

Despite the existence of the Press Council, many reporters working in regional journalism before the PCC[4] had little sense of regulation beyond the law. The National Council for the Training of Journalists' (NCTJ) qualification regime emphasised standards, accuracy and basic competence, but did not specifically address moral grey areas as long as they were within the law.

The notorious 'death knock' would be an excellent example of this, whereby a reporter would be sent out to visit the family of someone who had died unexpectedly. The instruction would be to 'get the story'. It was bad enough to have to knock on the door of bereaved people in the first place, but to have to go back again and again until they spoke to you was an ordeal for the journalist (never mind the bereaved).[5]

The regional press signed up to the new PCC Code with alacrity and one of the most noticeable changes was clause 5 covering 'intrusion into grief or shock' which meant reporters got one shot at the death knock and should not return. In this way the Code came as a relief and a protection to many reporters, who found the 'death knock' the most potentially morally unacceptable aspect of their job.

There was no doubt about the regional commitment to the new PCC Code. Speaking at the first Johnston Press Editors' Conference in York in 1998, company chairman Freddy Johnston unequivocally instructed all his editors to their faces to obey the PCC Code.[6]

Journalists in the regional press tried to work within the Code and transgressions from the Code were often accidental or unintentional rather than a deliberate attempt to take a story further or steal a march on rivals.

PCC complaints statistics by sector show the regional press for all its huge size attracted far fewer complaints than the nationals. The 2011 figures show from the total 7,341 complaints, 'cases where investigation was warranted i.e. the PCC requested a response from the relevant editor because the complaint appeared to raise a possible breach of the Code'[7] broke down as:

> 54.4% national newspapers
>
> 31.2% regional newspapers
>
> 8.4% Scottish newspapers
>
> 1.1% Irish newspapers[8]

In 2010 the picture was similar

> 50.3% national newspapers
>
> 33.7% regional newspapers
>
> 8.7% Scottish newspapers
>
> 2.1% Northern Irish newspapers[9]

And in 2009

> 51.51% national newspapers
>
> 33.33% regional newspapers
>
> 8.24% Scottish newspapers
>
> 2.13% Northern Irish newspapers[10]

If we accept the Newspaper Society's claim that 33 million people (or 71% of the adult population) read the regional press[11] and 56% read a national, we can see the smaller national newspaper readership generated more than half the complaints to the PCC consistently. Total regional complaints hover just over 30%, and that is without knowing the nature of the regional complaints, the seriousness or the outcome.

It can therefore be argued, as the regional press attracts significantly fewer complaints than the nationals, regulation would have less of an impact on it. Also, as Lord Justice Leveson pointed out during the hearings, in general, complaints to the regional press are less serious than those to the nationals, are more swiftly resolved and the complainants themselves are often more amenable to a timely apology.[12] Taking all these factors into account, the regional press has less, if anything, to fear from a stricter regulatory regime, as envisaged by Leveson.

The regional press suffers for the sins of the national press

Leveson said: "Although accuracy and similar complaints are made against local newspapers, the criticisms of culture, practices and ethics of the press raised in this Inquiry do not affect them: on the contrary, they have been much praised."[13]

But as can clearly be seen from the complaints statistics, the nationals were the major offenders and despite his praise, the relatively little time he gave the regional press to make its case and the fact it has suffered the same sanction as the nationals did attract criticism.

Although he took no verbal evidence from the editors of the largest single part of the regional press, weekly newspapers, Leveson did hear from the editors of some of Britain's biggest regional papers, Mike Gilson, editor of the *Belfast Telegraph*, John McLellan, then editor of *The Scotsman*, Spencer Feeney, editor of the *South Wales Evening Post*, Jonathan Russell, editor of the *Glasgow Herald*, Noel Doran editor of the *Irish News*, Peter Charlton, editor of the *Yorkshire Post*, Nigel Pickover, then editor of the *Ipswich Star*, and Maria McGeoghan, then editor of the *Manchester Evening News*.

After hearing from them Leveson said: "The presence of editors from outside the bubble that represents Fleet Street is, I think, extremely important to make the point that you have each in turn tried to make about the differences, about the value of your work and the important value of regional journalism."[14]

Gilson was disappointed by the way Leveson failed to differentiate between the nationals and what he (Gilson) described as 'newspapers outside London'.

In an impassioned piece in his own newspaper, he wrote: "For Leveson, the UK's regional press was but a bit part, an extra in a widescreen epic about clandestine meetings in the corridors of power, or in the fields of Gloucestershire and sinister, burly men chasing beautiful heroines down London streets in the dark of night.

> "He patted us on the head and said it wasn't really about us. But while some of the local press is in a pretty poor, supine state, in big cities like Belfast, Bristol and Newcastle and in Scotland and Wales, there are robust titles still lifting the rocks to find out what lies underneath.

> "Yet what did we really get from Leveson? A few paragraphs in his 2,000-page report and a proposal to put us under some form of statutory legislation for our pains.

> "Newspapers outside of London have a total of 33million readers every week, far above the combined circulation of those based in the capital.

"The problem was that, by not taking seriously enough the reading material seen by those 33million pairs of eyes, Sir Brian was bound to get a totally skewed picture.

"Putting aside the fact that most of the abuses of press power he heard about were already covered by laws, he denied himself evidence of the hundreds of stories that shed light on corruption, uncover miscarriage of justice, or reveal poor governance every week in the press, both in London and, as importantly, outside.

"Had he done so, his argument for some form of parliamentary involvement by statute in the running of the press would have been even weaker than it is now."[15]

Kevin Ward, editor of the *South Wales Echo*, pointed out: "More people read a regional or local newspaper at some point during a week than read a national.

"Yet the potential impacts of Lord Justice Leveson's recommendations for future regulation on the regional press are barely being mentioned in the wall-to-wall coverage that followed last week's publication of his Inquiry report.

"Television news constantly referred to the awful behaviour of the British press, as if all newspapers took part in the dreadful practice of phone hacking and other criminal acts.

"The reality is it was a tiny percentage of the British press that acted in a reprehensible manner."[16]

The essential argument is Leveson exhibited a patronising view of the local press and then saddled all of it with the same punishment as the nationals, despite happily conceding it had not committed the crimes which prompted it.

This made Gilson and other critics justifiably angry, but in the end what else was Leveson to do? The only 'fair' alternative might have been to set up a separate regulatory body for the regional press – so called 'two-tier regulation' – but this was never likely.

Lack of differentiation in the sanction, despite the evidence, was always going to be a problem, but if the regional press looks beyond this legitimate sense of injustice, there may be more reasons to be cheerful than glum.

Leveson emphasises the crisis in the regional press

Leveson's highlighting of the current plight of the UK regional press was an unexpected bonus. He praised the regional press, rightly celebrated its crucial role in communities up and down the UK and then tellingly warned of the threat to the future of local journalism caused by its present well-documented problems, before asking for the burden and cost of whatever new regulatory body is formed not to fall too heavily on local journalism.

Leveson concluded: "In relation to regional and local newspapers, I do not make a specific recommendation but I suggest the Government should look urgently at what action it might be able take to help safeguard the ongoing viability of this much valued and important part of the British press.

> "It is clear to me local, high-quality and trusted newspapers are good for our communities, our identity and our democracy and play an important social role. However, this issue has not been covered in any detail by the Inquiry and, although the extent and nature of the problem has been made clear, the Inquiry has heard no evidence as to how it might be addressed.

> "I recognise there is no simple solution to this issue. I also recognise many efforts have been made over the years to try to find a solution, and many of the options for public support that have been canvassed are not appropriate. This does not make the need to find a solution any less urgent."[17]

He addressed problems with falling circulation and revenue and – though there was little mention of the regional press owners' part in the creation of the current crisis because of the burden of debt imposed on some publishers by the large purchase prices during consolidation – he did point towards what some commentators have long thought, that without this debt, the future might be brighter for the sector[18] when he stated: "Despite this bleak picture, regional news provision remains essentially profitable, with the three of the top four regional newspaper groups for which figures are available posting profits of £154m between them in 2010."[19]

He added: "As to the commercial problems facing newspapers, I must make a special point about Britain's regional newspapers. In one sense, they are less affected by the global availability of the biggest news stories but their contribution to local life is truly without parallel...

"Many are no longer financially viable and they are all under enormous pressure as they strive to re-write the business model necessary for survival. Yet their demise would be a huge setback for communities (where they report on local politics, occurrences in the local courts, local events, local sports and the like) and would be a real loss for our democracy."[20]

This argument has subsequently been picked up by MPs[21] and it is to be hoped in their clamouring against statutory regulation, regional press leaders do not overshadow this more critical issue and waste this brief opportunity to highlight their current plight and seek help from a temporarily sympathetic political establishment and public.

So, what does it all mean for the UK regional press?
Simply stated, Leveson advocated punishment for the regional press for the sins of the nationals, but that punishment would only be a problem if the regional press was to be a major offender, just as toughening up the law against burglary would not affect anyone who doesn't steal things from other people's houses.

Though the precise shape of the future regulatory regime is not yet known, as long as it is not framed to stop the local paper exposing the councillor's fiddled expenses it is likely the regional press will have little problem staying within the new post-Leveson code of conduct, just as it did with the PCC.

In much of the regional press there is not the same competitive imperative as with the nationals, and if the local press transgresses it risks losing the respect of its community, a risk not faced in the same way by the nationals. It has its well-earned local integrity and trust built up over decades. It has its offices in its community where the staff are accountable to their readers face-to-face and it has the local commercial trade it relies on to stay in business. It has to play the long game and it has nowhere else to go.

Finally, as with its more cautious approach to the law of libel, in an environment of £1m fines, local papers simply don't have the resources to make a mistake of that magnitude.

The spectre of state regulation is not appealing, but it will happen, or it won't, and these great arguments of principle detract from the reality of the survival of the regional press, which must be more pressing.

So putting this aside, and the injustice of being kept behind after school because the naughty boys from the nationals misbehaved, the UK regional press has little to fear from tougher regulation because it is unlikely to be a major offender and if Leveson's comments about the value of local journalism do hit home, as they appear to have done for some MPs already, Leveson's impact is at worst neutral to the regional press and at best doubly positive in allowing it to be lauded as a responsible media while having overdue light shone on its positive role and current plight.

Notes

[1] The editorial columns of many regional newspapers the next day rang with the cry against statutory regulation.

[2] Linford, P., (2012) Local press boss calls for industry-wide deal on Leveson, http://www.holdthefrontpage.co.uk/2012/news/local-press-boss-calls-for-industry-wide-deal-on-leveson/ (accessed 05.12.12)

[3] See http://www.holdthefrontpage.co.uk/2012/news/editors-welcome-pms-stance-on-leveson/ where Jeakings and an array of regional editors are quoted in opposition to a new law. (accessed 05.12.12)

[4] Personal and anecdotal recollection of colleagues working in the industry in the 80s and early 90s.

[5] See Duncan, S. and Newton, J., 2010. How do you feel? Preparing novice reporters for the death knock, an exploration of attitudes and approaches. *Journalism Practice*, 4(4), pp. 439-453, and Newton, J. and Duncan S., (2012) Journalists and the bereaved: constructing a positive approach to the teaching of death reporting in Journalism Education, vol 1 issue 2, November 2012, Published online by the UK association for Journalism Education http://journalism-education.org for fuller discussions of the difficult moral area that is the phenomenon of the death knock. See also relevant

chapters of Keeble, R.L., and Mair, J., (2012) The Phone Hacking Scandal: Journalism on Trial, Suffolk: Abramis

[6] Speech by Freddy Johnston at first Johnston Press Editors' Conference, Royal York Hotel, York, January 1998, attended by author

[7] PCC 2011 figures preamble
http://www.pcc.org.uk/assets/80/PCC_Complaints_Statistics_for_2011.pdf

[8] PCC 2011 figures
http://www.pcc.org.uk/assets/80/PCC_Complaints_Statistics_for_2011.pdf

[9] PCC 2010 figures http://www.pcc.org.uk/review10/statistics-and-key-rulings/complaints-statistics/

[10] PCC 2009 figures http://www.pcc.org.uk/annualreports/annualreview.html The author is grateful to Catherine Spellar of the PCC for help in provision of sector complaints statistics

[11] www.newspapersoc.org.uk

[12] Leveson hearings, day 28, Jan 18, 2012, page 106.

[13] Leveson, The Rt Hon Lord Justice, (2012), An Inquiry into the Culture, Practices and Ethics of the Press, Executive Summary, London: TSO: page 6-7.

[14] Leveson hearings, day 28, Jan 18, 2012, page 112.

[15] http://www.belfasttelegraph.co.uk/opinion/columnists/mike-gilson/leveson-in-the-dock-over-handling-of-press-inquiry-16246145.html#ixzz2ECGzBRkx (accessed 05.12.12)

[16]
http://www.southwalesargus.co.uk/news/10092939.THE_EDITOR_S_CHAIR_Press_self_regulation_a_way_to_keep_legislation_at_bay/?ref=rss (accessed 05.12.12)

[17] Leveson, The Rt Hon Lord Justice, (2012), An Inquiry into the Culture, Practices and Ethics of the Press, Executive Summary, London: TSO: Chapter 10: The Regional Press Volume 1 page 152

[18] See Mair, J., Fowler, N., and Reeves, I., (2012) where the role of the regional press's own management in its present financial crisis is discussed in several chapters.

[19] Leveson, The Rt Hon Lord Justice, (2012), An Inquiry into the Culture, Practices and Ethics of the Press, Executive Summary, London:TSO: Chapter 10: The Regional Press Volume 1 page 150

[20] Leveson, The Rt Hon Lord Justice, (2012), An Inquiry into the Culture, Practices and Ethics of the Press, Executive Summary, London:TSO: page 11.

[21] See various articles on holdthefrontpage.co.uk especially
http://www.holdthefrontpage.co.uk/2012/news/act-now-to-save-local-newspapers-ministers-urged/ (accessed 05.12.12)

References
Clark, T., (2012a) 'The demand will remain, but what about the supply?' in Mair, J., Fowler, N., and Reeves, I., (2012) *What Do We Mean By Local: Grass-roots Journalism – Its Death and Rebirth*, Suffolk: Abramis

Clark, T., (2012b) 'Don't damn the many for the sins of the few' *Leicester Mercury*, June 18, 2012, Leicester: Northcliffe Media.

Clark, T., (2012c) 'National press should learn Leveson lesson' *Leicester Mercury*, December 1, 2012, Leicester; Northcliffe Media.

Duncan, S. and Newton, J., 2010. How do you feel? Preparing novice reporters for the death knock, an exploration of attitudes and approaches. *Journalism Practice*, 4(4), pp. 439-453

Gilson, M., (2012) Leveson in the dock over handling of press inquiry http://www.belfasttelegraph.co.uk/opinion/columnists/mike-gilson/leveson-in-the-dock-over-handling-of-press-inquiry-16246145.html#ixzz2ECGzBRkx

Keeble, R.L., and Mair, J., (2012) *The Phone Hacking Scandal: Journalism on Trial*, Suffolk: Abramis

Lambourne, H., (2012) http://www.holdthefrontpage.co.uk/2012/news/editors-welcome-pms-stance-on-leveson/

Leveson, The Rt Hon Lord Justice, (2012), *An Inquiry into the Culture, Practices and Ethics of the Press*, Executive Summary, London:TSO

Linford, P., (2012) Local press boss calls for industry-wide deal on Leveson, http://www.holdthefrontpage.co.uk/2012/news/local-press-boss-calls-for-industry-wide-deal-on-leveson/

Mair, J., Fowler, N., and Reeves, I., (2012) *What Do We Mean By Local? Grass-roots Journalism – Its Death and Rebirth*, Suffolk: Abramis

www.newspapersoc.org.uk

Newton, J. and Duncan S., (2012) Journalists and the bereaved: constructing a positive approach to the teaching of death reporting in *Journalism Education*, vol 1 issue 2, November 2012, published online by the UK Association for Journalism Education http://journalism-education.org

www.pcc.org.uk

Temple, M., (2008) *The British Press*, Maidenhead: McGraw-Hill/Open University Press

Ward, K., (2012) Press self-regulation: A way to keep legislation at bay? http://www.southwalesargus.co.uk/news/10092939.THE_EDITOR___S_CHAIR__Press_self_regulation_a_way_to_keep_legislation_at_bay/?ref=rss

Williams, K., (1998) *Get Me a Murder A Day*, London: Hodder Arnold

Note on the contributor

Tor Clark is Principal Lecturer in Journalism, BA Journalism programme leader and a Teacher Fellow at De Montfort University in Leicester. His main interests are political journalism, the UK regional media, the history of journalism, learning, teaching and the student experience. He was a previously a journalist in the regional press working on free, daily and weekly newspapers, two of which he edited. He is now a regular contributor to BBC Radio Leicester on political and media issues and also writes for *Total Politics* magazine.

Suffering for the sins of others? Leveson and local papers

Paul Marsden of Coventry University looks at the effect of the Leveson process on the largely innocent bystanders – the many local and regional papers in the UK to whom phone hacking,' blagging' and the other Fleet Street 'dark arts' were just that – dark and unknown

In the light of phone hacking, the closure of the *News of the World* and the resultant Leveson Inquiry, Fleet Street has just had its most turbulent eighteen months in a generation.

However, while the attention seeking national press seeks minor surgery its regional relation receives terminal care without many visitors at its' bedside. It is determined to fight another day but having endured several years of financial turmoil now waits to see what punishments it will have to serve for its' big brother's crimes.

In many ways, Leveson (2012) is just a minor inconvenience for the 'business' of regional titles – it's like arguing who is going to drive a car while forgetting it doesn't have an engine. In the last five years the number of regional reporters has shrunk by nearly a third[1] with 9,500 jobs being lost in a three and a half year spell from 2007 alone[2] .

From the outside the future for the regional industry certainly appears bleak.

Into the Intensive Care ward?

The race to consolidate the sector by the leading four players – Johnston Press, Trinity Mirror, Northcliffe and Newsquest – left them with 96% of regional newspaper readership[3] by 2004. But as recession has taken hold their managements have been left chasing unrealistic profit margins in order to pay back multimillion pound loans.[4]

This has meant that Chief Executives mindful of the need to satisfy shareholders, increasing the need for hundreds of staff[5] to be sacrificed in a bid to keep pace with these annual financial repayments. In a drastic bid to reverse the decline, daily titles in several towns and cities have gone weekly such as the

Northampton Chronicle and *Lincolnshire Echo*. In November 2012, Northcliffe sold its regional assets to the Local World consortium for £52m plus a 38.7% stake in the new company – significantly less than the £1.5 billion they attempted to sell it for in 2005.[6]

The thinning out of journalistic staff in the newsroom has led to fears of a lack of local oversight with fewer bodies to cover the courts, councils and the staple community parish pumps causing a so called 'democratic deficit'.

Hyper-local websites like *Lichfield Live* and *Saddleworth News* have sprung up to serve web-savvy locals – serving a need many titles are struggling to cater for – thus creating even more competition for vital readers and declining advertising revenue. Across the regional newspaper sector advertising revenue has fallen by around 50% in the last five years[7]. Regional newspapers are in the intensive care ward and it is feared many will cease to exist in ten years time.

A local toxic legacy?

With such an embattled landscape it is fair to say the phone hacking scandal engulfing the *News of the World* would not have been of massive importance to local newsrooms. But its legacy has already been toxic in communities up and down the country.

Maria McGeoghan, then Editor of the *Manchester Evening News* told Lord Leveson, regional reporters have been on the end of a public backlash against the press. "I've lost count now of the number of times I've been asked how you hack a phone or what the going rate for paying off a policeman is and it's not funny anymore. I'm very concerned about the perception we're all doing something shady."[8]

This viewpoint has been supported by other reporters who agree that the public's view of all journalists has been tainted by the scandal. Rob Parsons, of the (London) *Evening Standard*, has noticed 'subtle' differences to the way the general public relate to him. "I think more people than before, who might not have encountered a journalist previously, have the idea in their head that I will use the information they gave me for nefarious means, try to twist it or make stuff up that they haven't said.

"To members of the public, particularly those who are going through a traumatic period, for example those on the receiving end of a death knock, the difference might not be so obvious. I can imagine why they would read about what the *News of the World* hacks have been doing and imagine I am capable of doing the same thing."[9]

Regional newspaper editors appearing before Leveson said that phone hacking was a largely unknown practice in the local part of the industry. Only one had even heard of the practice prior to the *News Of The World* scandal.

They highlighted the different ethical standards of their newspapers. The editors stated public officials were not paid for stories and that subterfuge, including techniques such as 'blagging' (getting information using false identities or information), were never practiced at their titles.

Nigel Pickover, now Editor in Chief of the *Eastern Daily Press* and *Norwich Evening News*, outlined his opposition to being deceitful to stand-up a story.

"There's always a way round to ask your questions. We've had reporters in nightclubs swabbing for Class A drugs, which we've found, or we have tested security at the port of Felixstowe where we've literally gone in through barriers to find out what their security's like."[8]

Two tiers better than one?

The limited discussion of and blame attached to regional newspapers led some figures in that sector to call for 'two tier regulation'[10] of the press, segregating regional from national titles. The *Wolverhampton Express and Star*, warned that statutory regulation of regionals would leave even less cash to cover public meetings and courts and gained the support of several Midlands MPs (Labour and Conservative) for local papers avoiding any strict new rules[11].

Many within the industry understand public anger at the unethical and probably illegal activities at the *News Of The World* but feel the Press Complaints Commission oversaw their form of community journalism on a fair, consistent and appropriate basis. Many local journalists justifiably feel they are not to blame for the failures of national tabloids.

Roy Wright, Editor of the *Huddersfield Examiner*, believes most regional news chiefs understand the desire for tougher rules but wouldn't back new press legislation. "The issue is that it's a genie out of the bottle. When it goes out, it's very difficult to get back in. Once you start, what about the next government and the one after that? I think the industry has had a wake-up call. I think people have been shocked."[12]

Wright believes for local newspapers self-regulation, backed-up by the threat of public anger, was sufficient "In a community like Huddersfield if you door knock people who don't want to be door knocked your name is mud."

Management v The NUJ?

The lack of appetite for legislation among management at a regional level has once again pitched them against the National Union of Journalists, who surprised some of its own members by calling for statutory underpinning of the press in-line with the system already established in Ireland[13].

In her Leveson Inquiry submission, the National Union of Journalists' General Secretary Michelle Stanistreet attacked the greed of newspaper owners – who the union has been fighting with over job losses and working conditions for several years – and called for a Conscience clause to allow members to refuse assignments which breach the spirit of their code. Adam Christie, Vice President of the NUJ, says regulatory statutory underpinning is the only way to resolve the wider culture of the press.

"The message Leveson has given to politicians is if they don't get to [statutory regulation] it is not going to be long before his successor is appointed. We have just seen the beginning of the battle for what might go into legislation. If we don't go for some sort of statutory underpinning we'll be back in 10 or 15 years time."[12]

However like many other politicians and journalists, Christie is clear local reporters simply have no case to answer. He added: "The regional press does an entirely different job and has come out of Leveson unscathed. Because reporters live in the communities [they cover], we are incredibly accountable to the local communities."

Although proposals to regulate the regional and national press separately failed to gain traction, one positive result for the under-pressure local industry during the Leveson process has been the near universal praise for the work carried out by regional titles.

Ex-Prime Minister Gordon Brown highlighted that "a real problem" was developing about how regionals could continue their watchdog role. He felt a "radical solution" involving examining if the BBC licence fee was spent could form part of the solution. He told Leveson: "Every week I see a local newspaper going under. So we have a problem about how we finance quality journalism for the future. Without shining the light on potential corruption or maladministration or the abuse of power – and that's true at a local level as well as a national level – people get away with doing things in an unaccountable manner that are completely unacceptable, and that is why you need a local press."[8]

The Democratic Deficit?

The lack of reporters to effectively cover local communities is an issue which leading industry figures have highlighted[13]. Former Editor of the *Lincolnshire Echo* and *Derby Telegraph*, Neil Fowler, said in his Nuffield College Oxford Lecture in 2011, that "There are genuine fears of a [democratic] deficit as no-one is left to report on councils, courts and the police, let alone scrutinise them."[14]

There is hope that as the press' rises up the political agenda, albeit for all the wrong reasons, this could act as a trigger to urge MPs and ministers to examine the long-term viability of the local newspaper sector.

One solution proposed to ensure the survival of local newspapers in towns across Britain is to offer them tax breaks. Ex-MP Louise Mensch, whose former Corby constituency lost one of its daily when the *Northampton Chronicle* went weekly in 2012, said: "The local press performs a unique function in our democracy, as often only a local paper will hold a council or an MP to account. Government has to look at ways of preserving Britain's most popular print media – read by an estimated 33 million people per month. When we think of so many things that are subsidised that have only limited appeal, surely there is a case for tax advantages for local papers. And if a pure profit model doesn't work, government should look at ways to facilitate local communities and businesses owning their own papers – like the supporters trust model for football clubs."[15]

Investigating financial support for regionals was a topic touched on by Lord Justice Leveson himself: "It may be one has to be more imaginative about the way it is all funded. I make it abundantly clear I am a great believer, and always have been, in what local newspapers do."[8]

However with Sir Brian Leveson's overall verdict already being questioned, Ms Mensch – seemingly a rising star in the Conservative ranks – quitting her seat to move to New York and former PM Brown a diminished and infrequent visitor to the Commons since his 2010 General Election defeat, it appears these new found friends of the regional press will have little sway on future policy. It also appears fanciful that with the fear of a triple-dip recession on the cards and local services being squeezed more than ever that the government will dole out tax breaks for the large, very profitable companies that own the regional press.

This is not to say that local newspapers don't retain some powerful friends in Parliament. Cabinet Office minister Francis Maude, writing for the *West Sussex County Times*, stated his support for locals: "The contrast between national and local press [has been] highlighted more than ever – people trust local and regional press so much more than national papers…We trust [*The County Times*] to report on all local stories – both good and bad – unlike the national press."[16]

Support for the work of local journalists has also come from Labour MP Tom Watson, a prominent (former) member of the Culture, Media and Sport Select Committee. In 2012 this Committee stated that Rupert Murdoch, who testified before them in the wake of the phone hacking scandal, was, in their view, "not fit" to run his own company-News Corporation[17]. Watson believes the increasingly qualified and heavily unionised regional press had become the ethical standard bearer for the sector. "We don't need to change anything in the regional press, they are great papers. The NUJ had their code of conduct and Rupert Murdoch drove them out of Wapping. Had they had that code of conduct the [*NOTW*] cub reporters might have had the strength to shelter themselves from these activities."[12]

Action this day – or tomorrow?

It remains to be seen whether these warm wishes develop into empty platitudes and inaction as many regionals slide into oblivion. This will be the real test of the government's attitude to community journalism, a potentially key component of the Conservatives' much derided 'Big Society' now a seemingly discarded policy.

For the moment it appears pragmatism is the order of the day in government ranks. Looking forward to a difficult General Election in 2015 it appears the Conservative Party is more pre-occupied with staying in bed with the national press than assisting their local relatives out of their hospices.

As Lord Justice Leveson's Inquiry publication neared it was noticeable that leading Conservatives such as Michael Gove, Boris Johnson and Teresa May ratcheted-up the pressure that statutory regulation of the national press was not required[18]. This pre-empted David Cameron's rejection of the call for statutory regulation and it appears the ensuing split in the Coalition along with a bun fight in the Commons will now be allowed to polarise the debate on the future of all the UK's press.

The fear is that with further government cuts on the horizon talking up regionals, with their shrinking budgets, their owner's huge debts and falling circulations, is as far as ministers are prepared to go. Praised but underappreciated regional journalists are set to be left on the outside looking in alongside the genuine victims of hacking while the chastened but unbowed big nationals lobby Downing Street to retain their 'independence' and influence.

The local voice-muted at Leveson?

The Leveson Inquiry only heard from eight daily local newspaper editors – no weekly editors were included – in one afternoon on Wednesday January 18th, with three other written witness statements presented with the oral evidence. That day at the Inquiry was shared with the editors of celebrity magazines *Hello, OK* and *Heat.*

The entire regional press, which will be governed by Leveson's recommendations if they are accepted, was allotted one afternoon while politicians such as Jeremy Hunt, Jack Straw, Tony Blair, David Cameron and former Information Commissioner Richard Thomas were heard alone on set days.

Does this seem a fair way to assess the work of hundreds of newspapers around the UK?

If nothing else regional titles should have been afforded more time to differentiate themselves by showcasing the higher moral standards and ethics practiced in communities across the UK. As John McLellan, then Editor of the *Scotsman*, told Leveson the titillation sought by national tabloids is often a world away from the stories published by regionals. "The press serving smaller communities, while not perfect, has a very good reputation for behaving responsibly and ethically and should not be tarnished by recent scandals involving newspapers with an entirely different agenda."

Due to the deluge of sleazy tabloid behaviour showcased day-after-day and the constant presence of odious characters such as Paul McMullen spouting his 'privacy is for paedos' message, the image of every print reporter was suddenly reworked as a caricature of a weird desperado crawling through people's garbage.

Life outside the Leveson bubble?

Cut adrift from the Leveson spotlight many titles took the direct route to inform their readers of the truth. The *Blackpool Gazette* got readers to highlight the real power of the press explaining how they had fought campaigns for the introduction of stalking legislation, increased NHS funding to treat patients and to save the North Pier Theatre and the Grand.

Chief Feature Writer, Jacquie Morley, told readers: "We don't care about who's sleeping with who. We present real issues for real people. We've campaigned against knife crime, drugs, social blight, juvenile nuisance. We've not just banged the drum for the homeless this year but gone out and experienced a taste of it – one reporter spending two nights on the streets."[19]

Phone hacking revelations have certainly affected a degree of the public's trust in reporters leaving an unwarranted stain on innocent regional newsrooms. Indeed legislating against local titles is akin to punishing every corner shop in Britain for the misbehaviour of Tesco.

When geographical location is paramount to the survival of a newspaper it creates an inbuilt ethical standard in a newsroom. The *Sun* may have withstood a Merseyside boycott for 24 years after the Hillsborough Tragedy but the *Liverpool Echo* would not have. Once your name becomes mud it is a long road back for any regional paper. What reader wants their town to be unfairly repeatedly vilified by one of 'their own'? Nothing suggested by lawmakers will ever come close to the 'chilling' impact of unhappy readers cancelling their papers.

Ultimately, however new, tougher legislation is established local journalists will react in the same way as they have to every recent setback – by delivering the news to those communities who rely on them.

Notes

[1] Society of Editors (2011) *The future is yours: A survey of Editors attitudes*

[2] Nel (2010, pg.10) *Laid off: What do UK Journalists Do Next?* Published in collaboration with Journalism.co.uk.

[3] Greenslade, R (2004) *Have the regional takeovers run out of steam?* The Guardian. 29th November.

[4] Sweney, M (2011) *Johnston Press reports 8% fall in ad revenue* The Guardian. 15th November.

[5] Linford (2011) *Northcliffe profits down £10m as 600 staff axed* Holdthefrontpage.co.uk.

[6] Wembridge, M and Cookson, R (2012) *DGMT agrees Northcliffe newspaper arm sale* The Financial Times. 21st November.

[7] Source: Evidence of Spencer Feeney, Editor of South Wales Evening Post, to Leveson Inquiry. Available at www.levesoninquiry.org.uk.

[8] Quotations from the Leveson hearings taken from www.levesoninquiry.org.uk.

[9] Interview, 13th November.

[10] Greenslade, R (2012) *Flawed call by MPs who want regulation leniency for regional newspapers* The Guardian. 19th November.

[11] Wainwright, D (2012) *Unfair regulations on regional press* Wolverhampton Express & Star. 15th November.

[12] Remarks taken from *The Future of Journalism Conference* at Huddersfield University. 29th November 2012.

[13] Linford, P (2012) *NUJ faces industry backlash over new press laws* Holdthefrontpage.co.uk. 10th July.

[14] Fowler, N (2011) *Have they got news for you? The rise, the fall and the future of regional and local newspapers in the United Kingdom* The Guardian lecture at Nuffield College. 9th November.

[15] Burrell, I (2012) *Read all about it? Not in this once proud heartland* The i. 24th April

[16] Maude, F (2012) *Francis Maude: Column* West Sussex County Times. 6th November

[17] Peston, R (2012) *Murdoch 'not fit' to run News Corp* BBC News online. 1st May.

[18] Walters, S (2012) *Leveson 'to order press must be ruled by law'* The Mail on Sunday. 11th November.

[19] Morley, J (2012) *The real power of the press – our readers* The Blackpool Gazette. 4th December.

Note on the contributor

Paul Marsden is a former regional newspaper reporter who currently teaches Journalism and Media students at Coventry University. Prior to this he taught at Huddersfield New College and the Grimsby Institute of Further and Higher Education. He has experience of working at several regional newspapers, primarily in Yorkshire, Lancashire and Staffordshire. His most prominent role was as South Fylde reporter at the *Blackpool Gazette* where he covered the capsizing of HMS Riverdance, several murder trials, helped save a swimming pool from council cutbacks and also quizzed Nick Griffin at the BNP Summer conference. His chapter in *What Do We Mean By Local?* (edited by John Mair, Neil Fowler and Ian Reeves) entitled 'Autumn leaves: the sad and fast decline of the British regional press' was informed by his MA dissertation, Where did all the staff go? – A study of Journalists in the UK Regional Print Media

Section H. Do they mean us?
The view from elsewhere

John Mair

The Leveson Inquiry has been the reality must see show of the media chattering classes for the last eighteen months. It was live streamed and all testimony recorded, transcribed and cached on the Inquiry website. TV news and analysis programmes have used the video as evidence and some like 'rogue reporter' Rich Peppiatt have even put the testimony to music in 'mash-ups'.

The UK media agenda has been 'Leveson, Leveson and more Leveson' for much of 2012.But has it travelled beyond these shores. How has it played abroad?

Hugo De Burgh is a distinguished Professor of Journalism at the University of Westminster. For the last decade or more he has focussed his intellectual firepower on the emerging media landscape that is the PRC-China. Regulation rules there of course, especially by the ruling party-the Communist Party of China. They have a diagonally opposite take on Leveson to the British press barons; they like the thought of a regulated press as De Burgh explains with recent examples from China.

Jon Eilenberg is a visiting scholar to the UK from Denmark. He has come to study for a Masters in International Journalism at Brunel University in London. He has an outsider's view of the Leveson storm. He can see the wood for the trees and the obfuscation and fog put up by some of the Leveson sceptics and deniers. His analysis is clear, fresh and pointed.

Huw Hopkins already has his masters in Global Journalism from Coventry University. He looks at how others, especially in the Commonwealth, might look to post-Leveson Britain for examplars of press regulation for them to put into statute.

So, it seems the moving reality show in Court 73 of the High Court in the Strand might have echoes beyond the Westminster and Media Villages of London.

Leveson and China: The Leveson Inquiry as reference in China's debates over Media Regulation

Professor Hugo de Burgh is Director of the China Media Centre at the University of Westminster. He has been looking at how Lord Justice Leveson and his proposals for better regulating the British media are regarded in another and more regulated media land

In January 2012 the Chinese equivalent of Ofsted, the SARFT[1], promulgated restrictive regulations on entertainment television, following consultation on policy papers over the preceding year. These were reported in the Anglophone press as further examples of Chinese government repression of the media.

The new regulations would have been more accurately interpreted as a response to the widespread concern in China about the excesses of the media. The Leveson Inquiry in the UK has been followed with interest in China, because the issues it raises have long been discussed there (Li: 2005). The other media-related stories of 2012, from the Jimmy Savile case to the *Newsnight* mendacity and the case of the two Australian reporters' sting on the hospital where Prince William's wife was a patient, have all provoked comment and argument, because they have raised the issue of media regulation in terms which are familiar in China but not expected from the West.

The kind of things that Chinese people are worried about
In an essay reflecting on his experiences of television chat shows, the novelist, blogger and youth hero Han Han described his fury at discovering, on a programme purporting to discuss his own writings, that members of the audience had been primed to attack him as 'readers' and provoke dissension, and - to add insult to injury - they had not even read his works!

> On that programme, *How they moved me*, I stated that I disliked the stirring up of conflict on television programmes; good programmes should direct their attacks towards real problems and inequities in the world, rather than

manufacture dissension among studio guests. Today's programme makers only reckon a programme works if it produces discord and conflict. If this goes on, we will soon see satellite TV producing a programme in which they urge loving couples to divorce, and it'll be called *'I smash, I smash, I smash smash smash'*. (Han: 2012, 022)

What he is describing is a tendency to tabloidisation which has come about as China's media have become more commercial and more competitive. The phenomenon is known in China as 'eyeball journalism' and 'screaming media' (Li: 2008).

A leading professor of media studies, on being asked whether Taiwan's 'free' media offered China a model for the future, expressed a general anxiety when he replied:

> Taiwan has public media, but the majority of the media of Taiwan are commercial. So that's why they have many different voices. But there are two problems. One is that the media are overly commercial. Because it's a small island, a small market, with too many TV channels, the competition is ferocious. They have more than 120 channels, many of which are entertainment or news channels. They compete within this small market, so that the news programmes are becoming more and more 'tabloid'. They are increasingly sensationalised, yes,even more so than the Anglo-Saxon media. Even Taiwanese scholars criticise this. They describe today's Taiwan media with three Chinese words 'Xing', 'Shan', 'Xing'. ('Sexual', 'Sensational', 'Bloody'). (Hu: 2012)

The January 2012 regulations[2] are more a response to widespread concern, than constituting censorship in the way that China's Western attackers usually imply. If those regulations are censorship, then the *BBC Guidelines* on taste and decency constitute censorship (though by the media class, rather than by the political class).

Too much entertainment is bad for you?

What actually occurred was that SARFT ordered broadcasters to reduce the number of entertainment programmes and increase the time allocated to news and current affairs, to encourage other types of programme production such as documentaries, and limit commercial breaks (SARFT: 2012). Concern at the trashy and vulgar nature of many of the entertainment programmes, their licentiousness and promotion of greed and celebrity, was the main reason. However, it is possible that SARFT was also anxious about the success of regional television companies in competing for audiences with national 'public service' CCTV, and wished to remind the broadcasters, daily growing richer from huge advertising fees, that they were subject to higher authority.

Had such a policy been proposed in Italy, in an attempt to control Berlusconi's media, doubtless these regulations would have been welcomed by Western media as enlightened, but many Chinese commentators believe that the

Chinese media and their regulators are demonised by the West, in order to stymie the competition that the Chinese media are attempting to provide internationally (Dong: 2009, pp 141-142). The Chinese strategy of expanding their media internationally is in large part a response to the negative attitude to China that is endemic in the Anglophone popular press (Sparks: 2010).

Politics and the media

Some politically-minded journalists and commentators in China have long chafed at the limitations placed upon them by politicians and at the damage done to good journalism and therefore to the status of serious media in the eyes of the domestic audience. Political leaders are equally aware of the bad name that the Chinese media have abroad because of actual or assumed political interference in the media, and have discussed the matter openly on many occasions (Dong: 2009, pp 141-142). The importance of the media as a conduit for public opinion and as a vehicle of accountability and transparency were not lost, in 2002, on the then new President Hu and Prime Minister Wen, who talked forcefully about this in their early days of office, but who were unable to give practical support to journalists during their time in power, with one significant exception - the Freedom of Information Law.

Recent studies of Chinese journalists have found them committed to public service and enthusiastic about investigation, even when not optimistic about the actual possibilities (de Burgh: 2003;Polumbaum: 2008). As to their anxieties, journalists (according to a study of environment correspondents) are more concerned about their ability to gain public attention for, or editorial interest in, issues and events that they consider should be publicly known. They are also distressed by the obstructive behaviour of local governments, but their main concern is in fact their own lack of competence (de Burgh & Zeng: 2012).

The way in which Leveson has been reported

The Global Times reported the fierce opposition to Leveson's proposals by Britain's *Daily Express* and *Daily Mail* newspapers, quoting them as saying that they were the greatest threat to democracy for 30 years and would result in a bureaucratic nightmare.[3]

Focus Reports was one of at least three CCTV current affairs programmes (*Focus Reports* et al: 2012) that covered the topic in detail, including an interview with The *Guardian*'s Nick Davies. After a lucid account of the hacking issue, including an interview with actor Hugh Grant and various commentators in the USA and UK, the *Focus Reports* feature emphasised the power of the Murdoch empire and how it had influenced British public life, an interpretation provided by Jiang Fei, a Research Associate at the Media Research Institute of the Social Sciences Academy. Jiang Fei explained that the significance to the Western world of the hacking scandal was that the issue of politicians' relations with powerful media bosses had been raised. (*Focus Reports* et al: 2012)

His points were illustrated by an exposition of the personal links between British politicians and the Murdoch employees provided by CCTV's London correspondent which, in approach, hardly differed from those seen on British television.There were scenes of debates in Parliament and a quote to the effect that for 20 years politicians had been scared of running foul of Murdoch. Jiang Fei emphasised that Murdoch acknowledged error, but not responsibility, and a clip showed Prime Minister Cameron taking responsibility for hiring Andy Coulson as his spokesman. The emphasis on moral culpability was quite clear.

Houghton Street Media, a new company formed by a group of Chinese graduates of Anglophone media courses (LSE, Westminster, Columbia) has just completed a seven-part series on Western current affairs for China Central Television[4]. One programme is entirely devoted to the media. This half-hour documentary, scheduled for transmission at peak time, with its own discussion programme following on, not only discusses the hacking scandal and Leveson Inquiry, including interviews with the Editor of *Private Eye*, Ian Hislop, and *Guardian* journalists, but the widespread public unease about other aspects of the media, from their influence on US politics to the role of social media in the 2011 London riots. In each case, the arguments against media regulation were clearly stated, although the purpose of the programme was to demonstrate the issues raised when the media were 'irresponsible'.

In the discussion about regulation and censorship that have raged around this topic on *Weibo*, the Chinese Facebook-Twitter equivalent, Mo Yan, 2012 winner of the Nobel Prize for Literature and a former journalist, weighed in with these comments:

> I myself have never approved of press censorship, but it seems to me that every country has it. It's just that the extent and criteria are different. Were there no censorship, all could insult and slander others arbitrarily, which is something no country can permit. But I believe that censorship should respect the highest norms: truth and reality must not be censored. What betrays the truth should be censored.[5]

That would seem to be fairly representative of the Chinese point of view.

Management and regulation of the media in China

Ownership of media organs, with a few minor exceptions, rests with public bodies. These public bodies are diverse and the media organs they own even more so; after all, they cater to the varied tastes and interests of nearly a quarter of humanity. At the foundation of the Peoples' Republic of China, the very small number that survived the purges were expected to sing from one songbook, varying only in intonation or style, and were therefore controlled without difficulty. Today, when almost anything can be found being discussed in the media, the situation is rather more complicated.

The way in which the Chinese government deals with the media has usually been regarded as the result of Soviet influence, dating from the time when Russian consultants were building the Chinese Communist Party. Thus, it has been assumed, as Communist ideology and precedent lose their hold on Chinese imaginations, so the system it underpinned will disintegrate. However, although Communist ideas appear to have little place in China today, the attitudes to thought and information and the roles of the various players in the Chinese media world have not necessarily changed very much. They may appear less as products of a foreign ideology and more as expressions of traditional Chinese statecraft.

A presupposition widely adhered to in Chinese society is that the media must support authority, and that one of the duties of government is to use the media at its disposal to educate and inform the public as it sees fit. (MacKinnon: 1997). This has been the case at least since Han times, and the antecedents of current state institutions go back at least to Tang times. Several scholars have drawn attention to the ways in which institutions and behaviours traditional to Chinese culture have re-emerged (Zheng: 2010); observers often remark, for example, on the similarities between the present Inspection and Discipline Commission and the Imperial Censorate, in both theory and practice, and on the ways in which investigative journalism has been deployed to function as a Judge Dee of modern times.[6]

The Central Propaganda Department (CPD)

Nationally, the most important agency for the supervision of information is the Central Propaganda Department of the CCP. Quoting a Party publication, Shambaugh comments that its definition of the CPD

> 'means that virtually every conceivable medium that transmits and conveys information to the people of China falls under the bureaucratic purview of the CCP Propaganda Department. This includes all media organs, all schools and educational institutions, all literary and art organs and all publishing outlets'. (Shambaugh: 2009, p 107).

The CPD is responsible for (1) issuing instructions on content; (2) the professional development of content managers (editors, publishers); and (3) monitoring the content of communications to ensure that they do not cross the official line on topics that the Party considers important. It is particularly interested in any books, films or other publications which touch on foreign policies, the leadership, minorities and religion. It has units at every level of administration of which local newspapers and broadcasting channels must take account. The Propaganda Department answers for the network ('xitong'[7]) of information and cultural institutions to the most powerful decision-making body in China, the Standing Committee of the Politburo of the Central Committee of the CCP.

Responding to the new environment

Since 1978, the CPD has been faced with a number of challenges. In the 1980s, it became clear not merely that people no longer believed in the state ideology, but that few of the traditional methods of mobilising support or the values so forcefully propagated in China worked after the Cultural Revolution (1965-75).

By 1989, journalists were demonstrating in the street for freedom of information, 'freedom not to lie' (Polumbaum: 1990).

After the Tiananmen Square Massacre of 4th June 1989, the leadership of the Party was shaken. In its analysis of the causes and repercussions, it decided that much of the blame lay with a failure by the Party to remember that 'thought work' was the basis of everything (Brady: 2007, chapter 1). This, according to the leadership, had permitted pernicious ideas to take hold, in particular what they regarded as the fraudulent concepts of democracy and freedom of the press, as advocated by the USA and others. In those countries, they believed that only the rich enjoyed democracy and freedom to speak, and advocating them for China was a weapon in their battle to divide the Chinese people and bring down China. It was therefore decided that those who had been seduced into echoing this foreign line needed re-education. Thus, journalists and culture workers were ordered to go down to the factories and villages to learn from the people, to remind themselves that the media served the Party, the Party being the authentic representative of the people, while Western freedom was projected as a chimera.

The tone of speeches from senior leaders was uncompromising; not only was ideology to be returned to as the bedrock, but the CPD was to have its powers and authority enhanced. Li Ruihuan told the media that their job was to promote stability, provide less politics, and include more stories to attract the interest of ordinary people, motivating them to work towards China's economic development.

In an inspired analogy, Brady likens the hold of the Propaganda 'xitong' in China today to that of the Medieval Church in Europe (Brady: 2007, chapter 2 passim). Its lofty mandate is to attend to things spiritual and normative, to guide the minds of the people on to the right paths, and in particular to ensure that its emissaries, those employed in the media, do not deviate. We might add that the Church provided a parallel structure of authority, much as the CCP does. Brady argues, however, that whereas in Christendom the Church's authority has withered away, the Propaganda 'xitong', far from being an organisation whose usefulness in the era of the market society has passed, has in fact become ever more important. This has come about because the Party has understood that it is not by force but by persuasion that it must now exercise power, and because the system itself has adopted advanced theories and modern techniques in order to influence attitudes and behaviour.

The battle being fought by the 'xitong' today differs from that fought before 1989. Instead of seeing political subversion from abroad as the main threat, or instead of seeking to uphold a socialist ideology, the 'xitong' is seeking ways of coping with the new activism. What steps has it taken?

Towards an open society
First of all, the media are permitted to report an expanded repertoire of topics –
in fact, very few areas are out of bounds. The exposure of failures, corruption,

problems as yet unidentified by the government, were in the recent past mainly confined to the Restricted Circulation Publications. More and more revelations of this kind have found their way into the public media as investigative journalism has been encouraged (Tong: 2011, *passim*). Chat shows and opinion columns have multiplied, and journalism has been stirred and stimulated by the social media. Opinion polls are regularly conducted at both national and local levels by the Public Opinion Office of the CPD and its lower tier equivalents. The results feed into policy making and sometimes into the media. Starting with *Strong Country Forum*, the CPD began to use the Internet to set agendas, marshal opinion and direct discussion.

In the 1990s, the government introduced 'open government' programmes and prepared the ground for Freedom of Information legislation, enacted in 2008.

Finally, since 2002, the government has introduced and refined a 'Briefing and Spokesperson System', through which all government departments at all levels are expected to appoint – from among their career officials – people who will become specialists in dealing with media and public requests for information and comment from their organisations.

Regulation

Many proposals have been made over the years to provide a media law, but although the NPC has had a working group on this for at least 25 years, no media law has been enacted. Policies and regulations are created through orders issued by executives and agencies, rather than through formal law-making.

Administrative orders are classified into two types, the Administrative Directives issued by the State Council, the status of which is second to law, and the Administrative Rules, issued by SARFT. The rule-making process is 'not open to public engagement', but results from negotiation and co-ordination between different State Council departments, according to Chin Yik-Chan (Chin: 2007).

Regulation is not confined to these two categories of administrative order. There are also Internal Normative Documents, which include directives issued either by the State Council or SARFT, the legal status of which is determined by the courts and which are the result of negotiations between SARFT, its local bureaux and media organisations.[8]

However, decisions taken by senior Party officers may carry more weight than any written documents, whether they be laws, rules or directives. No matter what freedoms might be enacted by the NPC or enshrined in the Constitution, managers will always take their lead from the pronouncements of the most senior Party leader. Moreover, in the absence of such pronouncements, the speeches of the officer responsible for the Propaganda 'xitong' will have the force of law. China is, generally speaking, a relation-based rather than a rule-based society, to use the terms of the sociologists of politics (Li: 2009, pp 19-32). Openness has its limits, but in such a society it is never easy to determine where those limits are.

The day-to-day exercise of control

Control is enacted on a day-to-day basis, but it is not exercised in a completely predictable way. It varies according to circumstances, such as foreign policy exigencies or domestic crises; the personalities and politics of the leadership of the moment; who happens to be the editor at any particular time; and the local context, if the media involved are not national. Examples of the exercise of control are therefore not necessarily typical of all times and places.

However, there is a daily system which is in ordinary circumstances adhered to. In the CPD, a small group discusses which matters are to be emphasised in the media during the forthcoming week and how current issues may be treated. Once a decision has been made, the group calls in editors for 'synchronisation meetings' and then issues weekly guidelines. In the case of sensitive subjects about which the Party is leery, special instructions will be issued to publishers and editors as to what subjects cannot be covered and what should be. The angle to be taken in covering certain stories will be specified.

Television documentaries and major newspaper features may be submitted for pre-publication review, but the most common means by which control is exercised is post-publication, which takes place at the regular meetings when publications are analysed and evaluated, giving editors and their staff guidance on how to handle themselves in future. The CPD carries out its monitoring responsibilities by using teams, often of retired officials, to read, watch and listen to all publications considered relevant.

From time to time, managers in the media industries are obliged to attend away-days, at which they are made aware of the Party line on current issues and given guidance on how to deal with such issues.[9] There are many cases of editors being disciplined.

As far as the Internet is concerned, online dissent is monitored and from time to time is punished; government employees with disguised identities post anonymous commentary online; users of BBS websites and major web portals must register their real names and computers at schools, and Internet bars have software installed to prevent access to websites with politically sensitive, religious, and pornographic material.

Novel ways of control?

The novel *WoJu* (*Snailhouse*) (Liu: 2007) provides a good example of such means of control. China is experiencing a literary renaissance, and a very large number of novels deal with the darker aspects of society, much in the manner that Charles Dickens and Émile Zola exposed corruption, exploitation and suffering in northern Europe during the Industrial Revolution. Today, Chinese literature has its Mr Bumble, its Uriah Heep, its Circumlocution Office and its L'Assommoir in the works of Yan Lianke, Liu Liu, Chi Li and many others. Mo Yan and Yu Hua are deconstructing the history of Communism more than today's concerns.

WoJu tells the story of young professionals struggling to buy a flat in the jungle of Shanghai's property market, so that they can provide their baby with a home where they do not have to share a bathroom and kitchen with numerous other families, each confined to one room of a shabby old house. The seediness of the property developers and their crooked agents, the power of unscrupulous employers, the corruptibility of officials, and the ease with which young women can be exploited are all dealt with, and in such a manner that the reader empathises with the protagonists and is moved by their plight (Liu: 2007).

WoJu was acceptable to the authorities as a book, presumably because book circulation is relatively restricted. When the TV mini-series was screened, however, it was spiked midway. We cannot be sure of the reasons, but it would seem that, while a very pessimistic portrayal of young couples might be acceptable if read by fiction aficionados, a TV series would gain a considerably larger audience and could inflame many more passions against injustice and against the gulf between the profiteering developers, their government accomplices and the rest.

Freedom of information?
In the 1990s, the government introduced 'open government' programmes and also had officials examining foreign examples, with a view to China creating its own equivalent of Freedom of Information legislation implemented elsewhere in the world. There was probably more than one reason for this. Policymakers were aware of the benefits of greater transparency to the quality of decision-making, as well as to the political climate. The need to improve the accountability of officials, within the overall strategy of promoting involvement and better management, was already recognised by policymakers as an important objective, and transparency may have been seen as a means towards achieving this.

Opportunities for corruption may be limited by greater availability of information, and corruption is regarded as a major issue, with potential to slow down economic development. Given the number of demonstrations and riots and the dissatisfaction with government, as manifested on the Internet, freeing up information may be seen as a means of increasing public trust in the government. The government is only too well aware that it is often perceived as having failed to curb land-grabs or to enforce proper compensation for those who have suffered due to urban planning agendas; it is likewise conscious of having damaged its credibility over the mismanagement of information during the 2003 SARS crisis, the Songhua River case and the Sanlu Baby Milk case.

A very remarkable and impressive development, *Regulations on Open Government*, came into force on 1st May 2008. Freedom of information was to be achieved through two main policies. The first was that authorities at different levels are required to make information available on matters within their purview. This covers all regulations, particularly information on emergency planning, cost of public services, including economic and social programmes, government budgets and decisions, urban planning, land requisitions, and building demolition plans. The authorities must also publish the results of investigations into environmental protection, public health, and food and drug safety.

The second was the 'request function', by which citizens are given the right to request access to information. There is a long socialist tradition of withholding information, with the excuse that 'class traitors' or 'foreign enemies' might make nefarious use of it. Although this is often just a cover for official laziness or corruption, it will nevertheless take a long time to eradicate. Critics in any case suggest that the 'request function' is attenuated in scope, not giving adequate opportunities or rights to citizens.[10]

A story about regulation

An illustration of the type of problem thrown up by the somewhat unsystematic system of Chinese media regulation.

A woman in Nanjing, Jiangsu province, ('Mrs Lei') advertised her daughter Gan Lulu on the Internet as a potential companion for gentlemen desirous of the company of an attractive girl. Through the website, on which were posted photographs of the girl, wearing very little covering, many men got in touch and invited her out for dates.

By November 2012 the website had come to the attention of the general public and was being discussed in newspapers and on radio and TV shows. Some critics regarded Mrs Lei's activities as tantamount to prostitution, while many saw them as demeaning to her daughter and obscene in general for featuring women in this manner.

Jiangsu Television's Education Channel has a Question and Answer programme, named *Bang Bang Bang*, which was among many that discussed the story. By that time the younger daughter, Gan Maomao, was being advertised in the same way, and the programme featured a debate between a studio audience and the originator of the project, Mrs Lei, and both of her daughters. The studio discussion was heated and the mother became very angry with some of her critics, verbally hitting out at them and using foul language.[11]

SARFT decided that this was unacceptable and reacted with this statement:

> Jiangsu Education TV's Question and Answer programme, *Bang Bang Bang*, on 24th November, violated national broadcasting regulations, amplified ugliness, undermined media ethics and created a negative social impact. (Salter: 2012)

This referred to the bad behaviour and foul language on air, and stated that this was not only unacceptable but doubly unacceptable on an education channel! SARFT demanded that Jiangsu TV axe the channel - not just the programme – for an indeterminate period as a punishment for breaking regulations on indecency and obscenities.

The difficulty was that there were no explicit regulations on either of these topics; they are implicit. Media professionals were angry at what they considered a draconian punishment, a blatant example of killing the chicken to frighten the monkeys.[12]

Regulation and control of the media – a tentative conclusion

In Anglophone countries, we allow a great deal of influence to people who consider themselves media professionals. They are vested with the power to set the public agenda to a significant extent; to create or snuff out people and proposals; they determine how we look at ourselves and the world; they change our tastes and alter our levels of tolerance; we give them, in the famous phrase, 'power without responsibility'. As Nick Davies has demonstrated in *Flat earth news*, they themselves are all too fallible. Powerful interest groups pressurise them, they hunger for titbits of information from politicians, they regurgitate the press releases of unworthy companies, they investigate their political enemies and call it justice, they hype stolen correspondence and claim that this is in the public interest, and they join the fashionable side in wars and call it impartiality. It is also true that they give us relatively impartial information and, from time to time, reveal corruption we ought to know about, cruelty we must defeat and lies that shock. So far in the Anglophone world we have put up with the former as the inevitable price of the latter.

China's political class has so far not devolved such power to its media and it is not certain that the citizens want them to. In China, the agenda is in theory set by the CPD 'xitong', although in reality it is ever more influenced by the social media. It is of course also subject to pressure from political leaders and lobbying from self-servers in government and business. Like the Anglophone media executives who are their equivalent, the 'xitong' is unelected, claims it serves the public well, and is convinced that it is right.

While the mere fact that the national Chinese media reported, extensively, the hacking scandal and connected events and issues might be seen as a convenient way of reminding the CPD's critics that whatever may be the inadequacies of China's media the West is not as pristine as its admirers might think, it is also a contribution to debate. Many visitors to the China Media Centre ask us to arrange for briefings on Public Service Broadcasting, on media regulation in the UK, on Ofsted, and on such details as the Press Complaints Commission and the libel laws.

In January 2012, Jeremy Paxman and I were invited to a seminar on public service media in China in yet another indication of the anxious interest in how other countries do these things and in the model of a taxation-funded non-commercial broadcaster. Policy makers are struggling with transition from a hypodermic model of the media to a situation in which the Party claims to have the power to determine the agenda, but is more and more forced to cede that power to the opinionated disgruntled on *Weibo*.

In the Anglosphere, journalists are kept honest – when they are – by their professional pride, colleagues' values and by the market; in China there is a constant battle, a constant conflict between the CPD and journalists' sense of professionalism. In China, however, perhaps even more than in the West, digital media are pushing the conventional media to go straight; they are, in effect, changing accountability. Digital media are forcing the CPD to think very carefully not only about how it shapes opinion and promotes its line, but also about how much regulation is possible in the world ahead, and about the implications of how difficult it is to regulate, for government and for culture.

Reports on the Savile case, the Lord McAlpine case and the pranksters at the London hospital may well have further hardened opinion against media deregulation in China among the small proportion of the population paying attention to such things. Discussion of the hacking scandal and the Leveson Inquiry has shown up the differences in the Chinese and Anglophone worlds, but also the rather similar problems they face. In China the issue is, 'Should there be less regulation, and can it be made more enhancing and fortifying of professional journalists?' In the UK it is, 'Should there be more regulation, and if so can it be made less threatening?'

Notes

[1] SARFT, State Administration of Radio Film and TV 国家广播电影电视总局

[2] Efficiently summarised in:
http://www.marbridgeconsulting.com/marbridgedaily/archive/article/50698/sarft_curbs_satellite_tv_entertainment_programming

[3] http://www.weibo.com/1974576991/z7RgiirXh)

[4] I must declare an interest – I am the presenter and lead writer.

[5] (@莫言。12年12月7日01:37 新浪微博)

[6] Judge Dee is the protagonist of tales, in English, telling of the investigations of Examining Magistrate Di Renjie, a real character of Tang times on whose exploits Robert van Gulik based a series of novels.

[7] A 'xitong' or organisational network comprises all those Party and governmental units relating to a particular field of governance. Thus the Propaganda xitong contains every unit concerned with information and culture. Units derived from the State Council, including several in the business of information production and control, may be represented in a strategy co-ordinating body, the Leadership Small Group.

[8] http://www.javnostthepublic.org/media/datoteke/chin4-2003-5.pdf)

[9] http://blog.foreignpolicy.com/posts/2010/03/11/
chinese_journalists_to_get_refresher_course_in_marxism

[10] http://www.freedominfo.org/features/20070509.htm#3

[11] Mother Ms Lei video:.http://www.youtube.com/watch?v=BztS8w29RFg

The Question & Answer programme, Bang Bang Bang 棒棒棒:
http://www.youtube.com/watch?v=P-ZN-Z5ax0I
干露露参加竞猜节目《棒棒棒》与观众现场对骂 Her sister's name is Gan Maomao.

Comments from the SARFT:http://ent.sina.com.cn/v/m/2012-11-28/22083799107.shtml

Gan Lulu's mother's comment: http://ent.sina.com.cn/s/m/2012-11-29/15183799774.shtml

Comments from media people: http://blog.ifeng.com/article/21817735.html and http://www.bobaow.com/u/108/article/19442.htm

Another TV show:
http://et.21cn.com/gundong/etscroll/2012/12/04/13879967.shtml#6492479-tsina-1-60907-8e3d71476b17c48105a1179958d593ed

12 See comments about SARFT's later announcements in *Global Times*:
http://www.globaltimes.cn/content/725442.shtml

References

Brady, A.-M. (2007) *Marketing dictatorship: Propaganda and thought work in contemporary China.* New York: Rowman & Littlefield.

Chin, Yik-Chan (2007) From the local to the global: China's TV policy in transition. Manfred Kops & Stefan Ollig (eds.) *Internationalization of the Chinese TV sector.* Berlin: Lit Verlag, pp 221-240.

Davies, Nick (2008) *Flat earth news: An award-winning reporter exposes falsehood, distortion and propaganda in the global media.* London: Chatto & Windus.

de Burgh, Hugo (2003) *The Chinese journalist: Mediating information in the world's most populous country.* London: Routledge.

de Burgh, Hugo & Zeng, Rong (2012) *China's environment and China's environment journalists.* London: Intellect.

Dong, Steven Guanpeng (2009) *Governing China with the News: Television and National Development in China since 1958.* Unpublished Ph.D. thesis, University of Durham.

Focus Reports et al (2012) 焦点访谈

http://news.cntv.cn/china/20110721/117880.shtml

新闻一加一

http://news.cntv.cn/world/20110719/124453.shtml

环球视线

http://news.cntv.cn/world/20110722/120508.shtml

Hospital: http://www.weibo.com/1974576991/z8Q4PuRmp;

Savile: http://www.weibo.com/1974576991/z0qRcbwGl

Han Han (2012) *Qing Qun (Springtime).* Hunan Renmin Chubanshe, p 022.

Hu, Zhengrong (2012) Interview with the author. 101112, Peking.

Li, Shaomin (2009) *Managing international business in relation-based versus rule-based countries.* New York: Business Expert Press.

Li, Xiguang (2007) *A manual for spokespersons.* Peking: Tsinghua University Press.

Li, Xiguang (2008) *Journalism in transition.* Beijing: Tsinghua University Press.

Liu Liu (2007) *WoJu (Snailhouse).* Wuhan: Changjiang, CBS.

MacKinnon, Stephen R. (1997) Towards a history of the Chinese press in the Republican Period. *Modern China* 23 (1), pp 3-32.

Polumbaum, Judy (1990) 'The Tribulations of China's Journalists After a Decade of Reform' in Lee, Chin-Chuan, (1990) *Voices of China: The Interplay of Politics and Journalism* New York: Guilford Press, 1990.

Polumbaum, Judy (2008) *China ink: The changing face of Chinese Journalism.* Lanham, Md: Rowman & Littlefield.

Salter, Brian (www.chinadaily.com.cn) (2012) What does China's TV regulator do most of the time?

http://www.chinadaily.com.cn/opinion/2012-12/03/content_15979246.htm

SARFT (2012)

http://www.sarft.gov.cn/articles/2011/10/26/20111027084748180633.html

Shambaugh, David (2009) *China's Communist Party.* Berkeley: University of California Press.

Sparks, C. (2010) Coverage of China in the UK national press. *Chinese Journal of Communication,* 3 (3). Pp 347-365. ISSN 1754-4750.

Tong, Jingrong (2011) *Investigative journalism in China.* London: Continuum.

Zheng, Yongnian (2010) *The Chinese Communist Party as organizational emperor: Culture, reproduction and transformation.* London: Routledge.

Note on the contributor

Hugo De Burgh is Professor and Head of the China Media Centre at the University of Westminster. He is a frequent visitor to China and a Professor at Tsinghua University.

Leveson through a pair of foreign eyes

Danish Student Jon Eilenberg, who is studying for an MA in International Journalism at Brunel University, describes the responses to the Leveson Inquiry report seen through a pair of young foreign eyes

The report itself is not very relevant to outsiders, but the following debate shows how the British press, politicians and public perceive "press freedom". This is a general debate worthy of international interest. However, the international dimension is all but overlooked by British and foreigners alike.

> "Despite what will be said about these recommendations by those who oppose them, this is not, and cannot be characterised as, statutory regulation of the press." (Leveson 2012: 17)

For a foreigner living in Britain, the time around the release of the Leveson report was certainly a peculiar one. Other news was more or less put on hold, while the British media ran countdowns prior to the release, covered the presentation itself as if it was a political summit and afterwards cleared the front pages (both in paper and on screen) to give way to the responses.

I strictly write the *British media* here, because that is where it all took place. Even if the phone hacking scandal itself received some international attention, the ensuing inquiry by Lord Justice Leveson has largely been ignored outside Britain, except some sporadic coverage in the USA, Australia, Canada and a couple of other Anglophone countries (Becket 2012). Being *continental*, I, for one, had never heard of the Leveson Inquiry before arriving in Gatwick Airport and neither had any of the other 'foreigners' in the International Journalism programme at Brunel University.

Even if the Leveson Inquiry and its results are mostly, if not only, relevant to the British the responses to it have proven very interesting to foreigners. The debate immediately turned to Leveson's suggestion to introduce an independent regulator with some statutory underpinning. And the arguments quickly became quite polarised, with the pro- and anti-Leveson wings going at each other. It became clear that press regulation is a matter of great concern to many British and the discussion thereof actually can get quite passionate.

In this chapter I will focus more on the responses to the Leveson report than the report itself. The different arguments have shown different sides of British attitudes to press regulation. Through my foreign glasses I will take a look at some of the responses that came from three sides of the debate: the press, the politicians and the public. By going through the different responses to the Leveson report, I seek to capture how the British debate on press regulation appears to foreigners.

Response of the press: No!

Media organisations and journalists, self-evidently, have readily access to the press. This meant that some of the first reactions to the suggestion of an independent statutory underpinned regulator came from the press itself. The *Daily Express* editorial put it this way:

> "To put politicians in ultimate regulatory control of newspapers and then expect them never to seek to use that power to constrain criticism or scrutiny is to place in them a degree of trust they frankly do not deserve" (the *Daily Express* 2012).

A common theme in the press' criticism is struck here: Self-regulation without statutory underpinning is to be preferred to Leveson's recommendations, which are a slippery slope towards a politically controlled press. *The Telegraph*, the *Mirror* and the *Mail* went along the same lines and expressed concern over both the abilities and the intentions of the politicians. *The Sun*, with its usual simplicity, said: "No to censors" (the *Sun* 2012) – a statement difficult to disagree with. *The Guardian*, the *Independent*, the *Times* and the *Financial Times* all stated that the report held important points to be considered, but agreed with the rest of the press that the idea of statutory underpinned regulation was unfortunate. The rejection of Leveson's suggestion was thus an example of something very rare in the British press: complete accordance. However, there were a few individual dissidents. One of the most notable was the *Guardian* journalist Nick Davies (whose brilliant and diligent work on phone hacking had led to the setting up of the Leveson Inquiry) who openly criticised the press' response:

> "From a reporter's point of view, there is no obvious problem with the core of Leveson's report, his system of 'independent self-regulation'… This debate is not about to be settled with facts and reasoned argument. It will be conducted under the same old rules – of falsehood, distortion and bullying." (Davies 2012)

Self regulation - the only way?

The general response of the press to reject the solutions proposed by Leveson says a great deal about the self-perception of British journalism. At the heart of British journalism lies a conviction that only a self-regulated press is truly free. Lord Hunt, prior to his appointment as Chairman of the Press Complaints Commission (PCC) in 2011, put it this way:

> "A free press is the distinctive and indispensable hallmark of any truly free, civilised society. I have no desire to live in a country where the legitimate, lawful investigative activities of the press are fettered at the whim of politicians. That would not be freedom at all." (PCC 2011)

This paradigm of self-regulation would probably not be a problem if all branches of the British press did indeed adhere to their own rules. However, as the phone hacking scandal and Leveson's subsequent findings have shown, this is not the case. This leads me to another observation regarding the British press: the idea that rules and laws do not always apply to journalists.

Especially the more populist parts of the press – i.e. the 'redtop' tabloids – seem to value their very own codex of conduct. Among foreign journalists these publications are usually regarded with a combination of indulgence and contempt, judging from the comments of the Reuter's Institute Fellowship participants at a seminar on Leveson in Oxford in October 2012. However, the idea that rules and laws do not always apply for journalists is not only found in the 'red-tops'. The National Union of Journalists' (NUJ) codes of conduct states that a journalist:

> "Obtains material by honest, straightforward and open means, with the exception of investigations that are both overwhelmingly in the public interest and which involve evidence that cannot be obtained by straightforward means." (NUJ 2011)

In the British codes of journalistic conduct there always seems to be a back door that allows the adherents to break the rules. This door is only to be used in emergencies and only when public interest demands it. As a parallel I have, as a student in journalism, been taught that journalists are expected to "push the boundaries" in the public interest. But public interest is an ill-defined concept and it thus becomes unclear when illegal actions – such as, say, phone hacking – are acceptable and when they are not. If one truly was to be concerned over "slippery slopes" in British journalism, here is indeed an occasion to be.

The notion that a free press and its journalists cannot and should not be constrained by anyone has led to the British press' stark rejection of Lord Justice Leveson's suggestions. This notion has historical roots and presumably goes back to 1694 where press licensing was abolished in Britain. Ever since then British press has struggled to maintain and expand its autonomy from the state (Curran 2010). Perhaps the fact that the British press was the first in the world to gain freedom can explain its tendency towards self-congratulation and its suspicion of politicians, regulations and rules.

Response of the politicians: No and yes.
British politicians proved less unified than the press itself on the matter of press regulation. A great deal of the coverage of Leveson's suggestions centred around the fact that the three major political parties were not in agreement. Prime Minister David Cameron, the original initiator of the Inquiry, in his statement to the House of Commons said:

> "The issue of principle is that for the first time we would have crossed the Rubicon of writing elements of press regulation into the law of the land. We should, I believe, be wary of any legislation that has the potential to infringe free speech and a free press." (The Guardian 2012)

By referring to Rubicon and Caesar's overthrow of the Roman republic, Cameron was very much in line with the general stance of the press: a free press and its journalists cannot and should not be constrained by anyone – and especially not politicians. Deputy Prime Minister Nick Clegg, on the other hand, in his own statement embraced Leveson's suggestions:

> "The press does not operate in some kind of lawless vacuum. It has to abide by the law. In many instances it is already protected by the law and I agree with the report that we should actually go further in enshrining the freedom of the press in statute." (LibDems 2012)

Opposition leader Ed Miliband sided with Clegg, stating that:

> "Lord Justice Leveson's proposals are measured, reasonable and proportionate." (Labour 2012)

The political divide was thus complete, separating even the Coalition partners. Just as the press' responses to Leveson showed some interesting traits in British journalism, the political reactions reveal a thing or two about British politics. This disagreement reflects the relations between politicians and the press and between the parties themselves.

All three parties embraced the freedom of the press in a suitable democratic way. Politicians generally share the principled view that a free press is needed to scrutinise political conduct. Of course this is not always convenient, as the examination of MPs' expenses in 2009 has proved, but it is an indispensable part of a democratic society. However, some branches of the press have used its freedom to breach individuals' rights of privacy, which some politicians have experienced themselves. All parties are reluctant to impose press regulations. But the fact that they have different levels of reluctance reflects the parties' ideological hinterlands. Thus the Conservative party hails personal freedom, whereas the Liberal Democrats and Labour are more inclined to defend personal rights to privacy.

To me the British political system appears basically to be a two-party system with three parties. This observation has been supported by the impression that the British, including the politicians themselves, seem somewhat uncomfortable with having a Coalition government. The responses to the Leveson report from both Coalition and opposition parties have only confirmed this impression.

Leveson has highlighted the tensions in the political system and especially those between the Coalition partners. That the Coalition leaders could not agree on a common statement on such a significant thing as press regulation effectively exposed the government's difficulties with acting as a single body. As the opposition party, Labour could simply lean back and let the Coalition partners expose their differences in public. The Leveson report has thus been used as a pawn in the usual Westminster game of power, revealing the machinery of British politics.

Response of the public: Don't care, but OK.

Even if the closer definition of press freedom is under debate, press and politicians alike agree that a free press is vital for the public. Therefore it is interesting to see how the British public has responded to the Leveson report.

By-and-large the British public has not participated very much in the debate. This could be because the public does not care very much about press regulation. One poll suggests that people regard press regulation as significantly less important than for example economic growth, unemployment, inflation, immigration and health-care. In this specific poll, more than half of the respondents were more concerned about the BBC's handling of the Jimmy Savile case (not broadcasting one film they should have and broadcasting one they should not have..) than about phone-hacking or allegations of bribery (Morrison 2012).

However, when asked directly about press regulation an overwhelming majority backed Leveson's recommendations. In a YouGov survey no less than 82 per cent of the respondents did not trust that the press could regulate itself effectively. Simultaneously 79 per cent agreed with the statement:

> "There should be an independent press regulator, established by law, which deals with complaints and decides what sanctions there should be if journalists break agreed codes of conduct." (Media Standards Trust 2012)

There have also been voices from some of the victims of phone hacking, who have spoken in favour of Leveson's suggestions. One of those, the comedian Steve Coogan (2012), said:

> "The [Leveson] report is good enough. Lord Justice Leveson has produced a fair and non-Draconian set of recommendations that simply cannot be knocked back into the middle." (Coogan 2012)

The public response, insofar there was one, reveals a profound public distrust in both the press and its journalists. Given the recent transgressions by parts of the British press this is not surprising. However, this is not only a British phenomenon. As an up-an-coming journalist I have once and again been discouraged by the fact that journalists in many countries are placed somewhere between politicians and car salesmen with regards to trustworthiness.

It is a real problem that the public, whom the press claims to serve, does not trust journalists. However, the possibility exists that some of the trust might be regained if the British public felt certain at the press was being regulated satisfactory.

Who will triumph?

For me as a foreigner, the different responses to the report have proven to be a valuable insight to the relationships between the press, the politicians and the public in Britain. In that regard it is very interesting, how the self-perception of the press and some politicians seems quite far from the perception of the public and other politicians. It has been said that Britain offers both the best and the worst when it comes to the press. Following the post-Leveson debate it appears to me, that the different opinions are subject to how the press is perceived. If one thinks the best of the press, Leveson's recommendations are unnecessary. If one thinks the worst, they are essential. It is not my place to take sides, but it seems safe to say that the recent behaviour of the British press has given plenty of substance to both arguments.

Lord Justice Leveson foresaw that he would be accused of wanting to curb the freedom of the press. He has been proven absolutely right. However, the need for a free press is acknowledged by all parties: Leveson, the press, the politicians and the public. The disagreement is over different models of freedom. The press itself reject any interference in its self-regulation. The politicians are ideologically divided over the matter, but tend to use it in their own agendas. And the largely disinterested public distrusts the press and want it to be regulated more.

In all democratic countries freedom of the press is seen as a necessity, but the British interpretation of what "freedom" implies seems quite radical in comparison. Some degree of state regulation is accepted among many other countries recognised to have a free press. Both Ireland and Denmark, for instance, have independent press councils with statutory underpinning. These councils deal with complaints and can demand newspapers to print corrections. In Denmark the press council can even fine any newspapers that do not abide its code (Fielden 2012). In France, the press has been regulated by law since 1881. Thus no media organisation can control more than 30 per cent of the market, just as French journalists are limited in reporting court proceedings and public figures' private lives (Poirier 2011). All of these close neighbours to Britain have succeeded in maintaining a free *and* regulated press and valuable experiences could be drawn from them.

However, in the debate following the Leveson report, British press, politicians and public have only looked inwards and backwards in their discussion. The current discussion on how "press freedom" is to be understood has international relevance. Therefore it is in my opinion a shame; both that the British does not look abroad for inspiration, but also that other countries do not pay much attention to the British debate. It extends beyond the English Channel, the North Sea and the Atlantic Ocean.

References

Beckett, Charlie (2012) International perspectives on Leveson – what the non-UK media says, available online at
http://blogs.lse.ac.uk/polislevesonblog/2012/11/28/international-perspectives-on-leveson-what-the-non-uk-media-says, accessed on 14 December 2012

Coogan, Steve (2012) We've been betrayed by David Cameron, The Guardian, accessible online at http://www.guardian.co.uk/commentisfree/2012/nov/29/we-have-been-betrayed-by-cameron, accessed 17 December 2012

Curran, James (2009) Power Without Responsibility: Press, Broadcasting and the Internet in Britain, London, Taylor & Francis, seventh edition

Davies, Nick (2012) Leveson report: a nightmare – but only for the old guard of Fleet Street, The Guardian, 29 November, available online at
http://www.guardian.co.uk/media/2012/nov/29/leveson-report-nightmares-not-real?CMP=twt_gu, accessed on 15 December 2012

Fielden, Lara (2012) Regulating the Press – A Comparative Study of International Press Councils, Oxford: Reuter's Institute for the Study of Journalism

Labour (2012) Ed Miliband's Commons statement on the Leveson Inquiry, available online at http://www.labour.org.uk/statement-on-the-leveson-inquiry, accessed 17 December 2012

Leveson, Brian Lord Justice (2012) An Inquiry Into the Culture, Practices an Ethics of the Press – Executive summary and Recommendations, available online at
http://www.official-documents.gov.uk/document/hc1213/hc07/0779/0779.pdf, accessed on 14 December 2012

LibDems (2012) Nick Clegg's Leveson statement to the House of Commons, available online at
http://www.libdems.org.uk/speeches_detail.aspx?title=Nick_Clegg%27s_Leveson_stat ement_to_the_House_of_Commons&pPK=f9eb7b09-387c-42f2-b454-47f148068b59, accessed 16 December 2012

Media Standards Trust (2012) YouGov-Media Standards Trust Poll Results, accessible online at http://mediastandardstrust.org/mst-news/mst-poll-results/, accessed 17 December 2012

Morrison, Sarah (2012) Press regulation a minority concern, according to poll, The Independent, accessible online at
http://www.independent.co.uk/news/media/press/press-regulation-a-minority-concern-according-to-poll-8326434.html, accessed 17 December 2012

NUJ (2011) Code of Conduct, available online at
http://www.nuj.org.uk/innerPagenuj.html?docid=174m accessed 16 December 2012

PCC (2011) Lord Hunt appointed as new Chair of the PCC, available online at http://www.pcc.org.uk/news/index.html?article=NzQwMA, accessed 15 December 2012

Poirier, Agnès (2011) France can be proud of its resistance to media deregulation, The Guardian 16 July, available online at http://www.guardian.co.uk/commentisfree/2011/jul/16/media-law-france-phone-hacking, accessed on 16 December 2012

The Daily Express (2012) Our Verdict on Leveson: Freedom of the Press Must Be Used for Good, available online at http://www.express.co.uk/posts/view/361485/Freedom-of-the-press-must-be-used-for-good, accessed on 14 December 2012

The Guardian (2012) David Cameron statement in response to the Leveson Inquiry report, available online at http://www.guardian.co.uk/media/2012/nov/29/leveson-inquiry-david-cameron-statement, accessed 16 December 2012

The Sun (2012) No to Censors, available online at http://www.thesun.co.uk/sol/homepage/news/sun_says/article4675652.ece, accessed on 14 December 2012

Note on the contributor

Jon Eilenberg is studying for the MA in International Journalism at Brunel University in London. At present he is a contributor to Nucleus (nucleus.uk.net), which advocates British leadership in Europe. He has a BA and an MA in history and comparative religion from the University of Copenhagen and has published articles on cultural history, Vikings and drinking habits.

Après Leveson: How will the rest of the world react to changes in British press regulation?

Huw L. Hopkins looks away from the UK and the 'Fleet Street' Village to see how Leveson is viewed from afar

Two weeks after the *Sun* published naked photos of Prince Harry from a private party in a locked hotel room, calling it "vital" in the defence of Britain's free press[1], the same newspaper lambasted French, Italian and Irish publications for printing a long-lens invasion of Kate, the Duchess of Cambridge's privacy.

> "William and Kate were said to be "furious" over the "grotesque" intrusion in to their privacy and feel a "red line has been crossed... The Sun's editor Dominic Mohan confirmed the paper would not be running the shots. He said: "The *Sun* has no intention of breaching the royal couple's privacy by publishing these intrusive pictures."[2]

This double standard of what behaviour is expected from a 'free press', not just in Britain, but throughout the world, throws up a myriad of questions. If the famously brutal British press is aghast at the printing of these pictures, should it be considered tame in comparison to its European colleagues? Are Lord Justice Leveson's recommendations needed at all? But more importantly; how is the Inquiry seen by the rest of the world, and will it affect the way foreign media outlets are regulated?

Would the rest of the world care?

If Lord Justice Leveson's "necessary" recommendation for a statutory underpinning was adopted, it would undoubtedly change the way the British press operates, but would the rest of the world care? Despite Britain's diminished stature as a world leader since the rise of the United States, China and Germany, it is still heavily respected[3], and its' laws arguably set precedent for other countries around the world. Furthermore, the joining of many countries in to one political and economic system, such as the European Union (EU), is forcing countries to change the way they view particular national laws.

In 2005, Karen Murphy, a pub landlord was struggling to pay the increasing amount Sky were charging to air football games in public houses. According to the *BBC*, she was paying £700 (£8400 per year) a month for her customers to enjoy watching Premier League football, and instead bought a subscription to the Greek satellite broadcaster, NOVA for £800 a year. This breached UK copyright law, which stated Sky Sports were the only licensed UK broadcasters of Britain's most popular football league-the Premier League. In 2010 she took the matter all the way to the European Court of Justice who ruled in her favour, despite UK law initially suggesting otherwise[4].

If the EU can overrule British law on copyright, implementing Leveson's recommendations might prove a complicated matter. The current "will-they, won't-they" over Britain remaining economically tied to the EU throws up too many 'what-ifs', but one of Leveson's six assessors (wise men and women), Shami Chakrabati, was reported saying the recommendations could breach the Human Rights Act[5]. Adopted from the European Convention on Human Rights, most EU members do not take kindly to governments picking and choosing individual clauses for implementation or ignoring, a recent example being the right to give prisoners a vote[6]. If Leveson's proposals are accepted in Britain, the Human Rights issue could be flagged up, higher up the chain of the European Convention, and cause further distress for British governments. Chakrabati later clarified her comments and released a statement of five points; number four directly addressed the misunderstanding referring to a moment at Leveson's press conference, when he delivered the report.

> "He reflects on (without recommending) the possibility that Parliament and the public might feel the need to impose some level of compulsory statutory regulation on outlets that refused to play their part. It is this alternative that Liberty cannot support and which would in our view breach Article 10 of the ECHR and Human Rights Act"[7]

This distinction between what Leveson reflected on, and what he is recommending matters greatly in reference to the Human Rights Act. Without it, European countries with a free press would enjoy putting the British Inquiry, into the 'culture, practices and ethics of the press', into disrepute. With it, EU member states may wish to look at their own press laws.

It is highly unlikely any other European countries would change the way their own press is regulated to match post-Leveson Britain. The recent history of Europe has impacted hugely on attitudes toward freedom. Countries previously engulfed by Nazi and Soviet occupation are wary of censorship in any form, fearing a return to the days of authoritarian or Soviet Communist concepts of what the press should be and do (Siebert et. al. 1956). These days, Germany is in the Top 20 of the Press Freedom Index and moving up, as is the Czech Republic. Following the collapse of the Berlin Wall and the end of the Cold War, the latter of these countries stipulated quite clearly that the press has to remain free from censorship going forward (Smid 1999). France claim to have strict privacy laws but it was the French version of *Closer* that quite happily disregarded the 'rules' in publishing the 'peeping tom' photographs of the Duchess of Cambridge. Many believe this is a regular occurrence, and that legal payouts are simply filed under their annual budget[8]. press freedom in France is not just accepted, it is economically planned.

Foreign media concerns

Days before Lord Justice Leveson announced his recommendations, the British national press made attempts to discredit his recommendations before actually knowing the details. The *Guardian* reported how some foreign media were concerned about the effect Leveson might have in other countries[9]. The World Press Freedom Committee (WPFC) signed a letter to Foreign Secretary, William Hague, saying press legislation would send an appalling message to some of the world's "most illiberal regimes". This is partly true. Dictators often criticised by Western political elites, such as President Michael Sata of Zambia and President Bashar al-Assad of Syria, might use Leveson's statutory regulated British press law, no matter how limited, to claim carte blanche in silencing those who criticise them in their own countries.

Many British newspapers suggest this is what will take place if Sir Brian's Leveson's recommendations are implemented, the *Daily Mail* begged Culture Secretary, Maria Miller; "Don't muzzle the press"[10]. A muzzle is an object used on a dangerous dog; it is a term Amnesty International used to describe extremism toward the press in countries like Kazakhstan[11]. Yet, on regular occasions, campaigners like Hacked Off feel they have to insist muzzling is not something they are trying to achieve; they merely want to fix the problem of the behaviour of the mass media. The national press in Britain has been peddling misunderstandings of exactly what Leveson has recommended, and suggesting that crossing a legislative Rubicon means regulation will only get stricter. There has been an abstract failure to report the success stories behind some of the world's better regulated sectors like broadcasting in Britain.

... and the Chair of the organisation is a judge.

Those welcoming Leveson's suggestions draw upon positive journalistic examples from places like Sweden, which has been an advocate for press freedom since it introduced the Freedom of the Press Act in the country's constitution in 1776[12]. In 2011-2012, Sweden featured in the Top 15 of the World Press Freedom Index (Reporters Without Borders 2012). The Press Council there acts as an independent self-regulator, made up of a mix of press organisation representatives and the public. It holds the press to account and has powers to make them print retractions, and the Chair of the organisation is a judge[13]. In principle, the Swedish Press Council performs many of the same duties as the British equivalent, the Press Complaints Commission (PCC), but with one major difference, the person who chairs it. Lord Hunt of Wirral became Chairman of the PCC in 2011, his 'boss' the man who pays him as head of PressBof (The Press Board of Finance) is Lord Black, who had quite specific ties to the newspaper industry as the Executive Director of the Telegraph Media Group[14]. Both are former senior Conservative Party post-holders.

The rules of the PCC do not require a judicial head to sit on the panel and this decision might allow a conflict of interest to develop. The moment the committee does take disciplinary measures against one of the newspapers, it is all too easy for the unhappy owners to leave. With a track record of being one of the more volatile media proprietors, Richard Clive Desmond, owner of Northern and Shell and the *Daily Star* and *Daily/Sunday Express*, refused to pay his subscription to the PCC from 2011 and the Commission has not considered a complaint against his newspapers since. Despite Lord Hunt's attempts to generate a new, beefed-up regulator with professional contracts, critics argue the trust in self-regulation is not there. The success of the judicially chaired Swedish Press Council lingers.

The potential spread of statutory underpinning

Despite each side arguing their corner, the potential spread of any statutory underpinning to other countries is more limited than either will admit. The change in law is more likely to affect members of the British Commonwealth. Britain still holds sway with regard to the Commonwealth, despite the Imperial Conference of 1926 stating that "the UK and its dominions agree they are 'equal in status, in no way subordinate one to another in any respect of their domestic or external affairs, though united by common allegiance to the Crown"[15]. When William Hague took office as Foreign Secretary, he saw the necessity for the UK having a much bigger "global reach and influence"[16].In an effort to drag Britain out of recession, he preached stronger links with emerging economies, and in the autumn of 2012 he signed an agreement with Canada to assist in foreign affairs and even share embassies. Hague described the relationship like "first cousins under one Queen and united by a set of values"[17].

Another Commonwealth cousin, perhaps once removed, is Australia, which has a role in the world post -Leveson. Following the delivery of his report, the Judge lectured at the University of Melbourne, on press laws and how digital media should be included in future changes. Reports from Australia suggest support for the change in British press law; "[Leveson] criticised the relationship between the press and the politicians, saying it had been too close"; "The British press... currently regulates itself through the Press Complaints Commission, a body staffed by editors. Its critics say it is toothless"[18]. Australia has recently undergone its own media regulation inquiry in an attempt to tackle the new media. The quandary for the Australian government is whether or not to develop a public interest test in reference to media ownership and, in a separate review, give the press another chance at self-regulation. With a decision being delayed again and again, it may be that Australia is waiting to see how Britain plays its hand[19].

Deep-rooted attitudes toward the press

Every country in the world, regardless of its political, economic or moral connections, has its own deep-rooted attitudes toward the press. Should the government move forward with Leveson's recommendations in their entirety, it will make headlines globally but is unlikely to affect change in foreign views on legislation. If Australia follows Britain's lead, it may lead to a few others such as Canada and Ukraine reassessing their own situation, but only when a scenario develops that is as morally void and hideously illegal as journalists fishing for information and phone hacking. It also depends on the general public of these respective countries and if they feel legislation is required. The people of Britain were outraged at the hacking of Milly Dowler's phone; the same situation may not always provoke the same response on a national scale in a foreign country. Sovereign attitudes toward the press and a countries individual culture are inextricably linked, and a decision to change the law in Britain must be made with the focus of the British people in mind.

On Wednesday 28 November, 2012, one day before publication of the Leveson Report, Hugh Grant starred in a programme on Channel 4, in which John Whittingdale MP described Ukraine and other countries as "itching" to interfere with the press, waiting for the green light from Britain to do so[20]. If different nations plan on curtailing their own press behaviour, this should be a decision by their respective leaders. If a country is itching to change the law but does not, forms of censorship can become much less savoury than legislation, often resulting in the death of a journalist. These countries do not have an issue with the press; they have an issue with their leadership.

Notes

[1] *The Sun* http://www.thesun.co.uk/sol/homepage/news/sun_says/4502239/Prince-Harry-Vegas-Pictures-The-Sun-publishes-photos-of-naked-Prince.html. Accessed 4/1/2013.

[2] the Sun http://www.thesun.co.uk/sol/homepage/news/4538062/.html. Accessed 4/1/2013.

[3] The *Independent* http://www.independent.co.uk/news/world/europe/camerkel-a-love-affair-at-the-heart-of-europe-8348430.html. Accessed 4/1/2013.

[4] *BBC* http://www.bbc.co.uk/news/business-17150054. Accessed 4/1/2013.

[5] *Scotsman* http://www.scotsman.com/news/uk/leveson-inquiry-press-legislation-illegal-says-inquiry-aide-1-2671849. Accessed 4/1/2013.

[6] The *Independent* http://www.independent.co.uk/news/uk/crime/david-cameron-warned-on-votes-for-prisoners-8399522.html. Accessed 4/1/2013.

[7] Liberty http://www.liberty-human-rights.org.uk/news/2012/liberty-leveson-and-the-culture-practice-and-ethics-of-t.php. Accessed 4/1/2013.

[8] BBC http://www.bbc.co.uk/news/world-europe-19595796. Accessed 4/1/2013.

[9] *Guardian* http://m.guardian.co.uk/media/2012/nov/24/foreign-press-warn-over-leveson?cat=media&type=article. Accessed 4/1/2013.

[10] The *Daily Mail* http://www.dailymail.co.uk/news/article-2241266/Leveson-Report-Culture-Secretary-voices-grave-concerns-Leveson-proposals.html. Accessed 4/1/2013.

[11] Amnesty International http://www.amnesty.org/en/news/kazakhstan-must-not-muzzle-media-outlets-2012-11-22. Accessed 4/1/2013.

[12] Press Reference http://www.pressreference.com/Sw-Ur/Sweden.html. Accessed 4/1/2013.

[13] Swedish Press Ombudsman http://www.po.se/english/how-self-regulation-works. Accessed 4/1/2013.

[14] UK Parliament website http://www.parliament.uk/biographies/lords/guy-black/47111. Accessed 4/1/2013.

[15] The Commonwealth website http://www.thecommonwealth.org/Internal/191086/191247/140633/timeline/. Accessed 4/1/2013.

[16] *BBC* http://www.bbc.co.uk/news/10470857. Accessed 4/1/2013.

[17] *Daily Mail* http://leablog.dailymail.co.uk/2012/10/the-commonwealth-should-play-a-much-bigger-role-of-britains-future-an-interesting-snippet-of-news-slipped-out-recently-th.html. Accessed 4/1/2013.

[18] *Australian Broadcasting Company* http://www.abc.net.au/news/2012-11-30/leveson-hands-down-british-press-ethics-report/4399630. Accessed 4/1/2013.

[19] *Crikey* http://www.crikey.com.au/2012/10/25/when-will-the-government-tackle-media-regulation/. Accessed 4/1/2013.

[20] 4OD http://www.channel4.com/programmes/hugh-grant-taking-on-the-tabloids/4od. Accessed 4/1/2013.

References

Leveson (2012) *An Inquiry into the culture, practices and ethics of the press: report*, London : The Stationery Office

Reporters Without Borders (2012) *2011-2012 World Press Freedom Index*, Paris : Reporters Without Borders

Siebert, F. S. Peterson, T. Schramm, W. (1956) *Four Theories of the Press*, Chicago : University of Illinois

Smid, M. (1999) 'History of the Czech Press Law: The Missing Definition of Public Interest – The Ostacle to the new media legislation in the Czech Republic?' *International Journal of Communications Law and Policy* (2), available at http://www.academia.edu/698223/History_OF_THE_Czech_Press_Law. Accessed 4/1/2013

Note on the contributor

Huw L. Hopkins is a writer and journalist. In 2009 he graduated with a combination of degrees from Marjon University and in 2012 he passed his MA in Global Journalism with Merit, after completing a thesis titled *Post-Traumatic Journalism: How and why a major global event increases patriotism and reduces objectivity in journalism.* He has been published twice in the hackademic textbook series *The Phone Hacking Scandal: Journalism on Trial* by John Mair and Prof. Richard Keeble with titles 'Nobody likes a rotten apple, but someone picks them' and 'The rotten apple drops, bounces, rolls, and its seed spreads far and wide', the first of which was serialised in the *Guardian* by Roy Greenslade. His work has been published by *The Huffington Post, Autocar* magazine, *Wannabe Hacks, AltSounds* and the regional newspaper the *Coventry Telegraph*.

Appendix. The Leveson Report explained in infographics

Ændrew Rininsland

Through text corpus analysis, several of Leveson's themes can be brought to light. By glancing at the following visualisations, one can ascertain that the Leveson Report doesn't simply focus on the bad behaviour of the press, but also seeks to understand the impact the press has on the public, how the practices and ethics of the press affect this, and how the press should be regulated.

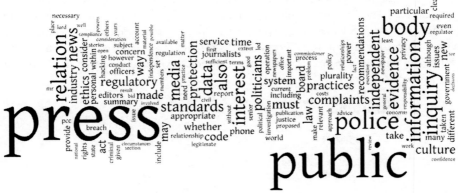

The basic way to visualise the report is through a "word cloud," which simply evaluates how many times a word is mentioned in a text and sizes it in relation to other words; bigger words appear more frequently. Evaluating the report's summary in such a manner, the words "press" and "public" dwarf everything else — given how a major component of the report is how the press impacts the public, this is fairly unsurprising. "Police" is also a major theme, which should also be unsurprising given a solid third of the Inquiry focused on how the press interacts with law enforcement. A fourth theme, "body", also stands out —

indeed, one of the biggest questions posed by the report regards what type of organisation will replace the Press Complaints Commission.

Digging deeper, one can use a "word net" to find the most prominent relationships between words. This uses a conjunctive phrase to find recurring themes within a text. For instance, "ethics of the press" is the most frequently-used phrase involving the conjunctive words "of the" in the summary, followed by "News of the World."

More straight-forward, the two words most frequently joined by the conjunction "and" are "practices and ethics", followed by "press and politicians," "confidence and data," and "police and politicians." Thus, the report isn't only about the "press" and "public" as identified from the word cloud, but can be seen as how the press interacts with not only individuals but also public bodies.

What else can be determined from simply analysing the frequency of words in the text? Using a classifier algorithm, commonly-used words are sorted into the following groups shared by all four volumes of the Leveson report:

A   view daily work relation newspapers chief reporting evidence press provided

B   lord interest clear public role subject current action case rights

C   police press public mps story officers evidence practices culture information

D   press murdoch ico media bid government hunt news decision political

E   information journalists point media hacking issue set national significant titles

F   witness police press statement hearing transcript lines investigation public dcs

G   press regulatory pcc regulation standards body industry complaints system code

H   time number news fact explained individual media clear private editor

I   evidence inquiry pcc made newspaper material code commission freedom

J   press report lines make issues evidence case general put public

These groupings are then weighted based on how closely they are tied to each volume of the Leveson Inquiry. This can then be fed into a network diagram layout to get an idea of how closely each topic grouping corresponds to each volume of the Leveson Report; see below. The strength of the relationship is depicted by the darkness and thickness of each line – the nodes in the middle of the graph are shared by all four volumes but have weak connections to each, while the topic groupings in the periphery are only relevant to one volume but are much more closely associated with that volume as a result. For instance, grouping "D" from the above table has a very strong connection to Volume III, likely due to that volume's emphasis on how politicians and the press interact. This can be seen by that grouping's inclusion of words such as "Murdoch," "ICO," "bid," and "Hunt" – all of which have to do with News International's attempt to acquire BSkyB.

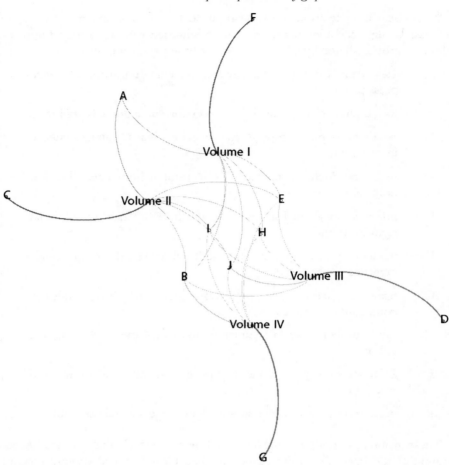

Note on the contributor

Ændrew Rininsland is a London-based data journalist with credits at *The Guardian* and *The Economist*. In addition to his visualisation work, he is also an active member of several open source software communities and maintains a blog at www.aendrew.com. He can be followed on Twitter via @aendrew.